Inclusion in Urban Educational Environments

Addressing Issues of Diversity, Equity, and Social Justice

Inclusion in Urban Educational Environments

Addressing Issues of Diversity, Equity, and Social Justice

edited by

Denise E. Armstrong
Brock University

and

Brenda J. McMahon
Nipissing University

INFORMATION AGE
PUBLISHING

Greenwich, Connecticut • www.infoagepub.com

Library of Congress Cataloging-in-Publication Data

Inclusion in urban educational environments : addressing issues of diversity, equity, and social justice / edited by Denise E. Armstrong and Brenda J. McMahon.

    p. cm.

 Includes bibliographical references.

 ISBN 1-59311-493-1 (pbk.) — ISBN 1-59311-494- X (hardcover)

 1. Education, Urban—United States. 2. Educational equalization—United

States. 3. Children of minorities—Education—United States. I. Armstrong,

Denise E. II. McMahon, Brenda J.

 LC5131.I465 2006

 370.9173'2--dc22

                                    2006005240

Printed in the United States of America

CONTENTS

Acknowledgments   *vii*

Introduction   *ix*

PART I: INTERSECTING EXCLUSIONS WITHIN
SCHOOL CULTURE

1. Exclusion in Urban Schools and Communities
   Jim Ryan   *3*

2. Understanding Urban School Culture: In/Exclusion Within
   Yearbook Discourses
   René Antrop-González, Debra Freedman, Jennifer L. Snow-Gerono
   Anne L. Slonake, Pey-chewn DuoPey-chewn Duo, and
   Hsiu-Ping Huang   *31*

PART II: SOCIOECONOMIC STATUS AND ABILITY

3. Reflecting on Mary H. Wright Elementary: Ideologies of High
   Expectations in a "Re-Segregated School"
   Susan L. Schramm-Pate, Rhonda B. Jeffries, and
   Leigh Kale D'Amico   *45*

4. Seeing the Glass as Half Full: Meeting the Needs of
   Underprivileged Students Through School-Community
   Partnerships
   Catherine Hands   *71*

5. Flipping the Special Education Coin: The Heads and Tails of
   Administering Schools for Students with Different Needs
   Lindy Zaretsky   *91*

PART III: GENDER AND SEXUAL IDENTITY

6. Gender: A H.O.T. (Higher Order Thinking) Link in Educating
   Urban Students
   Amy Barnhill   *113*

7. LGBTQ Students in Urban Schools: Sexuality, Gender, and
   School Identities
   Dominique Johnson   *137*

8. My Favorite Martian: The Cry for Visibility of Sexual Minorities
   in Urban Schools
   Kevin Alderson   *153*

9. Urban Girls Empowering Themselves Through Education:
   The Issue of Voice
   Gunilla Holm and Bill Cobern   *175*

PART IV: RACE AND ETHNICITY

10. Black Boys Through the School-Prison Pipeline: When "Racial
    Profiling" and "Zero Tolerance" Collide
    R. Patrick Solomon and Howard Palmer   *191*

11. "I'm Leaving!": White Fragility in Racial Dialogues
    Robin DiAngelo   *213*

12. Anne Frank Teaches Teachers About the Holocaust
    Lesley Shore   *241*

13. Addressing Multicultural and Antiracist Theory and Practice
    With Canadian Teacher Activists
    Darren E. Lund   *255*

PART V: TOWARD INCLUSION IN SCHOOLS AND COMMUNITIES

14. Supports That Matter: A Community-Based Response to the
    Challenge of Raising the Academic Achievement of
    Economically Vulnerable Youth
    Norman Rowen and Kevin Gosine   *277*

15. Framing Equitable Praxis: Systematic Approaches to Building
    Socially Just and Inclusionary Educational Communities
    Brenda J. McMahon and Denise E. Armstrong   *301*

About the Authors   *323*

ACKNOWLEDGMENTS

This volume is dedicated to the often nameless and voiceless urban students who persist in their heroic struggles in spite of oppressive school structures.

INTRODUCTION

This book is motivated by our experiences in working with students and their families in urban communities. We are particularly concerned about the urgent imperative to address the endemic educational and societal challenges that pervade the lives of urban students, particularly those who live in poverty, are of minority and immigrant backgrounds, and are otherwise marginalized within the current educational discourses and practices. In spite of the fact that over the last 3 decades policymakers, educators and communities across the globe have called for in depth structural changes, this is rarely evidenced in the discourses, practices, and structures within academic and practitioner spheres. This reluctance, despite articulations to the contrary, can be directly linked to normative theoretical and practical perspectives that are defined by assumptions that constrain urban students within restrictive boundaries. Fundamental to this debate is the paradox of equitable schooling since inclusive programs and practices disrupt the status quo and the meritocratic principles that undergird educational structures. Liberal democratic understandings of equality as equated with sameness directly contradict notions of diversity, equity and social justice. Anderson and Herr (1993) challenge these forms of myth-making that render issues of diversity invisible and hinder dominant groups understanding of urban realities: Ideals of color-blindness, meritocracy, and equal opportunity presuppose a world in which race, gender, poverty and sexual orientation are not factors in one's life chances. They are in fact myths which describe an ideal world that does not currently exist. These myths are dysfunctional in that they blind members of dominant groups from understanding the very real dilemmas of minority groups (p. 66). Dei and Karumanchery (2001) also dispute these urban myths, and point out that "equality of access does not result in equality of outcomes," since "access alone does not mean that students who occupy the margins of society will mysteriously find their culture, race and ethnicity reflected in the centre of their school experience" (p. 113). Narrow worldviews based on notions of what ought to be, combined with ignorance of the realties of students' lives focus on deviance and deficits. They blind prospective change agents to the strengths and richness that students bring, and they delimit the transformative potential of social justice praxis within urban environments. The resulting discourse, in the form of deficit beliefs, thoughts, actions, and dialogues shapes urban research, theory, and practice. We suggest that in order to counteract the debilitating impacts of these harmful constructions of urban and social justice, it is important to clarify this terminology.

Although the *Chambers Twentieth Century Dictionary* defines urban as "of or belonging to a city" (MacDonald, 1978, p. 1493), its usage in educational theory and practice is not this benign. In desconstructing the social mythology of the crisis of urban schooling, Miron (1996) points out that the concept of urban is socially constructed and has no inherent definition or meaning since it is derived from the social contexts and is inextricably connected to dominant social and power relations, and the political uses of knowledge. He argues that a more appropriate understanding of urban in a post modern climate is not confined to the inner city, but is embedded in the social construction of racial-ethnic identity. Haberman (2004) identifies a shift in American discourse during the second half of the twentieth century when urban areas moved from economically dynamic and attracting migrant populations to a "pejorative code word for the problems caused by the large numbers of poor and minorities who live in cities. Such negative perceptions of urban profoundly affect education and shape the nature of urban schooling" (p. 1) where what is viewed as urban is often seen as dysfunctional. Additionally, Steinberg and Kinchloe (2004) point out that "in contemporary U.S. society the use of the term *urban* itself has become in many quarters a signifier for poverty, non-White, violence, narcotics, bad neighborhoods, and absence of family values, crumbling houses, and failing schools" (p. 2).

In Canada, the concept of urban schools is fluid and evolving. In spite of differing historical and social contexts, Canadian configurations of urban have been largely influenced by American archetypes which impact negatively on school populations who do not fit notions of "good students." Urban transcends geographical boundaries. Often schools that are located within suburban areas are termed "urban" in negative ways that configure them as (sub)urban, that is, as lower or less than urban.

With an overwhelming focus on deficits, the strengths and possibilities existing in urban and suburban communities are often not highlighted in the media, educational research or practice. At the core of this dynamic, Canadians configure themselves as good and fair people and as a result reject the notion that systemic racist, classist, sexist, and heterosexist oppressions unfairly disadvantage students. Although Canadians do not articulate it, race as Black, and economics as poor are implicit in the use of the term urban within both countries.

Similar to shifting conceptions of urban, meanings of social justice are evolving concepts. Social justice recognizes real imbalances existing in the social, political, and economic power of lived experience. Contrary to configurations of justice as decontextualized and blind, social justice challenges as inequitable beliefs in justice and fairness which deny the significance of identity and location, and serves to counter what Fernandez-Balboa (1993) calls "social unjustness" (p. 62). As educational praxis, social justice is thus congruent with Freire's (1993, 1998) sense of emancipatory education. Theoharis (2004) reiterates Friere's call for public "educational systems to make bold possibilities happen for ... marginalized students" (p. 1). He then challenges educators to "advocate, lead, and keep at the center of their practice and visions the issues of race, class, gender, disability, sexual orientation, and other historically marginalizing conditions" (Theoharis, 2004, p. 2). In an attempt to consolidate senses of social justice in education Dantley and Tillman (2006) identify it as focused on issues of exclusion; including, race, diversity, marginalization, gender, ability, and sexual orientation. Attempts by educational theorists and practitioners to gain knowledge and redress inequity must respect what Narayan (1988) refers to as "insider knowledge" or the "epistemic privilege of the oppressed" (p. 35). We propose that in order to be freed from the constraints of mere articulation and to effect change for urban students, social justice must also include action.

While recent educational reforms have targeted the presenting symptoms of academic underachievement, little attention has been focused on the core intersecting issues that contribute to these gaps, and the ways in which they can be connected and addressed at multiple levels of implementation. This volume covers the spectrum of social justice issues related to urban schooling. It brings together a range of scholars from Canada and the United States, which, in spite of their unique cultures, share a number of similar characteristics in terms of demographic shifts, and the social and political impacts of educational reforms. The contributing authors present a variety of different lenses on "urban" education and its complexities, recognizing the diversity across urban schools. In addition, they examine how multiple theoretical and practical configurations of difference impact on students, their families and communities, and facilitate or hinder the creation of inclusionary learning environments.

CHAPTER OVERVIEWS

The 15 chapters in this volume present a wide range of understandings of urban communities. They integrate theory and practice, call for more critical humane approaches to education. Overarching themes focus on the challenges and possibilities inherent in: the complex, multilayered identities related to diversity, equity, and social justice within urban schools; competing discourses and the relationships between language and power; schools' responses to socioeconomic status and ability; school/ community partnerships; multicultural and antiracist pedagogy; sex and gender bias and initiatives; teacher training and activism; and solutions and possibilities. The authors identify exclusionary ideologies, policies, politics, and procedures as they impact on the lives of students in urban educational environments and existing practices which serve to either maintain existing hegemonic structures or to transform them. They call for educators and schools to reframe discourses and practices in order to create inclusive, equitable, and socially just environments for students, and to redress the urban achievement gap.

Part I focuses on intersecting exclusions within school culture and describes how they impact on students. Ryan and Antrop-González, Freedman, Snow-Gerono, Slonaker, Duo, and Huang connect their personal experiences to structures and practices which undergird school experiences. Using a wide angle lens, Ryan's article investigates multiple levels and forms of exclusion which are systemically and institutionally perpetuated within European, Canadian, and American environments. Despite rhetoric to the contrary, people configured as different routinely experience exclusion which continues to evolve in new and obstructive ways. He maintains that these exclusions occur in the new patterns in which work is organized, in recent responses to diversity and in complacency about perceived progress in economic, racial, gender, and sexual orientation matters. In the second chapter, Antrop-González, Freedman, Snow-Gerono, Slonaker, Duo, and Huang explore broad themes related to in/exclusion within the microculture of schools. Using students' yearbooks as artifacts, they illustrate how superficiality, reserved, elevated and special spaces, and compulsory heterosexuality are reinforced. They conclude with questions and comments relating to school cultural practices and implications for urban educators.

The three case studies in Part II examine intersections of socioeconomic status and ability as they are played out in urban elementary and secondary schools. Schramm-Pate, Jeffries, and D'amico's analysis of Mary H. Wright elementary school illustrates how high expectations, in conjunction with vision, caring, and purposive actions work toward social justice in a poor and predominantly Black school. Despite extreme poverty, a dismal record of school achievement, and demoralizing labels, the school's faculty believes that all students should clearly understand that there is no question of them performing poorly. The outcome of the study describes, illuminates, and attempts to improve understanding about how low-achieving schools may improve their performance by raising their expectations.

Hands' case study of an urban secondary school extends the connection between the importance of high expectations and community partnerships as correlates for effective schools. She addresses the liaisons and collaborative activities developed by a high school's personnel and the surrounding community to provide academic, social, economic, and emotional support to students from families of low socioeconomic status. Hands utilizes theoretical perspectives from education and ecology to frame the relationships and interdependencies of people. By moving away from deficit approaches, she highlights contextual issues within schools and communities which make partnering both necessary and possible. Zaretsky's case study examines the links between expectations for students identified with special needs and school community tensions during the transition from elementary to secondary school. Her conceptual critique of scholarly work on special education reveals deficit driven medical models juxtaposed with potentially more inclusive constructivist frameworks. In response to the theoretical debates and empirical evidence presented, she argues for critique of and dialogue about, practice and policy in special education and leadership. Furthermore she proposes a more inclusive notion of disability that allows for contestation and deliberation among parents and school staffs about inclusionary practice for all students.

Part III presents perspectives on gender and sexual identities. Barnhill's quantitative study provides links between academic processing and gender. She investigates the influence of gender orientation of text (male, female) and gender schema (masculine, feminine, androgynous) on cognitive complexity of responses. She finds that when a person's gender is matched with the gender-orientation of text, there is a greater likelihood that higher-level thinking will be elicited. In addition to achieving equity between genders, these findings are important for researchers and educators to know how readers are anticipating and building schemata rather than simply comprehending what they are reading. Expanding on notions of gender, Johnson provides a resiliency framework which offers insight into how LGBTQ (lesbian, gay, bisexual, transgender, and queer) youth create and negotiate identities within a variety of educational communities despite challenging circumstances. Adult-centered community centers, youth community centers, LGBTQ community bookstores, school-based groups such as diversity clubs are factors in creating, maintaining, and negotiating identity/identities outside of school. She identifies LGBTQ community support in such affirmative developmental outcomes as particularly salient in the present context of contention about the educational lives of LGBTQ youth. Alderson describes findings from the published literature in the area of [in]visibility in schools, and questions whether schools are ready to support youth who disclose their sexual identities as societal tolerance and acceptance of sexual minorities increases. He contends that sexual minority youth have remained invisible in urban schools primarily because of heterosexism and homophobia. He concludes with suggestions about what schools must do to reduce homo-negativity and create safe environments for LGBTQ youth of all ages.

Holm and Cobern's longitudinal study of gender explores what happens when a school articulates high expectations to assist marginalized urban girls to take charge of their own lives. Central to the philosophy in this school is a caring approach whereby the teachers attend to the girls in a holistic way and work with them as young women instead of only focusing on the subject matter. The complexities involved in inclusionary initiatives are highlighted in their illustrations of how the mostly White teachers struggle with providing a culturally congruent science classroom while giving different responses to the ways in which Black female students find and use their voices.

Part IV extends the discussion of social justice in urban educational environments by highlighting issues of race and ethnicity through an examination of teacher preparation and teacher and administrator practices in schools. While Holms and Cobern describe well-intentioned attempts to support Black females academically, Solomon and Palmer provide a perspective on the overt and covert structures that hinder the academic development of Black males. They analyze how the impact of racial profiling and authority structures within schools and law enforcement agencies perpetuate the systemic containment of Black males. To transform schools into more equitable, liberating, and empowering institutions, they suggest that educators, in partnership with members of Black communities, rethink their construction and implementation of safe schools/zero tolerance policies and their destructive impact on this segment of the school population. An integral part of this process entails disassembling preconceived notions about Black males, and reconstructing a more critical reflective practice in urban schooling.

DiAngelo focuses on the need to challenge White privilege as a way of changing the oppressive structures that Solomon and Palmer identify. Building on the construct of White fragility, she contends that Whites live in a social environment which protects and insulates them from race-based stress. This paper explores manifestations of the power dynamics in interracial dialogue between White teacher-education students and students of color. She argues that White preservice teachers are unprepared to explore their own locatedness or differences in racial perspectives that could facilitate their abilities to respond constructively to students in urban schools. This leads to a reinscription of White perspectives as universal and is antithetical to socially just practices. Like DiAngelo, Shore argues for a stronger antiracist approach to teacher education preparation. She proposes the Holocaust as a lens for approaching issues of equity and inclusion. This paper contends that facing anxious and uncomfortable histories is an important component to preparing student teachers for their urban classrooms in the current political landscape.

Focusing on to teacher activism, Lund presents an argument for further engagement between educational scholars and school-based social justice activists. He provides an analysis of one segment of social justice education which focuses on multicultural and antiracist education. A brief overview of the literature from Canada, England, and the United States highlights their complex and often overlapping concerns and the need for more dialogue to facilitate progressive social change. Excerpts from in-depth interviews with four Canadian teacher-activists reveal the challenges they face and the potential for educators to take up various debates and findings from the academic literature in their daily struggles to work for social justice.

Part V shows the possibilities for urban school and community partnerships. Through a discussion of the Pathways to Education Program^{TM} Rowen and Gosine illuminate the role that communities can play in enhancing the academic achievement and life chances of economically vulnerable youth. Their case study finds that Pathways has succeeded in reducing the number of Regent Park youth most in danger of not completing high school, specifically those with low credit accumulation and high absenteeism. They argue that the program's success provides strong evidence for the hypothesis that, if the right supports are provided, young people from economically disadvantaged communities can achieve as well as their more privileged peers. McMahon and Armstrong articulate a democratic leadership model that is designed to institutionalize inclusion within urban schools by addressing issues of diversity, equity, and social justice. Drawing on artistic and literary metaphors, this process model proposes approaches to the creation of equitable urban school environments. It addresses concerns arising from the impact of hegemonic structures on students, personnel, curriculum, and school and parent/ community interactions as they occur within diverse schooling contexts. Their model is structured to guide critical reflection, discussion, and action at each phase and recognizes that inclusionary praxis is a complex, nonlinear, and relational process.

REFERENCES

Dantley, M., & Tillman, L. (2006). Social justice and moral transformative leadership. In C. Marshall & M. Oliva (Eds.), *Leadership for social justice: Making revolutions in education* (pp. 16-30). New York: Pearson.

Fernandez-Balboa, J. (1993). Critical pedagogy: Making critical thinking really critical. *Analytic Teaching, 13*(2), 61-72.

Freire, P. (1993). *Pedagogy of the oppressed: Revised 20th anniversary edition.* New York: Continuum.

Freire, P. (1998). *Pedagogy of freedom: Ethics, democracy, and civic courage.* New York: Rowman & Littlefield.

Haberman, M. (2004, November 1). Urban education: The state of urban schooling at the start of the 21st century. *EducationNews.org*, 1-18. Retrieved April 23, 2005, from: http:www.educationnews.org/urban-edcuation-the-state-o-furb.htm

MacDonald, A. M. (1978). *Chambers Twentieth Century Dictionary.* Edinburgh: T & A Constable.

Miron, L. F. (1996). *The social construction of urban schooling: Situating the crisis.* Creskill, NJ: Hampton.

Narayan, U. (1998). Working together across difference: Some considerations on emotions and political practice. *Hypatia, 3*(1), 3–47.

Steinberg, S., & Kincheloe, J. (2004). *19 urban questions: Teaching in the city.* New York: Peter Lang.

Theoharis, G. (2004, November). *The rough road to justice: A meta-analysis of the barriers to teaching and leading for social justice.* Paper presented at the meeting of the University Council of Educational Administration, Kansa City, MO.

PART I

**INTERSECTING EXCLUSIONS WITHIN
SCHOOL CULTURE**

CHAPTER 1

EXCLUSION IN URBAN SCHOOLS AND COMMUNITIES

Jim Ryan

One of the most enduring memories of my childhood was of being excluded. Not yet 10, I still remember standing on the sidelines while boys two to 3 years older than I vigorously and with obvious pleasure played football. I recall with vivid clarity the graceful and the clumsy, the fast and the slow, the talented and the not-so-talented battling for their respective sides with everything that they had. And it was obvious to all who watched that they enjoyed every minute of it. But I also enjoyed playing the game, that is, when I had the chance, and I yearned to play with these older boys. But it was not to be. They only saw in me a smaller version of themselves and concluded that there could not possibly be a skilled athlete hidden within this undersized frame. That I was forced to watch troubled me greatly. It hurt. I was also convinced that being relegated to the sidelines was so unfair. I felt that I could play better than many of these boys and that if only I could be given a chance, I could make one of these teams better. I knew with certainty that it was not right to judge a kid's potential value by size or age.

My status as observer did not last. Before long, one of the more skilled players noticed that I could catch the ball better than most of his team-

Inclusion in Urban Educational Environments:
Addressing Issues of Diversity, Equity, and Social Justice, 3–30
Copyright © 2006 by Information Age Publishing
All rights of reproduction in any form reserved.

mates, and I became a regular participant and productive contributor. This exclusion/inclusion pattern would repeat itself in the years to come. While I may have been excluded from time to time from events, activities or privileges, in most cases I would eventually gain access. I also came to realize in time that this was not the case for everyone. There were, and still are, many people who continue to be excluded persistently from what life has to offer. A key difference between myself and these individuals is our respective social locations—locations that most of us have little control over. My position within gender, ethnic, class, and sexual orientation relationships pretty much guarantees me access to privileges that others do not have. My white skin, European heritage, mastery of the English language, comparatively comfortable economic position, masculinity, and heterosexuality has helped me to overcome most initial barriers—those that did happen to exist—to the various social institutions in the communities where I have lived and worked. This is not the case for others— women, those without white skin, non-Europeans, speakers of non-English languages, gays and lesbians, and the poor. They are regularly excluded from many things in life, forced to stand on the sidelines and watch the game unfold without them. And for many, the prospect of being asked to play is only a distant dream.

Many look to education to rectify this exclusion. The liberals among us believe that schools are beacons of opportunity for everyone, existing to ensure that everyone can acquire the knowledge and skills necessary to participate meaningfully in our equal opportunity community institutions. Other more critical observers, however, insist that schools are not the equal opportunity providers that they are purported to be. The latter consider them to be at least as exclusive as other institutions, riddled as they are with sexism, classism, homophobia, and racism. Unfortunately, too many continue to embrace the equal opportunity liberal view—that everyone is equally included in education processes and systems and that when they graduate they will have the same chances of making their way in the world as everyone else. Evidence to the contrary, I have heard some educators actually say that so much progress has been made in overcoming patterns of disadvantage that we no longer need concern ourselves with them. But these patterns of exclusion continue to evolve in new, complex, and obstructive ways—in the way in which work is organized, in recent responses to diversity and in complacency about perceived progress in gender and sexual orientation matters. Nowhere is this exclusion more apparent than in urban schools and communities where issues of race and class, and also gender and sexual orientation are so pronounced. In these settings, students and community members routinely find themselves excluded not just from educational processes but other community institutions.

This chapter describes this process of exclusion in urban schools and communities. It focuses, first, on the process of exclusion itself. Second, it illustrates how schools can exclude students. Next, patterns of exclusion that revolve around race, gender, class, and sexual orientation in schools and communities are described. Finally, I explore the idea and practice of inclusion as an alternative to exclusion. I argue that exclusion occurs with regularity in urban schools and can best be understood in the context of wider patterns of exclusion in local and wider communities. Combating exclusion requires that everyone be provided with the opportunity and the means to shape educational and community institutions that are truly inclusive.

UNDERSTANDING MARGINALIZATION AND EXCLUSION

Recently, those seeking to understand marginalization, deprivation, and social justice in schools and the wider community have employed the concept of exclusion. They have done so in two different contexts in studies of poverty in Europe and attempts to understand the plight of the differently-abled in schools. The idea of exclusion (and inclusion) has been part of education for some time now, generally associated with the education of "special needs," "exceptional" or "differently-abled" students (Bailey & du Plessis, 1997; Keys, Hanley-Maxwell, & Capper, 1999; Thomas, Macanawai, & MacLaurin, 1997). Researchers have used the term exclusion to refer to the common practice of removing these students from mainstream or "regular" classes. More recently, however, other scholars have expanded the notion of exclusion beyond the differently-abled to encompass other axes of disadvantage such as age, race, class, and gender (Boscardin & Jacobsen, 1997; Dei, James-Wilson, & Zine, 2002; Dei, Mazzuca, McIsaac, & Zine, 1997; Riley & Rustique-Forrester, 2002). Their basic premise is that students are excluded not just because of their ability, but also on account of the age, race, class, and gender relationships in which they participate. These studies are important because they draw attention to exclusion in education and help us understand the ways in which students are excluded and the patterns that this process follows.

Researchers studying poverty in Europe have also used the term exclusion (Byrne, 1999; Mandipour, Cars, & Allen, 1998; Munck, 2005). They prefer to see deprivation not in terms of poverty, but as a multidimensional process in which various forms of exclusion are combined. Among other things, they are interested in the extent to which men, women, and children have access to current social, economic, political, or cultural systems—to participation in decision making and political processes, to employment and material resources, and to integration in common cultural processes like education (Mandipour et al., 1998; Walker & Walker, 1997). In this view, people are excluded when they lack the resources to obtain certain types of diet, to participate in various activities and to enjoy the living conditions and amenities that are customary. The advantage of this approach is that it avoids blaming individuals, emphasizing instead the relational and structural nature of their misfortunes. Advocates of this approach contend that structural processes rather than individuals and groups systemically create barriers and inequalities that prevent the social advancement of the poor, disempowered and oppressed.

These two approaches complement one another and provide a useful framework for exploring exclusion in urban educational settings. First and most important, they shift blame away from individuals, and in doing so, clear the way for uncovering the often taken-for-granted role of institutions and systems in this process. They also allow us to explore the particular forms and patterns that this exclusion follows. Exclusion in these and other settings emerges in both physical and social forms and it follows patterns that transcend both local school and community contexts. Understanding how this occurs is an important first step in doing something about exclusion.

EXCLUSION IN SCHOOLS

Exclusion means to refuse to admit, consider, include; keep from entering happening or being; reject; bar; put out; force out; expel; or banish (Friend & Guralnik, 1960). When applied to social situations and to schools, exclusion becomes more complicated. In the case of schools, exclusion includes both the more apparent physical aspects and the more shadowy "social" ones. Students are excluded when they are physically absent and when they have difficulty in gaining entry to the school's various activities, experiences, and knowledge even when they may be physically present.

Most schools exclude students both physically and socially. The former happens through processes like suspension and expulsion. Suspension and expulsion rates in the United States and the United Kingdom are alarmingly high (National Center for Education Statistics, 2003b). In the United Kingdom, schools have formally expelled as many as 12,700 students in a single year (Riley & Rustique-Forrester, 2002). Some groups are more vulnerable to exclusion than others. For example, in the United Kingdom 8 out of 10 students who are expelled are males and 1 in 4 are in foster care. Also "Black and ethnic students" are 6 times more likely to be formally expelled than white students (Osler & Hill, 1998). The same is true for American schools. In 1999, they suspended or expelled 15%, 20%, 35%, and 38% of their respective White, Hispanic, Black, American Indian/Alaskan Native student populations (National Center for Education Statistics, 2003b). Students can also choose to remove themselves occasionally or permanently. Those who do this are generally youth who find themselves excluded from other aspects of school activities and learning processes.

More commonly, students are excluded in learning processes. In this sense, exclusion can be subtle. One way to understand this type of exclusion is in terms of "cultural capital" (Bourdieu, 1991). Cultural capital can be thought of as a set of valued resources. These include, among others, the ability to talk, act, and think in particular ways. By this explanation, schools reward students who can do these things. Those who possess this cultural capital will be able to take advantage of the best learning opportunities. Those who do not have these resources will find that they are unable to access learning in the same way. This capital, however, is not a neutral or universal commodity; not all students come to school with it. This is because the cultural capital required by schools has a social class element to it. It is, in fact, middle class (Bourdieu, 1991). Unfortunately, this does not bode well for those who are not from the middle class. Working class students will have difficulty accessing the best learning opportunities because they bring resources that differ from those favored by schools. This contrasts with middle class students whose cultural capital generally meshes with that favored by schools; their ways of talking, acting, and thinking enable them to get access to the best learning experiences. But differences in cultural capital are not just class-based. They also can have an ethnic dimension (Ryan, 2006), not to mention the additional dimensions of gender (Sadker & Sadker, 1994) and sexual orientation (Shapiro, Sewell, & Doucette, 2001). Students are routinely excluded from learning activities because they do not bring to school the same kinds of language and interaction skills that are required in the classroom context. The central point here is that schools exclude some students from their activities by requiring them to have attributes or resources that they do not possess.

Parents can also be excluded because they do not possess certain kinds of cultural capital. This is often the case in urban environments. The language, the interaction expectations, and the background knowledge that participants are expected to possess can exclude people. One Philadelphia parent, for example, expresses his frustration with what happens on the school council on which he serves.

> Due to the fact that the participants of the Governance Council are from a very specific situation—all are teachers/administrators, are from the same

school, and have been oriented through the years to a particular system and culture—the language, thinking and dialogue left me always playing catch up ball with such important subjects as meaning of words and concepts, philosophy of education, and contextual questions that relate [to this high school]. This promotes a high level of frustration. (Fine, 1993, p. 696)

Schools also exclude students by featuring knowledge in the curriculum that some students may have trouble identifying with. Knowledge is never universal or neutral. It will always be presented from a particular perspective and address a unique area of experience. It is not uncommon for school curricula to ignore aspects of community, indigenous and spiritual knowledge (Dei et al., 2002). Given the increasing levels of diversity in today's schools, it is inevitable that aspects of some students' knowledge will be absent.

Schools regularly exclude many from their processes of influence. Like many bureaucratic institutions in the Western world, schools are organized hierarchically. Those at the apex of the hierarchy have power over those in lower positions. This power is accompanied by a right to make decisions for others. Within the framework provided by legislation, most school principals routinely make choices for teachers, students, and community members. This does not mean that administrators never share power. Many, of course do. But this sharing is not always evident if not required by legislation, particularly in view of the responsibility that accompanies power. Administrators may be reluctant to share power with others who do not assume the same burden of responsibility that they do, not to mention the same level of expertise and experience or the same values.

Small wonder then, that exclusion and inclusion inevitably have an impact on important aspects of schooling. Perhaps most telling is the effect on the emotional health of students. When asked in one study how they felt when excluded, students responded that they felt angry, resentful, hurt, frustrated, lonely, different, confused, isolated, inferior, worthless, invisible, substandard, unwanted, untrusted, unaccepted, closed, and ashamed. On the other hand, when included they said that they felt proud, secure, special, comfortable, recognized, confident, happy, excited, trusted, cared about, liked, accepted, appreciated, reinforced, loved, grateful, normal, open, positive, nurtured, important, responsible, and grown up (Falvey, Givner, & Kimm, 1994).

To sum up: schools routinely exclude students. They do this by excluding them physically as well as through their selective learning processes, their curricula, and authority structures. This exclusion is not random; it plainly happens to certain groups more than others. Two things occur in the process. First, differences are identified and boundaries are erected.

People make distinctions between groups and the various characteristics associated with them. In some cases, differences are obvious; in other settings, they are not always so apparent. Second, values are attached to these differences. Those characteristics associated with middle class, Anglo/European, male, heterosexual cultures are generally valued more than others, and as a consequence, they are included in school activities more than others.

Needless to say, exclusion is not unique to schools. It also occurs as a matter of course in the local and global community. Exclusion and the circumstances that dictate people's fortunes originate in many respects outside of the school (Levin & Riffel, 2000). What happens in the global community affects what happens locally and this has an impact on what happens in schools. Despite a common perception that the local and global represent different realms of existence, the global and local are intimately related. "Globalization is not out there, but here and there in specific places where it is planned, implemented and contested" (Munck, 2005, p. 79). The accelerated movements of goods, capital, and people, and the increased connectedness that are part of this process consistently penetrate the political, economic, and cultural realms of localities where they shape how work is organized, how wealth in distributed, how people react to diversity and perceive gender and sexual orientation, and ultimately how individuals and groups are excluded or included.

EXCLUSION, POVERTY, AND WORK

Exclusion and poverty are related. Poor people are routinely excluded from opportunities to participate in both school and community activities. They do not have the power or ability to experience what others in better financial positions can. In school, these poor students are consistently unable to gain the better learning opportunities, and suffer accordingly. If there is any one finding that researchers in education have agreed on over the years, it is that educational experiences and achievement are related to economic position (Coleman, Campbell, Hobson, Mood, Winfield, & York, 1966; Goldstein, 1967; Jencks, 1972; Natriello, McDill, & Pallas, 1990). The children of parents who are financially secure do better in school than those who are not. Furthermore, the latter are more likely to drop out of school before graduation, and less likely to go on to postsecondary education than their middle-class counterparts (Sewell & Hauser, 1976). Those who do pursue education beyond the secondary level generally attend vocational institutions or colleges and take 2-year programs (Karabel, 1972).

Poverty and exclusion are also related to what people do. The nature of their work determines their economic position and the degree to which they are able to participate in the life of their communities. This is not new. It has been happening for many centuries. From feudal to modern times, people's fortunes have been associated with the kind of occupation they pursue. And even when the industrial revolution ushered in new forms of labor, poorer people stayed poorer and richer people remained better off. This occurred because poorer people were generally paid less than what their labor was worth. Employers made money from their employees' labor, and in doing so, helped to maintain a significant gap between rich and poor. However, economies of the West that were based on large-scale manufacturing enterprises did make some progress in reducing inequalities between rich and poor as the mid twentieth century came and went. Salaries and conditions of the working class gradually improved over the years and a middle class emerged and grew (Byrne, 1999). This progress, however, has now come to an abrupt halt.

In the United States, Canada, and the United Kingdom, the gap between the rich and poor has steadily increased since the 1970s, despite the fact that changing systems of production in North American and Europe may operate in different ways (Hutton, 2002). In the United States, most people in the bottom two-thirds of the income distribution ledger have seen their wages decline (Byrne, 1999). The income share of the lowest one-fifth of wage earners went from 4.4 in 1974 to 3.5 in 2001, while the top 5% went from 15.9% to 22.4% during this same time. Moreover, the lowest one-fifth brought in 3.5% of the total income, while the highest one-fifth took in 50.1% (U.S. Census Bureau, 2003a). Over the last year, poverty rates have increased. The number of people below the official poverty thresholds numbered 35.9 million in 2003, or 1.3 million more than in 2002, for a 2003 poverty rate of 12.5%, while the number of families in poverty increased from 9.6% and 7.2 million in 2002 to 10.0% and 7.6 million in 2003 (U.S. Census Bureau, 2004). The distribution of financial worth represents even a starker difference between the rich and the poor. In 1995 1 percent of the American population owned 47.2% of financial assets and 20% own 93.0%. On the other end of the spectrum, the bottom 40% own less than 1.3% of this same pie (Keister, 2000). Ironically, profits for United States businesses have never been higher (Byrne, 1999). The same is true for Canada and the United Kingdom. In Canada, the latest numbers indicate that the gap between the rich and poor has increased dramatically over the past 2 decades. Those with income levels in the top 10% saw the midpoint of their worth jump by 35% during this time, while the proportion of families with no net worth rose from 10% in 1986 to 16% in 1999 ("Rich getting richer," 2002a). In the United Kingdom, income in the lowest levels has decreased 25%, while the top 10% has increased by more than 60% (Byrne, 1999).

One reason for this reversal of fortune is the change in the nature of work. Shifts in production over the past 50 years have left more people than ever excluded. This is because there is now less need for the working poor (Byrne, 1999). At one time, many bodies were needed to do the routine tasks that kept factories running. This is no longer the case, at least not to the same extent, since technology now accomplishes many of the tasks that human beings once did. As well, many companies have expanded internationally. So when labor costs get too high, they just move their operations to distant lands. Changing work patterns have also contributed to this decrease in the need for workers. The economy no longer revolves around large-scale manufacturing. Instead, it relies more on flexible production and service industries. This allows companies to hire people for limited periods of time, to pay them lower wages and give them fewer benefits. More and more people today are being forced to accept part-time, temporary, and low-paying work. Although they are not completely excluded from the economy, many have only a marginal position within it. Even so, low wages, insecure employment, and dependence on benefits and supplements make it difficult for many people to participate socially and politically in their communities.

The most glaring form of contemporary exclusion is spatial, and it is ultimately related to the work people do (or do not do) and the material resources they are able to accumulate. People are excluded by virtue of where they live. Within cities, the poor are increasingly separated from the rich, the inevitable consequence of a current global economy that is unregulated by social mechanisms (Munck, 2005). Contemporary global cities contain the cutting of the new order, but also the worst of the old order, like poverty and marginalization, now made permanent. The decline of traditional industry, the prevalence of part-time and low paying service industry employment, and the negative impact of long-term structural unemployment have decimated many inner-city neighborhoods. High poverty neighborhoods in the United States have increased by 92% between 1970 and 1990 (Munck, 2005). Urban populations are polarized —on one hand, the disconnected and marginal neighborhoods and on the other, those linked to the new information economy and globalization. Anyone who lives in an urban area in North America can attest to these divisions. Chicago, for example, has displayed considerable polarization over time. Stable middle-class neighborhoods have been transformed into transient working-class ones (Morenoff & Tienda, 1997). Those forced to live in the less desirable locations have fewer opportunities to access crucial goods and services. Most important here are schools. For many people, where they live determines the kind of schooling their children will receive and that determines much of their future life course. Given the lack of resources and other difficulties that many urban schools face, students who live in these areas typically experience a poorer quality of education than those in more affluent areas. Inner city schools are particularly disadvantaged. Not only are they are plagued by an inability to attract talented educators, but they often do not have the resources to maintain the buildings themselves. A report commissioned by the Newark School System, for example, found that

> Physical conditions in most of the schools observed by the comprehensive compliance team reveal … neglect and dereliction of duty. Holes in floors and walls; dirty classrooms with blackboards so worn as to be unusable; filthy lavatories without toilet paper, soap or paper towels; inoperable water fountains; … and foul smelling effluent running from a school into the street, speak of disregard for the dignity, safety, basic comfort and sense of well-being of students and teachers. (New Jersey State Department of Education, 1994, cited in Anyon, 1997)

Work, poverty, and exclusion are intimately related to education. Today, the increasing number of people who must take part-time, temporary, or poorly paid work find themselves excluded from participating in many things that their communities have to offer. This has at least two consequences for education. First, students from poorer families are excluded from many of the (middle-class) school's learning experiences. Jean Anyon's (1980, 1981) classic work illustrates how approaches to curriculum content can produce very different experiences. The teachers she studied in two working class elementary schools excluded their students from conceptual, varied, challenging, and wide-ranging material—which their higher class counterparts in other schools received—by focusing on basic skills, repetition, a limited range of topics, and practical knowledge. The view of knowledge in these schools

> is not knowledge as concepts, cognitions, information or ideas about society, language, or history, connected to principles or understandings of some sort. Rather, it seems that what constitutes school knowledge here is (1) fragmented facts, isolated from context and connection to each other or wider bodies of meaning, or to activity or biography of the students; and (2) knowledge of "practical" rule-governed behaviors—procedures by which the students carry out tasks that are largely mechanical. Sustained conceptual or "academic" knowledge has only occasional, symbolic presence here. (Anyon, 1981, p. 12)

Anyon's more recent work illustrates that nothing much has changed in the interim (Anyon, 1997). Other developments, however, have exacerbated these inequities in other ways. One of these is the trend toward marketization (Whitty, Power, & Halpin, 1998). Simply put, the marketization of schools occurs when school systems favor practices that allow them to operate like markets. To do this, they make school boundaries permeable, while at the same time expanding options for parents and their children. This means that parents or students are not obliged to attend a particular school; they can choose from a range of them. There are two spin-offs that increase inequities. First, in order to make themselves attractive to potential "clients," schools engage in the practice of "cream-skimming." That is, they choose only those students who they feel will boost their performance, and in turn, make them attractive to potential "clients." But what happens is that not only do they select those who are likely to excel academically, but also they tend *not* to choose working class and non-White students (Whitty et al., 1998). These tactics also have consequences for other schools. The more successful ones tend to perpetuate their own success by attracting the best students. In doing so, however, they draw the better students from other schools in the area. Baker and Foote (in press) have illustrated this in their account of the city of "Bradford." They show how the attractive magnet school in the area drew the best students from another school, which steadily declined as the magnet school prospered. The neighborhoods in which many poorer families are forced to live have schools that do not offer what suburban schools are able to give their students. Chronic shortages of resources and less adequate facilities are common in schools that serve poorer communities (Persell, 1993). But it is not just the poor who are excluded from school and community life. Men, women, and children who belong to ethnic groups that are not European are also regularly left behind.

EXCLUSION, ETHNICITY, AND REACTIONS TO DIVERSITY

Exclusion also occurs across ethnic lines. Those who are not of European/Anglo heritage in Western countries like the United States, the United Kingdom, Canada, and Australia are often excluded from community affairs and school learning experiences. In schools, the knowledge, language, and community experiences of the local people are not always included in the curriculum, pedagogy, and leadership activities, particularly if they are not Anglo/European; educators and policy makers simply do not value them enough. The result of this exclusion is that many students either drop out of school or fail to master the curriculum. This exclusion is not restricted to schools and is driven, at least in part, by racism. Racism is as much of a problem as it ever was, surfacing in ever more subtle guises in an increasingly diverse and globalized world.

Exclusion has become more troubling as ethnic diversity continues to increase in Western countries. This diversity is not all the same. In some areas, immigration is swelling the number of different groups, while in other parts it is not so much the number of different ethnicities, but the increasing size of just a couple of groups. Canada, for the most part, represents an example of the former, while the United States, or at least parts if it, reflect the latter. Since the late 1960s, Canada has been receiving immigrants from all over the world. Before that time, most immigrants arrived from Europe, and in particular, the United Kingdom. Many of the new immigrants have settled in the larger cities, like Toronto, and the wide range of ethnicities is represented in local schools. Many urban and suburban schools in the Toronto area have upwards of sixty different ethnicities in their student bodies (Ryan, 1999). The United States has also been admitting people from places other than Europe over the past 3 decades. The more striking aspect of its diversity, however, is not the number of different groups, but the increasing numbers of Blacks and Hispanics (U.S. Bureau of the Census, 1995). As of 2000, people of African American and Hispanic heritage comprised 16.6% and 16.6%, respectively, of the total population (U.S. Bureau of the Census, 2001). In public schools, the number of students classified as "minority" increased from 29.3% in 1988 to 38.7% in 2000 (Merchant, 2000; National Center for Education Statistics, 2003a). The West and South had the highest concentrations of "minority" students, with 49% and 45% of the total student population, respectively (National Center for Education Statistics, 2003a).

The fallout from ethnically-based exclusion from schools is clear: more students who are not from the majority culture drop out and perform less well than their majority culture counterparts (Bennett, 2001; Darling-Hammond, 1995; Ogbu, 1994; Paquette, 1990). They are overrepresented in general and vocational tracks (Bennett, 2001; College Board, 1985; Oakes, 1985; Orfield, 1999) and attend colleges and universities in proportionately fewer numbers than their Anglo brethren in the United States (Bennett, 2001; Orfield, 1988, 1999). While there are exceptions to this pattern, these exceptions are not as universal as some may think (Lee, 1996; Macias, 1993; Paquette, 1990; Ryan, 1999). Although "minority" student achievement has improved over the years, the gap between the "White" students and others has more recently leveled off, and in some cases, begun to increase again. These numbers are reflected in the achievement scores of Hispanic and Black students in the United States. Both Black-White and Hispanic-White National Assessment of Educational Progress (NAEP) and Student Achievement Tests (SAT) score gaps narrowed by the early 1980s. By the late 1980s and early 1990s, however, these gaps had either stabilized or had widened (Lee, 2002). Many of these students therefore have to work harder than others to attain the same levels of achievement (Ryan, 1999).

Exclusive practices show up in the classroom in many ways. Curricula, for example, routinely leave out relevant perspectives. Jane, a Canadian student of African heritage who eventually dropped out of the school system, comments on how the history she took made little mention of the contribution of Black people.

> The curriculum ... was one-sided, especially when it came down to history. There was never a mention of any Black people that have contributed to society ... I mean, everything, it's the White man that did. History is just based on the European Canadians that came over ... There was no mention of the Africans that helped build a railway, that ran away from the South and came up to Nova Scotia and helped work and build Canada too ... no mention of that. (Dei et al., 1997, p. 139)

Behind the educational underachievement and general exclusion of "minorities" is a phenomenon that many "majority" culture members are often uncomfortable acknowledging—racism. Racism is not just a set of overtly negative beliefs and actions that are directed toward particular groups. It can also be subtle, showing up in the actions of well-meaning individuals, like teachers who patronize certain groups of students. Racism is also more than something individuals do or think. It is an integral part of general patterns, trends and institutional practices and beliefs that transcend individuals. These patterns may find expression in laws, school regulations, behavior codes, and just general or accepted habits of thinking, believing and doing. The values that are integral to these beliefs and practices, however, routinely penalize and exclude certain groups and individuals from the experiences that others are able to enjoy.

One way in which these beliefs find concrete expression is in stereotypes. The stereotypes held at Suburbia Secondary School, a diverse secondary school in a rapidly growing suburban area of a large North American city, are typical (Ryan, 1999). Both students and teachers subscribe to the belief that Asian students are academically gifted. Trina typifies the attitudes of other teachers when she says, "the Chinese, the Japanese, they all sit together at the front. They're bright, very bright. Brilliant" (Ryan, 1999, p. 106). On the other hand, many feel that while students of African heritage are gifted physically, they are also lacking in intellectual abilities. As a consequence, African male students sometimes feel pressure to join sports teams, while both males and females say that they have to work harder than other students to achieve comparable marks. Maria, for example, says that "You have to work as twice as every other kid in your class [to do well]. It shouldn't be that way" (Ryan, 1999, p. 105). Unfounded beliefs about groups of people, whether they be positive or negative, only make it that much more difficult for them to be included in learning in meaningful ways.

Racist belief and practice continue to exclude many people from both community and school life today. This exclusion was perhaps more obvious in the past. Not so long ago in the United States, Blacks were denied citizenship and education privileges (Lightfoot, 1978). This is no longer the case. African Americans now have the same rights and privileges as Whites, at least in principle. In practice, however, Blacks are still excluded from many privileges. For example, they do not have the same opportunities as others in the job market, even if they possess equal or superior skills (Ogbu, 1987). Blacks are also treated differently by the justice system. A study in Toronto, Canada, for example, revealed that for simple drug possession charges, Whites were released on the scene on a promise to appear in court at a later date 76.5% of the time, while Blacks were only released 61.8% of the time. Of those taken to the police station, Blacks were held for a court appearance 15.5% of the time, while only 7.3% of Whites were kept (Singled out, 2002b). Other evidence confirms this trend (Contenta, 2002, 2003; James, 1998; Ontario Human Rights Commission, 2003; Wortley, in press).

Recent reactions to increasing levels of diversity also threaten to exclude "non-Western" people from community life. Some see this diversity as a direct threat to their communities. They believe that efforts to recognize or include other cultures or ethnicities can only result in fragmentation and conflict. In the United States, Schlesinger (1991, p. 58) believes that what he refers to as the contemporary "cult of ethnicity" will leave his country "a society fragmented into ethnic groups." In his view, acknowledgement of this diversity "exaggerates differences, intensifies resentments and antagonisms, drives deeper the awful wedges between races and nationalities." Such a course risks "the disintegration of the national community, apartheid, balkanization and tribalization." Bissoondath (1994) provides us with a Canadian version of this view.

Others are even more definite about their wishes to exclude different others from their communities. Although their focus may be on preserving the sanctity of their community, their talk is clearly exclusionary. Adopting a fortress mentality, they emphasize patriotism, nationhood, and nationalism. This talk of home and homeland, what Morely and Robbins (1995, p. 89) refer to as *Heimat,*

> is about conserving fundamentals of culture and identity. And, as such, it is about sustaining cultural boundaries and boundedness. To belong in this way is to protect exclusive and therefore excluding, identities against those who are seen as aliens and foreigners. The "Other" is always and continuously a threat to the security and integrity of those who share a common home. Xenophobia and fundamentalism are opposite sides of the same

coin. For indeed *Heimat*-seeking is a form of fundamentalism. The apostles of purity are always moved by the fear that intermingling with a different culture will inevitably weaken and ruin their own.

Another example of this excluding frame of mind in the United States is reflected in the writing of Buchanan (2002, p. 2). He maintains that "for the first time since Andrew Jackson drove the British out of Louisiana in 1815, a foreign enemy is inside the gates, and the American people are at risk in their own country." For him, real Americans are not those of African, Hispanic or Asian heritage, but only those of Western, that is, European heritage. In fact non-Europeans are the enemy and they threaten not only his precious state, but the whole of Western civilization, as well. Buchanan believes that if something is not done to stem the "immigration tsunami rolling over America," it will become a Third World state. Whether or not we regard Buchanan's words as racist, his desire to exclude those who are not of European heritage from his American community is obvious.

The type of exclusion Buchanan advocates has threatened to become more than just rhetoric in the wake of the 9/11 terrorist attacks. The emotion of that moment has given way to responses designed to prevent this sort of tragedy from ever occurring again. Unfortunately, some of these measures also target certain groups and threaten to exclude them from aspects of community life in the United States. Among other things, they extend the racial profiling already underway before the attacks (Giroux, 2002). People from Arab countries and Muslims have been targeted, attacked, and watched. As many as 1,000 serious attacks were committed against people perceived to be "Arab" or "Muslim," and up to 11,000 immigrants were detained (Davis, 2001). Moreover, new legislation now permits increased surveillance of these and other groups and individuals that officials feel threaten national security. The USA Patriot Act of 2001 increases the power of law enforcement officials to conduct surveillance, order wiretaps without public disclosure, carry out secret searches, and detain immigrants indefinitely. It also authorizes the Central Intelligence Agency to spy on American citizens, conduct secret immigration trials and monitor attorney-client privileges (Giroux, 2002).

These new measures make it difficult for some groups to enter the United States in ways that Buchanan would likely approve. They discourage many people with some connection to Arab countries and others who are political activists. Professor Javad Mostaghimi is one such person (Szustaczek, 2002). Born in Iran, he completed a masters and doctoral degree at the University of Minnesota before settling in Canada in 1982. A respected scholar, Canada Research Chair and vice-dean, he was invited not long ago by the U.S. National Science Foundation to present a paper at a workshop. He declined when he learned what was expected of him at the Canada-United States border. New legislation now requires Canadian citizens born in Iran, Iraq, Libya, Sudan, or Syria to be finger printed, photographed, and questioned each time they enter the United States. After learning of these requirements, Professor Mostaghimi said "I declined to be treated like a criminal and cancelled my visit altogether.... I have decided not to travel to the U.S. again until such time as I am welcome" (Szustaczek, 2002, p. 3).

EXCLUSION, GENDER, AND SEXUAL ORIENTATION

Exclusion also surfaces in gender and sexual orientation relationships. These types of exclusions, however, appear to be less of a concern than they once were. This is because females and gay people are often seen as being included in more aspects of life than ever before. Women and girls are included in greater numbers in activities, occupations, and institutions once reserved primarily for their male counterparts. One of these areas is in the administration of schools. More women now occupy administrative positions in school districts than at any previous time (Blackmore, 1999; Young, 2002). One school district with which I am familiar reflects this trend. It has more women administrators than men. The top administrative position is held by a woman and so are two-thirds of the central office positions. Moreover, women administer half of the secondary schools and close to two-thirds of the elementary schools in the district. Pundits have also pointed to other kinds of progress, like the recent academic achievement of girls (Education Quality and Accountability Office, 2002; Wagemaker, 1996), as the basis for claims that there is no longer any need to be concerned with gender issues (Young, 2002). This sentiment has been displayed in government moves to stop such things as the collection of equity statistics (Young & Ansara, 1999).

Perceived progress on the part of gay men and lesbians has also brought about a kind of complacency. Once labeled as inherently flawed human beings (Shapiro et al., 2001), they are now celebrating their sexuality in greater numbers than ever before, and being accepted for it. Laws and regulations guarantee their rights, an increasing number of forums allow them to freely express their sexuality, and the public seems to tolerate their presence in ways that it has never done before. In Canada and Massachusetts, court decisions have cleared the way for gay people to marry, and more than a few have taken advantage of this opportunity. But despite this progress there is still cause for concern. Women, girls, and gay people are still marginalized and excluded in ways that men and heterosexual people are not.

Women continue to be excluded from the best jobs. While they have made progress getting into the job market, overall the positions that they hold pay less and generally have less power than those held by their male counterparts. Perceived improvements on the part of women over the years can be misleading because they are skewed by a minority which has entered the professions. Most women do not have access to such positions and the benefits that accompany them (Kodias & Jones, 1991). One consequence of this is that women tend to be poorer than men. This is particularly the case for single mothers. In the United States, 52% of poor families were headed by women in 1989, compared with 23% in 1959 (Rodgers, 1994). In the Western world, households headed by female single parents are likely to be poor (Byrne, 1999). Yet the cause of this poverty is not welfare dependency, as some contend, but the nature of the jobs available to, and forced upon, these women (Kodias & Jones, 1991). The flexible work patterns favored by contemporary employers that feature part-time, temporary, or subcontracted work leave these women particularly vulnerable to exploitation.

> Not only do the new labor market structures make it much easier to exploit the labor of women on a part-time basis, and so to substitute lower-paid female labour for that of more highly paid and less easily laid-off core male workers, but the revival of sub-contracting and domestic family labour systems permits a resurgence of patriarchal practices and homeworking. (Harvey, 1989, p. 153)

This type of exclusion also appears in education. It is women who tend to gravitate toward these increasingly flexible employment options. They do so in part to alleviate the stress related to job intensification (Young, 2002). In the past, women chose other options as a way of accommodating their domestic demands. Because they had fewer flexible options, they simply gave up their full-time contracts to spend time at home with their children. Now more school districts offer women the option of taking up part-time contracts. What happens in these cases is that districts will hire lower paid newer teachers, the majority of whom are women, on part-time contracts to fill the gaps as a cost-saving measure (Young, 2002). This in turn increases the number of part-time workers, widening the gap between core and casual workers.

Women also do not hold as many administrative positions in education today as some may believe. This is particularly the case for senior administrators. Women comprise only a small percentage of these positions in Canada and the United States (Grogan, 1996; Rees, 1990; Tallerico, 1999). After an increase in the early 1990s, the number of women in central office positions has now begun to decrease (Young & Ansara, 1999). Nevertheless, the number of women in school site administration is increasing. Men, however, still hold the majority of these positions, even in elementary schools. Recent data from Canada show that 31% of principals and vice principals of elementary schools are women. They also show that 65% of the teachers in those schools are also women (Statistics Canada, 1998). At the secondary level these numbers are lower. Women hold only 1 in 5 secondary school principalships and 3 out of 10 vice principalships (Canadian Teachers Federation, 1999). In the United States the story is much the same. Although the numbers of women administrators are increasing, they continue to lag behind men despite the greater number of women educators. As of 2000, women held 44% of the administrative positions as opposed to 70% of the teaching jobs (Digest of Education Statistics, 2002). Ironically, more women are coming into these positions at a time when these jobs are becoming more intense, complex, uncertain, and as a consequence, less attractive (Blackmore, 1999; Young, 2002).

Apart from employment opportunities, women and girls can be excluded in other ways. One of the most forceful ways is through sexual harassment. Despite efforts to eradicate sexual harassment, women and girls still experience its various forms in schools (Orenstein, 2002). Even at the elementary level, girls often have to endure the various misbehavior associated with sexual harassment (Stein, 2002). Women educators also may experience this same kind of harassment. Datnow (1998) describes a case where a group of male teachers used crass sexist discourse to disrupt reforms that they opposed. Seeking to undermine the authority and control of women who were leading the reform efforts, the "good old boys," as they were known in the school, characterized the women as less committed to their jobs, proposed that the reforms were "women's work," and made sexist jokes about the women in public contexts. Although the filing of sexual harassment suits put an end to the sexist jokes, the struggle continued. The men eventually brought a stop to the reforms by using their connections to get the support of outside people (men) with power.

Despite marginal progress over the past few years, gays and lesbians continue to be excluded in ways that straight people are not. Two examples illustrate this point. The first revolves around the troubles of a young boy. A friend of mine has a 7-year-old boy, Brian. Brian had been having a lot of trouble sleeping lately, the result of higher than usual levels of anxiety. After much prompting, Brian finally told his father what the trouble was. Last year, when he was 6 years old, he had mimicked words from a popular song, words that he undoubtedly did not understand, in front of a couple of friends. One of his companions, Paul, immediately picked up on the words, and called Brian a "fag." Paul then went to a teacher and told her what Brian had said. The teacher then admonished

Brian—and not Paul—for saying what he had said. That was last year. This year, the issue resurfaced, with Paul repeating what Brian had said, ridiculing him in the process. Now 7 years old, and understanding the meaning behind the ridicule a little better, Brian had become very upset, so much so that his sleep patterns were interrupted.

Here is another more shocking example. Jamie Nabozny knew by the age of 13 that he was gay (Lugg, 2003). Many others were also aware of his sexual orientation, and from Grades 7 through 10, Nabozny was repeatedly attacked. He was spat and urinated on, punched, and subjected to a mock rape. In the 10th grade, he was beaten so badly that he needed surgery to stop the internal bleeding and repair extensive abdominal damage. During one period, the abuse became so bad that he attempted to take his life on two separate occasions. All this occurred with the knowledge of administrators and teachers, most of whom did little to stop the abuse. The attitude of the administrators was that he had brought all this on himself. Eventually, Nabozny dropped out in his junior year after administrators told him he should go to school elsewhere.

Unfortunately, these incidents are not isolated. They happen all too regularly. In the most severe cases, people can be killed because of their sexuality (Lugg, 2003). But even though most gay students do not experience these extremes at school, nearly half of them do not feel safe when they are there. One poll indicated that 70% of those surveyed said they had been taunted, sexually harassed, shoved, kicked, punched, and even beaten (Young, gay, 1999). Another study reported that 97% of students heard homophobic comments from their classmates, and 57% heard similar comments from school staff (McFarland, 2001). This violence haunts them not only on school grounds, but also in their homes where family members abuse them for their sexual orientation (Tabor, 1992). These conditions can have devastating consequences for these young people. The U.S. Department of Health and Human Services indicates that one in three lesbian and gay youths attempt suicide, and one in four have serious substance abuse problems (Shapiro et al., 2001). They display many of the problems that other high-risk groups do at school. They tend to have discipline problems, and they often find that the school curriculum is irrelevant to their personal needs, family-related problems, self-esteem, and personal security (Sears, 1993).

Gay educators also suffer from the effects of homophobia. As recent as the 1960s Florida and California school officials conducted witch-hunts to weed out gay teachers (Blount, 2003). In the 1980s being suspected of being gay was sufficient to risk termination (Blount, 2003). Not surprisingly, both teachers and administrators are reluctant to advertise their sexual orientation if it is not heterosexual. Melissa, a participant in

Fraynd and Capper's (2003) study of sexual minority administrators, shares why she does not advertise her sexual orientation.

> We have a pocket of very conservative people. I know who they are ... they would fire me even if they suspected, or if they had more to go on that they would run me out.... I wouldn't want to be taken out of education at this level because of that ... I don't have a guarantee right now that I wouldn't be. (p. 108)

The administrators who conceal their sexual identities experience considerable stress from the risk of slipping up and being exposed. On the other hand, those who declare themselves feel that they have to perform at exceedingly high levels. Randy, another administrator in the same study, says:

> The hardest part is that I have to be a flawless principal to be taken seriously. Now, if I were straight and advocating for [sexual minority students], it would be different. But, when I am criticized, I've got to take the power away from them of criticizing me professionally. So, it puts a lot of pressure on me to not make mistakes in my role as principal because I am gay. (p. 104)

MULTIPLE EXCLUSIONS

It would be misleading to think of exclusion as something restricted exclusively and permanently to any one of the aforementioned categories. Exclusion works in more complicated ways. The various kinds of exclusion regularly overlap with one another and they may affect individuals and groups in different and fluid ways. This means that a person may be subject to more than one type of exclusion at the same time. Single mothers, many of whom lack the material comforts that others enjoy, are one example of this. This exclusion cuts across both gender and class lines; through double exclusion, these women are left out of the opportunities and privileges that males and those with more financial resources generally enjoy. The consequences of exclusion increase even more in those instances where single mothers are not members of the majority ethnic group. The U.S. Census reveals that Blacks and Hispanics suffer noticeably higher levels of poverty than Whites. In 2002, as many as 32.3% of Blacks and 27.7% of Hispanics were below the poverty line, as opposed to as few as 7.4% of Whites (U.S. Census Bureau, 2003b). Where these multiple exclusions find most force is in inner cities. It is here that gender, class, and race exclusions overlap with regularity; poverty rears its head most frequently among women of color in these settings.

At the same time, though, individuals may experience both exclusion and privilege. For example, poor males may be excluded by their class position, yet enjoy the advantages that come from being a male in certain contexts. The same is true of middle class women—excluded by their gender, yet privileged by their class. In a similar vein, young males of African heritage may suffer exclusion in schools because of "race" relationships (Cartledge, Tillman, & Johnson., 2001), yet experience advantages in some contexts because of their gender. Exclusion tends to get even more complicated when considering it on an international scale. Mexico and Mexican Americans tend to suffer disadvantages when dealing with American institutions, while indigenous people living in Mexico are themselves excluded in many ways (Osler & Hill, 1998). Japanese citizens were interred in North America during the Second World War, while Japan currently excludes Koreans. The Western world persecutes people from the Middle East, while a number of Middle East cultures persecute women. The West does not have a monopoly on exclusion; it is pervasive, existing in all societies and settings. Individuals occupy a range of different identities and as a result, may experience both inclusion and exclusion, depending on the circumstances that they find themselves in. Whatever the case, the challenge is to search out these multiple and complex forms of exclusion, expose them for what they are and work to change them.

WORKING TOWARD INCLUSION

Despite claims to the contrary, our schools and communities continue to be exclusive. Not everyone is able to participate meaningfully in decision making and political processes, or has access to employment and material resources, or to common cultural processes like education. This is particularly the case in urban environments. Here students are excluded physically and socially from school activities. Too many are forcibly removed or remove themselves. Too many find themselves unable to identify with, or participate meaningfully in the curriculum, favored pedagogies or decision-making processes. Parents are also excluded from school activities. Like their sons and daughters, many find it difficult to make their way to school-sponsored events, and in those instances when they do, to penetrate the social conventions that prevail. One of the most significant points about this exclusion is that it is not random; there are definite patterns to it. Students, parents, and educators are excluded by virtue of the class, race, gender, and sexual orientation relationships in which they participate. These relationships extend beyond the school to the local and global communities. What is happening at the global level today finds its way into local communities and schools, exacerbating already existing divisions between the rich and poor, majority and minority cultures, men and women, and hetero and homosexuals. Doing something about these injustices requires that we first recognize and then challenge them. Ultimately the goal should be inclusion. But how should inclusion be approached to ensure justice? Is it just a matter of seeing that people are entitled to play the game?

Proponents of social justice approach this idea of inclusion with caution (Munck, 2005). This is because inclusion can easily be configured conservatively. Proponents of the conservative take on inclusion believe that the central task is an engineering one—integrating outliers, the marginalized, and problematic into an already existing system. This included space, however, is "good," "clean," and unreservedly "white," middle class, male, and heterosexual, and people are to be included, that is integrated, so that the system can continue to run smoothly without unnecessary conflict or any fundamental change. The goal is to ensure that the game continues, absorbing new participants, without any significant disruptions or change in the rules. The problem with this view, of course, is that if there are to be no changes to the game, how are outsiders to be integrated. How will they be able to participate meaningfully in the game without adapting in ways that do not necessarily suit them, and for which they do not always have the resources, tools, or skills to participate?

The answer is that the game itself—the system—has to change. It has to acknowledge the contributions of not just the regular or traditional contributors, but also what others have to offer. Meaningful inclusion involves more than engineering minor problems; it can only be achieved when the structural and inherent features of an already unequal system are changed. Doing this means not only permitting access for all, but also allowing the accessed to shape the game so that they will be able to contribute and benefit from the game just like everyone else. New players need to be empowered so that they will be able to gain confidence and develop skills to control their participation and contributions and their own lives. Ultimately, participants need to see this as active process where change is generated not from "without" but from "within" (Munck, 2005). Everyone will only be able to be included in the game—in school and community life—when the game, that is the system, changes and this change will best be achieved with the input of everyone.

Changes of this sort require attending to both school life and life outside in the local and global communities. Inclusion in the classroom begins when educators honor different ways of knowing and sources of knowledge, allow students to write and speak in their own vernacular and employ culturally compatible communication styles. Educators can promote inclusion in the classroom when they express cultural solidarity with their students, demonstrate that they care about them and hold high expectations for all students (Riehl, 2000). Schools can encourage inclusion when they include everyone in decision- and policy-making process, develop ways of educating their school communities about inclusive issues, nurture critical ways of thinking, foster cultures of inclusion, emphasize student learning, promote dialogue among school, and community members, and advocate for marginalized groups and inclusive practices (Ryan, 2006). In all of this students, parents and educators need to find ways to recognize exclusive practices and discourses in schools and communities, understand them, and then contest them. Changes in the current exclusive system can only come about with the equal participation of everyone in these endeavors.

REFERENCES

Anyon, J. (1980). Social class and the hidden curriculum of work. *Journal of Education, 162*, 67-92.

Anyon, J. (1981). Social class and school knowledge. *Curriculum Inquiry, 11*, 3-42.

Anyon, J. (1997). *Ghetto schooling: A political economy of urban educational reform.* New York: Teachers College Press.

Bailey, J., & du Plessis, D. (1997). Understanding principals' attitude toward inclusive schooling. *Journal of Educational Administration, 35*(5), 428-438.

Baker, M., & Foote, M. (in press). Changing spaces: Urban school interrelationships and the impact of standards-based reform *Educational Administration Quarterly.*

Bennett, C. (2001). Genres of research in multicultural education, *Review of Educational Research, 71*(2), 171-217.

Bissoondath, N. (1994). *Selling illusions: The cult of multiculturalism in Canada.* Toronto, Canada: Penguin.

Blackmore, J. (1999). *Troubling women: Feminism, leadership and educational change.* Philadelphia: Open University Press.

Blount, J. (2003). Homosexuality and school superintendents: A brief history. *Journal of School Leadership, 13*, 7-26.

Boscardin, M., & Jacobson, S. (1997).The inclusive school: integrating diversity and solidarity through community-based management. *Journal of Educational Administration, 35*(5), 466-476.

Bourdieu, P. (1991). *Language and symbolic power* (G. Raymond & M. Adamson, Trans.). Cambridge, MA: Harvard University Press.

Byrne, D. (1999). *Social exclusion.* Philadelphia: Open University Press.

Buchanan, P. (2002). *The death of the West: How dying populations and immigrant invasions imperil our country and civilization.* New York: St. Martin's Press.

Canadian Teachers Federation. (1999, December-January). Female educators still underrepresented in school administration. *Economic Service Notes.* Ottawa: Canadian Teachers Federation.

Cartledge, G., Tillman, L., & Johnson, C. (2001). Professional ethics within the context of student discipline and diversity. *Teacher Education and Special Education, 24*(1), 23-37.

Coleman, J., Campbell, E., Hobson, C., Mood, A., Winfield, F., & York, R. (1966). *Equality of educational opportunity*. Washington, DC: Government Printing Office.

College Board. (1985). *Equality and excellence: The educational status of Black Americans*. New York: Author.

Contenta, S. (2002, November 8). U.K. to target police racism, *Toronto Star*. Retrieved November 8, 2002, from www.thestar.com

Contenta, S. (2003, October 23). Racism expose rocks U.K. police, *Toronto Star*. Retrieved October 23, 2003 from wwww.thestar.com

Darling-Hammond, L. (1995). Inequality and access to knowledge. In J. Banks & C. McGee Banks (Eds.), *Handbook of research on multicultural education* (pp. 465-483) Toronto, Canada: MacMillan.

Datnow, A. (1998). *The gender politics of educational change*. London: Falmer.

Davis, M. (2001). The flames of New York. *New Left Review, 12*, 34-50.

Dei, J., Mazzuca, E., McIsaac, & Zine, J. (1997). *Reconstructing "drop-out": A critical ethnography of the dynamics of Black students' disengagement from school*. Toronto, Canada: University of Toronto Press.

Dei, G., James-Wilson, S., & Zine, J. (2002). *Inclusive schooling: A teacher's guide to removing the margins*. Toronto: Canadian Scholar's Press.

Digest of Education Statistics (2002). *Elementary and secondary education*. Retrieved August 25, 2005, from http://nces.ed.gov/programs/digest/d02/tables/dt085.asp

Education Quality and Accountability Office (2002). *Ontario secondary school literacy test: Report of provincial results*. Toronto, Canada: Queen's Printer for Ontario.

Falvey, M., Givner, C., & Kimm, C. (1994). What is an inclusive school? In R. Villa & J. Thousand (Eds.), *Creating an inclusive school* (pp 1-12). Alexandria, VA: Association for Supervision and Curriculum Development.

Fine, M. (1993). [Ap]parent involvement: Reflections on parents, power, and urban public schools. *Teachers College Record, 94*(4), 682-710.

Fraynd D., & Capper, C. (2003). Do you have any idea who you just hired?!? A study of open and closeted sexual minority K-12 administrators. *Journal of School Leadership, 13*, 86-124.

Friend, J., & Guralnik, D. (Eds.). (1960). *Webster's new world dictionary of the American language*. New York: World.

Giroux, H. (2002). Democracy, freedom and justice after September 11th: Rethinking the role of educators and the politics of schooling. *Teachers College Record Retrieved November 10, 2004, from* http://www.tcrecord.org/Content.asp?ContentID=10871

Goldstein, B. (1967). *Low income youth in urban areas: A critical review of the literature*. New York: Holt, Rinehart & Winston.

Grogan, M. (1996). *Voices of women aspiring to the superintendency*. Albany, New York: SUNY.

Harvey, D. (1989). *The condition of postmodernity*. Oxford, England: Blackwell.

Hutton, W. (2002). *The world we're in*. London: Little Brown.

James, C. (1998). "Up to no good": Black on the streets and encountering police. In V. Satzewich, (Ed.), *Racism and social inequality in Canada: Concepts, controversies & strategies of resistance* (pp. 157-172). Toronto, Canada: Thompson Educational.

Jencks, C. (1972). *Inequality: A reassessment of the effect of family and schooling in America.* New York: Basic Books.

Karabel, J. (1972). Community colleges and social stratification: Submerged class conflict in American higher education. *Harvard Educational Review, 42,* 521-562.

Keister, L. (2000). *Wealth in America: Trends in wealth inequality.* Cambridge, England: Cambridge University Press

Keys, M., Hanley-Maxwell, C., & Capper, C. (1999). Spirituality? It is the core of my leadership: Empowering leadership in an inclusive elementary school. *Educational Administration Quarterly, 35*(2), 203-237.

Kodias, A., & Jones, J. (1991). A contextual examination of the feminization of poverty. *Geoforum, 22*(2), 159-171.

Lee, J. (2002). Racial and ethnic achievement gap trends: Reversing the progress towards equity. *Educational Researcher, 31*(1), 3-12.

Lee, S. (1996). *Unravelling the "model minority" stereotype.* New York: Teachers College Press.

Levin, B., & Riffel, J. (2000) Changing schools in a changing world. In N. Bascia & A. Hargreaves (Eds.), *The sharp edge of educational change: Teaching, leading and the realities of reform* (pp. 178-194). London: Falmer.

Lightfoot, S. (1978). *Worlds apart: Relationships between schools and families.* New York: Basic Books.

Lugg, C. (2003). Sissies, faggots, lezzies and dykes: Gender, sexual orientation, and anew politics of education. *Educational Administration Quarterly, 39*(1), 95-134.

Macias, J. (1993). Forgotten history: Educational and social antecedents of high achievement among Asian immigrants in the United States, *Curriculum Inquiry, 23*(4), 409-423.

Mandipour, G., Cars, G., & Allen, J. (Eds.). (1998). *Social exclusion in European cities.* London: Jessica Kingsley.

McFarland, W. (2001). The legal duty to protect gay and lesbian students from violence in school, *Professional School Counselling, 4*(3), 171-180.

Merchant, B. (2000) Education and changing demographics. In B. A. Jones (Ed.), *Educational leadership: Policy dimensions in the 21st century* (pp. 83-90). Stanford, CT: Albex.

Morely, D., & Robbins. K. (1995) *Spaces of identity: Global, electronic landscapes and cultural boundaries.* London: Routledge.

Morenoff, J., & Tienda, M. (1997). Underclass neighborhoods in temporal and ecological perspective. *Annuals of the American Academy of Political and Social Science, 551,* 59-72.

Munck, R. (2005). *Globalization and social exclusion: A transformationalist perspective.* Bloomfield, CT: Kumarian.

National Centre for Educational Statistics (2003a). *Racial ethnic distribution of public school students*, Retrieved October 17, 2004, from http://nces.ed.gov/programs/coe/2002/section1/indicator03.asp

National Centre for Educational Statistics (2003b). *Statistics and Trends in the Education of Hispanics: Grade Retention, Suspension and Expulsion* Retrieved October 17, 2004, from http://nces.ed.gov/pubs2003/hispanics/Section2.asp

Natriello, G., McDill, E., & Pallas, A. (1990). *Schooling disadvantaged children: Racing against catastrophe*. New York: Teachers College Press.

Oakes, J. (1985). *Keeping track: How schools structure inequality*. New Haven, CT: Yale University Press.

Ogbu, J. (1987). Variability in minority school performance: A problem in search of an explanation. *Anthropology and Education Quarterly, 18*(4), 312-334.

Ogbu, J. (1994). Racial stratification and education in the United States: Why inequality persists. *Teachers College Record, 96*, 264-271.

Orenstein, P. (2002). Striking back: Sexual harassment at Weston. In *The Jossey-Bass Reader on Gender in Education* (pp. 459-475). San Francisco: Jossey-Bass.

Orfield, G. (1988). Exclusion of the majority: Shrinking public access and public policy in metropolitan Los Angeles. *Urban Review, 20*(3), 147-163.

Orfield, G. (1999). Politics matters: Educational policy and Chicano students. In J. Moreno (Ed.), The elusive quest for equality [Special Issue]. *Harvard Educational Review*, 111-119.

Ontario Human Rights Commission (2003). *Paying the price: The human cost of racial profiling inquiry*. Retrieved October 17, 2004, from http://www.ohrc.on.ca/english/consultations/racial-profiling-report.shtml

Osler, A., & Hill, J. (1998). Exclusion from school and racial equality: An examination of government proposal in light of recent research evidence. *Cambridge Journal of Education, 28*(1), 33-59.

Paquette, J. (1990). Minority participation in secondary education: A fine-grained descriptive methodology, *Educational Evaluation and Policy Analysis, 13*(2), 139-158.

Persell, C. (1993). Social class and educational equality. In J. Banks & C. McGee-Banks (Eds.), *Multicultural education: Issues and perspectives* (2nd ed., pp. 71-89). Boston: Allyn and Bacon.

Rees, R. (1990). *Women and men in education*. Ottawa: Canadian Education Association.

Rich getting richer, middle class poorer. (2002a, March 15). *Toronto Star*. Retrieved March 15, 2002, from www.thestar.com

Riehl, C. (2000). The principal's role in creating inclusive schools for diverse students: A review of normative, empirical, and critical literature on the practice of educational administration. *Review of Educational Research, 70*(1), 55-82.

Riley, K. D., & Rustique-Forrester, E. (2002). *Working with disaffected students*. London: Paul Chapman.

Rodgers, J. (1994). The relationship between poverty and household type. In D. Papadimitiou (Ed.), *Aspects of distribution of wealth and income*. London: MacMillan.

Ryan, J. (1999). *Race and ethnicity in multiethnic schools*. Clevedon, England: Multilingual Matters.

Ryan, J. (2006). *Inclusive leadership*. San Francisco: Jossey-Bay.

Sadker, D., & M. Sadker (1994). *Failing at fairness: How America's schools cheat girls*. Toronto, Canada: MacMillan.

Schlesinger, A. (1991). *The disuniting of America*. Knoxville, TN: Whittle Direct.

Sears, J. (1993). Responding to the sexual diversity of faculty and students: Sexual praxis and the critical reflective administrator. In C. Capper (Ed.), *Educational Administration in a pluralistic society* (pp. 110-172). Albany, New York: SUNY.

Sewell, W., & Hauser, R. (1976). Causes and consequences of higher education: Modesof the attainment process. In W. Sewell, R. Hauser, & D. Featherman (Eds.), *Schooling and achievement in American society* (pp. 9-28). New York: Academic Press.

Shapiro, J., Sewell, T., & Ducette, J. (2001). *Reframing diversity in education*. London: Scarecrow.

Singled out. (2002b, October 19). *Toronto Star.* Retrieved October 19, 2002, from www.thestar.com

Statistics Canada (1998). *Education in Canada, 1997*. Ottawa, Canada: Minister of Supply and Services.

Stein, N. (2002). Bullying as sexual harassment in elementary schools. In *The Jossey-Bass reader on gender in education* (pp. 409-428). San Francisco: Jossey-Bass.

Szustaczek, C. (2002). U.S border law keeps professor home, *The Bulletin, 8*, 3.

Tabor, M. (1992, June 14). For gay high-school senior, nightmare is almost over, *New York Times*.

Tallerico, M. (1999). Women and the superintendency: What do we really know? In C. Brunner (Ed.), *Sacred dreams: Women and the superintendency* (pp. 29-48). Albany, New York: SUNY Press.

Thomas, R., Macanawai, S., & C. MacLaurin, C. (1997). Editorial. *Journal of Educational Administration, 35*(5) 385-396.

U.S. Census Bureau. (1995). *Statistical abstract of the United States: 1995* (115th ed.). Washington, DC: Author.

U.S. Census Bureau. (2001). *Projections of the resident population by age, sex, race and hispanic origin: 1999 to 2000*. Retrieved November 12, 2001, from http://www.census.gov/

U.S. Census Bureau. (2003a). *Poverty, income see slight changes; child poverty rate unchanged, census bureau reports*. Retrieved November 12, 2001, from http://www.census.gov/Press-Release/www/2003/cb03-153.html

U.S. Census Bureau. (2003b). *Historical income tables: Income equality*. Retrieved October 17, 2004, from www.census.gov/hhes/income/histinc/le3.html

U.S. Census Bureau. (2004). *Income stable, poverty up, numbers of Americans with and without health insurance rise, census bureau reports*. Retrieved October 17, 2004, from http://www.census.gov/PressRelease/www/releases/archives/income_wealth/002484.html

Wagemaker, H. (Ed.). (1996). *Are girls better readers? Gender differences in reading literacy in 32 countries*. Amsterdam, Netherlands: International Association for the Evaluation of Educational Achievement.

Walker, A., & Walker, C. (Eds.). (1997). *Britain divided: The growth of social exclusion in the 1980s and 1990s*. London: Child Poverty Action Group.

Whitty, G., Power, S., & Halpin, D. (1998). *Devolution and choice in education: The school, the state and the market*. Melbourne: The Australian Council for Educational Research.

Wortley, S. (in press). The usual suspects: Race, police stops and perceptions of criminalinjustice. *Criminology*.

Young, B. (2002). The Alberta advantage: "DeKleining" career prospects for women Educators. In C. Reynolds (Ed.), *Women and school leadership* (pp. 75-92). Albany, New York: SUNY.

Young, B., & Ansara, S. (1999). Women in educational administration: Statistics for a decade. *The ATA Magazine, 79*(2), 22-27.

Young, gay and scared to death at school. (1999, September 23). Message posted to http://www.cnn.com/US/9909/23/hate.crimes.gays/

CHAPTER 2

UNDERSTANDING URBAN SCHOOL CULTURE

In/Exclusion Within Yearbook Discourses

**René Antrop-González, Debra Freedman,
Jennifer L. Snow-Gerono, Anne L. Slonaker,
Pey-Chewn Duo, and Hsiu-Ping Huang**

Have a great summer and a wonderful life

2 cute+2 be=4 gotten

Call me 666-1234

Thanks for the memories you pot smoker

Finders (1997) explained that the school yearbook is a sign of belonging—a documentation of social roles and allegiances. Pictures are evidence of our popularity. The written messages become testament to our connection with others. The written messages, however, maintain more than just connection. Written messages are artifacts that speak to our participation with/in school culture. They become evidence of "hidden"

Inclusion in Urban Educational Environments:
Addressing Issues of Diversity, Equity, and Social Justice, 31–42
Copyright © 2006 by Information Age Publishing
All rights of reproduction in any form reserved.

social discourses that reinscribe hegemonic positionings, purposes, values, and intended course of action (Gee, 2001).

In this paper we explore the meanings of school culture, the ways we, as students, were in/excluded by looking through inscriptions found within/on/between the pages of our high school yearbooks. We are a diverse group of excavators. Our yearbooks come from a variety of places within the United States and throughout Taiwan. We are male and female. And our varied racial/class identities—Puerto Rican, Taiwanese, White, working class, and middle class—further add to the complexity of our understandings of school culture.

By looking at our yearbooks, we hope to uncover the hidden, complicated movements of our existence with/in school culture as well as take a more critical stance toward unnoticed social discourses that occur in schools: What did we value? What roles did we appropriate, desire, condemn? How did others construct our existence? As well, we see broader connections with issues of in/exlusion in urban school contexts. That is, while urban schools often propose to serve students of color who live in poverty, dominant structures actually work to actively marginalize students through culturally irrelevant pedagogy and inequitable access to activities and coursework (Antrop-González, 2003; Antrop-González, Vélez, & Garrett, 2005; Flores-González, 2005). We begin by exploring our yearbook experiences. Then we explore themes found within our yearbook signings: superficiality; reserved, elevated, and special spaces; and compulsory heterosexuality.

THE YEARBOOK EXPERIENCE

We all remembered the frenzy over purchasing the yearbook *before they all sold out*. We all remembered the urgent intercom announcements, beginning as early as October, highlighting the sale of yearbooks before they even made it to production. We all remembered the special *discount* and *sales* weeks. We remembered the much-cherished receipt—proof of our purchase, saved in a special place until the big day. We all remembered our belief that our picture would show up more often in the yearbook once the staff knew we were contributing our hard-earned allowances to their efforts.

Of course, the anticipation rose to an almost unbearable level when the intercom announcement proclaimed the yearbook had arrived. Time to stand in line with your friends, to discover your identity, to validate your belongingness. Our collective memories focused on the obtaining of our yearbooks and how our first reaction was to check for pictures of our friends and ourselves. The yearbook seemed to confirm our sense of belonging (Finders, 1997): the pictures become proof of our existence; the pictures become testament to our connections, our engagement with others, and our abilities to interact socially. In an attempt to demonstrate status, we would count the number of times our pictures appeared in the soon-frayed pages of the yearbook—and how many times our friends' pictures could be found as well. This meant that in order to belong, we had to find some way to make it onto the pages of the yearbook through, most often, extracurricular activities, whether they be athletic, academic, or through a particular talent for say, music or drama (Finders, 1997). The pictures and stories on the pages of the yearbook became a public indication of social status.

Our pictures were only one part of the experience, however. We knew that in order to belong we had to have evidence of how other people saw us, of how other people interacted with us—we had to have people sign our yearbook. For when the "right" people are signing your yearbook, you had arrived. Consider the story Finders (1997) tells where one of her participants, a popular girl, slides across the room privileging people with the opportunity to have her signature in their yearbook:

> It was easy to hear Tiffany's voice above the loud chatter. She leaped up from a crowd of girls, her long red hair flying back as she cackled loudly and ran full speed to the end of the hall, sloshing small amounts of her chocolate malt across the tan carpet as she went. She slammed into a group of friends and yanked a yearbook from one boy's hand, screaming, "Whose's this? You want me to sign it, don't you?" (pp. 34-35)

We signed our yearbooks as a form of graffiti. In fact, as we searched through our yearbooks for this project, Debra found the following words on an inserted piece of paper:

> *NOTICE! PLEASE CHECK FOR DAMAGE BEFORE WRITING IN THIS BOOK. THIS ANNUAL <u>CANNOT BE RETURNED</u> IF WRITING APPEARS IN ANY SECTION OF THE ANNUAL.

We laughed on finding this as we recognized this as the school's attempt at instilling its power over us as they would only accept books that were not "damaged"—that had no signings, no evidence of our cultural belonging and membership. The authors of this paper who came from Taiwan, Pey-Chewn, and Hsiu-Ping, had their friends write to them within the pages of a memory book. They remembered the yearbook as a place to house pictures and maybe a few autographs. Obtaining signings within the pages of the yearbook was not the norm. As such, their memory books became the signing space. Yet memory books became more than just signing spaces. Memory books were evidence of social class, indications of who could afford a "better" book created with a finer binding or material.

IN/EXCLUSION FOUND WITHIN OUR YEARBOOK SIGNINGS

Cultural belonging and membership seemed to be everything to us in high school. However, as we began looking back on our yearbook memories, the transparent nature of the signings became quickly apparent. Instead of belonging, we found an in/exclusionary discourse mired in nice and sweet phrases that in retrospect had and now have little or no meaning. At the time, we thought we would be friends forever, as evidenced by the signings embellished with the familiar "keep in touch," or "2 nice + 2 be = 4 gotten." On closer inspection, we now recognize that the signings were superficial, reserved for an exalted few, and situated within a culture of compulsory heterosexuality.

Superficiality

Superficial signings filled the void—vacuous words and phrases that permeated the yearbook pages only to imply and provide evidence of popularity. These signings occupied little or no relevant space. They were for show. We had no real relationship with the signer and the signer really did not know who we were and really did not care to know who you were. These types of superficial signings referenced no specific connections to experience and often provide only wishes for a good future, as evidenced by the following words found in Jennifer's yearbook: "Jennifer, I am glad we became good friends. I am also glad I met you. Love you lots."

How Jennifer became a friend with this signer is never recognized. And while the signer mentions—not once, but twice—how glad she was to know Jennifer, the nature of their relationship was not revealed. While most of these signings took up small amounts of space, there were instances where superficial signings took up significant amounts of space. For example, Anne had a signing that began at the top of the page and then had an arrow directing to the bottom:

> Anne Wuganny, What's up? Remember all the good times we have had and will have. You're a weirdo but that's o.k. [arrow drawn to the bottom of the page] Sorry I had to move to a new area. I am running out of things to say. You know! See you around always. And let's write to each other at college so that we will both have someone to write to at college. Love, your friend

Anne reflected on this meandering meaningless moment: "Why is her signing so shallow?" The shallowness of this particular signing surprised her: "Remember all the good times we have had and will have." "I am running out of things to say." Yet, the amount of space taken up by this superficial signing is impressive—evidence that space taking is more important than substance. We found evidence of this type of space taking in Pey-Chewn's memory book as well:

> Pey-Chewn, I wish you a bright future. Good Health [bookmark placed on the page taking up huge amount of space with Chinese characters on it that read "I'll care about you always."]

The message was short, sweet, and superficial. Interestingly, the space taken by the bookmark covered most of the memory book page, perhaps reflecting the sentiment of "I really do not know what to write to you, nor does it matter."

Often the signers of these superficial signings were hyper aware that they would never see the owner of the yearbook again. They boasted no false promises of friendship. The signers were matter-of-fact concerning their expectations with regard to future connections and friendships.

> Deb, it's been great knowing you this year. You're a lot of fun to be around and a very nice person. I'm sorry I kidded you so much. I hope you have a great summer and a wonderful life. Best of luck always.

These signings exhibited a realistic expectation, awareness with regard to the movements of life and the ways in which we lose contact after high school. As such, wishes for a wonderful life saturated these types of signings:

> Yo Anne What's happening! Those long years of school are finally over. It's been wild knowing you. Take it easy for the rest of your life.

Often, this realistic attitude provided closure and connection with high school memories.

> Pey-Chewn…. We are finally graduating…. It is possible that we might lose contact afterwards, but no matter what, let's not forget each other and the memories we shared together.

More often, a skewed sense of reality permeated these superficial signings. That is, there seemed to be the hope that superficial friendships might have the chance of turning into something more. If only there was some way of keeping in touch, perhaps we could become better friends.

Deb, I am glad we became friends! You are a super cool person and have a neat personality. Computer [class was] fun even though I didn't learn anything did you??!!! We will have to keep in touch over the years. Call me over the summer 666-1234.

The phone number was a standard tag line for these particular signings. We noticed as well, that area codes were not necessary as there was a strong assumption of permanency, a belief that you would always live within the boundaries of your hometown.

Reserved, Elevated, Special Spaces

We discovered that we all saved spaces for our closest friends. For most of us, the inside front cover was the most cherished space; often adorned with the words "Saved—do not write on this pleeeeeze" to ensure that no one less worthy than our *best* friend would autograph in this space. Pey-Chewn's memory book even had a page glued together after the signer had completed the message so that no one else could read or intrude on the special relationship shared between two friends. Anne remembered,

It seems to me that Colleen was the first to write on the inside front cover. Her face is escaping me right now, but by her words, we seemed to be close for our senior year…The last signing on the inside cover of my yearbook is from Sam… I know that I knew him for a long time. Probably connected since elementary school.

Most often, the signings found within these reserved, elevated, and special spaces had connections to memories, awareness and depth of friendship and acknowledgement of a specific context. For example, this signing from René's yearbook exhibited a deep connection and strong attachments:

René—What's up bud? Well, we've had some bad times and good times together but I just want to thank you for all your support and motivation (the key ingredient). You're a good friend and you stuck by my side when I was a jerk. I know I treated you bad but I like I told Kern … whatever our ups and downs came a friendship. Even though I don't see you much anymore doesn't mean you're not a close friend. But I would really enjoy seeing you at the meets next year if possible. You helped and I overcame a lot but I did screw up my dream [becoming All-Metro weightlifting champion] in the end and I apologize. Weightlifters stick together through *hell, war, victory.* Don't ever think you're not a good or strong lifter. Don't ever quit and I won't. To lift is a gift.

René reflected on this signing:

> My friend Derek and I were two of the smallest weightlifters on the high school team. We had often supported each other in the weight room and during competitions against other high schools. His yearbook message to me was quite passionate.

The passion exhibited within signings from best friends was quite apparent. There was a knowing, a connection, a hyper awareness of the yearbook owner's identity. And the signer was not afraid to acknowledge feelings publicly.

These public displays of affection were written for all to see. However, there were some moments when we found more private messages within the inner-pages of the yearbook. For example, we found the following signing hidden away in the middle pages of Debra's yearbook:

> Well dearie.... It really is too bad about our friendship but I realize that people do change over the years. Maybe when we both finish growing up, our relationship will get strong again. Who knows, like we say—people do change! I will always have fond memories about the years we shared—It was years—12 years to be exact. There're so many things I want to tell you about how much you mean to me and that you will always be a part of my life.... The tears and the joys we shared over all those silly boys sure sound crazy at times. Maybe we can share those again—you know we had something special—best friends—but we didn't have to be constantly around each other— you still are like a sister to me—there are times when I just want to call you up like olds times, but I'm afraid it would be awfully uncomfortable. I sit and think for hours about what I have done—but I never can come up with a solution. Maybe this summer we could get together.... Good Luck in all you do—Please keep in touch. Love & friends always.

Filled with memories and questions concerning a close relationship gone awry, Debra reflected:

> Katie and I had been friends since the first grade. Sometime in our junior year of high school we broke up with each other. She didn't appreciate me hanging out with friends other than Monique and her—funny how girls do that, funny that I asked her to sign my yearbook, funny that it was such a personal signing.

No space was saved for this signing. Yet, it was evidence of a close relationship, of a strong connection with a person. The personal nature of the content fascinated us—why did Katie feel so compelled to write such a personal message? It quickly became obvious to us that Katie only wanted Debra to read the message –messages in the middle sections of the yearbook were usually a bit more superficial as the front covers held the sign-ings of our closest friends. This signing was hidden because the message was not meant for the general public's consumption. Because Debra and Katie no longer spoke, the public spaces of the yearbook had become Katie's only means of communication with Debra. By placing the signing within the inner-pages the public space suddenly became a private space allowing for a very personal communication between two estranged friends.

Compulsory Heterosexuality

Throughout our yearbooks a discourse of compulsory heterosexuality persisted. Whether focused on virginity, dating, or attractiveness, these signings objectified us and placed us into definite positions that main-tained a hetero-normative social structure. For Debra her signings reflected the hope that she would soon be married, that she would follow the correct path, the only path available to her at that time:

> Hey shorty Deb, … I hope to see you in about 5 years. You will be married, 3 kids, a cute husband.

These types of signings seemed to stress a connection between happi-ness and marriage. As if to say that your life was meaningless unless you maintained the status quo and organized your life within a nuclear family construction.

> Debs … I hope your future holds so much happiness for you. And I hope that you find the tall, dark, handsome, sensitive, smart funny warm guy you've been looking for—and I hope he's Jewish, too!

These wishes for future connections and the possibility of marriage could be found throughout the yearbooks. In one case, these connections related to a crush that a student had for a teacher:

> Anne—I know you always liked Mr. Davis and want to get him next year because you liked to stay in his class and be in the same room with him even though he gave you thirteen detentions.

Anne's crush further exemplifies the heterosexual norms found within the pages of our yearbooks. Regardless of the fact that her crush was on a teacher, Mr. Davis, Anne's sexuality was seen through a hetero-normative lens.

Jennifer reflected that her yearbook signings exhibited objectification of her as an adolescent girl/young adult woman—even a majority of the signings received from girls wished her "good luck with the guys," invariably with the parenthetical comment ("even though you don't need it"). This seems to suggest that her major purpose and role in this school, the one thing that could make her happy was to be involved with a "guy," any "guy." The boys were not afraid to exploit this notion either. For example, one signer wrote "wish we could have been more than friends." And another signer penned the seemingly contradictory, "Stay Sweet and a Virgin (no prob)." Jennifer considered these signings,

> Undeniably it was "no prob" for me to "stay a virgin." I had no intentions of engaging in sexual activity at this point in my life. So why was my entire yearbook literacy based on sexual overtones and my body or womanhood as it pertained to boys' interest? I can only imagine what this did to my confidence or any ideas I had about sexuality. It is quite apparent that I am supposed "give myself" to a boy in order to find happiness or contentment.

René's yearbook signings resonated with hetero-normative sentiments as well. The contents of his signings made reference to his sexual prowess and his ability to demonstrate his machismo in the weight room:

> René (*blue balls*)—What's up, man? Nothing here! So how is your knew [sic] girlfriend? *I bet she's getting hot.* Thanks for helping in weightlifting this year. You were a big help. It was also killer hanging out with you. Good luck in college and I hope you come back and see us!

René reflected: "I realized that sex and sports were priority issues for those within my immediate social circle. Visions of sexual fantasies (and maybe realities) danced in the heads of those who wrote their messages in the yearbook."

Signings maintained this hetero-normative discourse at all costs. As in the following signing in Hsiu-Ping's memory book: "If you were a guy I would be crazy for you." The signer, a girl, could only be crazy for Hsiu-Ping if she were a guy. The other signings reflected similar constraints: marriage could only be understood within the confines of heterosexual relationships, sex could only be between females and males. Being gay, lesbian, bisexual, or transgender was never an option.

SO WHAT DOES THIS HAVE TO DO WITH SCHOOL CULTURE?

Within the spaces of our yearbook we enacted the hidden, underlying socializing purpose of schooling—the learning of norms, the doing of the dominant culture. That is, the superficiality, the elevated, special spaces, the compulsory heterosexuality found within the pages of our yearbook maintained hegemonic discourses that controlled our actions and constructed our identities within very narrowly defined cultural spaces. It seems that our desire to establish ourselves within this particular school cultural event clouded our understandings and maintained broader social structures that privileged the dominant class and maintained the status quo (Finders, 1997, p. 46).

Jennifer's memories as a former yearbook advisor are helpful here, as they help us to analyze student experience through a deeper understanding of the relationship between culture and power (Giroux, 1992, p. 16). She recounted that students had to have a yearbook in order to belong; students had to display their receipt of payment prominently in their wallet; students had to be seen standing in the distribution lines. This meant, however, that to own a yearbook a student had to have access to the necessary finances. It was inevitable that some students would have difficulty affording this all-important, highly visible, social signifier.

Yet, awareness of economic constraints was often unnoticed. Finders (1997) explains that school staff often ignore those students who cannot afford the yearbook and that there is an assumption that everybody gets a yearbook. Not surprisingly, authors of this paper have no memory of ever questioning why some students did not obtain yearbooks or why we so desperately needed a yearbook. At that time in our lives, hegemonic discourses were so ingrained in our understandings of the world. We did not question why signings denied race and class or why signings positioned us within the norm. Best & Kellner (1991) explain that Foucault described this type of power as being

> diffused throughout the social field, constituting individual subjectivities and their knowledges and pleasures, colonizing the body itself, utilizing its forces while inducing obedience and conformity ... individuals have been caught within a complex grid of disciplinary, normalizing, panoptic powers that survey, judge, measure, and correct their every move. (Best & Kellner, 1991, p. 54)

Our acceptance of the yearbook culture meant that we accepted these tacit cultural practices. We accepted in/exclusion as normal, as something to tolerate. This is different than many urban youth who are poor and feel excluded from the mainstream school environment as statistics show that current push-out rates in urban school districts in the United States consistently hover at 50% (Antrop-González, 2003).

Foucault recognized, however, that power is "a multiple and mobile field of force relations where far-reaching, but never completely stable effects of domination are produced" (Foucault cited in Best & Kellner,

1991, p. 51). Power relations, then, are always subject to contestation and struggle as new understandings are realized. These realizations have lead us to consider the ways that students navigate urban school culture and identity as well as wonder about membership in the larger culture outside of school. For us questions emerge specific to urban school cultures: How do urban school contexts offer pedagogical counter-narratives in an effort to include students? How do educators establish and maintain radical urban school cultures that recognize and uncover dominant structures in an effort to become true sanctuaries and second homes—places that promote and maintain interpersonal connections, places that honor race, culture, and our realities, places that afford psychological and physical safety, and places that have high academic expectations—for the students and the communities they strive to serve (Antrop-González, 2003; DeJesús, 2003)?

The notion of such a radical school culture exists through the work of the Dr. Pedro Albizu Campos Alternative High School (PACHS) located in Chicago, Illinois. A group of Puerto Rican students founded PACHS over 30 years ago in an effort to challenge Eurocentric curriculum practices and institutional racism. At PACHS, students and teachers actively work to construct and sustain cultural environments that include, rather than exclude, through curriculum and pedagogical practices that focus on sociopolitical and community realities (Antrop-González, 2003).

Curriculum at PACHS is situated in a project-based inquiry model. Students are encouraged to explore such topics as environmental racism, the economic and psychological effects of internal and direct colonialism, imperialism and neocolonialism, patriarchy, heterosexism, and homophobia. As a result of these inquiries, students and teachers work together, struggling to gain personal understanding in an effort to dismantle systems that maintain and protect the status quo. Students and teachers alike are thus encouraged to become change agents, questioners of the norm, activists in their school and in their communities.

The students and teachers at PACHS are hyper aware of issues of in/exclusion. As such, they maintain a psychologically and physically safe school environment; the wearing of gang colors, bullying, and racist and homophobic remarks are not tolerated. This type of environment engenders high quality interpersonal relationships between students and teachers as well as promotes high academic expectations. There is a strong sense of belonging at PACHS (Antrop-González, 2003).

We view the rereading our high school yearbook signing as an inquiry project, similar to ones that the students at PACHS accomplish. That is, our rereadings of our yearbook signings have become part of a larger process of reflection, negotiation, and understanding of the past and the ways we challenge and reclaim our present and future. Moreover, through this process we are learning to challenge broader notions of power and the status quo and to recognize the ways that others are struggling to overcome in/exclusion within school cultures—exposing the hidden curriculum within structures that in/exclude students based on class, race, gender identity, sexual identity, and ability and calling into question the subtle ways that the dominant culture maintains itself within our schools, within our curricula, within our cultural pedagogy.

REFERENCES

Antrop-González, R. (2003). "This school is my sanctuary": The Dr. Pedro Albizu Campos Alternative High School. *Journal of the Center for Puerto Rican Studies, 15*(2), 232-255.

Antrop-González, R., Vélez, W., & Garrett, T. (2005). *¿Dónde están los estudiantes puertorriqueños académicamente exitosos* [Where are the academically successful Puerto Rican students]?: Success factors of high achieving Puerto Rican high school students. *Journal of Latinos and Education, 4*(2), 74-95.

Best, S., & Kellner, D. (1991). *Postmodern theory.* New York: The Guilford Press.

DeJesús, A. (2003). "Here it's more like your house": The proliferation of authentic caring as school reform at El Puente Academy for Peace and Justice. In B. Rubin & E. Silva (Eds.), *Critical voices: Students living school reform* (pp. 132-151). London: Routledge Falmer.

Finders, M. J. (1997). *Just girls.* New York: Teachers College Press.

Flores-González, N. (2005). Popularity versus respect: School structure, peer groups, and Latino academic achievement. *International Journal of Qualitative Studies in Education, 18*(5), 625-642.

Gee, P. (2001). Readings as situated language: A sociocognitive perspective. *Journal of Adolescent & Adult Literacy, 44*(8), 714-725.

Giroux, H. A. (1992). Critical literacy and student experience: Donald Graves' approach to literacy. In P. Shannon (Ed.), *Becoming political: Readings and writings in the politics of literacy education* (pp. 15-20). Portsmouth, NH: Heinemann.

PART II

SOCIOECONOMIC STATUS AND ABILITY

CHAPTER 3

REFLECTING ON MARY H. WRIGHT ELEMENTARY

Ideologies of High Expectations in a "Re-Segregated School"

**Susan L. Schramm-Pate,
Rhonda B. Jeffries, and Leigh Kale D'Amico**

The myth contained in Ovid's *Metamorphoses* (1960) details a sculptor named Pygmalion praying to Venus, the Roman goddess of love, to transform his sculpture of a beautiful woman into flesh and blood. Greek and Roman myths were popularized and analyzed by Edith Hamilton (1953) who categorized the saga of Pygmalion and Galatea as a love story, but this particular folktale of a sculptor and his statue is also a story of not only transformation, but also that great human drama known as *becoming educated*. Since Galatea is the product of Pygmalion's expectation, the moral of the story is that the power of positive thinking can cause the impossible to come true. The Pygmalion theme has regularly recurred in English literature. The Elizabethan dramatist John Marston told the tale of Pygmalion in *The Metamorphoses of Pygmalion's Image* (1598), the Victorian socialist poet William Morris included it in *The Earthly Paradise* (1868-

Inclusion in Urban Educational Environments:
Addressing Issues of Diversity, Equity, and Social Justice, 45–70
Copyright © 2006 by Information Age Publishing
All rights of reproduction in any form reserved.

70), and it was the subject of a comedy by W. S. Gilbert titled *Pygmalion and Galatea* (1871). The most famous version is probably that of the popular play *Pygmalion* written by English playwright George Bernard Shaw in 1912.

Drawing on inspiration from the classical myth, Shaw's story deals with the complex issues of human relationships in a social world and beneath the comedy lies a satire on the superficiality of class distinctions. The Galatea in Shaw's version is Eliza Doolittle, a very cockney flower girl in turn of the century England and the Pygmalion is a cocky, sexist linguist, and phoneticist, Henry Higgins believes that diction is what really sets the classes apart. He wagers with his friend, Colonel Pickering, that through refinement of speech and transformation behavior, he can turn the lower class Eliza into a lady who will fool high society. What is in the wager for Eliza is the promise that she might be able to own her own flower shop and somewhat escape her lower class roots.

One of the major themes of Shaw's *Pygmalion* revolves around the benefits of acquiring an education. Part of the edification it bestows includes being able to reach new insights, being empowered to cultivate new awarenesses, and being endowed with new understandings of life and of self. Eliza begins the story as an unstable, insecure character who acknowledges her less privileged status and membership in the working class. She experiences a type of enlightenment as the result of undergoing a drastic change in social status which also increases her level of confidence as she gains a new perception of herself and a new outlook on life. Shaw uses the characters to demonstrate the necessity of human evolution—as Eliza's verbal ability increases, so does her self-esteem.

EDUCATIONAL SELF-FULFILLING PROPHECY

The term "self-fulfilling prophecy" first appeared in the essay, "The Self-Fulfilling Prophecy," by Robert K. Merton which was published in the *Antioch Review* in 1948, and is based on W. I. Thomas's famous dictum that "if men [sic] define situations as real, they are real in their consequences" (Wineburg, 1987, p. 28). A self-fulfilling prophecy is that which occurs when a person's expectations of an event make the outcome more likely to occur than would otherwise have been true. To paraphrase Henry Ford famous dictum: "If you think you can, you can. If you think you can't, you're right" (BrainyQuote, n.d.). Since Merton's publication the term has been used by everyone from American presidents to legislators to sports writers and in academic discourses as diverse as sociology, economics, political science, anthropology, public administration, and social work, but according to Wineberg (1987), it is American schooling where the term has garnered the most controversy.

The Pygmalion effect has been widely understood (if not practiced) by educators for decades (Feldman & Prohaska, 1979; Glasser, 1984, 1997; Ogbu, 1978; Rosenthal & Jacobson, 1968). Kenneth B. Clark, social psychologist and consultant to the National Association for the Advancement of Colored People (NAACP) in *Brown v. Board of Education* (1954), was prominent in influencing the court to dismantle American segregated school systems. In a description of Clark's desegregation work, Wineberg (1987) notes:

> Taught by society to be inferior, black children learned to feel and act inferior. Aided by the mechanism of the self-fulfilling prophecy, the effects of racism moved from 'out there' in society to inside people's heads and became in Clark's terms, "embedded in the personality." (p. 29)

Desegregationists like Clark realized that simply changing the social organization of schools would have little effect on the achievement of students of color unless a concomitant change occurred in the minds of their teachers. According to Wineberg (1987), the term "educational self-fulfilling prophecy" first appeared in the educational literature in Clark's 1963 report of a study of teacher attitudes in 10 inner-city desegregated schools. Clark's notion that teachers' low expectations for minority students caused them to do poorly in school filtered down to school personnel and became part of in-service training programs and the topic of educational research by the mid-1960s.

In their famous book *Pygmalion in the Classroom* published in 1968, Harvard psychologist Robert Rosenthal and elementary school principal, Lenore Jacobson detail their study of teachers in a low income southern San Francisco neighborhood where a testing program had identified some students as having high potential and others as having low potential. In fact, unbeknownst to the teachers, the students had been picked randomly and assigned to one of the two groups. The results after a year in school: the so-called high potential group showed "significant" gains in achievement and ability as measured by standardized tests. The implications of Rosenthal and Jacobson's (1968) study suggest that compensatory education needed to simply be more centered around the induction of positive expectancies in teachers where there previously existed negative expectations.

As Riessman (1962) had already noted of educational research and the education establishment, it was one thing to create a "positive myth" and quite another to have it accepted. While Rosenthal and Jacobson's study received criticism on statistical and design grounds from the scholarly community (Elashoff & Snow, 1971; Jensen. 1969, 1980; Thorndike, 1968), the educational Pygmalion effect as a *cultural ideal* was nevertheless embraced by the general public. A detailed discussion of the book made the front page of *The New York Times* on August 14, 1967 and Rosenthal himself was featured on the *Today Show* with Barbara Walters in 1969. The writers of the popular press embraced Rosenthal and Jacobson's theory that disadvantaged children did not possess some problem or have some deficit that must be remedied but that changing the attitudes and expectations of teachers toward disadvantaged children would be more effective.

BELIEF IN POTENTIAL CREATES POTENTIAL

Following *Pygmalion in the Classroom*, a barrage of educational studies in the 1970s suggested that everything should be done to create a highly positive attitude about students in the minds of teachers, administrators, and parents/guardians. These additional studies showed that teachers' positive and negative expectations affected student behavior if not IQ scores (e.g., Cornbleth, David, & Button, 1974; Rubovits & Maehr, 1971). For instance, Brophy and Good (1970) documented interesting patterns of student behavior resulting from the Pygmalion effect such as high expectations, students volunteering more answers, initiating more contacts with their teachers, raising their hands more often, and having fewer reading problems than their low expectation peers.

Some of the subsequent studies identified reciprocity as a missing link in the Rosenthal-Jacobson Pygmalion equation (Feldman & Prohaska, 1979; Rappaport & Rappaport, 1975; Zanna, Sheras, Cooper, & Shaw, 1975) and illustrated that *both* teacher behaviors *and* students' performances (i.e., student expectations) were key to influencing positive communication in classrooms. For example in *Student as Pygmalion: Effect of Student Expectation on the Teacher*, Feldman and Prohaska (1979) found that neither students nor teachers are the "sole Pygmalion in the classroom" and that "to examine only the teacher is overly simplistic given that both participants bring their own expectations, attitudes, and behavior to what is clearly a social situation" (p. 492).

If there are two types of self-fulfilling prophecy: those that are self-imposed and those that are imposed by others, then we can view how these impositions can influence both positively and negatively a person's life and consequently help to mold one's self-concept and ultimately one's self. Paulo Freire (1970/1997) in *Pedagogy of the Oppressed* argued that implicit in what he calls the "banking concept" of schooling is the assumption of dichotomies between human beings and the world and between teachers and students. Resolving the bipolar contradiction of teacher-student so that "both are simultaneously teachers *and* students," (p. 53) broadens expectations.

Imparting a positive motivating attitude that fosters a belief in the student's ability to perform, students should also have a clear understanding that there is no question of them performing well. We must be cognizant of the positive and negative ramifications of expectations—focusing on weaknesses will not bring out potential. Moreover, as Freire (1970/1997) has shown, by not treating persons who are not inside the dominant society as pathological we can challenge the school's "paternalistic social action apparatus" (p. 55).

According to John Ogbu (1978), cultural deprivation theory (Bloom, Davis, & Hess, 1965; Gottfried, 1973; Hunt, 1964) did not fully explain why Black children did poorly in school since the theory, "erroneously labels many aspects of black childhood experiences as 'pathological' and thus generates 'remedial programs' dedicated to the elimination of the presumed pathologies" (p. 46). Ogbu argued that teacher expectations were just one piece, albeit an important piece, of the complex cultural puzzle. Eliza Doolittle failed to speak "normal" English and act "normal" because she grew up in a "pathological" culture that was different from that of Higgins and Pickering and as such, Eliza did not acquire the values, attitudes, and learning styles required for success in mainstream bourgeois culture.

Just as Ogbu (1978) and Spradley (1972) noted, the criteria for measuring school performance and adequacy of cultural background is based on White, middle-class cultural values: tests, grades, skills, and tasks of middle-class American school children, so too was Eliza's remediation in the form of Higgins intervention aimed to "cure" or to "fix" the culturally deprived and marginalized Eliza. Higgins "belief" in her ability to change is thus linked to his desire to "fix" her shortcomings, to change her behavior patterns by changing her mentality so that she can fit into or "pass" within "healthy" society. His expectations are linked to the personal satisfaction he will get from winning the bet with Pickering that he can successfully pass Eliza off as royalty in high society. According to Freire (1970/1997),

> The truth is, however, that the oppressed are not "marginals," are not people living "outside" society. They have always been "inside"—inside the structure which made them "beings for others." The solution is not to "integrate" them into the structure of oppression, but to transform that structure so that they can become "beings for themselves." (p. 55).

Whether one believes in the doctrine of essentialism (i.e., that one is born with genetic gifts or the lack of them) or the concept of cultural deprivation theory, students clearly bring what Pierre Bordieu calls *habitus* (i.e., a collection of dispositions) to the classroom. The backgrounds, values, standards, linguistic codes, and worldviews of middle-class and upper-class children are often more analogous with those of teachers. As Bowles and Gintis (1977) have established, the so-called hidden agendas of schools, namely the socialization of oppression and sense of inferiority or defectiveness in the minds of students underscores academic and educational evolution. Like Shaw's *Pygmalion*, educational self-fulfilling prophecy represents not merely an idea but also a uniquely American *mythos*: Despite our social class, our previous experiences, and even our test scores the road to success is ultimately paved with the power of positive thinking. Contemporary research on effective schools indicates that there is a link between increased student achievement and higher teacher and administrative expectations (Glasser, 1997; Oakes, 1996; Sadker & Sadker, 1994).

Using the concepts of choice theory, Glasser's (1997) research in a seventh and eighth grade middle schools in Cincinnati, Ohio illustrates how he was able to create environments in which teachers stopped almost all coercion—"an approach that was radically different from the way most of these students had been treated since kindergarten" (p. 601). Glasser notes:

> When we asked the students why they were no longer disruptive and why they were beginning to work in school, over and over they said, "You care about us.' And sometimes they added, "And now you give us choices and work that we like to do." (p. 601)

Whether consciously or unconsciously, we inform students as to what our expectations are. We exhibit thousands of cues from the language we use to the body language with which we communicate. If expectations can create reality, there is an enormous incentive to have high expectations of the students in our spheres of influence. By communicating in a manner that will enable them to be their best, we impact students and it does not matter if the child is actually "smart."

Nel Noddings (1984) provides numerous examples to supplement her compelling argument for an ethics based on natural caring and recommends that we tap into a feminine sensitivity of receptivity, relatedness, and responsiveness. For her, the wholesale realignment of education impinges on an enhanced sensitivity in the moral matter of what it means "to care" and "to be cared for," she writes:

> The primary aim of every educational institution and of every educational effort must be the maintenance and enhancement of caring. Parents, police, social workers, teachers, preachers, neighbors, coaches, older siblings must

all embrace this primary aim. It functions as end, means, and criterion for judging suggested means. (p. 172)

The teacher and the student are engaged in the art of living and as such their task is to bring as much of their selves as they can to the process of schooling and have faith in themselves, others, and the culture in which they exist. Mary Caroline Richards wrote,

> It is a terrible thing when a teacher gives the impression that he [sic] does not care what the child does. It is false and it is unfaithful. The child hopes that an adult will have more sense and more heart than that. (1962, p. 101)

METHODOLOGY

The Research Site via Standards Based Movement

In the current standards based reform movement, educators continue to assign demoralizing labels to what they deem "poor" schools. According to the National Research Council Committee on Appropriate Test Use (1999) report on high stakes testing,

> [T]he lower achievement test scores of racial and ethnic minorities and students from low-income families reflect persistent inequalities in American society and its schools, not inalterable realities about those groups of students. The improper use of test scores can reinforce these inequalities. (p. 15)

Under the U.S. Department of Education's (2001) No Child Left Behind Act (NCLB), students are broken down into categories by characteristics such as race, income, and whether they are in special education classes. Schools must meet targets for each category and the more demographic categories a school has the more goals it must meet. If a school fails to meet its annual goal for Adequate Yearly Progress (AYP) it faces sanctions that grow progressively more severe.

In South Carolina, a program called *School Report Cards* attempts to meet the requirements for assessment in the current NCLB legislation in part by issuing a yearly four-page document that is publicized in the popular press. It determines "success" in schools by setting 15 objectives and then devising measures that decide whether or not schools achieve those objectives in order to meet the South Carolina 2010 Educational Goal of ranking in the top of states nationally. According to the South Carolina Education Oversight Committee's (EOC) (2004) Web site the 2010 Educational Goal is as follows:

By 2010, South Carolina's student achievement will be ranked in the top half of states nationally. To achieve this goal, we must become one of the five fastest improving systems in the country. (para 1)

The EOC claims to be an independent, nonpartisan group and it is made up of 18 educators, business people, and legislators who were appointed by the legislature and governor to enact the South Carolina Accountability Act of 1998. The Act sets standards for improving the state's K-12 educational system through ongoing reviews of the schools education improvement process.

The EOC's assessment of how the schools are doing is reported in the School Report Cards. The report cards are mandated by the Education Accountability Act of 1998. The Act also sets standards for what students need to "know" at each grade level and assesses how well they are learning those standards. School Report Cards provide ratings and information on factors such as school funding, teachers, and student attendance, student-teacher ratios, and parental involvement. The criteria used to calculate a school's rating depend on the grade levels included within the school. Student performance on the exit exam and the percentage of students eligible for LIFE scholarships are used to calculate high school ratings. Ratings for schools with students in Grades 3 through 8 are based on the results of the Palmetto Achievement Challenge Test (PACT).

Mary H. Wright Elementary School is located in Spartanburg, South Carolina, a mid-size city, and served 359 students in PreK through Grade 6 in Spartanburg School District Seven during the 2003-2004 school year (Free School Report, n.d.). Of those 359 students, 332 are Black, 15 are White, 3 are Hispanic, and 2 are Asian. Among the poorest children in South Carolina with 334 free-lunch students and 16 reduced price lunch students (Free School Report, n.d.), the per pupil expenditure is the highest in the state with $9,401 spent on each child in 2003-2004 (Public School Review, n.d.). In 2003-2004 the PACT results for Mary H. Wright Elementary School show that in mathematics 1.9% were classified as "advanced," 8.8% were classified as "proficient," 51.3% were classified as "basic," and 38.1% as "below basic," and in English/language arts 0.6% were classified as "advanced," 11.9% were classified as "proficient," 51.3% were classified as 'basic," and 36.3% were classified as "below basic" (GreatSchools.net., n.d.).

During the 2003-04 school year Mary H. Wright Elementary School received the following South Carolina School Report Card designations (GreatSchools.net, n.d.): Absolute Rating: *Average*; Improvement Rating: *Excellent*; Adequate Yearly Progress: *No*. These seemingly disparate ratings illustrate the ambiguity of the School Report Card system. One might ask how a school can be deemed "excellent" in improvement and yet "not adequate" in its yearly progress and merely "average" overall?

DATA REVIEW, COLLECTION, AND ANALYSIS

The researchers for this study collectively reviewed the existing data on the site under investigation and conducted open-ended, school history interviews with seven current teachers, the current principal, and the recently retired principal of Mary H. Wright Elementary. These interviews were collected via phone and electronic format and resulted in the production of verbatim or near verbatim transcripts. All researchers coded transcripts to identify thematic frameworks using the constant comparative method (Glaser & Strauss, 1967) across transcript data and archival document data. Interview transcripts and document data were compared and recoded to confirm and identify emergent themes. Member checks were conducted to confirm variability and trustworthiness within and among the narrative data (Merriam, 1998; Patton, 1990).

Specifically, this case study focuses intently on one elementary school site as the unit of analysis with purposeful sampling of the administrator(s), and purposefully selected samples of the classroom instructors who had significant time spent in the school environment during its transformation and to the present time. The case study method was used to revisit the site under investigation to explore the longitudinal data and confirm or refute the efficacy in the methods employed at the site. The participants' narratives were analyzed to gain an understanding of how external and internal policy and expectations impact one school's effectiveness from the perspectives of the administrator(s) and seven instructors. The outcome of the case study is evaluative in that it describes, illuminates, and attempts to provide a judgment and offer meaning to the reader about how low-achieving schools may improve their performances by raising their expectations. Additionally, the data show that the alteration and maintenance of expectations created a school culture that was able to sustain itself beyond the policy mechanisms put in place to begin the transformation.

Mary H. Wright Elementary and School Report Cards

The former principal of Mary H. Wright, Barbara Whitney who is credited with reconceptualizing the school over an eleven year period (Ballard, 2000) realized the strain the high stakes testing and standardization movement was placing on her teaching staff. She recalled:

> It is very difficult to "keep up the pace" when you are forced to continuously work at "breakneck speed" just to keep your head above water! I fear that the teachers will become distracted by all of the current demands of the profession and become discouraged to the point that many of those who are now dedicated to making a difference for these needy children will just "give up" and find alternative employment. (personal correspondence, October 11, 2004)

In the Winter 2001 publication of *In Our Schools* by the South Carolina Department of Education, State Superintendent of Education, Inez Tenenbaum described the report cards as "a great opportunity to celebrate our successes and address the challenges facing South Carolina's schools." She went on to say that, "We believe that every student can be a successful learner and that every school can achieve" (p. 1).

In an online "Chat" Tenenbaum (personal communication, December 4, 2001) said that the goal of the EOC and the State Department of Education was to "set fair challenging targets." In her address, "Involvement is Key to Accountability Success," Tenenbaum said that the report cards are just one aspect of South Carolina's multifaceted accountability system that includes curriculum standards, assessments, professional development, technical assistance, and rewards. The Mary H. Wright teachers recognize the progress they are making regardless of what South Carolina's School Report Cards have to say. Whitney concurs with Tenenbaum noting:

> School Report Cards or any other means of measuring school progress can never tell the whole story. It is but one tool used at one specific time that attempts to measure the learning for an entire year! It in no way can measure those times along the way when "children finally get it" or when they begin to see small but constant improvement in grades. (personal correspondence, October 11, 2004)

The explicit claims of accountability measures include equipping students with strong academic foundations, informing parents, and assuring parents that their children are getting a good education, providing teachers with measurable "proof" that their students are learning, and reassuring the general public that their tax dollars for schools are helping finance results. The moral undergirding of the accountability system are implicit expectations couched in the values and beliefs of school leaders. For South Carolina, ostensibly it follows that Tenenbaum's logic of the School Report Cards is based on her notion that "Pygmalion factors" of high expectations for performance, work habits, and test scores, can trigger an upward spiral in the performance of a school.

Tenenbaum declared, "Our accountability system raises *expectations* for our students and challenges communities to become more involved in helping our schools succeed" (South Carolina Department of Education, 2001, p. 3). Like many southern states with an inferiority complex where their nationally low ranked schools are concerned, State School Superintendent Tenenbaum plays into the hands of the state-to-state credibility gap that is part and parcel of NCLB's hidden curriculum to promote a national culture of competition. In her recent response to the U.S. Department of Education's approval of the state's NCLB accountability plan, she mused, "South Carolina schools will still have a steeper hill to climb than in other states ... but I believe we should be raising the bar for what we expect, not lowering it" (South Carolina Department of Education, n.d., p. 1).

However, for Tenenbaum, improvement of public schooling is linked to the "common good" and she has consistently argued that South Carolina's School Report Cards should reflect the combined efforts of both schools and communities noting, "All of us share the responsibility of ensuring the success of our schools. We invite everyone to become partners in this effort" (South Carolina Department of Education, 2001, p. 7). In her online "Chat," she said, "Every South Carolinian has a stake in improving the state's public schools because there is a strong link between the quality of a state's schools and its overall quality of life" (personal communication, December 4, 2001).

Within the reports, each school and school district receives one of five academic ratings—excellent, good, average, below average, and unsatisfactory. One rating is assigned to the school's performance level, one for the improvement rate, and one for the composite rating. The performance level is based on student performance within the past school year. The improvement rate is based on the academic progress of students from one year to the next. The improvement rating also takes into account the increase or decline of performance of all categories of students. The composite rating or absolute rating summarizes a school's performance level and improvement rating and evaluates its achievement at the end of the school year and the progress made over the year. The South Carolina Department of Education calculates the poverty composite—an index of students receiving Medicaid and/or reduced meal plans—for all schools. In 2002 almost 60% of schools with poverty composites of 80% or higher earned absolute ratings of "Below Average" or "Unsatisfactory" (South Carolina Department of Education, 2002).

The data used in the School Report Cards to recognize schools or districts with high performance and help make decisions aimed at targeting resources to assist schools or districts with low performance. Since the results are published in the popular press, they encourage public comparisons between schools (and thus, teachers and students) labeled "high" and schools labeled "low" around the state. Once assigned a label of either "below average" or "unsatisfactory," the expectations that educators and reformers have are also revealed. In other words, when demoralizing labels are used to identify students and schools they are more often than not used to identify non-mainstream students. Moreover, labels reveal the divisions and constructions of difference embedded in the structure of schooling just as much as they make claims at explaining and prescribing. According to Whitney,

> Although the Report Card reveals information that is less than desirable [for Mary H. Wright Elementary], we are viewed as a school that is doing the best job possible to provide the best education for our children. The number of congratulatory messages, visits, phone calls, and newspaper articles, and television spots attest to our status. (personal correspondence, October 11, 2004)

The labels assigned to Mary H. Wright Elementary School on the School Report Card indicate areas for improvement; however, the administrators and teachers received positive feedback from the community, parents, and most importantly, past and current students. Rather than dwelling on the School Report Card labels, Whitney and her team continually sought to improve the environment and encourage progress.

Mary H. Wright Elementary and the Accelerated Schools Program

Before the tenure of Whitney from 1994-2004, Mary H. Wright's dismal record epitomized what is lacking in South Carolina's public schools that serve the state's working class poor and people of color. With Whitney's help, Mary H. Wright chose to become an Accelerated School and underwent the demanding process in 1996. According to Ballard (2000):

> During the past six years, Mary H. Wright has pulled itself from the list of the 200 worst schools in the state, through teacher commitment and measures such as the implementation of the high academic and behavioral expectations of the Accelerated Schools Program.... The arduous process of becoming an Accelerated School energized the faculty and made the Mary H. Wright community aware that there were strengths that could be built upon. The leadership of Mrs. Barbara Whitney has been a tremendous asset for the school. (p. 204)

The concept of accelerated schools was introduced in 1986 at Stanford University as an effort to close the achievement gap between "at risk" and mainstream students (Hopfenberg & Levine, 1990). Economist and Stanford professor, Hank Levine founded the Accelerated Schools Program in an effort to radically change individual schools by redesigning and integrating curricular, instructional, and organizational practices so they can provide enrichment—not just remediation—for "at-risk" students (Finnan & Hopfenberg, 1997). For Levine, an "at-risk" student is one who is mismatched with an educational system (1997). The premise behind the Accelerated Schools Program is specific and simplistic:

> [A]t-risk students must learn at a faster rate than more privileged students—not at a slower rate that drags them farther and farther behind. An enrichment strategy rather than a remedial one, offers the greatest hope for achieving this goal. (Levine & Hopfenberg, 1991, p. 12)

Three overarching elements of the Accelerated Schools Program involve the following guiding principles and values: (1) unity of purpose; (2) empowerment and responsibility; and (3) building on strengths (Hopfenberg & Levine, 1990). The school community agrees on a common set of goals for the school and these goals focus efforts and serve as an organizational framework for curriculum and instruction. The members of the school community not only make collective educational decisions they also take responsibility for implementation and results thereby limiting the "blame game" that so often is associated with factors outside of their control for students' poor educational outcomes. The Accelerated Schools Program first identifies and draws on available strengths and learning resources in the school community such as youth organizations, senior citizens, and business and religious groups instead of exaggerating weaknesses typically associated with "at-risk" students. The strengths of the "at-risk" Mary H. Wright Elementary students are not the strengths typically associated with predominant whiteness and middle-classness.

According to Whitney, the Accelerated Schools Program provided Mary H. Wright with "the structure necessary to define, establish, and maintain the educational focus that was most beneficial to the teaching and learning in our school" (personal correspondence, October 11, 2004). The program's site-based management strategies that enabled her to initiate and implement changes at the local school level were the most valuable and she was able to bring parents, teachers, students, and administrators together to first take stock of where they were (baseline data) and then to agree on a common set of goals (changes) for the school. By creating a shared vision as a focus for change, Whitney and her teaching team were able to identify strengths, gaps, and needed changes and then to establish small groups to work on them (Ballard, 2000).

In addition to the Accelerated Schools Program, Whitney began her transformation of the school by asking her teachers to read the book, *A Framework for Understanding Poverty* (1996) written by Ruby Payne, a former teacher and school administrator. According to Payne, "I came to realize there were major differences between generational poverty and middle-class—and that the biggest differences were not about money" (p. 9). In her text, Payne makes accessible strategies for teachers to understand and to work with children and families living in generational poverty. Because the support systems and emotional resources tend to be weaker or unavailable to children living in generational poverty, Payne through a case study approach, presents stories that stress the importance of creating and continuously promoting a positive learning environment for students, including strategies for implementing school-wide homework support, supplemental school-wide reading programs, looping (i.e., keeping students with the same teacher(s) for 2 or more years), and the importance of parent training and contact. Following Payne, Whitney and her staff learned coping strategies for meeting the needs of physically aggressive students and ways to structure team interventions with parents to help the Mary H. Wright students be more successful in school.

Whitney required her teachers who chose to remain a part of the educational family at Mary H. Wright Elementary under the auspices of the Accelerated Schools Program to be willing to do whatever necessary to answer the call to transform the school culture. The internal culture of the school was positively transformed through the steps laid out by the Accelerated Schools Program and focuses on the following three key factors: (1) high expectations for performance, work habits, and test scores; (2) year-round calendar; (3) caring community/family atmosphere.

High Expectations for Performance, Work Habits, and Test Scores

The philosophy that it is "possible to have high expectations for all children and to reach even the most resistant learner through powerful curriculum, instruction, and organization" (Finnan & Hopfenberg, 1997, p. 489) made sense to Whitney. She wrote the following note to her staff at the beginning of the 1999-2000 school year:

> It truly exemplifies all of the warmth, caring, and nurturing that is the "rule" and not the exception here at Mary Wright.... You have a very high calling! Don't forget to touch their little lives with a word of hope and a

smile of encouragement. It may be the only one some will receive!... Have a great year and remember ... I love you, I respect you, and I trust you! Most of all ... the children depend on you! (Ballard, 2000, p. 211)

When Whitney inherited the school in 1994 it had continuously been dubbed "low performing" or "below average." The school's teachers and administrators had become accustomed to this label, and its students internalized a sense of demoralization and hopelessness in their intelligence and abilities. Whitney was determined to change the perception of the school among all stakeholders: the teachers, students, parents, community, and the state. In an interview with Robert Dalton published in the *Spartanburg Herald-Journal* in 1998, Whitney said, "'We have bright kids, wonderful kids here. We want to give them a chance to show what they can do,'" (Ballard, 2000, p. 88).

To begin the change process, Whitney instilled in her teaching staff a sense of pride in their own abilities and encouraged them to recognize and promote the individual abilities of all students. "Rita"[1] recalled how teacher attitudes were maintained at the school during the transition and even up to this point:

> When I was hired, they did mention that there were high expectations for the students and that Ruby Payne and her books were an influence in the school. We have discussed her books more in detail during in-service days which has been helpful. (personal correspondence, October 14, 2004)

Decisions impacting the school were made democratically, with teachers, parents, and students being active participants. The high expectations that included empowering the stakeholders through involvement in decisions prompted the growth of a family atmosphere in which the administrators, teachers, students, and parents felt like a team working to accomplish common goals.

The positive teacher expectations that grew out of the Accelerated Schools Program played a major role in Mary H. Wright Elementary School being identified as an American School of Promise in 2000. To become a School Of Promise, a school must demonstrate how it provides all Five Promises Of Caring Adults; Safe Place; Healthy Start; Marketable Skills; And Opportunities to Serve to a critical mass of students in that school (America's Promise, n.d.). Through the local environment, political leadership, related initiatives, and available resources Mary H. Wright provided the activities necessary to meet the Five Promises. A few of the assorted activities that enabled the school to meet its requirements as a School Of Promise included development programs that afforded much personal contact as well as extended school day activities, and a modified school calendar to provide continuous instruction and care giving to

Mary H. Wright students in times when they would normally be out of school. Mary H. Wright served as a national model School of Promise during the 2000-2001 school year.

The school was also one of 229 schools to receive Palmetto Gold status in 2003-2004 which was accompanied by a $2,644 reward and one of 22 Palmetto Gold schools with the highest levels of achievement and improvement to be showcased by the South Carolina Department of Education in the summer of 2004. These recognitions and awards prove that these children rose to the challenge when they knew the people who worked with them day in and day out really cared about them and were willing to go the extra mile to assure their preparedness.

Year-Round Calendar

Henry Higgins insists that Eliza Doolittle live under his roof while under his tutelage; in this way, the professor has an uninterrupted "school day" in which to transform his protégé. When he is not drilling Eliza with phonetics lessons into the wee hours of the morning (much to her chagrin) he is continually schooling her with the help of his staff and Pickering on proper etiquette of dress, manners, and conversation. While Eliza clearly yearns for a break from the overbearing Higgins, she also eventually not only appreciates her new home but thrives under the constant attention.

During the common school movement in the nineteenth century, many Americans lived in rural farming areas. The common school's traditional calendar with early morning start-times and 2 or 3 month summer breaks was designed to meet the growing nation's agrarian needs. School calendars revolved around the harvesting and planting of crops so that children could help at home during the busy summer months. One of the reasons why schools remained on the traditional schedule in the twentieth century after the United States transitioned from a primarily agrarian to an industrial economy is because it was difficult to hold classes during the summer months without air conditioning.

Over the past 2 decades, year-round schooling has gained popularity and acceptance. Year-round education (YRE) is a concept which reorganizes the school year to provide more continuous learning by spacing the long summer vacation into shorter, more frequent vacations throughout the year (Johnson, 2000). Students spend the same amount of days in class as students in traditional calendar schools—the days are just arranged differently with smaller, more frequent breaks throughout the year. The summer break for example may be only a month instead of 2 or 3 months.

The National Association for Year-Round Education promotes the idea that students and teachers will be more refreshed by frequent breaks and that they will not get burnt out as easily (Kneese & Knight, 1995). Some argue that too much time is spent reviewing in the fall after students have forgotten what they learned the previous year. Many immigrant children fall behind because they are not exposed to English during the long summer break. In the case of "at-risk" student populations, academic support in the form of remediation is continuous and timely.

Teachers' interests are met by offering extra days and extra pay for those who desire it through extended contracts, intersession employment, and substituting (Glines, 2000; Stenvall, 2000). Alternatively for teachers who prefer more personal time to money, it is sometimes possible for teachers to split 1 year-round contract or work fewer days per week (Rasmussen, 2000). Teachers in year-round programs generally believe that the quality of instruction is better than in traditional programs due to the continuity of instruction (Quinlan, George, & Emmett, 1987). Shields and Oberg (2000) found that teachers reflected more on their practice because they were able to plan instruction at regular intervals during the academic year when it is needed most. They find it more efficient and productive to plan curriculum for shorter blocks of time and feel that the year-round calendar provides ample time segments for instruction. Another advantage for teachers is that less review time is necessary at the beginning of each instructional block, as research has demonstrated that the shorter vacation periods reduce summer learning loss (Cooper, Nye, Charlton, Lindsay, & Greathouse, 1996). This is especially true for students of low socioeconomic status (SES) and high-risk students (Gandara & Fish, 1994; Kneese & Knight, 1995; Quinlan, George, & Emmett, 1987). This may be due to accessibility of immediate remediation in YRE (Curry, Washington, & Zyskowski, 1997).

Based on responses from students who wanted to spend more time at school, the long summer break in the traditional school year was recognized by Whitney and her teaching team as detrimental to the "at-risk" student population they serve (Ballard, 2000). The teachers and administrators sought support and district endorsement in implementing a modified year-round calendar. The school was granted the request and became the first school in Spartanburg to operate on a year-round calendar (Ballard, 2000).

While she acknowledges the difficulty some teachers had with adjusting to the year-round school schedule, Whitney credits the year-round calendar as instrumental to changing the cultural climate of the school as well as improving academic achievement. Referring to the year-round calendar as a "godsend," Whitney argues that this schedule was ideal for the children at Mary H. Wright since teachers could focus less on remediation and more on new skills. "In my opinion, selected school programs are centered around what is educationally sound and best suited for the children we serve" (personal correspondence, October 11, 2004).

Of the studies in which teacher attitudes have been explicitly examined, the research results clearly indicate that the majority of teachers in year-round schools favor the year-round calendar and believe it substantially enhances the professional environment (Shields & Oberg, 2000; Worthen & Zsiray, 1994). Due to the frequency of breaks on the year-round calendar, teachers exhibit improved morale and motivation, and less burn out and stress (Minnesota, 1999; North Carolina Center for Public Policy Research, 1997; Quinlan, George, & Emmett, 1987). "Mary Beth" a first grade teacher currently at Mary H. Wright said the year-round calendar helps with student and teacher burn out since "we all stay fresher ... not having so much review when the new school year starts" (personal correspondence, October 11, 2004).

At Mary H. Wright Elementary, the majority of teachers who are in favor of the year-round calendar approve of the continuity of education with shorter summer breaks and believe that students are benefiting both socially and academically from the continuous schedule. Those opposed see it as an unwanted intrusion into a family's traditional summer vacation and as unmanageable for working parents. "Don," a special education teacher who has been at the school for 3 years noted that a major concern for him centered around the school district offering extended calendar options for elementary school and middle school levels but not high school causing families with children falling in multiple grade levels to have to juggle different academic calendars.

He said:

> [We have] low enrollment [and] I know that it is because of [our year-round] schedule. Parents have a difficult time when several children in the family have different school schedules. At the beginning of our school year our students are very unhappy that friends from other schools are still enjoying a summer break or a brother or sister are still at home sleeping in. As far as making a student feel like family you do not need a different schedule to do that. Many of our students do not show up until after other schools start. At my previous year round or modified calendar school I stated [in an interview] to the *Charlotte Observer* newspaper a schedule is not what makes a great school. There is no research that says our [year-round] schedule is better. It can serve to get your school attention and some times your picture in the paper. (personal correspondence, October 18, 2004)

Critics like Don challenge the idea that year-round schedules improve grades and they raise concerns that scheduling can harm families. At Royal Oaks Elementary School in Cabarrus County, North Carolina,

The county school board agreed to put the school back on a traditional calendar, although [Principal] Winkler said, parent surveys have been positive on the year-round schedule, and test scores have gone up at Royal Oaks. But, Winkler said the year-round schedule didn't contribute to the higher test scores. (Smith, 2000)

Clearly there is plenty of debate. Supporters say year-round systems improve academic performance and enhance teacher praxis. Barbara Whitney was able to win the cooperation of her Mary H. Wright parents for a year-round calendar. While academic success was a concern of hers and the school district's, Whitney believed that fighting tradition and switching to a year-round schedule was in the best interest of the Mary H. Wright students.

Caring Community/Family Atmosphere

Dissolving the dualism between human beings and the world requires considering how the expectations of the broader school community impact learners and vice versa. Professor Higgins does not single-handedly turn his cockney protégé into a "lady." Eliza herself plays a part in her own transformation—she desires it, she wishes it so, she works hard toward her goals. Further, Eliza is also the product of an informal hidden curriculum as myriad people contribute to her education in both formal and informal ways. For example, the educational culture as it were for Eliza is affected by Higgins's housekeepers' kindnesses and their daily words of encouragement to Eliza, by the positive lessons that Higgins's colleague Colonel Pickering brings to the mix, and by the acceptance and encouragement of the people at the high society gatherings Eliza attends with Higgins and Pickering. Thus, all in the school community must take a hand in highlighting a student's potential and making clear their expectations.

For many children there is no Professor Henry Higgins or Colonel Pickering either inside or outside of the classroom to believe in them or to care about them. Their (mis)educators are often the streets or the juvenile detention center, where they may learn to hustle to survive in an atmosphere that is anything but geared to building self-esteem. Furthermore, their lack of support can even be found within the very classrooms that are charged with providing students with the information they need to be successful thinkers and citizens. Following Glasser (1997) and Noddings (1984), the Mary H. Wright staff believes all that should matter is that teachers and others in the school community believe in the child and care about the child. The staff goes to great trouble to enable the children to believe that they think their ideas are clever. They listen to them and believe in them and attempt to make them feel more comfortable. In short, they believe in the children. In a recent interview, Whitney, who retired last year, discussed her role in promoting the family atmosphere that has been noted as a key element of the success of the school:

> I grew up in a big family where everyone was always made to feel special....
> I have taken this feeling with me into the educational setting.... They say,
> "children don't care how much you know, until they know how much you"
> care! (personal correspondence, October 11, 2004)

Enabling the children to feel a sense of belonging, a sense of family, and a sense of ownership in the school was one of her primary goals and continues with the current administration and staff. While "Don" the teacher of self-contained classes of third, fourth, fifth, and sixth graders, bemoans the year-round calendar, he finds the family atmosphere conducive to his special education students. "We have an open door policy and continually work with parents as partners in their child's education" (personal correspondence, October 12, 2004). By reinforcing the school as the children's "home away from home," the Mary H. Wright staff is able to change the school culture from one of defeat to one of pride and improved learning.

Whitney did the hard work of getting her teachers to "buy into" the self-fulfilling prophecy effect that is now a taken for granted part of the school culture. Working through the school's bureaucratic administrative system for personnel, Whitney had teachers reassigned who did not adopt the cultural norms inherent in her Accelerated Schools program's great expectations. As an African American woman in a leadership position, Barbara Whitney's leadership style was to, "lead by example so there will be no doubt about your expectations" (personal correspondence, October 11, 2004). "Louise," currently a first grade teacher at the school noted that Whitney was always very personal in her leadership style and she loved the students. Another first grade teacher, "Mary Beth" said,

> I have enjoyed my years here because of the family atmosphere and the way
> we have always pulled together for the student's sake even though we
> haven't always agreed on everything.... You can feel the love and concern
> the teachers have for the students and for each other throughout the build-
> ing. (personal correspondence, October 11, 2004)

Finally, second grade teacher "Caroline" said,

> We [teachers] really become the parents of our students.... We show them
> love many times not seen at home and we give them POSITIVE feedback

constantly. They need to know they are worth something! (personal correspondence, October 13, 2004)

The children who attend Mary H. Wright Elementary are perhaps more fortunate than many children who live in poverty and one of the reasons is because Whitney and her staff not only care about the students but also work to cultivate new partnerships and expanded existing community partnerships. Several local organizations and churches embrace the spirit and energy exuded by Mary H. Wright and donate time and resources. For example, there is an active aftercare program everyday until six o'clock sponsored by the Boys' and Girls' Club of America and money from the Episcopal Church of the Advent provides enriching activities through an Adventure Program. The school also enjoys the active partnerships of Spartanburg Technical College and the mentorship of an African American male student group at Wofford College (Ballard, 2000).

CONCLUSION

If schools are really to be communities as John Dewey (1909) described in *School and Society*, it is clear that they should offer much more opportunity for highlighting students' potential and making clear their expectations. Through the Accelerated Schools Program, Whitney was able to organize Mary H. Wright Elementary on a year-round calendar, significantly increase community involvement, and most importantly, raise academic and behavior expectations. The idea of creating climates of high educational expectations presented in the present study was prompted by Shaw's *Pygmalion*. Throughout the years, Shaw's play has been read as a moralizing drama about the power of phonetics in the English language and the artificiality of class and social status. But, as Shaw himself argued (1963) and as Jane Roland Martin (2002) has recently pointed out, it is also a didactic drama about the power of education to *transform*.

Drawing inspiration from the Greek myth, Shaw's construction of the relationship between Henry Higgins and Eliza Doolittle is also a story of powerful influence of one person's expectations on another's behavior. James Macdonald (1995) explored schools and curriculum from a utopian desire for social justice, equity, and fairness. He wrote:

Education [is] a moral enterprise rather than simply a set of technical problems to be solved.... Thus, the struggle for personal integration, educational integrity, and social justice go on, necessitating a constant reevaluation of oneself [sic], one's work and one's world ... the act of theorizing is an act of faith, a religious act.... Curriculum theory is a *prayerful act*. (1995, p. 10-11, italics added)

Mary H. Wright is representative of a prayerful act, an act of faith. As a "re-segregated" school, it moved away from the taken-for-granted and the everyday and is still keeping pace under the most challenging of circumstances. "Moral judgments tell us what we ought to do and what we ought not to do" (Strike & Soltis, 1992, p. 7). A good consequentialist is concerned with "maximizing the *good*, that is, producing the most *good*" (1992, p. 12, italics added). As a consequentialist, Barbara Whitney choose the *moral* actions that had the best set of consequences for her school. Once she set up reasonable expectations and refused to deviate from a framework of democratic rights, responsibilities, and practices that would lead to a better realization of justice, equality, and liberty for the children of Mary H. Wright, her staff and students began to struggle (and continue to struggle) and refused (and still refuse) to give up hope.

Antonio Gramsci's notion of the *organic intellectual* (Forgacs & Nowell-Smith, 1985) typifies Whitney and her staff—immersed in the everyday, these school workers integrate great expectations and caring into the very fabric of the lifestyles, language, and traditions of the environment of Mary H. Wright Elementary. Their activities, efforts, and expectations focus on the ideas, values, attitudes, and morality of the persons in the school and in the context of their lived experiences. Whitney's solution is to physically hug each child she comes into contact with and to say the words, "I love you." While this may not be an option for everyone, in the case of Mary H. Wright the children respond by showing respect for themselves and for others. If more often than not, the outcomes of events that occur in our lives are the product of expectations we have of ourselves or that others have for us, then the Pygmalion effect has implications for educators.

NOTE

1.   Pseudonyms are used to protect the confidentiality of teachers.

REFERENCES

America's Promise: The Alliance for Youth. (n.d.). *Schools of promise*. Retrieved September 16, 2004, from http://www.americaspromise.org/community/schooldetail.cfm

Ballard, A. M. (2000). School success in the inner city: Exploring the components of curriculum, the calendar, and care in educational improvement (Doctoral dissertation, University of South Carolina, 2000). *Dissertation Abstracts International, 61*, 2570.

Bloom, B. S., Davis, A., & Hess, R. (1965). *Compensatory education for cultural deprivation*. New York: Holt.

Bowles, S., & Gintis, H. (1977). *Schooling in capitalist America: Educational reform and the contradictions of economic life*. New York: Basic Books.

BrainyQuote (n.d.). *Henry Ford quotes*. Retrieved October 11, 2005, from www.brainyquote.com/quotes/authors/h/henry_ford.html

Brophy, J. E., & Good, T. L. (1970). Teacher's communication of differential expectations for children's classroom performance: Some behavioral data. *Journal of Educational Psychology, 61*, 365-374.

Cooper, H., Nye, B., Charlton, K., Lindsay, J., & Greathouse, S. (1996). The effects of summer vacation on achievement test scores: A narrative and meta-analytic review. *Review of Educational Research, 66* (3), 227-268.

Cornbleth, C., David, O. L., Jr., & Button, C. (1974). Expectations for pupil achievement and teacher-pupil interaction. *Social Education, 38*, 54-58.

Curry, J., Washington, W., & Zyskowski, G. (1997). *Year-round schools evaluation, executive summary*. Austin, TX: Austin Independent School District Department of Accountability, Student Services, and Research.

Dewey, J. (1909). *The school and society*. Chicago: University of Chicago Press.

Elashoff, J., & Snow, R. E. (1971). *Pygmalion reconsidered: A case study in statistical inference: Reconsideration of the Rosenthal-Jacobson data on teacher expectancy*. Belmont, CA: Wadsworth.

Feldman, R. S., & Prohaska, T. (1979). The student as Pygmalion: Effect of student expectation on the teacher. *Journal of Educational Psychology 71*(4), 485-493.

Finnan, C., & Hopfenberg, W. S. (1997). Accomplishing school change. *Journal for a Just and Caring Education, 3*(4), 480-493.

Forgacs, D., & Nowell-Smith, G. (Eds.). (1985). *Antonio Gramsci: Selections from cultural writings*. Cambridge, MA: Harvard University Press.

Freire, P. (1997). *Pedagogy of the oppressed*. New York: Continuum. (Original work published 1970)

Gandara, P., & Fish, J. (1994, Spring). Year-round schooling as an avenue to major structural reform. *Educational Evaluation and Policy Analysis, 16*, 76-85.

Glasser, W. (1984). *Control theory: A new explanation of how we control our life*. New York: Harper & Row.

Glasser, W. (1997, April). A new look at school failure and success. *Phi Delta Kappa, 78*(8), 597-602.

Glaser, B., & Strauss, A. (1967). *The discovery of grounded theory*. Chicago: Aldine.

Glines, D. (2000). *Reflecting year-round education: Traditions and innovations*. San Diego, CA: National Association for Year-Round Education.

Gottfried, N. W. (1973). Effects of early intervention programs. In K. S. Miller & R. M. Dreger (Eds.), *Comparative studies of Blacks and Whites* (pp. 273-293). New York: Seminar Press.

GreatSchools.net. (n.d.). *Mary H. Wright Elementary School*. Retrieved August 23, 2004, from http://www.greatschools.net/cgibin/cs_compare/sc/?street=309+Caulder+Avenue&school_selected=100

Hamilton, E. (1953). *Mythology.* New York: New American Library.

Hopfenberg, W. S., & Levine, H. M. (1990). *Accelerated schools.* Stanford CA: Stanford University Press.

Hunt, J. M. (1964). The psychological basis for using preschool enrichment as an antidote for cultural deprivation. *The Merrill-Palmer Quarterly, 10,* 209-248.

Jensen, A. R. (1969). How much can we boost IQ and scholastic achievement? *Harvard Educational Review, 39,* 1-123.

Jensen, A. R. (1980). *Bias in mental testing.* New York: Free Press.

Johnson, K. (2000). *Frequently asked questions about year-round education.* San Diego, CA: National Association for Year-Round Education.

Kneese, C., & Knight, S. (1995). Evaluating the achievement of at-risk students in year-round education. *Planning and Changing, 26,* 71-90.

Levine, H. M. (1997). Raising school productivity: An X-efficiency approach. *Economics of Education Review, 16*(3), 303-311.

Levine, H. M., & Hopfenberg, W. S. (1991). Don't remediate: Accelerate! *Principal, 70*(13), 11-13.

Macdonald, B. J. (Ed.). (1995). *Theory as a prayerful act: The collected essays of James B. Macdonald.* New York: Peter Lang.

Martin, J. R. (2002, November). *Educational metamorphoses.* George Kneller lecture at the annual meeting of the American Educational Studies Association Annual Meeting, Pittsburgh, PA.

Merriam, S. (1998). *Case study research in education.* San Francisco: Jossey-Bass.

Merton, R. K. (1948). The self-fulfilling prophecy. *Antioch Review, 8,* 193-210.

Minnesota Department of Children, Families, & Learning. (1999, February). *Working group on alternative calendars: Report to the legislature. Twenty-sixth reference directory of year-round education programs for the 1999-2000 school year.* San Diego, CA: National Association for Year-Round Education.

National Research Council Committee on Appropriate Test Use. (1999). *High stakes: Testing for tracking, promotion, and graduation.* Washington, DC: National Academy Press.

Noddings, N. (1984). *Caring: A feminine approach to ethics & moral education.* Berkeley: University of California Press.

North Carolina Center for Public Policy Research. (1997, May). *North Carolina Insight, 17*(1).

Oakes, J. (1996). *Keeping track: How schools structure inequality.* New Haven, CT: Yale University Press.

Ogbu, J. (1978). *Minority education and caste: The American system in cross-cultural perspective.* San Diego, CA: Academic Press.

Ovid. (1960). *The metamorphoses.* New York: Mentor Book.

Patton, M. (1990). *Qualitative evaluation and research methods.* Newbury Park, CA: Sage.

Payne, R. K. (1996). *A framework for understanding poverty.* Highlands, TX: aha! Process.

Public School Review: Public Elementary, Middle, and High Schools (n.d.) *South Carolina School Agencies.* Retrieved October 19, 2004, from http://www.publicschoolreview.com/agency_stats/stateid/SC/level/0/stat/3

Quinlan, C., George, C., & Emmett, T. (1987). *Year-round education: Year-round opportunities*. A study of year-round education in California. Los Angeles: California State Department of Education.

Rappaport, M. M., & Rappaport, H. (1975). The other half of the expectancy equation: Pygmalion. *Journal of Educational Psychology, 67,* 531-536.

Rasmussen, K. (2000). Year-round education: Time to learn, time to grow. *Education Update, 42*(2), 46.

Richards, M. C. (1962). *Centering*. Middletown, CN: Wesleyan University Press.

Riessman, F. (1962). *The culturally deprived child*. New York: Harper & Row.

Rosenthal, R., & Jacobson, L. (1968). *Pygmalion in the classroom: Teacher expectation and pupil's intellectual development*. New York: Rinehart & Winston.

Rubovits, P. C., & Maehr, M. L. (1971). Pygmalion analyzed: Towards an explanation of the Rosenthal-Jacobson findings. *Journal of Personality and Social Psychology 19,* 197-203.

Sadker, M., & Sadker, D. (1994). *Failing at fairness: How America's schools cheat girls*. New York: Scribner.

Shaw, G. B. (1963). *Complete plays with prefaces*. New York: Dodd, Mead & Co.

Shaw, G. B. (1975). *Pygmalion*. New York: New American Library.

Shields, C., & Oberg, S. (2000). *Year-round schooling: Promises and pitfalls*. London: The Scarecrow Press.

Smith, G. (2000, November 21). Cabarrus school to drop out of year-round plan: Too few opt for schedule principal says. *The Charlotte Observer,* p. B1.

South Carolina Department of Education (n.d.). *U.S. Department of Education approves revisions to state's NCLB accountability plan*. Columbia, SC: Author.

South Carolina Department of Education (2001). Significant PACT improvements made: Educators praised for hard work. *In Our Schools, 2*(1), 3. Author.

South Carolina Department of Education (2002, October 31). *Schools receive higher absolute ratings on report cards: 80% average or better*. Retrieved September 28, 2004, from http://www.myschools.com/news/more.cfm?articleID=264

South Carolina Education Oversight Committee (2004). *South Carolina's 2010 education goals*. Retrieved September 28, 2004, from http://www.state.sc.us/eoc/

Spradley, J. P. (1972). The cultural experience. In J. P. Spradley & D. W. McCurdy (Eds.), *The cultural experience: Ethnography in complex society* (pp. 1-20). Chicago: SRA.

Stenvall, M. (2000). *A checklist for success: A guide to implementing year-round schools*. San Diego, CA: National Association for Year-Round Education.

Strike, K. A., & Soltis, J. F. (1992). *The ethics of teaching*. New York: Teachers College Press.

Thorndike, R. L. (1968). Review of Pygmalion in the classroom. *American Educational Research Journal, 5,* 708-711.

U.S. Department of Education (2001). *No Child Left Behind Act*. Washington, DC: Author.

Wineberg, S. S. (1987). The self-fulfillment of the self-fulfilling prophecy. *Educational Researcher, 16*(9), 28-37.

Worthen, B. R., & Zsiray, S. W. (1994, March). *What twenty years of educational studies reveal about year-round education*. Chapel Hill: North Carolina Educational Policy Research Center.

Zanna, M. P., Sheras, P. L., Cooper, J., & Shaw, C. (1975). Pygmalion and Galatea: The interactive effects of teacher and student expectancies. *Journal of Experimental Social Psychology, 11*, 279-287.

CHAPTER 4

SEEING THE GLASS
AS HALF FULL

Meeting the Needs of
Underprivileged Students Through
School-Community Partnerships

Catherine M. Hands

In our economically and culturally diverse society, the gap in student achievement between advantaged and disadvantaged groups is widening (Davies, 2002). Some scholars note that "current social circumstances in inner cities militate against the ability of urban schools and families to provide, unaided, enough support to stem academic failure" (Keith, 1996, p. 238). As a result, schools are finding it increasingly difficult to create educational program to address the diverse needs of the students (Merz & Furman, 1997) with the finances and the resources available to them.

For several decades, educational researchers have been advocating the benefits of partnerships between schools, families, and communities as a means for promoting student achievement (Davies & Johnson, 1996; Epstein & Sanders, 1998; Henderson, 1987; Swap, 1993). With frequent

Inclusion in Urban Educational Environments:
Addressing Issues of Diversity, Equity, and Social Justice, 71–90
Copyright © 2006 by Information Age Publishing
All rights of reproduction in any form reserved.

interactions between the partners, it is more likely that common sentiments regarding the importance of school, of exerting academic effort, of assisting others, and of staying in school will be reiterated and subsequently reinforced by a variety of influences on the students (Epstein, 1995). Similarly, researchers demonstrate that a lack of attention and support from the adults in the students' lives, an absence of discipline, and not "staying on them" or prodding the students are considered the most important barriers to educational success by educators, community mentors and students in a poor, inner city environment (Shapiro, Ginsberg, & Brown, 2002).

A number of schools and their boards are arriving at the same conclusion that collaboration is an avenue through which students' needs may be met and achievement promoted. Consequently, some school personnel are looking to garner not only financial, but material resources, as well as social support and educational experiences, from the surrounding geographic communities in order to supplement students' in-school learning opportunities. These principals and teachers view partnerships as a way to provide a support net for each student. For secondary school students, it may be particularly important to cultivate partnerships with community organizations and citizens along with parents to address the students' needs. The advantage to community involvement in their present schooling is two-fold, enhancing students' learning opportunities and easing the transition from high school.

The study on which this chapter is based sought to yield insight into the process of initiating communication with potential partners and establishing school-community partnerships. In doing so, I examined a secondary school situated in a town characterized as low income by federal government standards. Yet, this school had established numerous partnerships with the surrounding community, the material, intellectual, and emotional needs of the students were being addressed, and student achievement was being promoted. This chapter takes a close look at the role that this school's views on community involvement in education, as advocated by the educators and their community partners, played in the establishment of partnerships. The partnerships that were developed illustrate that financial resources are not the only valuable product of partnering for schools. I depict how a broad spectrum of the students' needs was met through school-community liaisons, and I underscore the value of partnering regardless of a community's general socioeconomic status. I begin with an overview of existing sociologically based education literature to provide a framework for the concepts of community and partnering as well as the interaction between individuals establishing liaisons.

THE NATURE OF SCHOOL-COMMUNITY PARTNERING

Prior to describing the characteristics of partnerships between school personnel and community members, it is helpful to define community. The concept of community is multifaceted, with many possible meanings (Beck, 1999; Merz & Furman, 1997). Steiner (2002) points out that communities are characterized and limited by the human interactions and geographic distance between populations, and are therefore both physical locales and social processes. It is this depiction of community which is useful for this chapter. For the purposes of school-community liaising, the community is made up of the school personnel and all of the individuals and organizations external to the school with a common interest in education (National Network of Partnership Schools, n.d.). As such, the boundaries vary from community to community and across schools within a geographic region. They may include the for-profit sector such as businesses, the public sector such as educational institutions, government and military organizations and health care facilities, as well as the nonprofit sector such as faith organizations, cultural, and recreational facilities, in addition to other community-based organizations and individuals in the community (Epstein, 1995; Hands, 2005; Sanders, 2001; Wohlstetter, Malloy, Smith, & Hentschke, 2003).

A working definition of school-community partnerships can be described as the "connections between schools and community individuals, organizations, and businesses that are forged to promote students' social, emotional, physical, and intellectual development" (Sanders, 2001, p. 20). Thus, with a central focus on students' wellbeing, the collaborative activities between individuals in schools and the surrounding communities constitute partnerships. They are characterized by efforts of all parties toward mutually desirable goals, which are unattainable in the absence of cooperation (Hargreaves & Fullan, 1998).

Partnering From Positions of Equity

Keith (1999) provides a useful conceptualization of relationships to facilitate the communication and cooperation essential for establishing partnerships (Darling-Hammond & Lieberman, 1993; Epstein, 2001; Sanders & Harvey, 2002). A broader understanding of partnerships, and the promotion of parent and community engagement efforts is achieved through the redefinition of social roles (Keith, 1999). Neighborhood residents are considered agents with resources, rather than as individuals without assets and needing services. Further, the notion that schools are a collection of professionals serving the students, parents, and community members (Keith, 1999; Merz & Furman, 1997) must be shed in order for families, schools, and community members to be able to approach partnerships as equals. "This means respecting each as both knowledgeable and needing to learn, without resorting to the power games of expert authority" (Keith, 1999, p. 230).

To combat power discrepancies that may exist, an inclusive approach must be taken (Robinson, 1994). As Davies (2002) and Epstein (1995) note, for partnerships to be created, they must be designed and implemented with the input from all individuals and groups involved. Conflicts of interests may arise between two or more individuals or groups; however, this does not mean they cannot collaborate, and views to the contrary are barriers to the creation of environments in which diverse groups gather to address problems or issues in ways that benefit all parties (Robinson, 1994). Keith (1999) advocates working together toward common goals which are unattainable individually. Further, it may be appropriate to view all educational goals, not only community projects to which Keith refers, as unattainable in isolation if we are to meet the educational needs of all students and establish partnerships broadly across the school system.

The Establishment of Partnerships

Toward that end and the practical realization of school-community partnerships, several scholars have provided insight into implementation strategies and resources. In her discussion of effective implementation, Sanders (2001) notes that identifying goals, defining the focus of the partnerships and selecting potential community partners are key steps for building successful collaborations. Both the school personnel and potential partners engage in a negotiation process to determine the goals and activities of the partnerships, and "win-win" situations are created whereby both partners benefit (Hands, 2005). Once collaborative activities are established, they are monitored and evaluated (Sanders, 2001). If they do not meet the expectations for the partnerships, the liaising terms are renegotiated; however, if the student, school, program and community partner needs are met, the liaisons are maintained over time (Hands, 2005).

Epstein provides a description of the areas of possible interaction between educators and members of the community with her six-part typology of activities (2001) and examples of partnership activities (1995). While Epstein targets parent involvement activities as her primary focus for interaction between schools and their external environments, Sanders (2001) provides further categorization of activities established between individuals in the schools and members of their communities. Activities reported in her survey of schools had a focus on student support, family support, school improvement, or community development (Sanders, 2001). This categorization may be broadened. Wohlstetter and colleagues (2003) found activities centered around curriculum, facilities, financial assistance, business and management expertise, and to a lesser degree, liaisons with community, assistance with administrative procedures, and enhancing schools' legitimacy.

Hence, the existing literature addresses the nature of partnerships, and provides examples of the variety of collaborative activities currently pursued by schools and their community partners. Further, the initial steps toward identifying and selecting the desired potential partners are outlined, as are the stages of partnership development. With the liaising process thus clarified, the sections that follow address the benefits yielded to the students and the community when school personnel partner with individuals and organizations beyond the walls of the school.

METHODOLOGY

Noting the need for a deeper understanding of participants' experiences of the phenomenon, I chose a research design to allow for cross-site analyses of how school-community partnerships are established within differing real-life contexts (Yin, 1994). With this goal in mind, this chapter draws on data collected in a qualitative case study of two secondary schools within a southern Ontario school board. In order to examine the techniques by which educators and community members successfully established school-community liaisons, the primary criterion for sample selection was the presence of numerous and strong school-community partnerships. The schools were identified through the school board as schools that had a reputation for establishing strong partnerships and numerous collaborative activities with community members. Grassmere High School,[1] located in a low socioeconomic, culturally homogeneous community, and Wicklow Secondary School, situated within a multicultural, low- to middle-income community, were the two schools selected. Preliminary conversations with the principals of the schools ensued, to confirm the presence of numerous strong community links. Both schools had cultivated between 75 and 80 school-community liaisons.

During the data collection process, 25 interviews were conducted with the principals, teachers, and school support staff during three site visits at Wicklow and four site visits at Grassmere, as well as with members of the community who were involved in partnership activities with the schools (e.g., individual community citizens, and contact people for businesses, government offices, senior citizens' organizations and health care institutions). In total, the 30 individuals participating in the study were involved in one semistructured, open-ended interview of approximately 45 minutes in length. While three focus group interviews were conducted, the majority of the interviews were individually conducted. Additionally, observations were conducted at the schools and documents that were pertinent to the partnership activities, including the schools' mission statements, memos, school plans and meeting minutes, were gathered from school staff and community partners over four site visits to each school.

Off-site visits were also conducted with the community partners with whom the educators reported having the strongest links. A snowball technique (Merriam, 1998) was used to obtain community participants for the study. During interviews with school personnel, the names and contact information of their community partners were requested. The community partners were then contacted by the researcher, and interviews were conducted and documents were collected. Multiple sources of data were sought to establish construct validity through the triangulation of the data (Merriam, 1998; Rothe, 2000; Yin, 1994).

Once the interviews were transcribed verbatim, they were sent to the participants for review and clarification. The collected data were coded and analyzed for emerging categories and themes. The constant comparative method was utilized in which the data obtained from each participant were continuously examined and incidents were compared across the data (Bogdan & Biklen, 1982; Merriam, 1998). In this way, new categories and themes were developed and existing ones were evaluated and modified. Once the within-case analysis was completed, the cross-case analysis (Merriam, 1998; Miles & Huberman, 1994) was conducted to yield the categories which emerged across the data from Wicklow and Grassmere.

The case that I subsequently describe is based upon the archival data, fieldnotes, and transcripts of audio recordings generated by interviews with the principal of Grassmere High School, the school office manager, five teachers, and 14 community members who partnered with the school. I begin the discussion with an examination of the community and school contexts in which the partnerships occurred.

Grassmere High School and the Surrounding Community

Grassmere High School is located in the town of Queenstown. Centrally situated near Queenstown's main street, Grassmere is within walking distance of the business district, hotels, restaurants, and boutiques as well as local community resources such as a public library, a sports complex and art gallery. The institution operates as a full-service semester school with a wide range of programs, in keeping with Principal Monica Kenny's focus on meeting the needs of all of the students in the area, and with the understanding common among the educators that the majority of the students would transition from school to work.

As a small urban centered, the town of Queenstown was economically resource-poor. The majority of Queenstown's families were considered low-income, with lower per capita income than other regions in the province (Statistics Canada, 2001). Further, the business landscape was characterized by small corporations, many of which required a skilled labor force, with no large industry in the area. Many of the town's citizens sought employment outside of the community. Consequently, commuting and job obligations presented challenges to parenting and community volunteering by virtue of constraints on parents' and community members' time.

Moreover, the school board had identified all of Grassmere's feeder schools as institutions requiring extra resources since the students were at risk of academic failure as a result of their underprivileged backgrounds. The low socioeconomic status of the students and their families as well as the accompanying living conditions were recognized by school personnel and community members alike. Many students were unable to afford to purchase school supplies such as physical education uniforms and art materials. Further, the study participants were aware of a number of Grassmere students who regularly went without meals. In response, the school had a bursary program with donations from teaching staff and community members from which the principal and teachers would provide the necessary funds to the students.

Other poverty-related issues were prevalent in Queenstown, and not as easily addressed by school personnel. The director of a child and youth mental health organization serving Queenstown noted chronic generational issues and domestic violence as issues she and her organization addressed with the students at Grassmere. A theater costume-maker and Grassmere partner noted that many families were comprised of "single parents, out working. The students are home alone all of the time. There are siblings at home with them, they're babysitting." In her view, many of the students' difficulties such as poor self-esteem stemmed from their families' lack of available time to attend to their needs. The social director of a seniors' club involved with Grassmere observed the same phenomenon in her experience with Grassmere students.

Although Grassmere's principal and teaching staff were sensitized to these issues, they recognized that they could not address them alone. Further, the effective delivery of school programs and the school personnel's focus on meeting the wide range of students' needs required the involvement of others beyond the school walls.

"HAVE NOTS" ARE PERCEIVED AS "HAVES":
THE IMPORTANCE OF COMMUNITY INVOLVEMENT

Despite the prevalence of underprivileged youth and their families in Queenstown, the educators in particular noted that the community members had a great deal to offer the school and the students in terms of resources.

Cultivating a School Culture That Supports Community Involvement

Monica was very cognizant of the context of the community, the low economic status of its citizens in general and the resultant impact on the students and the school.

> When I talk with our staff, and whenever I interview a new teacher, I tell them, that "You will learn you will be involved with kids probably on a scale in some cases more so than in other schools.... Some of our students are so entirely needy in many areas."

Yet she did not equate the economic circumstances of the students and many community members with an inability to meet the needs of the students.

> I believe that all else can be going on out there, but when you walk through this door, it's our responsibility to make sure that that student gets everything he can, we don't use excuses. Yes, we have needs up here, but our students are going to do as well as everyone else.

Monica advocated for the development of numerous partnerships and links throughout the community to ensure that the academic, physical, and emotional needs of the students were addressed. Through Monica and her team of department heads, an outward-looking perspective was promoted among the teachers. A school culture was propagated which encouraged and supported the teacher capacity and agency necessary to procure external support for the students and the school. This was consistent with Sanders's (1999, 2001) and Sanders and Harvey's (2002) findings that the principal's support and vision were essential for the development of school-community partnerships.

For all of the participants, schools were perceived as part of a larger entity. As such, the provision of education was regarded as a common responsibility that bound schools and their surrounding geographic communities together.

In voicing his philosophy regarding the need for community involvement, community-based education department head, Tom, stated that close links between the school and community were

> very important ... for support ... for being able to offer programs.... We have a small school, we have 900 young, developing, eager, energetic minds here. We have lots of potential.... And the community has this infrastructure of opportunity ... and jobs and experience that they can offer to these energetic students.

In this and other participants' opinions, schools and communities need to work together for maximum educational gains. As the director of the child and youth mental health organization serving Queenstown stated, schools and communities need to work

> together, to make it work for the kids, because we have an obligation to these kids.... As a community, as a mental health centre in a school board, as a school ..., as a teacher ... from the macro [level] right on through.

Thus, schools cannot and should not educate alone. A willingness on the part of community members to collaborate on educational issues was considered influential in the development of the numerous partnerships the school had cultivated with Queenstown citizens and organizations.

INTERACTION BETWEEN SCHOOLS AND THEIR COMMUNITIES

The school culture combined with teachers' and community members' personal philosophies of the active role communities should take in education, enabled the educators and their partners to address the students' needs through partnerships. Typically the partnership initiators, the teachers assessed their school's internal capacity. If the students' and their program needs were not satisfied in terms of the resources available within the school, they sought outside assistance. The relationship was viewed as being a "a two-way street. Something's going out, something's going back into the school," according to life skills teacher, Sandra.

For the participants, free-flowing activities across school and community borders were envisioned. Alternate education teacher, Rhonda, noted,

> If we can have it more seamless, if we can have the community in and out of the school, and the school involved in different things in the community, then our kids'll benefit. And I think that's what needs to [take place] for real education to happen. For it to be as meaningful as it should be.

From the community member perspective, the director of the youth mental health organization and a coordinator for an abuse prevention organization voiced comparable opinions in terms of the creation and benefits of a two-way exchange between schools and communities through their activities. These findings are consistent with those of Mawhinney (2002) and Crowson and Boyd (2001). In her study, Mawhinney found that education was considered a "partnership of mutual responsibility and benefit among schools, parents, governments, community agencies, and the private sector" (pp. 245-246).

Of Grassmere and the existing partnerships that had been developed between the school and Queenstown, a rehabilitation coordinator from a nearby nursing home observed that

> They are a part of the community. And it makes them more a part of the community. You know, working, interacting and working together and fulfilling the needs of the students, the teachers, the residents. It's just kind of a continuous interaction that benefits all.

Grassmere had effectively established a reciprocal relationship with its surrounding community. The school personnel and the community members had access to resources that could benefit their partners. Yet for partnerships to be developed, each side needed to first recognize the other's potential contributions to the relationship.

WHAT THE COMMUNITY WAS ABLE TO PROVIDE THE SCHOOL AND THE STUDENTS

In particular, the educators in this study challenged a deficit perspective of the community. They noted that the resources available in the community extended beyond monetary ones. This was not to say that the liaisons were one-sided; rather, they were partnerships in the manner described by Hargreaves and Fullan (1998), Sanders and Harvey (2002) and Keith (1999). Community partners realized benefits from their collaboration, such as access to school resources and public recognition for their efforts. Community partners also acknowledged that they exposed the students to a broader range of resources and experiences than the school or its personnel alone could provide. Thus, the partnerships were mutually beneficial.

In the next section that follows, however, the focus is on the benefits of partnering realized by the students and the school. This was the primary rationale for all partnering efforts, according to the study participants. Also, the notion that predominantly low-income communities have much to offer schools and the education system is clearly demonstrated in this manner.

Community Involvement: Material and Social Resources Provision

A conclusion commonly voiced by the teachers interviewed acknowledged that their program could not function without their partnerships in terms of resources and student experience. Sandra required community involvement in her life skills program:

> We have a very wide range of abilities in our classes, some of the students are non-verbal, we have some who are using wheelchairs for getting around, and some of them work independently in the summertime, earning real dollars. So that's the wide range we have. Using community resources helps us cope with that wide range.... We'll start [the students] with the work ethic kind of thing. But things like lunch hour, and what you do at break time, is where most of the students really fall down. It's those social skills and that kind of thing. We can't artificially set that up in the classroom effectively. But if they're going to be in a real community, they have to learn to be in a real community. That's where they're going to be, that's where it has to take place.

The community-based education head and the alternate education teacher concurred that the survival of their program depended on community involvement to provide work experiences, skills development, and social interaction.

The history and family studies department heads also noted both a lack of material resources and social opportunities within the schools prompted them to partner with community members. For the hospitality and food services program in particular, the students required exposure to the community organizations and businesses as clientele in order to hone their food preparation and catering skills. They had catered business lunches and birthday parties in the past, and were currently hosting weekly luncheons at the school for a local senior citizens' organization. Also, the school's parenting program benefited from the teachers' partnership with a community day care center. Through this relationship, the students were able to gain experience interacting with and caring for children of a variety of ages. Thus, the teachers saw community involvement as a means by which their students' needs were most appropriately met.

In another partnership, a local grocery store owner introduced the students to values they would not have the occasion to fully appreciate within the school. Through their work placements in the various departments within his grocery store, he exposed the students to a broader understanding of some of the concepts theoretically presented at the school level. As a business owner, he focussed on teaching the students about work ethics and occupational responsibilities. In his words,

> If you want to be working in my store, in my business, I feel I have an obligation to teach you what the workforce is really about. I have an obligation to teach you about responsibility in the workplace. And not only for you today, but it will help you all the way through your life. If you're going to do it right, respect your job today.... Because ... if you learn a good work ethic, it will help you no matter what you do. Even in your studies.

Thus, community involvement was not important solely because of the ability to address programming needs; rather, it provided exposure to the broader community and the values held by its citizens.

Community Participation and the Creation of Social Capital

For their part, several community members expanded on the social value their involvement had for the students and the schools. A general practitioner, a rehabilitation coordinator of a nursing home and an executive director of a church-affiliated conference center had provided work placements for students in the community-based education program. In their view, community involvement provided the students with social experiences beyond those offered at the school. Students working at the nursing home accompanied the home's residents on walks, assisted in their transportation to program at the home, and helped residents during meals and social activities. At the doctor's office, the students answered the telephone and booked appointments, showed patients to their examination rooms, recorded information in the patients' files, and learned some nursing procedures under the supervision of the staff. In the general practitioner's opinion,

> I think that getting the kids out and working in businesses, and trying to help them understand how businesses work, and [introducing them to] ... people outside of the classroom, is very important to them. Especially if they're interested in fields like we are here, in nursing or medicine, where you're going to be seeing people every day, and you have to deal with people. And so I think it's really important that they spend some time out of the classroom.

It was paramount for the students to be exposed to learning opportunities external to the school and broader sets of social situations out in the community, especially since many of the students would be engaged in careers beyond the school walls. The community partners took the time necessary to coach the students in appropriate workplace behavior. They encouraged constructive working relationships within the organizations as well as positive relations between the students and the clients from the community who used the organizations' services.

Through their experiences with community partners and the citizens within the broader geographic community, the students expanded their opportunities to build relationships with other community members. In so doing, the provision of student support was facilitated. "By building dense sets of networks" (p. 251) of relationships between schools and communities, student access to community facilities and organizations is enhanced and access to knowledge for the success of all students in schools is fostered (Mawhinney, 2002). In this way, the students developed social capital through their engagement with their community, for they expanded their resources through their positive, collaborative relationships with community members which facilitated subsequent productive activity (Coleman, 1988).

Opportunities to Contribute to Society Encouraged Hope Among Students

Partnering was considered as a step toward contributing to improved relations within the community, and more broadly, the society. In particular, the grocery store owner and the town's leisure services manager, who coordinated the lunch program for a senior citizens' club with the club's social director and Grassmere's family studies department head, talked of reducing the amount of vandalism caused by the youth via partnership activities involving the students. From the municipal manager's perspective,

> since we've done these program within Queenstown, I don't have the vandalism at the seniors' centre.... I can rhyme you off the other buildings that are just a nightmare for me for vandalism, but the seniors' center is not on the list at all.

In the store owner's words,

> it's all part of giving to the society, to make it a better society. I think that's what the achievement should be, and maybe businesses and so on have to be told that. We all talk about our storefronts getting kicked in at night, but

maybe we have to play a better role in order to see if we can't stop that. And this is through education, through opportunity, and so on.

According to these partners, community involvement and partnership activities involving the students encouraged citizenship and community-oriented values that demonstrate respect for persons and property, and a desire to contribute to community wellbeing were promoted.

More than this, the community involvement and interest in the students' welfare to which the grocery store owner alluded provided the youth with a sense of hope. The school council chair concurred. As a community, "we do have a responsibility to [the students] ... having each kid able to do what they can, and making sure they understand what's out there for them." Similarly, Grassmere's principal observed the importance of a perspective for the students "that's optimistic in all senses, that they can achieve, that they can go where they need to go.... We want kids to know that they can succeed.... So optimism for some of our kids is very important." Through partnerships, these educators and community members attempted to stem the despair, anger and feelings of hopelessness that can lead to vandalism and an inability for the students to reach their educational and life goals.

Personal Support for the Students

Moreover, community involvement was valued on its own merit, as a tool for influencing the growth and development of the students as people and community citizens. As the general practitioner pointed out,

> the experiences you have, and not just the ones in the classroom, will shape where you go in the future. And ... if you do a co-op [placement], and it's not something that you actually end up doing, it doesn't mean it's not of value to you.

In the same manner, a program coordinator in a provincial ministry department with a modest budget provided an autumn work placement for students to assist ministry workers in conducting angling and fisheries surveys on a nearby lake. He noted,

> I think we all at some point, need a starting place. And so this is, in my mind, probably a pretty good place. This would be a good chance for a kid to begin his work career, even if he did not end up working in the [Ministry].

Other community partners were more specific regarding the personal development provided by the partnerships. The director of a child and youth mental health services organization noted that youth mental health issues needed to be addressed with multidisciplinary treatment which required partnerships between the school and her organization. In the director's words, "We have a responsibility to ensure that kids can actively participate in society.... We all do. As a society." In order to deal with behavioral, social, and emotional issues affecting some of the students at Grassmere in many cases due to their families' poverty, and to enhance their ability to learn and to make positive contributions to their social environment, services and counselling were brought into the school through a partnership established by the principal and the director. In this way, student mental health and wellbeing was promoted to enable productive participation in society.

In other liaisons, student involvement in partnership activities within the community provided the students with occupational skills and emotional support. This was particularly true of work placements arranged with community organizations by Grassmere's community-based education, alternate education, and life skills teachers. Here, community members assisted the students in developing their skills base in a work environment. A theater costumer recruited the Grassmere students into costume-making for both the amateur and professional theaters in an effort to involve the students in the community. Through their work with the costumer, the students contributed to the community's cultural activities and provided a needed service to the cash-strapped theater companies. In return, they gained an appreciation for the arts, learned about historical periods, garnered some practical skills, and in some cases, obtained subsequent employment in the costuming departments at the theaters. In general, both educators and their partners reported that obtaining employment following work placements or after participating in partnership activities with community members was a common occurrence.

Further, through their exposure to caring community members, students' involvement with the community elevated their self-esteem. According to the theater costumer, many of the youth "have baggage." In her view, the students

> have no respect for themselves, so through partnerships and working with the community, I try to get them out and to respect themselves, and feel good about what they're doing. A lot of them are never told what they're doing is right.

Similarly, the grocery store owner noted the importance of including the community-based education placement students as "part of the team" in his business.

When a kid comes in, you give him a name tag, give him a hat, get him a shirt. The kid just lightens right up. He just can't believe that you're recognizing him. Because a lot of these children have got a problem.... But when you pay a little attention to them, and so on, I find you get it back. Then they take an interest in you. They say, "You know what? This guy cares about me. People care about me." And I think one of the biggest things is letting them know you care about them.

Therefore, through a compassionate approach, caring relationships were cultivated and the youths' self-esteem was enhanced, which facilitated the acquisition of skills to further augment their self-worth. In the words of the executive director of a church-affiliated conference center,

We feel that everyone is worth something. Sometimes we get kids who feel they're worth nothing. And our mandate would be to increase their self-worth. Our mandate would be to give them something that's productive, to give them the ability to learn to do different things. Our staff here, we are a family and we are a team. When [the students] walk in here, they walk in knowing that they're part of a team. And they feel good about coming here.... I think it's our approach to these folks: "Hey, you're a part of us. We want you here. You're not sent here. We want you here."

At the center, the adolescents assisted the director and his community coordinator in the day-to-day running of the conference center, from setting up meeting rooms and painting the buildings, to chopping wood and clearing the center's grounds. Whether they were youths assigned to community service as part of a court order, or Grassmere students engaged in a work placement, the focus was on building personal skills and fostering self-esteem. Further, it improved their attitude toward community members, their work and their efforts toward the acquisition of skills.

In sum, a partnership "gives [the students] an idea that the people outside the school care," according to a Queenstown senior citizen and Grassmere community partner. The partnership activities provided the students with opportunities to develop their interpersonal and vocational skills and self-esteem. At Grassmere, then, the school-community partnerships enabled youth to cultivate positive relations with others in their community and to meet with success in their educational and occupational endeavors.

What the Students Gave Back to the Community

Additionally, students' involvement in their communities encouraged civic responsibility. In the theater costumer's opinion, "besides themselves, there are other people out there that they can help. And really get involved in their communities." The Queenstown leisure services manager noted that partnerships were one way to achieve this goal:

> We always say we have to give, give, give to the youth. But I think if they take a partnership in it, and help work towards the outcome of something, then I think they do take pride in it and care more about it.

Consequently, over the course of her tenure with the town, the leisure services manager frequently recruited youth to volunteer for Queenstown events, such as setting up or participating in an annual winter carnival. By the students taking part in partnerships or volunteer activities in the community, the partners felt the activities discouraged an egocentric focus and stimulated students' outward looking attitudes, as well as a sensitivity to and an interest in citizenship called for by scholars such as Keith (1999), and Westheimer and Kahne (2002).

The same focus on reciprocation was expressed by teachers Sandra and Frances, with the community contributing to the school, and the students contributing to their community as much as they are able. Of her life skills class, Sandra noted that,

> Our students tend to get a lot. So we try and say that, "If you can, it's a good idea to give back." That's kind of my philosophical bias, though. We talk about voting and citizenship and being part of the community, and part of that is that we do give back.

For her part, family studies department head, Frances, involved her students in several volunteer activities to encourage citizenship.

> A lot of the stuff that we do is sort of on a volunteer basis. I want them to understand that when they get older, it's nice to give back to the community. And they're at that age in their lives, "It's all me, me, me, me."… We partner with the Boy Scouts of Canada, we make their scarves for two Boy Scout packs every September…. We sewed for the whole of Queenstown minor hockey, all the letters and patches on the back of the jerseys…. So they were dropped off here, and my kids sewed them on…. Then all of a sudden the figure skaters for their little carnivals came and we designed a whole show for little kids and all the clothing for that…. Once a week we go over [to a seniors' club] and we do crafts with the seniors and then the crafts are sold at their bazaar…. And for Queenstown, now we're working to do sails for the light standards down the middle of the road in the spring.

Athough not considered strong partnerships due to the sporadic nature of the activities, these activities were part of a reciprocal, mutually beneficial relationship between the school and the community. Through participation in these volunteer activities, the students gained an appreciation for the broader community and the people in it. An informal component of civics training, these activities effectively sensitized the students to community events, and promoted an outward-looking approach to the students' attitudes and subsequent behaviors.

The school and its students were able to provide useful services to the community, a finding consistent with those of Mawhinney (2002). Further, the partnering practices in this study promoted students' acquisition of "the knowledge, skills and attitudes necessary to function effectively as citizens in a democracy" (Westheimer & Kahne, 2002, p. 14).

CONCLUSIONS

This chapter traces the benefits yielded from school-community partnerships with an economically depressed town. The liaisons and collaborative activities developed and discussed illustrate the value of engaging community involvement regardless of the participants' financial means. The findings of this research indicate that even within low-income communities, there is a wealth of resources available to the students. In addition to receiving support, students and their schools also may provide valuable resources to the community.

Through community participation in schooling and the creation of partnership activities involving youth, the students not only received material support such as financial aid and access to community resources, they were guided in their personal development. The community members' involvement provided social support in the form of expanded social networks, social capital, and experience with broader sets of values than the students were likely to have experienced in school or with their families. Further, the partnership activities facilitated the students' acquisition of skills and self-esteem over the course of their personal development, and encouraged civic involvement. In these ways, optimism for the future was fostered among the students through the partnerships.

While not presented as a quick fix to the issues experienced by students from low-income families, the findings of this research indicate that the support from partnership development and community involvement assists schools in addressing the needs of these students. Partnerships and the accompanying community support represent one avenue through which skills and hope for the future are developed along with the resilience necessary for the students to overcome their issues and to become productive participants in society.

NOTE

1. Pseudonyms have been used for the schools', participants', and communities' names in order to protect their anonymity.

REFERENCES

Beck, L. G. (1999). Metaphors of educational community: An analysis of the images that reflect and influence scholarship and practice. *Educational Administration Quarterly, 35*(1), 13-45.

Bogdan, R. C., & Biklen, S. K. (1982). *Qualitative research for education: An introduction to theory and methods.* Boston: Allyn & Bacon.

Coleman, J. S. (1988). Social capital in the creation of human capital. *American Journal of Sociology, 94*(Suppl.), S95-S120.

Crowson, R. L., & Boyd, W. L. (2001). The new role of community development in educational reform. *Peabody Journal of Education, 76*(2), 9-29.

Darling-Hammond, L., & Lieberman, A. (1993, April). *James P. Comer, M.D., on the School Development Program: Making a difference for children.* New York: National Center for Restructuring Education, Schools, and Teaching.

Davies, D. (2002). The 10th school revisited: Are school/family/community partnerships on the reform agenda now? *Phi Delta Kappan, 83*(5), 388-392.

Davies, D., & Johnson, V. R. (Eds.). (1996). Crossing boundaries: Family, community, and school partnerships. *International Journal of Educational Research, 25*(1), Special Issue.

Epstein, J. L. (1995). School/family/community partnerships: Caring for the children we share. *Phi Delta Kappan, 76*(9), 701-712.

Epstein, J. L. (2001). *School, family, and community partnerships: Preparing educators and improving schools.* Boulder, CO: Westview Press.

Epstein, J. L., & Sanders, M. G. (1998). What we learn from international studies of school-family-community partnerships. *Childhood Education, 74*(6), 392-394.

Hands, C. M. (2005). *Patterns of interdependency: The development of partnerships between schools and communities.* Unpublished doctoral dissertation, University of Toronto, Ontario, Canada.

Hargreaves, A., & Fullan, M. (1998). *What's worth fighting for out there?* New York: Teachers College Press.

Henderson, A. (1987). *The evidence continues to grow: Parental involvement improves student achievement.* Columbia, MO: National Committee for Citizens in Education.

Keith, N. Z. (1996). Can urban school reform and community development be joined? The potential of community schools. *Education and Urban Society, 28*(2), 237-259.

Keith, N. Z. (1999). Whose community schools? New discourses, old patterns. *Theory Into Practice, 38*(4), 225-234.

Mawhinney, H. B. (2002). The microecology of social capital formation: Developing community beyond the schoolhouse door. In G. Furman (Ed.), *School as community: From promise to practice* (pp. 235-255). Albany: State University of New York Press.

Merriam, S. B. (1998). *Qualitative research and case study applications in education.* San Francisco: Jossey-Bass.

Merz, C., & Furman, G. (1997). *Community and schools: Promise and paradox.* New York: Teachers College Press.

Miles, M. B., & Huberman, A. M. (1994). *Qualitative data analysis: An expanded sourcebook* (2nd ed.). Thousand Oaks, CA: Sage.

National Network of Partnership Schools. (n.d.). *Type 6: Challenges and redefinitions for collaboration.* Retrieved March 24, 2004, from http://www.csos.jhu.edu/p2000/challenges/type6cha.htm

Robinson, V. M. J. (1994). The practical promise of critical research in educational administration. *Educational Administration Quarterly, 30*(1), 56-76.

Rothe, J. P. (2000). *Undertaking qualitative research.* Edmonton, Canada: The University of Alberta Press.

Sanders, M. G. (1999). Schools' program and progress in the National Network of Partnership Schools. *The Journal of Educational Research, 92*(4), 220-232.

Sanders, M. G. (2001). The role of "community" in comprehensive school, family, and community programs. *The Elementary School Journal, 102*(1), 19-34.

Sanders, M. G., & Harvey, A. (2002). Beyond the school walls: A case study of principal leadership for school-community collaboration. *Teachers College Record, 104*(7), 1345-1368.

Shapiro, J. P., Ginsberg, A. E., & Brown, S. P. (2002, October). *Family and community participation in urban schools: The ethic of care.* Paper presented at the Values and Leadership in Education conference, Toronto, Ontario, Canada.

Statistics Canada. (2001). *Earnings statistics.* Retrieved May 18, 2004, from http://www12statcan/english/Profil01/Details/details1inc2.cfm

Steiner, F. (2002). *Human ecology: Following nature's lead.* Washington, DC: Island Press.

Swap, S. M. (1993). *Developing home-school partnerships: From concepts to practice.* New York: Teachers College Press.

Westheimer, J., & Kahne, J. (2002). Education for action: Preparing youth for participatory democracy. In R. Hayduk & K. Mattson (Eds.), *Democracy's moment: Reforming the American political system for the 21st century* (pp. 91-107). Lanham, MD: Rowman & Littlefield. Retrieved October 8, 2004, from http://www.democraticdialogue.com/DDpdfs/EducationForAction.pdf

Wohlstetter, P., Malloy, C. L., Smith, J., & Hentschke, G. (2003). *Cross-sectorial alliances in education: A new approach to enhancing school capacity.* Unpublished manuscript, University of Southern California, Rossier School of Education, Center on Educational Governance at Los Angeles.

Yin, R. K. (1994). *Case study research: Design and methods* (2nd ed.). Thousand Oaks, CA: Sage.

CHAPTER 5

FLIPPING THE SPECIAL EDUCATION COIN

The Heads and Tails of Administering Schools for Students With Different Needs

Lindy Zaretsky

Special education has been the focus of extensive scholarly scrutiny and debate for several decades, particularly because school systems are generally accorded the responsibility of endorsing and privileging particular conceptions of *normal* and *abnormal* (Ferguson & Ferguson, 1995; Skrtic, 1995; Thomas & Loxley, 2001; Tomlinson, 1995). Whether they recognize it or not, many educational professionals, including school administrators, have traditionally worked from a medical model of disability. Professionally vested interests in the fields of medicine, psychiatry, and psychology have contributed to much of the theoretical and empirical knowledge in special education (Barnes, Mercer, & Shakespeare, 1999). Currently educational professionals appear to rely heavily on this knowledge base, generally considered stable, objective and helpful knowledge in making decisions about appropriate instruction, assessment, and placements for students with disabilities. This is perhaps understandable, con-

Inclusion in Urban Educational Environments:
Addressing Issues of Diversity, Equity, and Social Justice, 91–110
Copyright © 2006 by Information Age Publishing

sidering school policies and practices concerning special education have typically constructed, reinforced, and legitimized the categorization and designation of particular students as *special*. There are, of course, no shortage of scholars who propose the need to critically examine this dominant discourse and its use of such essentializing norms in order to confront the perceived contradictions and dilemmas that the special education practice of scientific labeling yield (Barnes, Mercer, & Shakespeare, 1999; Clark, Dyson, & Millward, 1998; Skrtic, 1995; Thomas & Loxley, 2001). These scholarly efforts suggest that traditional and commonplace approaches to special education locate children's differences and disabilities unproblematically within students' pathologies.

Currently, there is little engagement in dialogical interactions about special education theorizing in the practitioner's arena. For example, few practitioners understand what theoretical underpinnings are associated with the practice of *full inclusion* or why others might favor a range of alternative placement options from segregated to integrated special education settings for students with special needs. To this end, there is a considerable need to support practitioners in understanding how they have come to know and understand special education, disability, and inclusion in different ways. In the absence of these theory and practice connections, special education in practice will remain a highly contentious and conflicted school arena.

In this paper, I examine competing conceptions of disability grounded in medical and social theoretical models and propose an epistemological shift in the scholarly conversations. A more inclusive account of special education is offered that I suggest recognizes, appreciates, and incorporates both the traditional sciences and social sciences together—something the scholarly field has failed to do. Such a perspective may serve to harmonize current themes of *medicalized* and *social/holistic* conceptions of disability and special education in the field. This paper in no way discounts or dismisses the knowledge contributions of, for example, medicine and psychology to special education, but rather calls for greater appreciation and ultimately inclusivity of the sociocultural means of arriving at different understandings. A single perspective is plainly inadequate for developing a more sophisticated understanding of what might constitute valid knowledge and expertise in special education. My aim is to also encourage greater clarity among theories and practices regarding the knowledge claims we make, the evidence assembled in support of those claims and the logic employed when linking that evidence to such knowledge claims. These principles can (and should) underpin our scholarly and practical work in order to provide for greater methodological understandings that invite sound decision-making practices in, for example, the design and delivery of instructional programs based on high expectations for academic achievement for *all* students.

This paper begins with an overview of current trends in special education theorizing. The balance of this paper is devoted to discussing some of the potentially harmful effects on practice that may arise when holding to a particular unitary conception of special education. These constructed understandings dichotomize special education into conceptual opposites creating adversarial stances among practitioners, who for the most part, are unaware of the theoretical orientations in which their beliefs, attitudes and practices are embedded. Such effects are reported on through a discussion of overall findings from a study of one inclusion project. A parent advocacy association joined in partnership with a large urban district school board over a 3 year period in an effort to promote inclusive thinking, practices, and learning environments in secondary schools for students with disabilities. I contend that concepts such as disability and inclusion remain extremely controversial especially because they relate to core educational and social values. I conclude the paper with a discussion of the benefits to both scholarship and practice when different approaches to knowing are validated.

Revisiting the Theoretical Debate in Special Education

Special education theorizing about disability typically involves a functionalist paradigm oriented toward a medical/behaviorist model which pathologizes disability and seeks appropriate interventions and *cures*. Disability is usually held to be a phenomenon consistent with the medical model, and as such can be treated and accommodated. There are numerous scholars who claim that categories of disability remain stable over time and across context (Kauffman & Hallahan, 1990; Mostert & Crockett, 2000; Sasso, 2001). These scholars purport that medicine and psychology have contributed a substantial knowledge base developed through the scientific method of inquiry which in turn has produced the best technologies of science-based practices delivered by well trained special education professionals that include educators, psychologists, speech pathologists, occupational therapists, and numerous other support personnel in special education. In turn these professionals support special education teachers with the development of sound and promising instructional strategies to enhance the learning of students with disabilities. The scholars show how research findings have supported many children with disabilities in learning to read and write through well-defined task appropriate strategies. It is their understanding that foundational *truths* of physical and biological phenomena have most definitely supported researchers and practitioners in furthering an understanding of psychological and social aspects of teaching and learning that have benefited many students with disabilities in special education classrooms. Logical inquiry involving direct adherence to this traditional *scientific* method continues to influence policy and practice in special education. The current state of knowledge in special education, developed through the scientific method of inquiry, remains promising and provides a solid foundation on which to build more knowledge and best practices.

In sharp contrast, the postmodern thought in special education clearly rejects the apparent determinism of science in favor of a socially constructed view of disability, emphatically claiming that the medical model of disability is fraught with serious difficulties and even morally questionable conceptions of difference. This alternative postmodern paradigm advocates for a social-constructivist model that typically treats disability as difference with the ultimate aim of inclusion. Recently, postmodernism and cultural relativism have been accorded critical attention in special education both in the literature on inclusion (Giangreco, 1997; Kerzner-Lipsky & Gartner, 1997; Thomas, Walker, & Webb, 1998: Villa & Thousand, 2000) and disability studies (Brantlinger, 2000; Danforth & Rhodes, 1997; Gallagher, 1998; Peters, 2004).

Postmodern thinking in special education is largely a reaction to the assumed certainty of *scientific* or *objective* efforts to explain the reality of disability. Many scholars (Danforth & Rhodes, 1997; Peters, 2004; Skrtic, 1995) are, for example, highly skeptical of explanations of *normal* and *deviance* within stated categories of exceptionalities that are considered to be *valid* and *truthful*. Their views of disability are derived through the valuing of relative truths of each individual and his or her own particular construction of reality. Several other scholars agree that reality and truth are only created through individual interpretations of what the world means to us through concrete experiences as opposed to abstract and universal principles (Gallagher, Heshusius, Iano, & Skrtic, 2004). This view of disability is underpinned by notions of there being multiple versions of reality. Meanings can only be derived through an interactional process.

Like all disciplines, special education embodies particular sets of values and broadly shared assumptions emerging from the social context. Still, one basic tenet of modernism is that research must always be value-free (Hallahan, 1998; Kauffman, 1994, 1999; Kavale & Mostert, 2003; Sasso, 2001). In contrast, postmodern thinkers in disability studies argue that it is virtually impossible to conduct value-free research because values cannot be readily separated from facts (Barton, 1998; Brantlinger, 2000; Ferguson & Ferguson, 1995; Peters, 2004; Skrtic, 1995; Slee, 2001). What is more, the language surrounding the competing models of special education further complicates the issue. As proposed in the literature, many of the basic tenets of postmodern thought in special education are in direct conflict with the tenets of modernism. These two major contenders for theoretical superiority articulate in their writing just how diametrically opposed they are in their scholarly missions and visions for special education practices in our schools.

The Dominant Discourse: In Pursuit of Objective Truths

It is often the position of modernist inquiry that true answers and *facts* should be sought lest special education run the risk of compromising its *truthfulness* as evidenced through a large body of special education literature that has historically been generated through empirical research based on accepted scientific methodology and design (Sasso, 2001; Schrag, 1992). Scholars in the fields of special education argue that postmodern thinking in disability studies discounts *objective* truth and relevant evidence gathered through legitimate scientific processes of logical inquiry. They argue that logical inquiry has obvious criteria for judging *scientific practices* using empirical research based on sound scientific methodology and design (Kavale & Mostert, 2003; Sasso, 2001).

Many scholars in pursuit of *objectivity* (Sasso, 2001; Schrag, 1992) emphatically insist in their writing that postmodernists' research findings, for the most part, can be reduced to assumptions and rhetoric related to attitudinal or emotional responses which are not serving the academic needs of students with disabilities. Others consider the adoption of interpretivist and or constructivist paradigms to be dangerous and destructive to the education of children with special needs (Hockenbury, Kauffman, & Hallahan, 2000; Kavale & Mostert, 2003). It is wrong, they argue, to relinquish the symbolic orderliness of modernism in favor of postmodern thinking where there are merely *stories* or *narratives* with which to make sense of the world. Such scholars contend that logical inquiry must be more than descriptive notions of acceptance achieved through individuals' participation in social negotiation processes. From their perspective, engagement in logical inquiry through experimentation and evidence produced by it is essential to the healthy preservation of special education as a distinct and necessary alternative to regular education.

These scholars often attempt to portray postmodernists in special education and disability studies as *full inclusionists* who allegedly take the moral high ground in their assertions that all children belong in regular education classrooms in their neighborhood schools. Kauffman (1999) contends that *full inclusionists* dismiss science as untrustworthy and prefer to supplant reason with rhetoric which he considers harmful to practice.

In his view, such an ideologically-driven approach to special education ignores the practical challenges of educating all children in a regular education setting. A common argument put forth against inclusion is that its practice may provide students with superficial physical access in a regular education classroom but it does not necessarily provide the kind of instructional access required (Crockett & Kauffman, 1998; Hallahan, 1998). From this perspective, sound instructional interventions grounded in *legitimate* and *valid* special education research need to be implemented in classrooms to meet the needs of exceptional learners. Social values *can* and *must* be separated from validity claims. Furthermore, such a perspective extols the need to embrace the normative spirit in measuring how valid evidence is for this or that claim.

Introducing a Different Discourse: In Pursuit of Socially Negotiated Truths

Postmodernists and critical theorists frequently include the perspective of the *other* (Vincent, 2000; Ware, 1999). They recognize that students with disabilities are often required to negotiate and resolve tensions between themselves and their socially constructed identities in schools. These tensions are likely to be generated via competing individual, social, and biomedical perceptions of disability. Historically, parents of children with disabilities have had to mediate many conflicts that characterize such social encounters in the special education arena (Fiedler, 2000; Turnbull & Turnbull, 2000; Zaretsky, 2004). Slee (2001) refers to power-knowledge relationships when describing the communicative processes of assessment and decision making about learners with disabilities. He argues that they predominantly takes place within a context of evidence-based claims made by professional groups to a scientific expertise based on their rational application of knowledge about a wide range of syndromes and disorders. In this way the medical discourse remains the dominant and privileged one that formalizes the exclusionary practice of dismissing other ways of knowing.

The primary focus of postmodern theorists in special education is on changing social constructions that limit the advancement of individuals with disability. The cause for concern is that concepts of *deficits* and *needs* can potentially serve to reinforce concepts of disadvantage, marginalization, and exclusion. In their writing, many scholars actively resist the functionalism and determinism associated with the *science* of special education. Ferguson and Ferguson (1995) encourage us to begin defining disability in more holistic terms and to think critically about how disability is constructed, and which attributes in people are more highly valued.

Notions of *normal* and *abnormal* should also compel theorists and practitioners to interrogate unexamined value judgments used to represent what is right and desirable in special education program and placements. We may be best served by being more accepting of multiple interpretations and ways of knowing than presently embraced by more traditional forms of scientific inquiry.

A constructivist or social model of disability focuses on how classifications are constructed and which attributes and people are most highly valued, based on an assumption that the competitive and hierarchical structures of schooling and society make it necessary to define normality against abnormality and deficiency (Jordan, 2001; Skrtic, Sailor, & Gee, 1996; Starratt, 2003). According to Vincent (2000) normative assumptions continue to be informed by a medical discourse that emphasizes dependency and loss as defined by special education professionals. As suggested by Burrello, Lashley, and Beatty (2001) constructs of difference could replace constructs of deviance, allowing a greater focus on changing disabling structures and not the individual himself or herself.

Several scholars suggest that it is time to take a questioning disposition to the special education knowledge base derived from the disciplines of medicine, psychology, and psychiatry which purport to best understand learning and learners, and of course, why some students appear to fall short of allegedly *normal* educational expectations (Jordan, 2001; Skrtic, 1995). As noted by Clark, Dyson, and Millward (1998) there is a core assumption that an overreliance on this medical model perpetuates deficit-driven and impoverished instruction irrelevant to the strengths and needs of individual students. Ballard (1999) writes that "faith in certain kinds of knowledge provides the credence, the believability behind special education's status. Trust in this knowledge secures special education's reputation as a rational, sensible way of educating a portion of the population" (p. 1).

Clinical descriptions of disability continue to carry greater weight in making decisions about program and placements in special education than the identification of systemic environmental barriers encountered by students with disabilities in schools (Barton, 1998; Ware, 1999). As many of the postmodernists in disability studies point out (Gallagher, Heshusius, Iano, & Skrtic, 2004) disability is the product of both biological and social factors. Facts should not be seen as separate from values, as truths can only be relative to the individuals who hold them. All *scientific* knowledge must be viewed as socially constructed through interactions where meanings are constantly in negotiation.

FROM THEORY TO PRACTICE

The presentation of overall research findings from a qualitative study of one inclusion project illuminates the practical challenges that arise from the *us versus them* theoretical debate. Findings are presented from a 3 year inquiry involving the extensive planning of the transition of a group of adolescent learners with moderate to severe intellectual disabilities and autism spectrum disorders into secondary school settings. Throughout their elementary school careers, these particular students had been fully included in regular education classrooms alongside their *typical* peers. The primary goal of the project was to create spaces where multiple and varied interpretations of inclusion could be expressed and accepted. The 18 participants in this process included 12 parents of the students with disabilities, one regular and one special education teacher in the elementary panel, one elementary and one secondary school principal, the secondary school special education coordinator, and the principal responsible for special education (Kindergarten through Grade 12) for the district school board.

Engaging all participants in a series of individual conversations, focus group dialogues, and monthly steering committee meetings, helped me to identify recurring themes interwoven throughout the conversations. Efforts were made to ensure all participants' voices were included in the design of new models of inclusion in secondary schools within a large district school board in Ontario, Canada. Efforts were also made to varying degrees to resist the temptation of imposing a singular and dominant view of inclusion. This paper places an emphasis on exploring how these participants understood and responded to *inclusion* (or the lack thereof) in the unique contexts of their individual lives, local classrooms, schools, and larger organizations with which they are affiliated. The focused conversations offered valuable information about their thinking, perceptions, attitudes, evaluative judgments, and practices regarding inclusive education in both elementary and secondary schools.

Practitioners' Understandings

The parents of the children with disabilities entered the dialogue with initial hopes of working alongside school staff to achieve a sense of belonging and acceptance as partners in a shared commitment to cocreating inclusive programs in secondary schools. They expected some freedom of choice among options available for their children, as well as some power and influence over processes to the extent that school personnel would listen to them and value their input. Through their role as political activists seeking educational change, these particular parents articulated their desire to challenge prevailing understandings of parents as passive recipients of school personnel's professional knowledge and expertise in special education. A questioning disposition was precisely the attitude adopted by many parents in this study who considered it their responsibility to challenge and critique the pervasive assumptions which dominated current educational programs and services in the secondary school settings.

All parents argued that the socially democratic goal for all students with disabilities should be their full participation in rich and meaningful curricular experiences tailored to their individual strengths and needs, and maximizing their potential for learning. The parents contended that all students needed immersion in creative and innovative instruction and inclusive assessment practices that would promote their independence and self-advocacy in addition to honoring and recognizing differences and diversity as beneficial to everyone's learning. They viewed disability more as a manifestation of human difference rather than as a lack of capabilities. The parents did not deny the significance of possible impairments in their children's lives yet preferred to focus on the organizational structures in schools that they considered to be the real barriers to inclusion. They wanted to see more of an emphasis placed on the child in relation to his or her learning environment. Many voiced their concern that secondary schools, in particular, lacked such a focus. This was the rationale for preferred placement in the regular education classroom where they articulated a preference for appropriate accommodations and modifications to the regular education curriculum expectations.

The regular and special education teacher, assigned to the inclusive classroom in the elementary school, described their explicit team teaching instructional model that over time successfully blended the rich knowledge traditions of regular and special education. For example, they claimed that their combined knowledge of pedagogical approaches enhanced their ability to address issues of disability as well as cultural and linguistic differences among children in the classroom. In order to achieve this quality education, the teachers reported that they had to focus on delivering explicit instruction, strategies, and tactics grounded in research and planned for in the original design of the regular classroom and special education teachers' collaboratively created units of study. Using the analogy of architecture, Hehir (2005) points that "we often attempt to retrofit the child with inappropriate interventions after they have failed in school, rather than design the instructional program from the beginning to allow for access and success" (p. 35). For example, poor readers may still be able to access grade level materials in history or science if they have access to adaptive technologies that include digital text read from computers with screen readers or taped. These strategies are echoed by Pivik, McComas, and LaFlamme (2002) in their research on barriers and facilitators to inclusive education.

The elementary school principal reported that special education continued to present one of the key challenges facing him as an educational leader within the context of diversity and comprehensive school reform. He claimed this put a great deal of pressure on the local school administrator to inspire all staff and students to *perform* well. From his perspective, what helped him to balance and mediate this pressure was the creation of relational networks with many partners who had combined their knowledge pool to support all learners with improved student achievement. According to this principal, the school leader's relational role was essential to facilitating a collective mobilization and distribution of social, political, and economic resources in special education, which in his opinion, never came close to matching current student need. This principal also claimed that inclusive practice required that roles and responsibilities remained fluid and flexible in schools. Based on his own experiences, he suggested that this necessitated an individual and collective attitudinal shift where the school leader, parent, student, and teacher positioned themselves as colearners and not always the experts in any one particular school improvement process. Knowledgeable and skillful principals were, in his opinion, able to further nurture collaborative relationships and networks within this context of accountability.

Responses from both the secondary school principal and the secondary school coordinator indicated that they positioned inclusion in regular education classrooms for students with moderate to severe developmental disabilities as somewhat of a countervailing force to certain school improvement efforts that included high expectations for academic achievement among the regular education student population. As a result, only the students diagnosed with autism spectrum disorders who were currently able to meet the Grade 6 to Grade 8 curriculum expectations outlined in core academic areas of the curriculum were initially accorded entry into some credit bearing regular education courses for grade nine. In contrast the students diagnosed with moderate to severe developmental disabilities who were assessed at a Grade 1 to Grade 3 level of performance were placed in partially self-contained special education settings for Grade 9 where a special education teacher delivered a nonaccredited and alternative literacy and math curriculum. These particular students were invited to choose among elective courses that had been prepackaged as part of this placement. The courses focused on *functional life skills* development. When some of the parents strongly resisted this package, a compromise was reached. The students were invited to take part in other credit bearing courses (i.e., ninth grade geography or science, etc.) as auditors of the course yet there would be no credit earned for their participation. The secondary school principal and coordinator claimed that the *integrity* of the courses would be compromised if extensive modifications to program were allowed. Their attitudes and beliefs about the learning capacity of students with developmental disabilities appeared to determine the limited extent to which they were going to promote adjustments to teaching methods and learning environments that would allow these particular students to access regular education curriculum in general with their faculty.

As the parents of the children with moderate to severe developmental disabilities continued to question and critique some of the current special education practices in the partially self-contained classroom settings, the principal and coordinator began to label these particular parents as aggressive, unrealistic, overly demanding, and bullies. The ongoing dialogue indicated that the secondary school principal and coordinator remained somewhat reluctant to participate in a reconceptualization of legitimate and politicized parent involvement when it demanded a revisioning of current inclusive educational practices within an accountability context. They perceived it as a challenge to the professional autonomy they had enjoyed in making what they perceived to be responsible and well informed decisions in the best interests of *all* students. Similar findings were reported in research conducted by Zaretsky (2004) when investigating interactions associated with special education processes between parent advocates and principals. These issues are also consistent with previous research examining inclusivity at the secondary school level. For example, Johnson, Stodden, Emanuel, Luecking, and Mack (2002) reported many of the same institutional and attitudinal barriers towards parent involvement, accessibility to the full range of curricula and programs, and coordination of services as important factors in facilitating or impeding inclusivity in classrooms and schools.

The principal responsible for special education (K-12) in the school district articulated her desire to focus her efforts on supporting schools in the management of program implementation, services, and personnel in special education that would allow all students to maximize their learning and achievement in a variety of inclusive learning environments while simultaneously honoring the district school board's continued commitment to offering a full range of placement options for students with disabilities. She also expressed the need to forge stronger partnerships between elementary and secondary school teachers and administrators so that they could build and share their knowledge and expertise, in for example, explicit literacy instruction and assessment. In her view, successful collaboration between individuals who may never have worked together in the past required the development of trust in the relationships. However, she also understood that transforming practices associated with curriculum, instruction, and assessment required a shift in how each participant in the process reflected upon learners, the learning process, forms of knowledge, and the goals of inclusive education. There is a growing recognition of just how critical this intentional focus on teaching and learning are to such a change process (Riehl, 2000; Thurlow & Johnson, 2000; Weiss & Lloyd, 2002). Schools are currently acknowledging that they cannot address the varied needs of students and their families and foster such a culture of inclusivity without building more coalitions of support among school staff, regional support staff, community providers in education, health and social services, and university faculty (Ainscow, Farrell, & Tweddle, 2000; Booth & Ainscow, 1997; Vernon & DiPaola, 2004).

Towards Inclusion of Perspective in Theory and Practice

The participants' dialogical interactions involved a critical evaluation of self, role, interaction with others and institution. In this sense, educational leadership, political activism of parents, and development of partnership and community not only intersected but often collided through deliberate acts of resistance in response to the escalating tensions resulting from competing conceptions of disability embedded in different paradigms. The inclusion project highlighted that the over-emphasis on the differences between perspectives obscured any potential consideration of what the perspectives actually have in common, and unfortunately hinders our capacity for interdisciplinary inquiry and honest and critical dialogue in practice.

In light of principals', parents', and teachers' underlying assumptions about what is *normal, deviant,* and *inclusive* in an accountability context, it should not be surprising that seemingly insurmountable dilemmas continue to arise in their attempts to resolve highly problematic issues around programs and placements in special education. If anything, these complexities demand that scholars and practitioners begin to take more of a questioning disposition to the theoretical knowledge base in special education and think more critically about the ways in which special education and disability are typically framed at the microlevel of local school practices (Gallagher, Heshusius, Iano, & Skrtic, 2004).

The inclusion of parental voice, previously marginalized or excluded in special education and educational research, could also engender a change in thinking and practice among principals and parents engaged in the interactive processes of resolving problems of mutual concern in special education. Most optimistically, we might hope it can also provide the impetus for a deeper interrogation of the notion of a professional and what should constitute professional knowledge. It might also unearth assumptions about self, others, and issues of power and ideologies. The participants in this study emphasized that this form of interrogation has inevitably presented them with more challenges and, at times, even conflicts. However, they agreed that it had been a necessary prerequisite to the creation of a more socially just space for participatory dialogue. Future inquiry into this area might also afford the larger community of scholars and practitioners in special education and disability studies the opportunity to more clearly understand and address the debates and conflicts that lie across the different fields of study and how they impact upon the debates and conflicts in the practitioner's arena. It is particularly evident that practitioners have little knowledge of how the literature has fuelled this bifurcation of perspectives.

Through an examination of theories and practices, it is apparent that alternative knowledge should complement empirical data. Shared beliefs and practices, as well as personal and professional experiences can and should be usefully employed. Personal meanings and intentions that individuals construct in their everyday lives should contribute to the knowledge base of special education that involves complex socially constructed meanings. As such we need to apply critical examination and reflexive methodologies in our practices. The inclusion project has emphasized that engagement in special education requires the careful mediation of tension between what are pursued as social and biomedical conceptions of disability. It should not be about negating or embracing one particular set of values over another. Perpetuating an *us versus them* division between scholars in special education and disability studies is counterproductive and damaging to attempts by practitioners to attend to multiple interests and ways of knowing. If scholars continue to compete in this way and are not willing to become more theoretically inclusive, then the chances of practitioners achieving greater inclusivity in their practice is sensibly reduced.

Certainly in my work as an educational leader and scholar I am continually confronted with norms for student achievement, for the "successful" learner, and for the instruction and assessment of students. To succeed with diverse populations within a context of standards-based reforms, educators and administrators need to model for others how it is possible to view different forms of sociocultural capital as valued resources rather than deficits. The education of students with disabilities has been traditionally associated with lowered expectations and far less of a focus on educational outcomes (Thurlow & Johnson, 2000). The dominant discourse in special education remains a medical one that links disability exclusively with biological factors. Students who are thought to be disabled are deemed to have different physiological attributes not considered to be social constructs. This type of discourse serves particular interests and has been very influential in shaping special education (Tomlinson, 1995; Van Rooyen, Le Grange, & Newmark, 2002). It has given us the prevailing medical perspective that pathologizes students with disabilities. As Slee (2001) points out, special education knowledge in schools continues to emphasize deficit-driven understandings of exceptionalities most often associated with professional scientific knowledge. There is little consideration of the perspective of the *other*—the one who does not hold the power derived from participation in the dominant discourse.

I submit that we need to pay far greater attention to the inequities embedded in the ways that schools are organized and operated. Little attention in special education meetings is ever drawn to organizational features and barriers that may be impeding the learning of students with disabilities (Barton, 1998; Thomas & Loxley, 2001). The focus remains on strategizing curative and remedial approaches to improving the individual rather than the environment in which the individual is located. The implication for *inclusion* as constituted by the medical discourse necessitates *exclusion* for those identified or assessed as having needs that transcend what the regular education classroom can offer.

School practitioners are in the best position to model a genuine appreciation for the contributions others can bring to the social process of knowledge construction (Begley & Zaretsky, 2004; Ryan, 2003; Schoeman & Schoeman, 2002; Shields, 2004). As debates continue, and as new scientific advances lead to new understandings of disability, scholars and practitioners are being asked to engage in more interdisciplinary efforts and inclusive practices. They are being asked to reconceptualize their perceptions of disability as part of the overall diversity of the school. Subsequently they are focusing their attention on improving student access to curriculum and student achievement through universal design processes. There is an explicit paradigm shift from process to achievement.

> Viewed in this light, special education should not mean a different curriculum, but rather the vehicle by which students with disabilities access the curriculum and the means by which the unique needs that arise out of the child's disability are addressed. This role requires a good deal of specialized knowledge and skill. (Hehir, 2005, p. 30)

Extending the Boundaries of Study and Practice in Special Education

Without question, the fields of science and medicine have contributed to the development of a large body of research on teaching and learning that underpin highly effective instructional practices and have produced highly innovative technologies that allow students in both regular and special education classes to maximize their learning and achievement. However, an institutional inclination toward medical discourses persists. It is worth recognizing that an expansion of the clinical scientific research base to reflect a wider appreciation of disability and impairment might appreciate these phenomena as socially constructed rather than individualized or pathologized, and that can provide us with more inclusive theories of special education.

The divisiveness in the special education literature in and of itself is a constructed phenomenon. The question, then, is whether we have erected battle lines that are defensible in and of themselves. Thus a claim that disability is socially constructed, as currently understood in postmodern terms, is not an inevitable result of just biology, but contingent on many sociocultural processes as well. Science is but one discourse among many today. Its knowledge claims, just like those from the social sciences and humanities can (and should) be held up to the standards that define their particular discursive communities. The medical model or the social holistic model have been developed for use within *their* unique interpretive communities where they too adhere to a particular set of conventions, ideologies, and sociopolitical and economic circumstances endemic to their own cultures of inquiry. It is difficult to find many who would attempt to even refute that most (if not all) of our reality is socially constructed regardless of the research community to which an individual belongs. All would agree that understandings are socially created.

Clearly, scientific knowledge is socially moderated, yet it can still be a powerful and effective tool for social and academic improvement. It would appear, then, to a large extent, scholars have chosen to misrepresent one another in pursuit of their own theoretical superiority (Richmon, 2004). *They h*ave left us with seemingly only two options from which to choose— determination by nature or determination by society—ignoring the populist view that we can *determine* ourselves by exercising our free will.

It is not so much a rejection of existing scientific literature in special education or empirical research based on accepted scientific methodology and design as some scholars would have us believe (Kauffman, 1999; Kavale & Mostert 2003; Sasso, 2001), but a rejection of some of the *interpretations* associated with this research when such interpretations are considered the *objective* truth with little consideration for the inclusion of other *truths* (Gallagher, Heshusius, Iano, & Skrtic, 2004). Decisions appear to be driven by scientific and objective analyses, yet when translated into instructional practices, appear inescapably subjective in nature. Logical inquiry is a matter of seeking out, checking, and assessing the worth of evidence. It is not about subordinating science—it is about critically examining a claim and its plausibility. A more in-depth examination and deconstruction of both assumed objective truths and perceived subjective truths relating to special education needs to be promoted. Most optimistically, we might hope it can also provide the impetus for extending the traditional boundaries of expertise (Zaretsky, 2004).

The fundamental point here is that critical dialogue about special education issues must better attend to bridging scholarly perspectives with actual classroom practices in order to be more responsive to the professional needs of practitioners and the educational needs of students and their families. The initiation and sustaining of dialogue is dependent upon approaching our own learning in a critical manner (Begley & Zaretsky, 2004; Faircloth, 2004). Theorists can support practitioners in developing their capacities to examine their own beliefs, practices, and taken-for-granted understandings. They can also support them in understanding that their values, beliefs, attitudes, and practices are social in nature. They do not originate exclusively with individuals. Rather, they have a history and are influenced through interactional processes. Although adopting a multiperspectival approach can be daunting, it is nonetheless essential when undertaking research that examines the complexities of special education. Furthermore, this engagement would allow the larger community of scholars and practitioners in special education and disability studies to clearly see where the debate or conflict lies, albeit in the definition of concepts or the logic used to link evidence to claims.

I have come to understand that no one theory can direct my administrative actions as a school and system leader in the sense that it can prescribe foolproof strategies or solutions to problems. In my experiences in schools as a teacher, administrator, and researcher, I have found that appreciating different perspectives on, for example, inclusion, resulted in a complementarity and richness that provided a deeper understanding of how this concept was understood differently, and hence how it might be better realized in practice. I would suggest, then, that dialogue across theoretical orientations better serves the interests of our schools and most effectively captures the complexity of issues relating to social difference and inclusive education currently confronting school personnel and families. My practical experiences and scholarly research remind me that there are no easy means for arriving at a shared understanding of what might constitute "inclusive education," but I have attempted to work with families, researchers, educators, administrators, and others who are committed to the collaborative endeavor of finding such understandings with me.

There is a wide range of theoretical positions related to different underlying ideologies, philosophies, and competing discourses in special education and disability. Still, while these varied interpretations are expected (if not desirable) from an "inclusion" standpoint, my intention has not been to reconcile or merge these differences but to use them to extend the boundaries of the study of special education and disability. I believe that any significant differences in interpretations of scholarly and practical perspectives on special education and disability can only assist us in better realizing inclusive ends in our schools and the communities they serve.

REFERENCES

Ainscow, M., Farrell, P., & Tweddle, D. (2000). Developing policies for inclusive education: A study of the role of local education authorities. *International Journal of Inclusive Education, 4*(3), 211-229.

Ballard, K. (1999). International voices: An introduction. In K. Ballard (Ed.), *Inclusive education: International voices on disability and justice* (pp. i-iv). Philadelphia: Falmer.

Barnes, C., Mercer, G., & Shakespeare, T. (1999). *Exploring disability: A sociological introduction*. Cambridge, England: Polity Press.

Barton, L. (1998). *The politics of special educational needs*. London: Falmer Press.

Begley, P. T., & Zaretsky, L. (2004) Democratic school leadership in Canada's public school systems: Professional value and social ethic. *The Journal of Educational Administration, 42*(6), 640-655.

Booth, T., & Ainscow, M. (1998). *From them to us: An international study of inclusion in education*. London: Routledge.

Brantlinger, E. A. (2000). Using ideology: The politics of research and practice in special education. In S. Ball (Ed.), *Sociology of Education, 3,* 425-460. New York: Routledge-Falmer.

Burrello, L. C., Lashley, C., & Beatty, E. E. (2001). *Educating all students together: How school leaders create unified systems*. Thousand Oaks, CA: Corwin.

Clark, C., Dyson, A., & Millward, A. (1998). Theorising special education: Time to move on! In C. Clark, A. Dyson, & A. Millward (Eds.), *Theorising special education* (pp. 156-173). London: Routledge.

Crockett, J. B., & Kauffman, J. M. (1998). Taking inclusion back to its roots. *Educational Leadership, 56*(2), 74-77.

Danforth, S., & Rhodes, W. C. (1997). Deonstructing disability. *Remedial and Special Education, 18,* 357-366.

Faircloth, S. C. (2004). Turbulent policy demands and ethical dilemmas: The impact of federal education policies on special education programs and services. *Values and Ethics in Educational Administration, 2*(3), 1-6.

Ferguson, P. M., & Ferguson, D. L. (1995). The interpretivist view of special education and disability: The value of telling stories. In T. M. Skrtic (Ed.), *Disability and democracy: Reconstructing (special) education for postmodernity* (pp. 104-121). New York: Teachers College Press.

Fiedler, C. R. (2000). *Making a difference: Advocacy competencies for special education professionals*. Boston: Allyn & Bacon.

Gallagher, D. J. (1998). The scientific knowledge base of special education: Do we know what we think we know? *Exceptional Children, 64*, 493-502.

Gallagher, D. J., Heshusius, L., Iano, R. P., & Skrtic, T. M. (2004). *Challenging orthodoxy in special education: Dissenting voices.* Denver, CO: Love.

Giangreco, M. F. (1997). *Quick guides to inclusion: Ideas for educating students with disabilities.* Baltimore: Paul H. Brookes.

Hallahan, D. P. (1998). Sound bytes from special education reform rhetoric. *Remedial and Special Education, 19*, 67-69.

Hehir, T. (2005). Defining ableism in education. In T. Hehir (Ed.), *New directions in special education: Eliminating ableism in policy and practice* (pp. 14-42). Cambridge, MA: Harvard.

Hockenbury, J. C., Kauffman, J. M., & Hallahan, D. P. (2000). What is right aboutspecial education? *Exceptionality, 6*(1), 3-11.

Johnson, D. R., Stodden, R. A., Emaunel, E. J., Luecking, R., & Mack, M. (2002). Current challenges facing secondary education and transition services: What research tells us. *Exceptional Children, 68*(4), 519-531.

Jordan, A. (2001). Special education in Ontario, Canada: A case study of market-based reforms, *Cambridge Journal of Education, 31*(3), 349-371.

Kauffman, J. M. (1994). Places of change: Special education's power and identity in an era of educational reform. *Journal of Learning Disabilities, 2*, 610-618.

Kauffman, J. M. (1999). Commentary: Today's special education and its messages for tomorrow. *Journal of Special Education, 32*(4), 244-254.

Kauffman, J. M., & Hallahan, D. P. (1990). What we want for children: A rejoinder to REI proponents. *The Journal of Special Education, 24*(3), 340-345.

Kerzner-Lipsky, D., & Gartner, A. (1997). *Inclusion and school reform.* Baltimore: Paul H. Brookes.

Kavale, K. A., & Mostert, M. P. (2003). River of ideology, islands of evidence, *Exceptionality, 11*(4), 191-208.

Mostert, M. P., & Crockett, J. B. (2000). Reclaiming the history of special education for more effective practice. *Exceptionality, 8*, 133-143.

Peters, S. (2004, April). *Origins and development of the social model: An historical deconstruction.* Paper presented at the American Educational Research Association (AERA) Conference, San Diego, CA.

Pivik, J., McComas, J., & LaFlamme, M. (2002). Barriers and facilitators to inclusive education. *Exceptional Children, 69*(1), 97-107.

Richmon, M. J. (2004, May). Naïve constructivism: *Epistemological laxity for the sake of school improvement.* Paper presented at the annual meeting of the Canadian Association for the Study of Educational Administration, Winnipeg, Canada.

Riehl, C. J. (2000). The principal's role in creating inclusive schools for diverse students. A review of normative, empirical, and critical literatures on the practice of educational administration. *Review of Educational Research, 70*(1), 55-81.

Ryan, J. (2003) *Leading diverse schools.* Dordrecht, Netherlands: Kluwer.

Sasso, J. M. (2001).The retreat from inquiry and knowledge in special education. *Journal Of Special Education, 34*, 178-193.

Schoeman, M., & Schoeman, M. (2002). Disability and the ideology of professionalism. *International Journal of Special Education, 17*(1), 15-20.

Schrag, F. (1992). In defense of positivist research paradigms. *Educational Researcher, 21*(5), 5-8.

Shields, C. (2004). Dialogic leadership for social justice: Overcoming pathologies of silenced voices. *Educational Administration Quarterly, 40*(1), 111-134.

Skrtic, T. M. (1995). The functionalist view of special education and disability: Deconstructing the conventional knowledge tradition. In T. M. Skrtic (Ed.), *Disability and democracy: Reconstructing [special] education for postmodernism* (pp. 65-103). New York: Teachers College Press.

Skrtic, T. M., Sailor, W., & Gee, K. (1996). Voice, collaboration, and inclusion: Democratic themes in educational and social reform initiatives. *Remedial and Special Education, 17*, 142-157.

Slee, R. (2001). Social justice and the changing directions in educational research: The case of inclusive education. *International Journal of Inclusive Education, 5*(2/3), 167-177.

Starratt, R. J. (2003). *Centering educational administration: Cultivating meaning, community, responsibility.* Mahwah, NJ: Erlbaum.

Thomas, G., & Loxley, A. (2001). *Deconstructing special education and constructing inclusion.* Buckingham, England: Open University Press.

Thomas, G., Walker, D., & Webb, J. (1998). *The making of an inclusive school.* London: Routledge.

Thurlow, M., & Johnson, D. R. (2000). High stakes testing for students with disabilities. *Journal of Teacher Education, 51*, 289-298.

Tomlinson, S. (1995). The radical structuralist view of special education and disability: Unpopular perspectives on their origins and development. In Skrtic, T. M. (Ed.), *Disability and democracy: Reconstructing [special] education for postmodernity* (pp. 92-111). New York: Teachers College Press.

Turnbull, A., & Turnbull, H. R. (2000). *Families, professionals, and exceptionality: Collaborating for empowerment* (4th ed.). Upper Saddle River: NJ: Prentice Hall.

Van Rooyen, B., Le Grange, L., & Newmark, R. (2002). (De)constructions of functionalist discourses in South Africa's education white paper 6: Special needs education. *International Journal of Special Education, 17*(2), 1-24.

Vernon, L. J., & DiPaola, M. (2004, April). *The impact of school leadership teams on inclusive services to students with disabilities.* Paper presented at the American Educational Research Association (AERA) Conference, San Diego, CA.

Villa, R. A., & Thousand, J. S. (2000). Collaborative teaming: A powerful tool in school restructuring. In R. A. Villa & J. S. Thousand (Eds.), *Restructuring for caring and effective education: Piecing the puzzle together* (2nd ed.). Baltimore, MD: Paul Brookes.

Vincent, C. (2000). *Including parents? Education, citizenship and parental agency.* Buckingham, England: Open University Press.

Ware, L. (1999). My kid, and kids kinda like him. In K. Ballard (Ed.), *Inclusiveeducation: International voices on disability and justice* (pp. 86-116). Philadelphia: Falmer Press, Taylor & Francis.

Weiss, M. P., & Lloyd, J. W. (2002). Congruence between roles and actions of secondary school educators in co-taught and special education settings. *Journal of Special Education, 36*(2), 58-72.

Zaretsky, L. (2004). Responding ethically to complex school-based issues in special education. *International Studies in Educational Administration, Journal of the Commonwealth Council for Educational Administration & Management, 32*(2), 63-72.

Zaretsky, L. (2004). Advocacy and administration: From conflict to collaboration. *Journal of Educational Administration, 42*(2), 270-286.

PART III

GENDER AND SEXUAL IDENTITY

CHAPTER 6

GENDER

A H.O.T. (Higher Order Thinking) Link in Educating Urban Students

Amy Barnhill

The current study is an examination of three areas of research which, as of yet, have not been linked: gender schema, gender elements found in texts, and cognitive complexity. Gender schema, which is defined as the degree to which individuals organize their self-concepts and behaviors on the basis of their gender (Bem, 1981), influences the way males and females interpret and understand literature, and relate to school and one another (Belenky, Clinchy, Goldberger, & Tarule, 1986; Magolda, 1992; Perry, 1970). In addition, elements of text also influence how males and females make sense of text (Bleich 1986; Day, 1994; Flynn 1986; Halpern, 1985). Both of these areas of research are based on the theory of constructivism. Constructivism (Gruender, 1996) recognizes that it is a combination of the reader's prior knowledge and experiences as well as the text that creates meaning for the reader. So, the theory of constructivism plays a significant role in developing a rationale for the current study.

Inclusion in Urban Educational Environments:
Addressing Issues of Diversity, Equity, and Social Justice, 113–135

The final area of research that lays the foundation for the current study is cognitive complexity. Ernest McDaniel's (1991) description of cognitive complexity is used in the current study. It refers to a thinking process based on cognitive structures that range on a continuum from "simplistic categorization and evaluation of information to the ability to generate theoretical frameworks that organize complex events and relations" (McDaniel, 1991, p. 18). It is another way to look at higher levels of thinking. McDaniel is unique in his description of cognitive complexity in that he provides an evaluation tool for measuring higher levels of thinking. He attempts to quantify levels of thinking.

Each of these three areas of research is important to understanding how we read and how our reading influences our thinking. However, there is a lack of research attempting to connect these areas together in order to examine the effect of gender schema and elements of text on various levels of cognitive complexity. Is gender schema, or even simply gender, a piece of the puzzle in understanding how we, as readers, can approach a text using higher levels of thinking? The following study addresses this issue in an urban educational environment; the subjects were taken from a large Midwestern metropolitan area. More specifically, it addresses why researchers and educators should utilize knowledge gained from this study to create equitable learning experiences and resourceful students.

BACKGROUND

As recently as the 1950's, reading specialists described reading as the process of transmitting knowledge from the text to the reader. Some researchers recognize that reader factors such as intelligence and attitude play a part in this process; however, they fail to connect the important role of the reader's prior experience with the reading process (Lyman & Collins, 1990). In the past 3 decades there has been a surge of reading comprehension research, and, most recently, research in the area of higher-order reading and thinking. Jean Piaget (1959), perhaps the best-known theorist of cognitive development, explains cognitive development in terms of a person's interaction with their environment. The basic premise of his theory is that knowledge is constructed through interaction with the surrounding environment (Ginsburg & Opper, 1988). This interest in how people gain meaning from text and the world has resulted in a new movement in the field of education termed "constructivism" (Gruender, 1996).

The philosophy of constructivism assumes that the individual actively constructs knowledge; knowledge is not simply transmitted from the text to the head of the reader. As with many philosophies, constructivist philosophers vary in their focus on certain issues. There is one school of thought that focuses on the cognitive contents of the individual learner while others attend to the social and political forces that impact human knowledge (Phillips, 1995). Those who belong to the first school of thought stress that knowledge is a result of a learner's cognitive activity and not the passive reception of information. Those from the other school of thought focus their concern on the construction of human knowledge in general and the sociopolitical forces that impact it. For the purposes presented here, knowledge is actively constructed by the individual, but not without social and political forces influencing that construction.

Every person brings a host of unique experiences to the reading of text. These experiences, as well as the ability of the individual and their disposition—or inclination to read and learn, interact to create meaning. Because each person is inherently different and comes to the text with different schemata (prior knowledge structures), the meanings they draw from the text are different. Constructivism, then, involves a substantial amount of subjectivity. The act of constructing meaning, since it is highly subjective, can often lead to cognitive distortions. A person may accept a view that is false due to their subjective interpretation of reality (Gruender, 1996). For example, one might believe that gang members are minorities and come from poverty-stricken homes or that members of a certain race are not as intellectually capable as others. These cognitive distortions arose, not because they were scientifically proven, but because human beings make "truths" for themselves based on their past experiences, abilities and dispositions. On the other hand, this same subjectivity can lead to highly imaginative and creative thinking. One of the goals of education is to encourage and facilitate creative and inventive thinking while discouraging such cognitive distortions as are bound to arise in the course of living and learning.

Overcoming severe, or pervasive cognitive distortions can be difficult because it requires the restructuring of existing schemata. One such schema is gender schema. According to Bem (1981), gender schema refers to the degree to which individuals organize their self-concepts and behaviors on the basis of their gender. For example, children learn what society expects from them in terms of which attributes are to be linked with their own sex. The gender schema that develops becomes a kind of guide or standard for the child. In turn, gender schema affects behavior as the individual begins to conform to society's idea of maleness or femaleness. Gender schemata, then, is a cognitive structure and potential distorter, that lead one to perceive and encode information in ways that are bound to stereotypic representations of an individual's gender. Some individuals will develop a highly sex-typed gender schema and others will develop a more androgynous gender schema. Those who are highly sex typed will behave in ways that are stereotypic of their gender. Those who are androgynous may behave in ways that represent aspects of both male-ness and femaleness.

Empirical research on gender schema and recall has shown that gender schemata are used to store information in memory (Day, 1994). For instance, Martin and Halverson (1983) found that, when kindergarten children were shown pictures of actors doing something, they made few errors in identifying the sex of the actor. However, 84% of the mistakes that were made occurred when the actor was doing something sex-incon-sistent. Day (1994) interprets these findings as evidence that consistency with schemas is critical for information to appear real in memory. A study by Halpern (1985) also examined gender schema and recall in a sample of high school students. Students read two stories and then answered questions about them. Male and female students both answered signifi-cantly more questions correctly when the protagonist was his or her own sex. The researchers suggest that subjects are more likely to identify with same-sex characters. These findings also suggest that identification is a way of making information meaningful, thereby facilitating knowledge retention (Day, 1994).

Other studies have also demonstrated gender-related differences in people's responses to narrative fiction. Bleich (1986) and Flynn (1986) found that male college students referred to the author of the work more so than females, while women were more inclined to involve themselves in the lives of the characters. Day (1994) suggests that men tend to draw boundaries between themselves and the piece of literature while women tend to become a part of the world described in the book. This interpreta-tion is consistent with other data on developmental differences between men and women. Men tend to draw their self-esteem from their ability to achieve results, primarily by themselves (Belenky, et al., 1986; Gray, 1992). Autonomy appears to be important to men which may explain why men draw boundaries between themselves and the piece of literature. Women, on the other hand, tend to develop their self-esteem through their feelings and the quality of their relationships, therefore lending sup-port to the reason women become a part of the world described in the text (Belenky, et al., 1986; Gray, 1992). It may be suggested that certain texts have a gender orientation. Some tend to include elements that males will find meaningful (plot and action-centered, male protagonist) while others tend to include elements that females will find meaningful (centered around relationships and emotions, female protagonist).

Research by Manzo, Manzo, Barnhill, and Thomas (2000) indicates that there may be "reader subtypes," or clusters, among proficient readers that may also be divided along gender lines. They found four possible subtypes in their research. The first subtype they discovered was titled mature, or androgynous progressing readers. These readers tended to have good concentration, critical analysis, and concept formation with an ability to read and think between and beyond the lines. The second subtype appeared to have a more conventionalized, entrepreneurial male orientation often associated with males in western cultures. They had fair transfer-of-training, preferred doing repetitive and predictable tasks, and were not inclined to self-examination. However, these readers tended to be action-oriented and entrepreneurial. Entrepreneurial, in this case, is referring to a willingness to take risks, particularly when using new information in reaching pragmatic goals. The third type of reader had a conventionalized, story-reading female orientation associated with females in most cultures. They maintained solid literal comprehension and often read for pleasure. While reading seemed to comfort them, they rarely thought deeply about what they read nor did they use the new information toward practical goals. The final subtype was titled detail dependent, rule followers. This subtype tended to be passive readers with some possible emotional immaturity and unsophisticated patterns of thought. To the surprise of the researchers, it appeared that gender factors were a strong possible element in distorting reading and thinking. Since gender schema is a principle for organizing and making sense of information and is not always consistent with the sex of the individual, it would seem that gender schema rather than the sex of the individual was the influential element as both men and women fell into all categories. This research further validates ethnographic findings (Magolda, 1992) that gender schema influences the way males and females interpret and understand literature, and relate to school and one another.

In addition, we must keep in mind our knowledge about how individuals construct meaning from text. Constructivism recognizes the role of the reader in constructing meaning, but it does not abandon the idea that the text also plays a role. The interaction between text and reader creates meaning. Therefore, it makes sense that the nature of the text will also be an important element in studying how individuals create meaning and move to higher levels of thinking/reading. In dealing with the nature of a text, it is important to consider the role of rauding. Rauding is a term defined by Carver (1997) as the process that most readers use regularly. It is "simple reading" (Carver, 1997, p. 6). Another explanation is that the rauding process is similar to simple comprehension. It is often helpful for teachers and researchers to know whether a student has comprehended a passage, skimmed a passage, or even moved to higher levels of thinking. This is traditionally assessed by evaluating responses.

Carver (1997) proposes a formula for predicting the accuracy of text comprehension without evaluating responses but by manipulating the text itself and elements surrounding the reading of the text. This formula involves the following: (a) the reading level and rate level of the individual, (b) the difficulty level and length of the text, and (c) the time spent reading (p. 3). There are specific methods that researchers can use to induce certain levels of thinking. The first method concerns the relative difficulty of the material involved. If the material presented is easy for the reader, then the rauding process (comprehension process) is more likely to be used by the reader. If the material is more difficult than the ability level of the student then he/she will not likely engage in the rauding process (Carver, 1997). The second method involves the way in which the instructions are presented by the researcher. Instructions prepare subjects for the type of learning they are going to do. If the researcher says that the subjects should read the material as they usually do, then they will most likely use the rauding process. If the researcher tells the subjects to learn the important parts of the text, then they will probably shift out of the rauding process and move to a higher level of reading, the learning process. The subjects' reading moves from passive to active. The third method is the subjects' knowledge of the consequences following reading of the text. If the subjects know that they will be asked to identify incomplete thoughts, then they will probably use the rauding process. However, if the subjects know that they will need to answer difficult multiple choice questions, they may shift up to the learning process. If the subjects know that they will be asked to write down as much as they can remember about the text, they will likely move to the highest level of reading, memorizing (Carver, 1997).

This particular study focuses on higher levels of thinking. Knowledge of the rauding process was used to enhance the possibility that subjects did engage in higher levels of thinking. The subjects must have rauded the material before they were able to read on higher levels. It was important to make sure that the subjects were rauding, and therefore were prepared to move to higher levels of thinking. Higher level thinking can be defined a number of ways. One popular method used by many schools and teachers utilizes Bloom's Taxonomy (Sax, 1997) which includes six levels of thinking and reading: knowledge, comprehension, application, analysis, synthesis, and evaluation. The last three levels on the taxonomy —analysis, synthesis, and evaluation—are considered higher levels of thinking. Another popular taxonomy is Barrett's Taxonomy of Reading (Sax, 1997) which involves five levels of reading: literal comprehension, reorganization, inferential comprehension, evaluation, and appreciation. Again, the last three levels are considered higher level thinking. These taxonomies are useful in that they assist teachers in their development and use of questions.

Their limitations, though, are quite significant and should spur educators to consider alternative definitions of higher order thinking. Schemata, or the information processing structures in our brain, are not included in those traditional descriptions of higher order thinking. Our schemata impact our intellectual growth and tendency to think on higher levels and, therefore, should be at the core in any description of thinking. Ernest McDaniel (1991) uses the idea of schema in his definition of cognitive complexity. Cognitive complexity, or higher-order thinking, is defined as a thinking process marked less by inductive and deductive reasoning, which suggests a progression of logical sequences, and more by associative and elaborative processes. As individuals grow and encounter learning experiences, their schema, and therefore their thinking processes, become more mature and complex. They build associations and elaborations based on their experiences. Thinking processes then can be described in terms of immature and mature. Perry (1970) uses this dichotomy in his description of thinking. Immature thinking is when students appear to view the world as divisible into simple "black-white" categories. Authorities have all the answers and there is the feeling that everything will work out if one relies on hard work and obedience. Mature thinking, on the other hand, stresses the ability to imagine alternative solutions not suggested by the problem situation and the ability to see knowledge as relative from person to person and place to place.

Belenky et al. (1986) create a similar definition of complex thinking, only this definition is based on interviews and research with women. Perry's (1970) research was based on interviews and research with men. Both definitions include a scale from immature to mature thinking. Both describe thinking in terms of how people look at the world and how they view knowledge. One of the major differences between the two definitions of complex thinking is how men and women align themselves with authority and how they utilize their personal knowledge. As people progress to more mature thinking, men tend to align themselves with authorities more so than women. Because women see themselves as separate from the "theys," or authorities, their personal knowledge becomes a strong element in constructing new knowledge. This difference may be accounted for by women's rootedness in a sense of connection and men's emphasis on separation and autonomy (Belenky et al., 1986). Even though there is a difference between men and women in their thinking, both types of thinking can be described in terms of immature and mature. The term cognitive complexity can be used for both genders to describe higher level thinking.

In order to elicit a cognitively complex response, the type of prompt used must be carefully selected. If one wanted to test "formal reasoning" (Galotti, Kozberg, & Appleman, 1990), a well-defined problem would be set forth and the student would follow logically sound rules of reasoning and use the information provided to obtain the correct answer. If one wanted to test "everyday reasoning" (Galotti, Kozberg, & Appleman, 1990), the statement would be open-ended and all of the needed information might not be provided. "In everyday reasoning, the way information is perceived, selected and interpreted plays a major role in formulating solutions" (McDaniel, 1991, p. 6). Most texts and assessments call for formal reasoning where the students logically assess the statements provided. However, formal reasoning does not allow students an opportunity to formulate their own problems and come to their own conclusions. Much can be determined about a student by assessing their typical responses. These responses will most likely represent their inclination to think on an immature or mature level, in other words their cognitive complexity. It can also give insight into the operating gender schema of the person. Everyday reasoning, or typical responses, was the purpose behind prompts used in this study to measure cognitive complexity.

While much research has shown a gender-related connection between reading and thinking, other studies have indicated that the link between gender and higher-order thinking may not be significant. One study into mathematical and scientific higher-order thinking looked at gender differences in the role of inquiry (Kelly, 1999). The results indicated that *both* genders had similar perceptions about inquiry and approaches to higher-order thinking. Another study attempted to explain the involvement of gender in higher-order thinking (Noble & Powell, 1995). This study looked at various factors and their influence on a higher-order thinking test called PLAN. The factors included: course work taken, educational needs and plans, high school attended, as well as gender and ethnicity. The results suggested that course work taken, students' educational needs and plans, and high school attended were major factors in explaining students' achievement of higher-order thinking skills. Gender and ethnicity explained 2% or less of the variance in PLAN scores over and above these factors.

Both of these studies seem to cast some doubt on the connection between gender and higher-order thinking; however, there are some aspects of the design in these studies, as well as some theoretical differences, that were different than the design and theoretical basis of the study being discussed here. In the first study by Kelly (1999) the type of higher-order thinking involved in the study was different than the higher-level responses elicited from subjects after reading a fictional text. Inquiry may be a partial factor in responding to fictional texts, but other types of higher-level thinking would include interpretation of the literature, relating the text to one's own life, evaluating the decisions of the characters, and questioning the author. These are just a few of the types of higher-level thinking a person may explore when reading fictional text. In the second study by Noble and Powell (1995), the assessment of higher-order thinking involved the PLAN test. This test is often used in educational planning and in program and curriculum evaluation. It measures higher-level thinking, but does not target the type of higher-level thinking proposed in this paper. In addition, both studies looked only at gender, not gender schema, which we have established may be different from one's gender. The purpose of this study was to investigate the influence of gender orientation of text (male, female) and gender schema (masculine, feminine, androgynous) on cognitive complexity of responses to selected text.

METHODOLOGY

The following provides a look at the methodology applied to this research. Data concerning the subjects is presented; information regarding the texts used in this study is discussed; and measures for the variables of cognitive complexity, gender schema and reading ability are described.

Subjects

Ninety male and female freshman high school students at a mid-Western suburban high school participated in the study. The school district was located on the outer edges of a large urban city. The high school where this study was conducted was one of three high schools maintained by the district and was approximately 10 driving minutes from the city's downtown. Even though this high school was in a suburban school district, it could be said that it experienced many of the same issues prevalent in urban school districts. This high school, of the three high schools, had the most economically disadvantaged families with 33.6% of students qualifying for free/reduced lunch. In addition, there was ethnic diversity among students. Students in the high school were predominantly Caucasian (77%) with some African American (8%), Asian (7%), Hispanic (7%), and Native American (1%) students. The boundaries for this high school included an area of town that housed a large population of immigrants; therefore, the school provided an English Language Learner (ELL) program for students as well as evening ELL classes for adults.

The students participating in this study were taken from an honors English course at the high school. All students attending class participated in the study as the English teacher required it. The students were able to self-enroll in this honors course without recommendations or other requirements. The course was developed for students who planned on attending college. However, the teacher indicated that some of the students realized that the material was too difficult and did not enroll in the honors English program during their sophomore year. In fact, based on The Accuracy Level Test (Carver, 1990), a test that determines reading ability in terms of grade equivalent scores, 16 of the 90 students participating in the study had a reading level below the readability level of the texts. The readability level cutoff point was set at a grade equivalency (G.E.) of 6.0; the data from those subjects with a readability score of 6.0 or below were eliminated from the study and were not considered in the results. Therefore, 74 students provided results that could be utilized in this study. The racial/ethnic mix in the sample was predominantly Caucasian (86%) with some African American (5%) and some Asian (9%) but no Hispanic or Native American students. Table 6.1 describes the background of the subjects.

Text

The texts used for this research study were chosen based on their strong evidence of a particular gender-orientation, either male or female. Gender-orientation of text was determined by selecting criteria suggested by research to indicate a male-orientation or a female-orientation. The criteria selected for a male-oriented text were: plot and action-centered with a male protagonist (Gambell & Hunter, 2000; Halpern, 1985). The criteria selected for a female-oriented text were: relationship-centered and emotionally based (Bleich, 1986; Day, 1992; Flynn, 1986), with a female protagonist (Gambell & Hunter, 2000; Halpern, 1985). The

Table 6.1.   Demographics of Subjects

Number of Subjects Providing Usable	Total (n = 74)	Female (n = 35)	Male (n = 21)
Average age	15 years old		
Racial/ethnic background	Caucasian (86%)	Asian (9%)	African American (5%)
Rauding data	# of subjects rauding above G.E. 6.0, n = 74 (usable data)		# of subjects rauding below G.E. 6.0, n = 16 (nonusable data)

selected texts were also chosen due to their readability level. It will be necessary for the subjects to read texts that are below their own reading level.
The reason for this can be explained through rauding theory. If the subjects read text that is below their reading level, the likelihood that they
will raud the text, or comprehend the text, increases. Each subject must
be able to raud the text in order to move to higher levels of thinking.

The male-oriented text included three excerpts taken from *Life on the
Mississippi* by Mark Twain. These excerpts were written about Twain's adolescent life as a riverboat pilot. Two of the excerpts described Twain's difficulties with his pilot, Mr. Brown, and how he takes revenge on him. The
last excerpt described an explosion on the riverboat and the fate of some
of the passengers as the boat burst into flame and sank. These excerpts
were written from Twain's point-of-view. The researcher took a sample of
689 words from the excerpts and used the Flesch-Kincaid readability formula to determine a grade level equivalency of 5.1

The female-oriented text was a short story called *Red Dress* by Alice
Munro. The theme of this short story was a rite-of-passage. The narrator,
an adolescent girl, goes to a school dance. Some events happen that test
her courage and confidence. Another element in the story was the girl's
relationship with her mother. As in the male-oriented text, the researcher
took a sample of 690 words and used the Flesch-Kincaid readability formula to determine a grade level equivalency of 5.7. Both texts were taken
from the English literature book, *Elements of Literature: Third Course* by R.
W. Anderson (1989). Every effort was made to find two texts that were
similar in length in order to control for length of text as a distracting element for the subjects. *Red Dress* was six and a half pages long, and the
excerpts from *Life on the Mississippi* were seven pages long. In addition, it
was desirable to find two texts having similar grade equivalency levels.
However, in order for the current study to apply in the classroom, the
classroom textbook was chosen as the source for the two texts needed. It
would be nearly impossible to find two texts that met the criteria for a
male- or a female-oriented text as well as have exact grade equivalency
scores. Therefore, the two stories that were chosen were the best choices
given the limitations of the study and the textbook.

Measures

Cognitive Complexity.   In order to measure "everyday reasoning" (Galotti, 1990), which is closer to a person's typical response than "formal reasoning" (Galotti, 1990), an open ended question/statement followed each
passage. The question/statement was: "Write a summary statement
describing your reaction and interpretation of this situation." The sub-

jects' answers were evaluated using two raters. The raters used McDaniel's (1991) Cognitive Complexity Strand Scale to rate the subjects' level of cognitive complexity. The raters assigned scores to the subjects' responses using the five levels of thinking identified by the MCCSS. The levels are described below:

Level 1: Unilateral Descriptions.   A person at this level simplifies the situation. Focuses on one idea or argument. Does not identify alternatives. Brings in no new information, meaning, or perspectives. Makes good/bad and either/or assumptions. Appeals to authority or simple rules. Simply paraphrases, restates or repeats information.

Level 2: Simplistic Alternatives.   A person at this level identifies simple and obvious conflicts, but the conflicts are not pursued or analyzed. Develops a position by dismissing or ignoring one alternative and supporting the other with assertions and simple explanations rather than by making a deeper assessment of the situation.

Level 3: Emergent Complexity.   A person at this level identifies more than one possible explanation or perspective. Establishes and preserved complexity. Introduces new elements. Supports position through comparisons and simple causal statements.

Level 4: Broad Interpretations.   A person at this level uses broad ideas to help define and interpret the situation. Manipulates ideas within the perspective established. Has a clearly recognizable explanatory theme. Integrates ideas into "subassemblies," each supporting a component of the explanation.

Level 5: Integrated Analysis.   A person at this level restructures or reconceptualizes the situation and approaches the problem from a new point of view. Constructs a network of cause-and-effect relationships. Integrates and extrapolates ideas. Arrives at new interpretations by analogy, application of principles, generalizations, and world knowledge. Constructs an organizing framework, sketches connections, and predicts consequences.

Research in the areas of thinking skills and cognitive processes has been handicapped by the lack of valid instruments to test these areas. Rather than develop a new instrument to measure cognitive complexity for the direct purposes of this study, it made sense to use a measure that already had established reliability and validity—McDaniel's Cognitive Complexity Strand Scale.

Gender Schema

The Bem Sex-Role Inventory (BSRI) was used to measure gender schema. The BSRI separately assesses psychological femininity and masculinity, and therefore, can possibly identify individuals who are "androgynous"—those who have both feminine and masculine traits. Bem, the author of the inventory, asserts that the results of the test could identify those individuals who organize their self-concept and behavior on the basis of a culturally defined gender.

Reading Ability

The Accuracy Level Test (ALT) developed by Carver (2000) was used to measure reading ability. It was important to determine each subject's reading level to insure that the text in the passages was below their reading level. According to rauding theory, if the text is below the reading level of the subjects, they will likely be rauding as they read. It is necessary to raud before moving to higher levels of thinking. Any subject with a reading ability below 5.9 was discarded from the research. Those subjects with a reading ability of 6.0 and above were considered as part of the data. The most important aspect of the ALT is its validity in measuring the highest level of material difficulty that individuals can raud. Carver (1990) determined that the ALT does predict comprehension quite well and is relatively accurate in estimating rauding accuracy level (individual's reading level in G.E. units).

RESULTS

The results are organized into two areas of inquiry. The first area, which was the initial line of inquiry, is the effect of gender schema and gender-orientation of text on cognitive complexity. The second area is the effect of gender and gender-orientation of text on cognitive complexity. After evaluating the results based on gender schema, a second analysis was conducted identifying the subjects by gender rather than gender schema. The effect size measure, Eta squared, based on Cohen's criteria (1977) is included for each measure. Cohen determined that an Eta squared value of .01 was considered a small effect, .06 was a medium effect, and .014 was a large effect. The following is a presentation of results from both lines of inquiry.

Bem Sex-Role Inventory (BSRI)

The Bem Sex-role Inventory was utilized to determine subjects' gender schema. Gender schema was an independent variable in this analysis. A brief note needs to be made about the data that was utilized from the BSRI. The BSRI allows for subjects to be classified into four sex-role groups: feminine—a person's femininity score was significantly higher than her or his masculinity score; masculine—a person's masculinity score was significantly higher than her or his femininity score; androgynous—a person's femininity and masculinity score were approximately equal and the score on both was high; undifferentiated—a person's femininity and masculinity score were approximately equal but the score on both was low. In this study 19 subjects had a masculine sex-role, 12 had a feminine sex-role, 25 had an androgynous sex-role, and 18 had an undifferentiated sex-role. For the purposes of this study, the data from the undifferentiated individuals was not analyzed because it was not relevant to the research. Therefore, 56 subjects provided analyzable data for this study.

McDaniel's Cognitive Complexity Strand Scale (MCCSS)

The McDaniel's Cognitive Complexity Strand Scale was utilized as a measure of cognitive complexity and was the dependent variable in this study. Two independent raters were required to make subjective judgments when scoring subjects' written responses to both female- and male-oriented texts. Two measures were used to examine inter-rater reliability of 56 responses to selected texts. The first measure was to calculate the average difference between rater 1 and rater 2 based on the original scale in MCCSS of a 1–5 rating. This would attempt to demonstrate how closely the rater's scores were to each other when rating the passages using the 1–5 scale. On the female-oriented passage responses the average difference was .6. This means that the rater's scores were not even 1 off from each other when rating the female-oriented passage responses. On the male-oriented passage responses the average difference was .2. This means that the rater's scores were quite close to each other when rating the male-oriented passage responses.

The second measure of reliability was percent agreement, that is, how often the two raters had agreement when scoring the written responses. The percent agreement was 88% when the rating was equal or +1 or -1. This means that 88% of the time the two raters agreed on a score for the written responses or their scores only varied either positively or negatively by 1 point. For example, one rater may have rated a written response 3 out of 5 using the MCCSS. The other rater, when reading this same written response, rated it either 2, 3, or 4 88% of the time. Therefore, based on these two measures of inter-rater reliability, consistency in the raters' use of the MCCSS scoring rubric was supported.

Descriptive statistics for the MCCSS using gender schema and gender-orientation of text as independent variables are shown in Table 6.2. The cognitive complexity score was higher on the female-oriented passage than the male-oriented passage for all subjects—male, female, and androgynous gender schema. Androgynous gender schema subjects had more similar results on both the female- and male-oriented texts than

**Table 6.2.   Means and Standard Deviations for
the McDaniel's Cognitive Complexity Strand Scale (MCCSS)
Using Gender Schema and Gender Orientation of
Text as Independent Variables**

	Number of Subjects	*Male-Oriented Text*		*Female-Oriented Text*	
		Mean	*SD*	*Mean*	*SD*
Male gender schema	19	4.2	1.6	5.1	1.7
Female gender schema	12	4.3	1.1	5.7	1.7
Androgynous gender schema	25	4.4	1.8	5.1	1.9

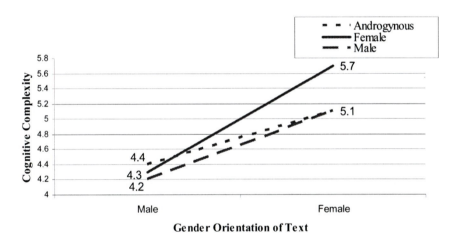

Figure 6.1.   Interaction of the means for gender schema and gender orientation of text on cognitive complexity.

male or female gender schema subjects. Figure 6.1 displays the means for the interaction of gender schema and gender orientation of text on cognitive complexity.

Descriptive statistics for the MCCSS using gender and gender orientation of text as independent variables are presented in Table 6.3. The cognitive complexity score of male subjects did not change whether reading the male-oriented passage of the female-oriented passage. The cognitive complexity score did change for the female subjects. It was lower on the male-oriented passage and higher on the female-oriented passage. Figure

**Table 6.3.   Means and Standard Deviations for the
McDaniel's Cognitive Complexity Strand Scale (MCCSS)
Using Gender and Gender Orientation of
Text as Independent Variables**

	Number of Subjects	Male-Oriented Text		Female-Oriented Text	
		Mean	SD	Mean	SD
Male subjects	21	4.6	1.6	4.6	1.6
Female subjects	35	4.1	1.6	5.6	1.8

6.2 displays the means for the interaction of gender and gender orientation of text on cognitive complexity.

A two-way analysis of variance was completed for the interaction between gender schema and gender orientation of text. The difference between means for the interaction between gender schema and gender orientation of text was not statistically significant, $p = .636$ where $p < 0.05$. The effect size (Eta squared) was .01, or small, for the interaction between gender schema and gender orientation of text on cognitive complexity. A two-way analysis of variance was completed for the interaction between gender and gender-orientation of text. The difference between means for the interaction between gender and gender-orientation of text was statistically significant, $p = .012$ where $p < 0.05$. The effect size (Eta squared) was .04, or approximately medium, for the interaction between gender and gender-orientation of text on cognitive complexity.

The results from the interaction between gender schema and gender-orientation of text on cognitive complexity indicate that this interaction is not statistically significant. There are, however, some results worth noting here. Subjects with an androgynous gender schema had a smaller change in cognitive complexity when reading either the male- or female-oriented text than subjects with either a male or female gender schema. In addition, the means for cognitive complexity using the female-oriented text was higher for subjects with all three types of gender schema (male, female, and androgynous) than the means for cognitive complexity using the male-oriented text. Interestingly, the female-oriented text had a higher readability level (5.7 G.E.) than the male-oriented text (5.1 G.E.).

The results from the interaction between gender and gender-orientation of text on cognitive complexity indicate that the interaction is statistically significant. From looking at the effect size measure, Eta squared = .04, this interaction does have a larger effect than the previous interaction which used gender schema instead of gender as an independent variable. Another notable point to be made with this particular interaction is that

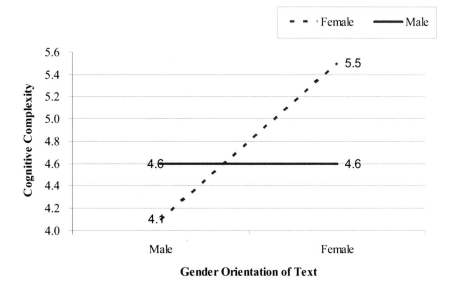

Figure 6.2.   Interaction of the means for gender and gender orieintation of text on cognitive complexity.

males had no change in cognitive complexity whether reading the male- or female-oriented text. The females did have a change in cognitive complexity. For females, their cognitive complexity score on the female-oriented text was higher than their cognitive complexity score on the male-oriented text.

However, it has been established in the analysis using gender schema as an independent variable that the female-oriented text elicited more cognitive complexity from all three gender schemas (female, male, and androgynous). This may have been because of some inherit difference between the texts. In order to accurately interpret the results for the interaction between gender and gender-orientation of text on cognitive complexity one should adjust the means in order to account for the inherit differences between texts. The overall mean difference between the male-oriented text responses and the female-oriented text responses was 1.0 (5.3–4.3 = 1.0). The means for the male-oriented responses was adjusted by adding 0.5 to the male-oriented text means and the means for the female-oriented text responses was adjusted by subtracting 0.5 from the female-oriented text means. The results indicate that males had higher cognitive complexity on the male-oriented text than the female-oriented text (5.1 vs. 4.1, approximately), and that the females had higher cognitive complexity on the female-oriented text than the male-oriented text

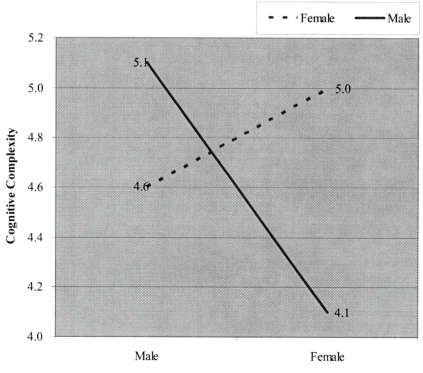

Figure 6.3.   Interaction of the adjusted mean for gender and gender orientation of text on cognitive complexity.

(5.0 vs. 4.6, approximately). Figure 6.3 displays the adjusted means for the interaction between gender and gender orientation of text on cognitive complexity.

DISCUSSION

These data indicated that the gender-orientation of text *does not* affect complex thinking differently for varying types of gender schema. Very little research has been done which investigates the connection between gender schema and higher levels of thinking. Previous studies have made a connection between gender schema and lower levels of thinking such as recall and comprehension (Halpern, 1985; Martin & Halverson, 1983). Some previous studies have also attempted to make the connection between gender and higher levels of thinking (Kelly, 1999; Love & Guthrie, 1999; Magolda, 1992; Noble & Powell, 1995). But very few exist that venture into the untapped area of gender schema and higher levels of thinking.

This research attempted to extend Manzo's et al. (2000) research by beginning the exploration of gender schema and it's affect on higher levels of thinking. These results were gathered from a group of freshman students enrolled in an English honors course at a mid-Western suburban high school. The Bem Sex-Role Inventory (BSRI) was administered in order to determine the gender schema of individual subjects and The Accuracy Level Test in order to determine individual student's grade level equivalent in reading. During the pilot study, the researcher and English teacher realized that the ninth grade students needed some definition of terms in the BSRI. Therefore, before administration of the BSRI, the teacher and researcher discussed some terms that were confusing for the students. It was hoped that this would increase the accuracy of the BSRI as the students were not just guessing but were making informed decisions.

Some interesting conclusions can be drawn by looking at the results of the interaction of gender schema and gender orientation of text on cognitive complexity. Subjects, whether male, female, or androgynous gender schema, utilized higher levels of thinking when reading the female-oriented text than when reading the male-oriented text. A possible explanation for this could be differences between texts. Some differences were (1) the female-oriented text had a higher readability level (5.7) than the male-oriented text (5.1); (2) the female-oriented text included topics that dealt with feelings, emotions, and relationships, and the male-oriented text included action and plot-centered topics. Perhaps topics such as relationships and feelings lend themselves to more variety in interpretation and encourage the reader to think on higher levels as opposed to topics that are plot-centered and action-oriented.

Another possible explanation for the subjects utilizing higher levels of thinking on the female-oriented text could be error in the labeling of gender schema. If the subjects' gender schema were mislabeled this could change the results. One confounding factor in this labeling was that the subjects were ninth grade students, approximately 15 years old. Bem (1981) reports in her test manual, that "although it has been used primarily with college students and adults, the items in the BSRI should be comprehensible to most high school students" (p. 6). However, as noted above, the researcher and English teacher needed to clarify some terms used in the BSRI in order to increase informed decision making of subjects while taking the test. This could have introduced error into the administration of the BSRI which could result in mislabeling of gender schema. Even though some interpretations of the data can be drawn from closely analyzing the results, the overall conclusion based on the data is that gender orientation of text does not affect complex thinking differently whether the subject has a male, female or androgynous gender schema.

Because research also exists dealing with gender and its connection to higher levels of thinking (Love & Guthrie, 1999; Magolda, 1992), it was decided to look at the results when the subjects were divided along gender, or sex of the individual, rather than gender schema, a principle for organizing and making sense of information. As discussed earlier, the analysis using gender schema as an independent variable produced results which indicated higher levels of cognitive complexity from all three gender schemas (female, male, and androgynous) when the subjects read the female-oriented text. This may have been because of some inherent difference between the texts. In order to accurately interpret the data when the subjects were divided along gender rather than gender schema, the means for the interaction between gender and gender orientation of text were adjusted so as to account for the inherit difference between texts. These results indicated that gender orientation of text *does* affect complex thinking, or cognitive complexity, differently for males than it does for females, that is, males have higher cognitive complexity for male oriented text than female oriented text, and females have higher cognitive complexity for female oriented text than male oriented text.

CONCLUSIONS

This research study provides support for a connection between gender and higher levels of thinking. The connection appears to be quite similar for males and females. Several conclusions can be drawn from this study. The data from the study supported the interaction between gender and gender orientation of text and its effect on cognitive complexity, but these results did not support an interaction between gender schema and gender orientation of text in their effect on cognitive complexity. Bem (1978, 1981), the leading theorist of gender schema, may have a sound basis in discussing gender schema as a theory, but the current form of the BSRI probably does not effectively label high school students in regard to their gender schema. Some error may have been introduced in the administration of the Bem Sex-Role Inventory (BSRI) as the researcher and cooperating teacher attempted to explain confusing terms for the students. This could have skewed the labeling of gender schema in this study. A conclusion that can be drawn from this experience is that the creators of the

BSRI should reevaluate its use with teenagers or create an alternate form to better diagnose high school students.

A second conclusion can be drawn from this research study. When a person's gender is matched with gender-orientation of text then the likelihood that higher-level thinking will be elicited is greater as opposed to when the gender and gender-orientation of text does not match. This relates to the theory of constructivism—or the idea that the individual actively constructs knowledge; knowledge is not simply transmitted from the text to the head of the reader. An individual utilizes prior experiences, as well as his/her ability and disposition—or inclination to read and learn, to interact and create meaning. In this research, the prior experiences considered were related to gender.

The implications for these interpretations of male and female patterns of complex thinking can be far reaching. Gender inequalities exist in our world and in our schools and have for centuries. But, if research such as the current study, brings forward possible methods to even the playing field for both males and females, should not educators take notice? No one questions the importance of exposing students to a variety of literature and reading material; but if a teacher is attempting to teach a new skill or practice a concept that is difficult to learn, such as higher level thinking, the current study suggests that scaffolding by aligning the student's gender with corresponding gender elements of a text may help them reach the goal of higher level thinking and reading.

In addition to achieving equity between genders, it is important that researchers and educators know how readers are anticipating and building schemata rather than simply comprehending what they are reading. This knowledge will help us better understand the path to higher-order literacy—or reading beyond the lines. The goal of educators is to create students who cannot only participate in society but impact it. This can be accomplished through teaching students how to think and read "beyond the lines." Knowing information about how to elicit higher levels of thinking from our students does not only impact teaching today, but molds the citizens of tomorrow.

REFERENCES

Anderson, R. W. (1989). *Elements of literature: Third course*. Austin, TX: Holt, Rinehart, and Winston.

Belenky, M. F., Clinchy, B. M., Goldberger, N. R., & Tarule, J. M. (1986). *Women's ways of knowing: The development of self, voice, and mind*. New York: Basic Books.

Bem, S. L. (1978). *Bem sex-role inventory*. Redwood City, CA: Consulting Psychologist Press.

Bem, S. L. (1981). Gender schema theory: A cognitive account of sex-typing. *Psychological Review, 88*, 354-364.

Bleich, D. (1986). Gender interests in reading and language. In E. A. Flynn & P. P. Schweickart (Eds.), *Gender and reading: Essays on readers, texts, and contexts* (pp. 3-30). Baltimore: Johns Hopkins U.P.

Carver, R. P. (1990). Predicting accuracy of comprehension from the relative difficulty of material. *Learning and Individual Differences, 2*, 405-422.

Carver, R. P. (1997). Reading for one second, one minute, or one year from the perspective of rauding theory. *Scientific Studies of Reading, 1*, 3-43.

Carver, R. P. (2000). *The accuracy level test.* Kansas City, MO: Revrac.

Cohen, J. (1977). *Statistical power analysis for the behavioral sciences.* New York: Academic Press.

Day, S. X. (1994). Gender schema and reading. *Reading Psychology, 15*, 91-107.

Flynn, E. A. (1986). Gender interests in reading and language. In E. A. Flynn & P. P. Schweickart (Eds.), *Gender and reading: Essays on readers, texts and contexts* (pp. 3-30). Baltimore: Johns Hopkins U.P.

Galotti, K. M., Kozberg, S., & Appleman, D. (1990). Younger and older adolescents' thinking about commitments. *Journal of Experimental Child Psychology, 50*, 324-339.

Gambell, R., & Hunter, D. (2000). Surveying gender differences in Canadian school literacy. *Journal of Curriculum Studies, 32*, 689-719.

Ginsburg, H., & Opper, S. (1988). *Piaget's theory of intellectual development/Herbert P. Ginsburg, Sylvia Opper.* Englewood Cliffs, NJ: Prentice-Hall.

Gray, J. (1992). *Men are from Mars, women are from Venus.* New York: HarperCollins.

Gruender, C. D. (1996). Constructivism and learning: A philosophical appraisal. *Educational Technology, 36*, 21-29.

Halpern, D. F. (1985). The influence of sex-role stereotypes on prose recall. *Sex roles, 12*, 363-375.

Kelly, C. A. (1999). Gender and inquiry: An investigation into identifying and defining the role of inquiry in higher-order thinking. *European Journal of Teacher Education, 22*, 101-114.

Love, P. G., & Guthrie, V. L. (1999). Perry's intellectual scheme. *New directions For student Services, 88*, 5-15.

Lyman, B. G., & Collins, M. D. (1990). Critical reading: A redefinition. *Reading Research & Instruction, 29*, 56-63.

Magolda, M. B. (1992). *Knowing and reasoning in college: Gender-related patterns in students' intellectual development.* San Francisco: Jossey-Bass.

Manzo, A. V., Manzo, U. C., Barnhill, A., & Thomas, M. (2000). Proficient reader-subtypes: Implications for literacy theory, assessment, and practice. *Reading Psychology, 21*, 217-232.

Martin, C. L., & Halverson, C. F. (1983). The effects of sex-typing schemas on young children's memory. *Child Development, 54*, 563-574.

McDaniel, E. (1991, April). *Levels of cognitive complexity: A framework for the Measurement of thinking.* Paper presented at the Annual Meeting of the American Educational Research Association, Chicago, IL.

Noble, J., & Powell, D. A. (1995). *Factors influencing differential achievement of higher-order thinking skills, as measured by PLAN.* ACT Research Report Series, 95-104, American College Testing Program, Iowa City, IA.

Perry, W. G. (1970). *Forms of intellectual and ethical development in the college years: A scheme (by) William G. Perry, Jr.* New York: Holt, Rinehart & Winston.

Phillips, D. C. (1995). The good, the bad, and the ugly: The many faces of constructivism. *Educational Researcher, 24,* 5-12.

Piaget, J. (1959). *The language and thought of the child.* London: Routledge & Kegan Paul.

Sax, G. (1997). *Principles of educational and psychological measurement and evaluation* (4th ed.). Belmont, CA: Wadsworth.

CHAPTER 7

LGBTQ STUDENTS IN URBAN SCHOOLS

Sexuality, Gender, and School Identities

Dominique Johnson

The physical structure of the gay metropolis as a visible city community is often identified through its center city neighborhood boundaries, frequently an influential site of city planning and phenomenal gentrification. Through community advocacy and agency, and a unique set of dynamic circumstances in concentrated neighborhood establishment, the gay metropolis is an active participant in the interactional processes of urban planning and development and a force for change. Of particular interest to the gay metropolis are the ways in which the education of urban youth, especially LGBTQ (lesbian, gay, bisexual, transgender, and queer) youth, can embody collaborative community agency and advocacy as a strategy for urban social change and as a lens of urban life.

Theories of the city suggest that urban life can be conceptualized across many dimensions (LeGates & Stout, 2003). For urban theorists using economics or evolution as a lens, cities rise and flourish due to matters of finance, defining urban space mainly in terms of size and density.

Inclusion in Urban Educational Environments:
Addressing Issues of Diversity, Equity, and Social Justice, 137–151
Copyright © 2006 by Information Age Publishing
All rights of reproduction in any form reserved.

Scholars such as Mumford (2003) propose an alternate view, suggesting that human dimensions of cities are the means by which they thrive. As dynamic spaces embodying the human spirit and drive for innovation, Mumford (2003) argues that cities even drive human civilization. To create enhanced, more humane cities fundamentally furthers the development of humanity itself (Mumford, 2003). What it means to be urban, therefore, is an essential question to the progress of civilization. Wirth (1938/2003) poses this question, offering a sociological solution of the distinct urban "way of life" that creates "urban types" of people (Wirth, 1938/2003).

For North American gays, "going to the city" (both presently and historically) required making a journey to New York, Los Angeles, and the self-described cultural mecca of San Francisco. In these instances, as in prominent notions of the city, urbanity is synonymous with sophistication, culture, refinement, and style. Influences of LGBTQ people and gay communities on urban experience, planning, and life are demonstrated in the call to the city as a safe refuge, the possibility of the city as a site of resistance to violence through critical population mass, the concentrated neighborhood communities of center cities, and the changes these communities create through neighborhood settlement and gentrification.

Of particular interest to the human dimensions of city life are the notions of urban heterogeneity, where individualism is replaced by categorical identities in a circumstance of physical contact and social distance. The city, when conceived as a social entity with its own personality and as a community with collective behavior, offers challenges and opportunities for the structural issues inherent in urban life. The gay metropolis is both a site of and force for urban change. Categorical identities of race, sexuality, ethnicity, gender, religion, age, and socioeconomic status are embodied, organized around, and performed by active participants on the urban stage. What these experiential, practical, and theoretical ideas might contribute in particular to this urban landscape are a framework for understanding the gay metropolis that expands beyond the narrative of gay urbanity toward one that encompasses both built and human structure and the processes of community interaction with the city environment, exemplified in educational communities of urban youth that empower LGBTQ youth and their identities.

Urban America offers a critical mass of LGBTQ students and an arguably more prominent LGBT community than suburban and rural America. Indeed, the lived experiences of LGBTQ youth can be classified into the geographical categories of rural, suburban, and urban. Much, if not the majority, of the existing literature does not emphasize such geographic contexts (Szalacha, 2003, 2004), even though many of these studies are based upon students in programs and services offered in North

American cities (Schwartz, 1994), however there unequivocally are LGBTQ student experiences in *urban* schools.

Part of a special issue of *Education and Urban Society* on LGBTQ students, an article by LeCompte (2000) describes how one high school struggled for 20 years to create a safer school climate. Decisions as to how to manage race riots and the sexual harassment of young women set the pattern for the emerging school safety initiatives for LGBTQ students. When ideas about inclusion in urban schools are informed by the various identities urban LGBTQ youth create and negotiate as students, sexuality, gender, and school identities are located into a broader urban educational context. Among the results can be a safer school climate for all urban students.

THE ROLE OF URBAN SCHOOLS IN CREATING A SAFER SCHOOL CLIMATE FOR LGBTQ YOUTH

One of the first times gay youth demanded their rights to inclusion in school policies and practices occurred in 1972 in the Bronx, New York City. As predominantly gay students of color, the members of George Washington High School's gay group organized boldly within their classrooms, hoping to enact change using their school as a site of activism. Their unequivocal call to political, identity-based action within their school also suggests that their goal was to create a safer, more tolerant school climate for all students (Johnson, 2006). The Stonewall Riots—the riots ensuing after a police raid of New York City's Greenwich Village gay bar the Stonewall Inn in 1969—were the defining historical moment of a modern movement for LGBT civil rights. This resistance catalyzed and made visible the social movement for Gay Liberation and the modern LGBT rights movement, creating the sociopolitical climate necessary in order for the gay student group at George Washington High School to form in 1972 (Cohen, 2003, 2005).

Stonewall and its influence as a watershed for identity, the politicization of identity struggles, and the emerging visibility of the gay community on a national level made activism for gay students' rights within the site of the North American school a possibility. Though differences between the experiences of gay students at George Washington High School in 1972 (only 3 years after the watershed of Stonewall) and those of today's LGBTQ students do exist, the work for tolerance by these early LGBTQ students in this earliest school-based effort offers lessons for the continuing struggle for tolerance for LGBTQ youth and a safer school climate for LGBTQ students in North American schools (Johnson, YEAR?), particularly urban schools.

Today, there are over 2000 school-based extracurricular clubs, gay-straight alliances (GSAs), in American schools (Cianciotto & Cahill, 2003). Students who have sought to form GSAs in their schools have sometimes met with a series of legislative and policy decisions denying them access to public school facilities in order to form their club, with one instance where an urban school board banned all extracurricular organizations rather than authorizing a GSA (Burrington, 1998; Platt, 2001). George Washington students discussed issues faced by today's GSAs: verbal and physical abuse, the need for straight allies to engage in student civil rights efforts in order to enact change at the school-wide level, and the resistance of the school administration toward the creation of gay student organizations. There are also 275 LGBTQ out-of-school community-based youth groups around the United States, and most are concentrated in urban areas like New York City and San Francisco (Platt, 2001). In 1984, Project 10 was founded in a Los Angeles high school, marking the establishment of the first school-based program (McCready, 2001; Uribe, 1994; Uribe & Harbeck, 1992). Urban public and private alternative and community-based schools provide "separate and safe educational environments" for LGBTQ students "while addressing social service needs" (Cohen, 2003, p. 32). During the current climate of contention where LGBTQ students are on the front lines of the culture wars, they continue to use activism as a site for education and continue to define for themselves the roles education might play in their own liberation as well as in the construction of their own identities (Johnson, YEAR?).

Schools are certainly the greatest sites of resistance to equal rights for LGBTQ youth (Rofes 1997; Woog, 1995). It remains that LGBTQ students are perhaps the most underserved students in the entire educational system (Uribe, 1994), feeling confined by the pressure to conform while believing that an essential part of them is being dismissed, despised, or deleted from school life (Khayatt, 1994). Lugg (1997) reminds us that both teachers and academics have only recently begun to address the boundaries that exist between both sexual and gender identity, and education. Despite the post-Stonewall movement strategy of including sexual orientation in the debate over school reform (Irvine, 2001), education and the schools are for the most part dismissed centers of activism for adults in the LGBT movement (Rofes, 1997). As a social movement, "we are not organized to work politically where people live culturally," a fact that remains from the time of Stonewall and before (Vaid, 1995, p. 221).

ANTIGAY AND GENDER-BASED VIOLENCE IN SCHOOLS

Three out of four students targeted by bullies are incorrectly identified as LGBTQ (National Mental Health Association, 2002), and 2 million students are bullied every year because they are, or are thought to be, LGBTQ (Human Rights Watch, 2001). According to a comprehensive statewide 2004 Gay, Lesbian, and Straight Education Network (GLSEN) report, a large majority of U.S. students attend schools in states with no legal protections against anti-LGBTQ bullying and harassment (Gay, Lesbian, and Straight Education Network, GLSEN, 2004). The U.S. federal hate crime statute (Title 18, U.S. Code, Section 245, U.S. Department of Justice, 2005) has yet to include sexual orientation and gender identity or expression (including those students who identify as transgendered, or who are gender-questioning and gender nonconforming) as protected categories, and a federally protected activity such as attending a public school therefore does not cover LGBTQ and other students who are victims of hate crimes while at school (Department of Education and Justice, 2000). According to GLSEN's 2004 report,

> more than seventy-five percent of the approximately 47.7 million K-12 students in the U.S. go to schools that do not include sexual orientation and gender identity/expression as statewide protected classes alongside federally mandated protections based on religion, race, and national origin. (GLSEN, 2004)

There are only eight states and the District of Columbia that currently have statewide legal protections for students based on sexual orientation. Only California, Minnesota, and New Jersey include protections based on gender identity or expression as well (Cahill & Cianciotto, 2004; GLSEN, 2004).

LGBTQ students are twice as likely as others to feel unsafe or afraid at school and are approximately 2 to 7 times more likely than their peers to report skipping school because of feeling unsafe (Safe Schools Coalition, 1997, 1999). Some LGBTQ youth, particularly students of color, choose to stop attending school (GLSEN, 2003). Fifty-five percent of transgender youth reported being physically harassed because of their gender, gender expression, or sexual orientation (GLSEN, 2004). These violent conditions put trans youth at great risk of suicidal feelings and behavior (GLSEN, 2003). Consequently, preventing violence and harassment in schools is a crucial issue in ensuring a positive school climate for all students. Approximately one-half of perpetrators of antigay violence are age 21 or younger (Comstock, 1991), with young White males of lower socioeconomic status committing the greatest number of hate crimes.

Indeed, gender-based harassment affects entire school populations, and all students—both heterosexual and LGB (lesbian, gay, and bisexual) —are affected by rigid gender roles, often limiting their choices in academic classes and extracurricular sports and activities (Grayson, 1987). This gender-based harassment is most often overlooked in explanations of extreme school violence, even though it is present in every case: anti-gay and gender-based bullying and harassment preceded some of the most notable incidents of school violence—school shootings—in the U.S. (Kimmel, 2004). What is more, existing safe school interventions, particularly those concerning the safety and well-being of LGB students, might not be as effective as they could be, given their exclusion of gender identity/expression and the lived experiences of transgender and gender nonconforming students (Johnson, 2005).

Comstock (1991) describes how a "boys will be boys" attitude fortifies the permission already granted by familial, religious, and social norms that "exclude, disapprove of, or are hostile to lesbians and gay men … [and] the failure or refusal of high school educators to protect lesbian and gay students" and teach about the diversity of human sexual identity (p. 105). Indeed, American law has epitomized this position: homosexuality itself was criminal until the 2003 U.S. Supreme Court decision in *Lawrence v. Texas* (Supreme Court of the United States, 2003). It is not surprising that many schools have yet to acknowledge the significance of gender and the importance of confronting sexism and transphobia as a part of the daily realities of all students.

Mac An Ghaill (1994) describes how British Black gay youth conceive of gender and sexual identities as unstable identities. Their schools along with other social institutions they encounter in adolescence attempt to regulate, maintain, and strengthen these categories of identity. The most extreme consequence of the expectation associated with adhering to gender boundaries is illegal behavior such as criminal violence. When in the form of gender-based and antigay persecution, these actions "appear to be extensions, exaggerations, or socially premature demonstrations, rather than violations, of the gender role behavior" young men learn while coming of age in American society (Comstock, 1991, p. 106). Safe school initiatives can therefore be compromised when antihomophobia work is not considered in a broader context of multiple oppressions and marginalized populations. When safe school initiatives create an educational climate where students can reject gender-stereotyped roles such as hypermasculinity, the result can be increased visibility, support, and awareness of LGBTQ people, their experiences, and the issues they face in school (Johnson, 2005). A safer school climate can also offer a space where students can consider means by which they construct their own identities.

LGBTQ STUDENT IDENTITIES IN URBAN SCHOOLS

The struggle for identity development in urban schools affects all students. Recent work portrays emerging urban LGBTQ identity and economic and political life in U.S. cities (Bailey, 1999), and LGBTQ identity development among students in an urban educational context (Barry, 2000). Between 1972-1999, a review of the professional literature found 166 publications on LGB youth. This represents 1% of journal articles serving school practitioners published during this period (Ryan, 2000). Of the 1%, only 3.6% focused on LGB youth of color, and none addressed transgender youth of color (Ryan, 2002). These youth, who lack the access to elite sites of knowledge production (including peer-reviewed journals and university presses), and the academic language they use (including a highly specialized, theoretical vocabulary, and a PhD and a tenure-track or tenured position in academia) "are effectively barred from participation in the construction of the theoretical discourse which helps shape public understanding of their very identities" (Park, 1998, p. 10).

LGBTQ youth often focus upon either their developing sexual orientation and/or gender identities or their academic pursuits (Morrow & Campbell, 1997, as cited in Morrow, 1997). Their experiences in life and as students are often framed with the themes of impaired self-esteem and emotional growth, isolation and the downward spiral of depression, school difficulties, substance abuse and chemical dependence, foster care, group care, and homelessness, prostitution, and survival sex, HIV/AIDS and STIs, and self-destructive behaviors/suicide (Owens, 1998). Most of the research literature available addresses these resulting risk factors. Discussion of any possible developmental benefits for LGBTQ youth both in and away from school is unfortunately few and far between.

An emerging literature is, however, speaking to the protective factors and resiliency of LGBTQ youth. A great number of these articles, books, edited volumes, and studies discuss implications for the safety of LGBTQ students in North American high schools, offering a variety of small, convenience samples with statistical results (many from social service organizations), case examples, nonempirical information (including journalistic accounts), advocacy pieces, policy recommendations, and resources for teachers and counselors (Russell, Seif, & Truong, 2001).

Research attesting to the effort put forth in managing the person-based stigma of same-sex attraction indicates that the normative challenges of adolescence, when coupled with the challenges of a queer adolescence, are striking. Emerging adolescent sexuality assumes an important and fundamental challenge for young people (Katchadourian, 1990). For LGTBQ youth, this developmental process often is augmented by a need to negotiate a gay, lesbian, or bisexual adolescence, reified by encounters with cultural and social stigma of same-sex romantic attraction, behavior, and identity (Rotheram-Borus & Fernandez, 1995). The identity development of LGBTQ youth, particularly youth of color (Greene 1998; Savin-Williams & Rodriguez, 1993), is distinctive in that multiple, intersecting identities are not accounted for in existing LGBTQ identity development models. Comprehending intersections of identity and the complexities of adolescent life are essential in order to understand the educational experiences of urban LGBTQ youth.

Lasser and Tharinger's (2003) concept of visibility management, whereby youth negotiate growing up and coming out, relates to many dynamics of the creation and maintenance of separate school and sexual/gender identities. Coming out as lesbian, gay, bisexual, and/or transgendered is often a marker of identity development as well as a site of pedagogy and critical self-reflection. As for the school identities of these youth, many of these youth are high- or overachievers on campus as a means of survival, acceptance by others, and/or to divert attention away from sexual/gender identities. Tully (2000) and Evans and D'Augelli (1996) have addressed the absence of role models as a significant problem in the development of queer youth.

Schools are indeed academic communities: students do not merely *go* to school—they *create* their school experiences. These communities are dynamic educational spaces where students negotiate the essential right to be who they are. Urban classrooms, providers of information, are more than just sources of instruction: these entities influence ideas about social identity by providing a space for their articulation, transformation, and elaboration, both overtly and covertly, explicitly and implicitly (Hall, 1981). The privileging of identities forces students to choose the one most salient to their individual experiences. Gender, racial, ethnic, sexual, and academic identities develop in relation to one another, and the tensions that arise from these coconstructions present challenges to the students that negotiate them. For example, developmental challenges for urban LGBTQ youth of African descent (Parks, 2001) reveal distinctive LGBTQ and same gender-loving (SGL) urban youth cultures. Cohen (2003) suggests that, "[y]outh elect to join or avoid programs based upon actual and perceived rules of eligibility (rules that are entangled with definitions of sexual and other identities). Membership is strongly influenced by identity" (p. 85). Cox and Gallois (1996) propose that if youth are asked to choose one identity over another or deny one altogether when it might appear to be incompatible with another, there are psychological and social costs.

Educational institutions must acknowledge and address the fact that the intersections of race, sexuality, class, ethnicity, and gender together inform identity development and practical experiences (Gutierrez, 2004). As youth construct their identities and work toward a sense of self, self esteem, a positive life outlook, and self-assurance, some aspects of their identity development might include: a value and understanding of cultures, the recognition of diversity/difference as a basis of self-appreciation and pride in oneself, and an exploration of the full ramifications of difference while striving to appreciate the diversity of others. During their identity development, youth may also choose to fight oppression, integrate their identities into a balanced view of themselves and others, and see multiple frames of reference.

Students might construct and negotiate identity using community-based spaces in relation to their lives in and out of school more often than bringing or carrying it with them to school. For example, LGBTQ students could use an LGBT community center or bookstore to help them create and negotiate their sexual and gender identities out of school, particularly if their schools are not supportive and affirming environments. Various community spaces can be an educational means and resource for academic and identity development outside of school for LGBTQ youth. Accordingly, these community spaces could be a viable method for educational support for educational institutions and programs. The educational space of LGBT community organizations and spaces may affirm and encourage educational development beyond school.

Adult-centered community centers, youth community centers, LGBT community bookstores, and school-based groups such as GSAs and/or diversity clubs are all factors in creating, maintaining, and negotiating an identity/identities outside of school. The role of LGBT community support in such affirmative developmental outcomes is particularly salient in the present context of contention about the educational lives of LGBTQ queer youth. The debates surrounding the expansion of the Harvey Milk High School in New York City, a public high school affirming and supportive of LGBTQ youth, the continued establishment of gay-straight alliances in American schools, legal enforcement of equal educational access and school safety for LGBTQ youth, and the emergence of separate schooling of these youth by educational advocates from the LGBT community all contribute models for intervention in order to encourage successful educational experience.

GENDER, SEXUALITY, AND THE CITY: IMPLICATIONS FOR URBAN SCHOOLS

While forming a grief support group named in memory of their friend, Sakia Gunn,[1] Newark, New Jersey lesbian students were denied their request to have a moment of silence in her honor at the public high school they attended (Wang, 2003, as cited in Franklin, 2004). The principal, who denied the request, did not respond to press inquiries regarding the hate-motivated murder of her student. McCready (2003) describes ways in which urban schools (such as the Newark high school these young women attend), through a commitment to address institutional homophobia and transphobia, might assist students and teachers to overcome such challenges in order to create and maintain safe spaces in their schools. Racial segregation and de-normalizing Whiteness both present significant challenges to LGBTQ youth programs in urban schools, especially those with high levels of disorder and student delinquency.

In particular, McCready (2003) suggests three strategies for creating, strengthening, and/or maintaining safe havens for LGBTQ students in urban schools: students and teachers should both be aware of the social and cultural contexts of cities, specifically the school and its surrounding community, and the way these contexts affect participation in extracurricular activities; challenge (de-normalize) the perceived Whiteness of LGBTQ youth identity by making a conscious effort to use speakers bureaus and workshop facilitators that are racially and ethnically diverse, decorating the meeting room with LGBT historical figures from diverse racial and ethnic backgrounds, and having books, magazines, and other reading materials on hand that reflect a range of racial and ethnic experiences about LGBTQ identity; and, emphasizing coalition building, antiracism, and social justice, build alliances with other students and teachers who are concerned with the ways multiple forms of oppression (e.g., institutional racism, sexism and heterosexism, and poverty) make schools unsafe for all students (pp. 43-45).

It is important to remember that homophobia not only targets students with queer sexual orientations, but with queer *genders* as well, particularly those youth who are more visibly queer. Homophobia cannot therefore be fully addressed until there is a genuine commitment to address issues of gender, such as transgender identity and gender nonconformity in education (Kumashiro, 2001). Because issues of gender prejudice are substantial components of the very basis of homophobia and sexual prejudice, safe school initiatives will never be fully effective until gender-based school safety and gender-based antiharassment and violence work are integrated into existing efforts. Approaches that consider notions of sexuality *and* gender specifically relate sexual prejudice and homophobia as defining factors of heterosexuality and masculinity in American culture. Violence prevention and intervention initiatives for safer schools that are more inclusive of entire school populations, and consider the possibility of *both* gender-based and antigay harassment and violence as *interrelated* entities, can work toward establishing a more comprehensive school-wide effort to ensure safer schools for all.

Kumashiro (2001, 2002) addresses these intersections in the context of educational theory and practice contributing to an antioppressive pedagogy. Antioppressive approaches to education are juxtaposed with contemporary education-based queer youth activism, constituting a framework of theories that "offer ways of thinking and talking about education, oppression, identity, and change" helpful for "working against traditional ways of thinking and acting, teaching and learning" (Kumashiro, 2002, p. 9). Kumashiro (2001) posits that educators and students should create safe spaces based upon what is needed now, yet constantly recreate these spaces in order to question whom the space might harm or exclude. He also argues that building upon the research literature should not be done to fill critical gaps, since a lack of knowledge is not the only problem. Research should disrupt the knowledge that already exists, using questions to move beyond what is already known in order cultivate inquisitive practices that break intellectual boundaries and establish new approaches and paradigms.

Researchers, educators, and adult allies must move from the language of risk to one of developmental benefits and resiliency, and coordinate support for youth empowerment. What the purpose of education is for LGBTQ youth and how we conceptualize LGBT education for liberation leads to challenging intersections: all educational contexts, particularly school-based programs, must be antioppressive (Kumashiro, 2001, 2002) in theory and practice, and community-based initiatives for LGBT education must work from a youth empowerment perspective.

NOTE

1. African American urban high school student Sakia Gunn was murdered in 2003 while waiting for a bus in Newark after returning with friends from a night out in Manhattan's Greenwich Village.

REFERENCES

Bailey, R. (1999). *Gay politics, urban politics: Identity and economics in the urban setting.* New York: Columbia University Press.

Barry, R. (2000). Sheltered "children": The self-creation of a safe space by gay, lesbian, and bisexual students. In L. Weis & M. Fine (Eds.), *Construction sites: Excavating race, class, and gender among urban youth* (pp. 84-99). New York: Teachers College Press.

Burrington, D. (1998). The public square and citizen queer: Toward a new political geography: Gay/straight Alliance, Salt Lake City, Utah. *Polity, 31*(1), 107-131.

Cahill, S., & Cianciotto, J. (2004). U.S. policy interventions that can make schools safer. *Journal of Gay and Lesbian Issues in Education, 2*(1), 3-17.

Cianciotto, J., & Cahill, S. (2003). *Education policy: Issues affecting lesbian, gay, bisexual, and transgender youth.* New York: The National Gay and Lesbian Task Force Policy Institute.

Cohen, S. (2003). *Conclusions: Definitions of membership, praxis, social change, and identities.* Unpublished manuscript, Harvard University, Cambridge, MA.

Cohen, S. (2005). Liberations, clients, activists: Queer youth organizing, 1966-2003. *Journal of Gay and Lesbian Issues in Education, 2*(3), 67-86.

Comstock, G. D. (1991). *Violence against lesbians and gay men.* New York: Columbia University Press.

Cox, S., & Gallois, C. (1996) Gay and lesbian identity development: A social identity perspective. *Journal of Homosexuality, 30*(4), 1-30.

Departments of Education and Justice (2000). *Annual report on school safety.* Washington, DC: U.S. Departments of Education and Justice.

Department of Justice (2005). Federally Protected Activities, Title 18, U.S. Code, Section 245, U.S. Department of Justice, Civil Rights Division, Criminal Section. Retrieved October 22, 2005, from http://www.usdoj.gov/crt/crim/245.htm

Evans, N. J., & D'Augelli, A. R. (1996). Lesbians, gay men, and bisexual people in college. In R. C. Savin-Williams & K. M. Cohen (Eds.), *The lives of lesbian, gays, and bisexuals* (pp. 201-226). Fort Worth, TX: Harcourt Brace.

Franklin, K. (2004). Enacting masculinity: Antigay violence and group rape as participatory theater. Sexuality research and social policy. *Journal of NSRC, 1*(2), 25-40.

Gay, Lesbian, and Straight Education Network (GLSEN) (2003). *National school climate survey.* Retrieved July 7, 2004, from www.glsen.org

Gay, Lesbian, and Straight Education Network (GLSEN) (2004). *State of the states 2004: A policy analysis of lesbian, gay, bisexual, and transgender LGBT safer schools issues.* Retrieved July 7, 2004, from www.glsen.org/cgibin/iowa/educator/library/record/1687.html

Grayson, D. A. (1987). Emerging equity issues related to homosexuality in education. *Peabody Journal of Education, 64*, 132-145

Greene, B. (1998). Family, ethnic identity, and sexual orientation: African-American lesbians and gay men. In C. J. Patterson & A. R. D'Augelli (Eds.), *Lesbian, gay, and bisexual identities in families: Psychological perspectives* (pp. 40-52). New York: Oxford University Press.

Gutierrez, N. (2004). Resisting fragmentation, living whole: Four female transgender students of color speak about school. In Y. Padilla (Ed.), *Gay and lesbian rights organizing: Community-based strategies* (pp. 69-80). New York: The Haworth Press.

Hall, S. (1981). The whites of their eyes: Racist ideologies and the media. In B. Bridges & R. Brunt (Eds.), *Silver linings: Some strategies for the eighties* (pp. 28-52). London: Lawrence and Wishart.

Human Rights Watch (HRW) (2001). *Hatred in the hallways: Violence and discrimination against lesbian, gay, bisexual, and transgender students in U.S. schools.* New York: Human Rights Watch.

Irvine, J. M. (2001). Educational reform and sexual identity: Conflicts and challenges. In A. R. D'Augelli & A. R. Patterson (Eds.), *Lesbian, gay, bisexual identities and youth: Psychological perspectives* (pp. 251-266). Oxford, England: Oxford University Press.

Johnson, D. (2005, April). *Fragmented safety: Envisioning safe schools initiatives for transgender students*. Paper presented at the American Educational Research Association Annual Convention, Montreal, Quebec.

Johnson, D. (2006). *Young and gay at Stonewall: Lessons from the earliest school-based gay youth group for current LGBT safe school initiatives*. Manuscript submitted for publication.

Katchadourian, H. (1990). Sexuality. In S. S. Feldman & G. R. Elliot (Eds.), *At the threshold: The developing adolescent* (pp. 330-351). Cambridge, MA: Harvard University Press.

Khayatt, D. (1994). Surviving school as a lesbian student. *Gender and Education, 6*(1), 47-61.

Kimmel, M. S. (2004). "I am not insane; I am angry": Adolescent masculinity, homophobia, and violence. In M. Sadowski (Ed.), *Adolescents at school: Perspectives on youth, identity, and education* (pp. 69-78). Cambridge, MA: Harvard.

Kumashiro, K. (2002). *Troubling education: Queer activists and anti-oppressive pedagogy*. New York: Routledge Falmer.

Kumashiro, K. (Ed.). (2001). *Troubling intersections of race and sexuality: Queer students of color and anti-oppressive education*. Lanham, MD: Rowman & Littlefield.

Lasser, J., & Tharinger, D. (2003). Visibility management in school and beyond: A qualitative study of gay, lesbian, and bisexual youth. *Journal of Adolescence, 26*(2), 233-244.

LeCompte, M. D. (2000). Standing for just and right decisions: The long, slow path to school safety. *Education and Urban Society, 32*, 413-429.

LeGates, R. T., & Stout, F. (Eds.). (2003). *The city reader* (3rd ed.). London: Routledge.

Lugg, C. A. (1997). *No trespassing: U.S. public schools and the border of institutional homophobia*. Paper presented at the annual convention of the University Council for Educational Administration. Orlando, FL. (ERIC Document Reproduction Service No. ED429252)

Mac An Ghaill, M. (1994). (In)visibility: Sexuality, race, and masculinity in the school context. In D. Epstein (Ed.), *Challenging lesbian and gay inequalities in education* (pp. 152-176). Buckingham, England: Open University Press.

McCready, L. (2001). When fitting in isn't an option, or, why Black queer males at a California high school stay away from Project 10. In K. Kumashiro (Ed.), *Troubling intersections of race and sexuality: Queer students of color and anti-oppressive education* (pp. 37-53). Lanham, MD: Rowman & Littlefield.

McCready, L. (2003). Some challenges facing queer youth programs in urban high schools: Racial segregation and de-normalizing whiteness. *Journal of Gay and Lesbian Issues in Education, 1*(3), 37-51.

Morrow, S. L. (1997). Career development of lesbian and gay youth: Effects of sexual orientation, coming out, and homophobia. In M. B. Harris (Ed.), *School experience of gay and lesbian youth: The invisible minority*. New York: The Haworth Press.

Mumford, L. (2003). What is a city? In R. T. LeGates & F. Stout (Eds.), *The city reader*. (3rd ed., pp. 92-95). London: Routledge. (Original work published 1937)

National Mental Health Association [NMHA] (2002). *National survey of teens on Anti-gay teasing and bullying.* Alexandria, VA: National Mental Health Association.

Owens, R. E. (1998). *Queer kids: The challenges and promise for lesbian, gay, and bisexual youth.* New York: The Haworth Press.

Park, P. (1998, March). *The radically constructive turn: An academic activist's reflections on race and culture in the theorizing of the transgender.* Paper presented at Transpositions, A Conference Towards Transgender Studies. Ithaca, NY.

Parks, C. W. (2001). African-American same-gender-loving youths and families in urban schools. *Journal of Gay and Lesbian Social Services, 13*(3), 41-56.

Platt, L. (2001). Not your father's high school club. *American Prospect, 12*(1).

Rofes, E. (1997). Schools: The neglected site of queer activists. In M. B. Harris (Ed.), *School experiences of gay and lesbian youth: The invisible minority* (foreword) (pp. xiii-xviii). New York: The Haworth Press.

Rotheram-Borus, M. J., & Fernandez, M. I. (1995). Sexual orientation and developmental challenges experienced by gay and lesbian adolescents. *Suicide and Life-Threatening Behavior, 23*, 26-34.

Russell, S. R., Seif, H., & Truong, N. L. (2001). School outcomes of sexual minority youth in the United States: Evidence from a national study. *Journal of Adolescence, 24*, 111-127.

Ryan, C. (2000). *Analysis of content and gaps in the scientific and professional literature on the health and mental health concerns of lesbian, gay, bisexual youth.* Report prepared for the American Psychological Association, Healthy LGB Students Project, Washington, DC.

Ryan, C. (2002). *A review of the professional literature and research needs for LGBT youth of color.* Washington, DC: National Youth Advocacy Coalition.

Safe Schools Coalition (1997). *Safe Schools report from Washington state.* Retrieved July 7, 2004, from www.safeschoolscoalition.org

Safe Schools Coalition (1999). *Eighty-three thousand youth: Selected findings of eight population-based studies.* Retrieved October 22, 2005, from www.safeschoolscoalition.org/83000youth.pdf

Savin-Williams, R. C. (1995). Lesbian, gay male, and bisexual adolescents. In A. R., D'Augelli & C. J. Patterson (Eds.), *Lesbian, gay, and bisexual identities over the lifespan: Psychological perspectives* (pp. 165-189). New York: Oxford University.

Savin-Williams, R. C., & Rodriguez, R. G. (1993). A developmental, clinical perspective on lesbian, gay male, and bisexual youths. In T. P. Gullota, G. R. Adams, & R. Montemayor (Eds.), *Adolescent sexuality: Advances in adolescent development* (Vol. 5, pp. 77-101). Newbury Park, CA: Sage.

Schwartz, W. (1994). *Improving the school experience for gay, lesbian, and bisexual students.* ERIC Digest No. 101. New York: ERIC Clearinghouse on Urban Education, Institute for Urban and Minority Education, Teachers College, Columbia University. (ERIC Document Reproduction Service No. ED377257)

Supreme Court of the United States (2003). Retrieved October 22, 2005, from www.supremecourtus.gov/opinions/02pdf/02-102.pdf

Szalacha, L. A. (2003). The research terrain: A brief overview of the historical framework for LGBTQ studies in education. *Journal of Gay and Lesbian Issues in Education, 1*(2), 77-87.

Szalacha, L. A. (2004). Educating teachers on LGBTQ issues: A review of research and program evaluations. *Journal of Gay and Lesbian Issues in Education, 1*(4), 67-79.

Tully, C. T. (2000). *Lesbians, gays, & the empowerment perspective.* New York: Columbia University Press.

Uribe, V. (1994). Project 10: A school-based outreach to gay and lesbian youth. *High School Journal, 77*(1&2), 108-113.

Uribe, V., & Harbeck, K. M. (1992). Addressing the needs of lesbian, gay and bisexual youth: The origins of Project 10 and school-based intervention. In K. Harbeck (Ed.), *Coming out of the classroom closet: Gay and lesbian students, teachers and curricula* (pp. 9-28). New York: The Haworth Press.

Vaid, U. (1995). *Virtual equality: The mainstreaming of gay and lesbian liberation.* New York: Anchor Books.

Wirth, L. (2003). Urbanism as a way of life. In R. T. LeGates & F. Stout (Eds.), *The city reader* (3rd ed., pp. 97-104). London: Routledge. (Original work published 1938)

Woog, D. (1995). *School's out: The impact of gay and lesbian issues on America's schools.* Los Angeles: Alyson.

CHAPTER 8

MY FAVORITE MARTIAN

The Cry for Visibility of Sexual Minorities in Urban Schools

Kevin G. Alderson

My Favorite Martian was an American television sitcom that aired on CBS from 1963 to 1966 (Harison, 2005). Tim O'Hara (actor Bill Bixby) unexpectedly found Mr. Martin, the Martian (actor Ray Walston), after his spaceship crashed on Earth. One of Mr. Martin's supernatural powers was that he could become invisible after raising his retractable antennae, an action often taken to avoid discovery by others. In this chapter, I argue that sexual minority youth have largely remained invisible in urban schools because of several factors, but especially in consequence of heterosexism and homophobia. As societal tolerance and acceptance of sexual minorities increases, concomitant increases in youths disclosing their sexual identities at school becomes likely. Such trends are already being witnessed anecdotally. Are urban schools ready to deal with the increased visibility of sexual minority youth? Are they ready to assist these teens in increasing their visibility while at the same time providing a safe environment for them at school? Shockingly, evidence suggests that most urban

Inclusion in Urban Educational Environments:
Addressing Issues of Diversity, Equity, and Social Justice, 153–174
Copyright © 2006 by Information Age Publishing
All rights of reproduction in any form reserved.

Source: Photo courtesy of MPTV.net.

Figure 8.1.   Bill Bixby and Ray Walston, stars of *My Favorite Martian,*
1963-1966.

schools are not much further along on this path compared to when *My Favorite Martian* aired on television 40 years ago.

"The assumption and expectation in our society, however – politically, economically, and religiously—is that all people are inherently heterosexual."

—Kozik-Rosabal (2000, p. 369)

"What schools fail to realize, however, that by not confronting homophobia, they are likely condoning it."

—Loutzenheiser, cited in Little (2001, p. 105)

"Schools allow a hostile environment for gay and lesbian youth."

—Callahan (2001, p. 2)

On July 20, 2005, Canada became the fourth country in the world to legalize same-sex marriage (Department of Justice, Canada, 2005), following the lead taken by the Netherlands in 2001, Belgium in 2003 (Alderson, 2004b), and Spain in 2005 (Green, 2005).

Canada is one of the most socially progressive nations on earth regarding the provision of legal rights to sexual minorities. However, when it comes to the treatment of sexual minority youth within urban grade schools, we remain stuck within an archaic ideology that continues to defame their very being. This ideology inflicts great harm to the psychological, emotional, and spiritual development of sexual minority youth, and it is time to create significant change within our educational systems to provide them with equitable and fair treatment. Before reviewing the published research to support these statements, the first section provides definitions for the terms that are used here.

TERMINOLOGY

Sexual minorities include individuals who have a gay, lesbian, bisexual, transgendered, transsexual, or queer identity. *Gay* and *lesbian individuals* are defined as males and females, respectively, who have come to identify themselves as having primarily homosexual cognition, affect, and/or behavior, and who have adopted the construct of gay or lesbian as having personal significance to them (Alderson, 2003).

The term *queer* was once used against gay men and lesbian women (and sometimes still is) as a pejorative term. Today, some individuals have reclaimed the term and given it a positive connotation. In effect, queer individuals are those who refuse to be classified on the basis of sexuality (Herdt, 1997), and the term "encompasses lesbians, gay males, bisexual males and females, transgender persons, and even those heterosexual allies who support liberation efforts for sexual minorities and who actively struggle against the limited societal notions of 'normalcy' " (Blumenfeld & Raymond, 1993, pp. 350-351). The author's experience suggests that the reaction to use of the word queer remains variable, and consequently, it is not used here, except within the inclusive definition of sexual minorities offered above.

Bisexual individuals are defined as those who have come to identify themselves as having primarily cognition, affect, and/or behavior directed at both genders. Bisexual individuals have not established a substantive bisexual community (McKirnan, Stokes, Doll, & Burzette, 1995), so many define themselves as gay, lesbian, or heterosexual (McKirnan et al.). *Transsexual individuals* are those who believe "that they are really a member of the other gender trapped in bodies of the wrong gender" (Herring, 1998, pp. 161-162), while *transgendered persons* refer to "individuals who do not comply with the either/or, female/male construction in society" (Ormiston, 1996, cited in Herring, p. 162).

Some other terms used here are *homophilia*, which is the propensity to fall in love romantically only with members of the same gender (Money, 1988). A homosexual orientation refers to a sexual orientation created through the interaction between affect and cognition such that it produces homoerotic attraction, homoaffiliative desire, and ultimately homophilia (Alderson, 2003).

Coming out can mean one of two things, and usually the context provides the appropriate connotation. First, coming out can be used to refer to the process of self-identifying as gay. Second, coming out can refer to disclosing one's gay identity to others. The term *disclosing* is more specific than coming out and refers to telling other people that he or she identifies as belonging to a sexual minority.

Heterosexism refers to the many ways individuals in our society consciously or unconsciously minimize sexual minorities, either by assuming that they do not exist or by projecting a belief that they are somehow inferior compared with their heterosexual counterparts. *Homophobia* is the fear, dislike, or intolerance of gay individuals (Blumenfeld & Raymond, 1993). *Internalized homophobia* refers to sexual minority individuals fearing, disliking, and/or hating themselves or others who they perceive to belong to a sexual minority. Finally, *reorientation therapy* (Spitzer, 2003), also known as reparative or conversion therapy, is therapy directed at changing a homosexual or bisexual orientation into a heterosexual orientation.

HEARING THE CRY

When I first joined the University of Calgary, I wrote that above all else, I wanted my children to be safe. "If my children are raised believing in themselves, and if they are provided nurturant environments, then I believe their post pubescent search for identity and the concomitant exploring that occurs will be productive and meaningful to them" (Alderson, 2001, p. 1). From my readings and observations, it appears that little has changed within the urban schools they attend—I do not feel they will be safe if either turns out to be a member of a sexual minority. That is clearly wrong. At university, I feel supported for who I am. Why are my children, who are far more vulnerable than me, unable to enjoy the same degree of safety, acceptance, and nurturance within their grade schools?

We expect schools to be safe places for everybody, yet that was not my experience growing up, and it is not the experience of children today either who happen to have different sexual proclivities, gender identities, or for those who happen to embrace nonconforming gender roles. So called "gay bashings" are often not gay bashings at all: they are people bashings, and the targets are often heterosexual males who do not present as fitting the hegemonic masculine role (Kimmel & Mahler, 2003). Epstein (1997) argues that because boys are often targeted for homophobic attack since they do not demonstrate characteristics of "real manhood," homophobia cannot be separated from misogyny. In Epstein's words, "misogyny is homophobic and homophobia is misogynist" (p. 8). Consequently, the devaluation of those males who do not present with hegemonic masculine traits are, in effect, presenting with feminine traits: the only two choices available within a binary system that genders human traits as either masculine or feminine.

Dempsey (1994) points out that, "Although some males are obviously effeminate and some females obviously masculine, homosexual adolescents cannot generally be identified by outward physical or behavioral characteristics" (p. 161). In effect, the stereotypes of how gays and lesbians look and sound is only true of some individuals, and most effeminate males and masculine females are heterosexual. "Gender-role orientation is often confused with sexual orientation" (Richardson & Hart, 1981, p. 75). In effect, then, there is not a one-to-one relationship between sexual orientation and an individual's gender role presentation. Preventing, stopping, and punishing homophobic slander and homophobic physical attacks would help all students feel better about themselves, regardless of their sexual orientation or gender role presentation.

While we continue to embrace such old stereotypes of how a male is supposed to look, talk, and act, we keep all males within a prison cell of narrow walls. While such gender-nonconforming lads continue to receive their daily punishment for being who they are within their schools, occasionally a crack in the cosmic egg shatters more than just yolks. Of the 28 random school shootings witnessed in the United States since 1982, 27 of these occurred in rural or suburban schools while only one occurred in an urban center (i.e., Chicago).

Despite the finding that every one of the perpetrators was reportedly heterosexual (Kimmel & Mahler, 2003), nearly every one of them had been continually teased, bullied, and beat up as though they were gay, barraged with the typical homophobic epithets that we all know too well—until they could take it no longer.

Reporting on the famous Columbine shootings, one of the school's football team members said after the incident:

Columbine is a clean, good place, except for those rejects," [he] said. "Sure we teased them. But what do you expect with kids who come to school with weird hairdos and horns on their hats? It's not just jocks; the whole school's disgusted with them. They're a bunch of homos.... If you want to get rid of someone, usually you tease em. So the whole school calls them homos. (Gibbs & Roche, cited in Kimmel & Mahler, 2003, p. 1,447)

Canada and the United States are countries where individual liberty and freedom are taken for granted by the majority culture. Although the rights of all are enshrined within such legislative documents as the Constitution and the Charter of Rights and Freedoms, the vision contained within them is not always translated into observable action. Such is the case with the treatment of sexual minorities within the grade school system. It remains within the common vernacular that nearly every boy is called a faggot or sissy for transgressing any of several traditional masculine gender roles. Homophobic insults are frequently levied at young people, regardless of whether they belong to a sexual minority or not. This was evident in the Canadian Public Health Association Safe School Study that was conducted in fall 2003 and spring 2004 with 2,806 and 2,755 respondents, respectively (Totten, 2004). Seven schools located in Manitoba, Quebec, British Columbia, New Brunswick, and Ontario were selected using very strict criteria to ensure student safety and support. Of these seven schools, two were within large urban centers (600,000+ residents), three were within small urban areas (25,000-50,000), one was within a small town (< 25,000), and one school was situated in a rural area (< 1,500).

The surveys used included a Grades 4–7 survey and a Grades 8–12 survey. There were equal numbers of males and females in each sample. Statistical differences between the schools based upon geographic region were not reported—however, as noted above, five of the seven schools were situated in urban environments. Nearly one out of five students reported that they rarely or occasionally felt safe, regardless of their sexual orientation.

Homophobic harassment was common in the seven schools, and 1 in 10 students stated they had been called a fag, lesbian, and so forth on a weekly basis. More than a third of the students reported homophobic harassment on a monthly basis. Of the students surveyed, 3% identified as gay, lesbian, or bisexual; 4% reported that they were questioning their orientation; and 93% said they were heterosexual.

Another Canadian study included a sample of 3,636 adolescents from 17 high schools situated within three sizeable urban centers: Toronto, Kingston, and Montreal (Williams, Connolly, Pepler, & Craig, 2003). Gay male, lesbian, bisexual, or questioning youth comprised approximately 3-4% of the participants. The researchers found that the sexual minority and questioning youth reported more experiences of victimization by bullying, sexual harassment, and physical abuse than their heterosexual peers. Sexual minority children are often beaten up, sometimes murdered (Thernstrom, 1999), simply because they are different and because they do not fit into the hegemonic masculine or feminine ideal. Aside from the two Canadian studies mentioned above, "homophobic harassment is an understudied and frequently overlooked form of sexual harassment in Canadian schools" (Totten, 2004, p. 11). Consequently, I need to rely on American evidence for most of the data in this chapter, which is not ideal as the United States has a different culture from Canada.

A survey conducted by the Roper Center for Public Opinion Research (Kiener, 2000) compared adolescents in the United States with Canada, and they found that 45% of American teens favor laws permitting same-sex marriage versus 67% of Canadian teens, suggesting that Canadian youth are less homophobic compared to our Southern neighbors. The recent reality of same-sex marriage legalization in Canada compared to the enactment of Defence of Marriage Acts—defining marriage as only between a man and a woman—throughout many states in the United States (Lahey & Alderson, 2004), and the opposition to same-sex marriage expressed by their current President, suggest that the American people are generally more conservative and potentially homophobic compared to Canadians.

The situation in American grade schools is truly frightening. I am not convinced, however, that the situation in Canada is remarkably different. Some of the best research occurring in the United States is being done by the Gay, Lesbian and Straight Education Network (GLSEN). They conduct the *National School Climate Survey* biennially, and have done so since 1999. The 2003 survey was completed by 887 lesbian, gay, bisexual, and transgendered (LGBT) youth from 48 states and the District of Columbia attending community groups, and another 579 students who completed the survey via the Internet (total $n = 1,466$) (Gay, Lesbian and Straight Education Network, 2003). Their key findings were (a) 84% of LGBT students report experiencing verbal harassment; (b) 91.5% report hearing homophobic remarks, such as "faggot," "dyke," or "that's so gay" frequently or often; (c) 82.9% report that faculty or staff never intervened or intervened only some of the time when overhearing homophobic remarks; (d) 39.1% report being physically harassed because of their sexual orientation; (e) 64.3% report feeling unsafe at their school because of their sexuality; (f) 28.6% report missing at least one entire day of school in the past month because they felt unsafe; (g) those who experienced frequent harassment had GPAs more than 10% lower than those who did not. They were half as likely to plan on attending college as well; (h) 37.3% do not feel comfortable discussing LGBT issues with their teachers, and those who could not identify supportive teachers were also half as likely to plan on continuing their education; and (i) LGBT students in schools with gay-straight alliances (GSAs) were more likely to feel safe in school than students whose schools do not have a GSA. Overall, the authors conclude that "violence, bias and harassment of LGBT students continue to be the rule—not the exception—in America's schools" (p. 2).

The prejudice levied against gays is more frequent compared to ethnic minority groups (Savin-Williams & Cohen, cited in Ginsberg, 1999), leading Unks (cited in Ginsberg) to conclude that "high schools may be the most homophobic institutions in American society, and woe be to anyone who would challenge the heterosexist premises on which they operate" (p. 3). Not only do students hurl their hateful homophobic comments at each other, but teachers are also sometimes implicated in joining in the laughter or making homophobic comments themselves (Buston & Hart, 2001; Peters, 2003). Teachers often do not intervene when gay pejorative nouns are thrown around at school: in classrooms, in hallways, in the cafeteria, in the washrooms, in the gym, and in the locker room (Buston & Hart). A study of 307 teachers in the United Kingdom found that although they were aware of homophobic bullying, they reported being confused, unable, or unwilling to deal with the issue (Warwick, Aggleton, & Douglas, 2001). In Peter's study of school climate, based on 1,166 completed surveys, 44% of the students reported that no one ever intervened when anti-gay epithets were overheard, and another 42% said that someone intervened rarely.

Sexual minorities are not subjected to only teasing in schools, however. Findings from studies done by the National Gay and Lesbian Task Force indicate that more than a third of individuals surveyed suffered from violence due to their sexual identities (Elia, 1993). "While homophobia is rampant throughout society, it is more concentrated in the high schools" (Elia, p. 179). The U.S. Department of Justice reported that "gays and lesbians were the most frequent victims of hate crimes, and that school was the primary setting for hate crime violence" (Callahan, 2001, p. 2).

Many of our sexual minority children experience physical assault because of who they are. A 14-year-old boy in Niagara Falls, Ontario, made the mistake of telling his best friend that he was gay. Word spread, and over the next 2 years, Christian Hernandez:

> was teased and harassed almost daily. One day, a group of boys waited for him after school. Their leader had a knife, and, says Hernandez, "He told me he didn't accept faggots, that we brought AIDS into the world." The boy then cut Hernandez on the neck, putting him in the hospital for a week. When Hernandez told his parents the reason for the attack, his father, who has since moved back to his native El Salvador, said he would "rather have a dead son than a queer son." (Fisher, 1999, p. 3)

Schools appear to be ambivalent when it comes to dealing with sexual minority youth (Macgillivray, 2000). For example, although New York City has a very large concentration of sexual minorities, Peters (2003) found that as he approached 56 school districts on the east side of the city to participant in his school climate study, only six agreed. Representatives from the 50 school districts that refused participation replied that the subject matter was too "provocative" for them to consider participating. Often teachers do not want to deal with the subject of homosexuality, fearing a backlash from parents and administrators (Macgillivray; Warwick, Aggleton, & Douglas, 2001). Other reasons that lead to the invisibility of discussions or curriculum on homosexuality include a belief by some administrators and teachers that schools should not teach homosexuality, or that values concerning human sexuality should be left for parents to discuss (Macgillivray).

Regardless of the reason, the ethos of making homosexuality nonexistent in school discussions or curriculum only serves to further perpetuate heterosexist thinking. Furthermore, it does little to encourage sexual minority youth to unveil their sexual identities and be proud of them. The invisibility of sexual minorities in urban schools has occasionally been perpetuated by banning books containing nonheterosexual content. The Surrey School Board in British Columbia banned three books depicting same-sex families in 1997 (Fisher, 1999) and book banning occurred in the same year by the Calgary, Alberta Public School Board who claimed two books promoted homosexuality. Many of us remember the courageous young gay teen, Marc Hall, who found out that he could not take his boyfriend to the high school prom in Oshawa, Ontario in 2002 (Fisher, 2002). The fight he went through to simply attend the prom with his date was unimaginable, and even still we wait for the Supreme Court of Canada to render its ruling on whether individual rights supersedes religious doctrine within publicly funded school systems.

The Salt Lake City School Board took an interesting action on February 10, 1996. To prevent a club from forming that would explicitly include gay and lesbian students, they chose to ban all extracurricular clubs, including "the closure of young men's and women's associations; ethnic clubs; volunteer councils; Kiwanis clubs; human rights groups; and hiking, skiing, rugby, soccer, chess, and environmental clubs" (Henning-Stout, James, & Macintosh, 2000, p. 182). At least they treated everyone equally—if one group could not have a club, neither could anyone!

Sexual minority teachers live in their own terror, fearing they may lose their jobs if students or school districts discover their identities (Macgillivray, 2000; Peters, 2003). Everyday, most of us overhear people talk about their opposite-sex mates or spouses, and they are especially proud (as they ought to be) of talking about their children. Sexual minority teachers, however, are expected to shut up about their mates or spouses. In effect, both the teacher and his or her mate are expected to remain invisible.

Urban schools are not the only ones to blame for the invisibility of sexual minority youth, of course. When I interviewed a 15-year old for my dissertation and my first book (Alderson, 2000), at the end I asked him if there was any information I could provide him, knowing possibly more about this subject than he did. He asked, "Where can I meet other young guys like myself?" After mentioning the one gay youth group in Edmonton, Alberta, to which he had attended and found himself not fitting in, I was dumbfounded. One club for gay youth in a city of 800,000 people! For heterosexual youth, there are hundreds of clubs they could join where they would feel the camaraderie of other heterosexual young people. No wonder isolation is the number one problem reported by sexual minority youth (Hetrick & Martin, 1987).

How do sexual minority youth cope with their invisibility in urban schools? They manage their [in]visibility by closely monitoring their surroundings and deciding when and with whom to disclose their sexualities (Lasser & Tharinger, 2003).

> Participants monitor and modify dress, speech, and body language to manage their visibility. They use subculture symbols, euphemisms, humour, and references to pop culture to manage their visibility. Some change the pronouns of their boyfriends or girlfriends, while others withdraw socially at home and school. (Lasser & Tharinger, pp. 237-238)

However, having to pretend brings with it consequences.

The devaluing of sexual minorities in urban schools is contributing to the mental health problems of LGBT students. Sexual minority youth report and experience many problems in greater proportion compared to their heterosexual counterparts. These include acting out or externalizing of their problems (Williams et al., 2003), high-risk sexual behaviors (Blake, Ledsky, Lehman, Goodenow, Sawyer, & Hack, 2001), depression (Lock & Steiner, 1999; Williams et al.), diminished self-esteem (Galliher, Rostosky, & Hughes, 2004), alcohol and substance use (Bradford, Ryan, & Rothblum, 1994; Chesir-Teran, 2003; Orenstein, 2001), homelessness (Lock & Steiner, 1999), HIV/AIDS (Rotheram-Borus, Murphy, Kennedy, Stanton, & Kuklinski, 2001), and internalized homophobia (Chesir-Teran; Omizo, Omizo, & Okamoto, 1998). These problems have been linked to heterosexism (Chesir-Teran).

Regarding suicides, gay and lesbian youth are reported as being 2 to 6 times more likely than heterosexual teens to attempt suicide, and they may account for as many as 30% of completed suicides (McFarland, 1993). In 1993, the World Health Organization (cited in Sussman &

Duffy, 1996) reported that 60% of new HIV infections worldwide are found in 15- to 24-year-olds. The Centers for Disease Control & Prevention (2005) more recently reported that from 2000 through 2003, the estimated number of HIV/AIDS cases in the United States increased in the 13-14 and 15-24 age groups. The evidence is clear: sexual minority youth are a more vulnerable population compared to heterosexual individuals, yet they are "perhaps the most underserved students in the entire educational system. For many of them, school is a lonely and frightening place to be" (Uribe, 1994, p. 171). The ones who are especially harassed do more poorly at school compared to the more fortunate who have an easier time passing (Gay, Lesbian and Straight Education Network [GLSEN], 2003). The dropout rate for sexual minority students in Canada is 28%, compared to the national average of only 9% (Shelby, cited in Little, 2001).

Although most sexual minority youth navigate their adolescence reasonably well (Anderson, 1998; Savin-Williams, 2001a), a sizeable percentage do not. They succumb to the verbal abuse that resonates in their ears or the physical abuse that breaks their bones. Many sexual minority youth lose friends when they disclose their sexual identities (Flowers & Buston, 2001; Hart & Heimberg, 2001). Compared to heterosexual youth, sexual minority youth report less companionship with their best friends (Williams et al., 2003). Furthermore, they often have trouble relating to heterosexual peers because they fear discovery or because they do not share typical interests for their gender (Marinoble, 1998). Combined, the problems that sexual minority youth face with peers only serves to deepen their feelings of isolation.

Gay and lesbian youth are disclosing their sexual identities at younger ages than in the past (Platt, 2001; Taylor, 2000), and as Canada and the United States become more tolerant and accepting of sexual minority youth, we can expect this trend to continue. In the 1970s, the average age of self-disclosure occurred during the mid to late 20s, whereas now the mean age is 18 (Floyd & Stein, 2002; Platt, 2001). Furthermore, it is not unusual to find gay and lesbian students disclosing their sexual identities while still in high school (Platt, 2001). The mean age of disclosure in a sample of 116 gay, lesbian, and bisexual youth was 16.8, 16.0, and 16.8 years, respectively (Maguen, Floyd, Bakeman, & Armistead, 2002). Additionally, Floyd and Stein (2002) studied the milestones of gay, lesbian, and bisexual youth and found that the mean age by which their participants became aware of same-sex attraction was 10.39 years. The mean age at which they had sex with someone of the same gender was 16.31 years. Another study reported awareness of same-sex attraction at 9.6 years for gay males, 10.9 years for lesbians, and 13.2 years for bisexuals, while same-sex sexual contact occurred at ages 14.9, 16.4, and 16.7 years, respectively (Maguen et al., 2002). Notably, all of these statistics pertain to children who are school-aged.

I believe that we will also see more sexual minority youth demanding services and recognition of their identities in the very near future within urban school systems. In 1986, the average age that gay males became aware of their homosexual attractions was 12.8, followed by their first homosexual relationship at age 21.9 on average (Obear & Reynolds, cited in Pope, Prince, & Mitchell, 2000). The achievement of a positive gay identity occurred, on average, at age 28.5 (Pope, et al.), about 16 years after first recognizing their same-sex feelings. More recently, the average age of same-sex attraction was 10.39 years, and the first same-gender serious relationship occurred at age 18.48 on average (Floyd & Stein, 2002). Getting involved in serious relationships is viewed as an important aspect of having a positive gay identity in at least three gay identity acquisition theories (Alderson, 2003; Coleman, 1981-1982; Troiden, 1979). Consequently, it would appear that in less than 20 years, the age that gay men and lesbians are acquiring a positive gay identity is lessening. Along with a positive identity comes strength of character and a refusal to remain invisible in many if not most settings (Alderson, 2000).

Teachers know little about sexual minorities (Floyd et al., cited in Chung & Katayama, 1998), and most prospective teachers harbor negative attitudes toward sexual minority youth (Roffman, 2000). Most counselors have received little training themselves in how to work with this population (Alderson, 2004a). Are schools prepared to deal with the issues that will arise as more sexual minority students demand recognition, acceptance, and equitable treatment? The answer is self-evident from the research that has been done to date. In truth, if we do not act soon, our legal system will act for us.

Jamie Nabozny of Ashland, Wisconsin admitted to another student in the early 1990s while he was attending middle school that he was gay. For years, he was brutally persecuted verbally and physically in his school, culminating in an incident where several boys threw him to the floor and kicked him so hard in the stomach that he ended up in hospital with internal bleeding. At age 16, Jamie never returned to public school again – however, this did not mean he was about to roll over and die. Instead, he took the school district to court. In a landmark ruling in the United States, Jamie was awarded $900,000 in damages (Buckel, 2000).

In Canada, similar events do not bring the same dollar amount in damages. In June 1996, Azmi Jubran, a student in a secondary school in North Vancouver, filed a complaint with the B.C. Human Rights Commission. Jamie had been repeatedly teased by his peers, called all the homophobic pejoratives one can imagine. Jamie, like many others who are similarly attacked, was not gay. On April 6, 2005, Jamie was awarded

$4,500 in damages, sending a strong message that if schools do not act, judges will (B.C. court of appeal supports bullied student, 2005).

I think you can see by now that all is not well—far from it. Sexual minorities continue to be mistreated in significant ways at every level within the school systems to which they must attend. It is akin to a compulsory form of defamation and persecution for those who cannot quit school because they are underage. Nazi Germany persecuted gays and lesbians, and many were put to death. Is this the message we want to uphold, even if the death we are referring to here is more psychological?

Every piece of research I have read about gays and lesbians in school offers the same message: it is time we did something about their plight. I am sick of reading the message. Either we do something, or we sit on our laurels and continue to pretend all is well. One of my interviewees in Beyond Coming Out (Alderson, 2000) with the pseudonym of Alex stated it well:

> My friend Roger and I went to a school near our house and inquired into beginning there in the fall. The principal was completely atrocious. He called us faggots. Roger had a Caesar cut, and he wore makeup and a tight shirt with nipple rings showing through. We both wore earrings. The principal just didn't know how to handle us, and he said that it would be a cold day in hell before homosexuals started coming to his school. We went to the school board, and they forced him to let us in. (p. 169)

Alex continued to experience harsh moments of heterosexism and homophobia throughout his school years, and he eventually had an opportunity to share some of its impact with one individual who could have made a difference:

> One of my saddest memories is thinking about the many people who have failed me in my life. When I called out for help, the education system didn't do anything. I actually ran into that principal [note: a different principal from the one described previously] two weeks ago when I was at a conference in Toronto. There were fifteen hundred people at this luncheon, and I ended up sitting at the table next to her. In front of probably eighteen people who were listening, I told her, "You need to be aware of what you did by ignoring the abuse that happened. You need to know the pain that I went through because you chose to ignore it." She started to cry, and I felt bad for her. But that happened, after all, in the eighties. That was yesterday. (Alderson, 2000, p. 175)

If I have given you the sense that urban schools remain difficult establishments for sexual minority youth, even worse is their treatment in rural ones. Rural settings are generally acknowledged as being more conservative (Cody & Welch, 1997) and homonegative (Bohan, 1996; Goldfried &

Goldfried, 2001) compared to urban areas. It is not surprising that significant numbers of gay and bisexual males migrate from rural to urban centers (Bagley & Tremblay, 1998) in their search for greater connectedness and acceptance (Cody & Welch).

Furthermore, educational institutions are not the only places in which sexual minority youth are poorly treated. Although Savin-Williams (2001b) found that parents do not react as negatively to their gay or lesbian youth's disclosure of their identity status to them as popular literature suggests, half of the gay and lesbian adolescents who report being physically assaulted because of their sexual orientation are beaten by family members (Bohan, 1996; Flowers & Buston, 2001). Most parents are not overjoyed to hear that their son or daughter is part of a sexual minority (Goldfried & Goldfried, 2001).

The mistreatment of sexual minority youth in rural schools and by their families is not the focus of this chapter, however. The argument here is that urban schools throughout the United States and Canada, most of which are publicly-supported institutions, remain—for the most part—deeply entrenched in heterosexist and homonegative practices. Such practices continue to keep sexual minority youth invisible at the start of the twenty-first century, and this invisibility is hurting them mentally, emotionally, spiritually, and for some, even physically. The abuse must end, and it is imperative that urban schools take the lead if they are to fulfill their mandates of providing a safe and secure environment for all students.

WHAT URBAN SCHOOLS CAN DO TO INITIATE EQUITABLE TREATMENT FOR SEXUAL MINORITY YOUTH

Some schools have done exemplary jobs of helping sexual minority students feel welcome. Some notable projects in the United States are Project 10 (Uribe & Harbeck, 1991), the Massachusetts Governor's Commission on Gay and Lesbian Youth, and Washington's Safe Schools Project (Henning-Stout, James, & Macintosh, 2000). Here are a few practical ideas of what urban schools can do to help:

1. Include teaching about sexual minorities in the curriculum. Athanases and Larrabee (2003) found that most students in their study knew very little about lesbian and gay youth. Written responses from those who received instruction about lesbian and gay youth indicated a strong appreciation for what they learned. Furthermore, 85% of Canadian parents want sex education in schools, and most of them want this instruction to include teach-

ing about sexual orientation (McKay, 2005). Similarly, 92% of students want sex education to be included in schools. Suggested curricula for content regarding sexual minority clients can be found in Alderson (2004a), D'Augelli (1991), and Stein and Burg (1996).

2. Schrader and Wells (2004) mentioned a national project in the United States called the No Name-Calling Week and a similar initiative in Canada called the National Day Against Homophobia, which occurs the first Wednesday of each June. According to Scharder and Wells, the National Day Against Homophobia has targeted the field of education for June 6, 2007. Bringing awareness to the harm caused by homophobic epithets and pejorative names used against minority groups is a positive step toward ending this practice.

3. Bring in guest speakers who belong to sexual minorities. Nelson and Krieger (cited in Athanases & Larrabee, 2003) found that bringing in a panel of lesbian and gay peers can significantly increase the positive attitudes of college students towards lesbians and gays. Other research has also found that exposure to lesbians and gays improve people's attitudes toward them.

4. Take action when witnessing antigay remarks or antigay aggression. The Safe Schools Anti Violence Documentation Project (Reis, cited in McFarland, 2001) recommends five strategies. First, intervene immediately. Second, make it safe to report incidents by identifying a "safe" person in the school to whom school personnel and students can report. Third, think about educating and disciplining the offenders. Fourth, consider the safety, support, and recovery of the victim(s). Fifth, consider the needs of the witnesses and others in the school community by offering reassurance that such behavior will not be tolerated, and that when it occurs, it will be dealt with.

5. Establish a gay-straight alliance (GSA) at your school. Most of these were created following the widely publicized murder of Matthew Shepard in 1998 (Platt, 2001). About 50 of these were organized between 2000 and 2002 in Canadian schools, mostly in the provinces of British Columbia, Manitoba, Ontario, and Nova Scotia. Although most members of GSAs are gay or lesbian, some heterosexual youth join as well (Robinson, 2002).

6. Purchase appropriate readings about sexual minorities for your library. Taylor (2000) recommends several books, but the most exhaustive list I have seen of gay-themed books, educational vid-

eos, and curriculum development materials is found in Schrader and Wells (2004).

7. Get used to saying and hearing the words lesbian and gay (Casper, Schultz, & Wickens, 1992). Recently I shocked one of my gay undergraduate students with how open I was in using these words. If he was shocked, I can only imagine how those who are not gay react.

8. Provide in-services to school personnel. Blake et al. (2001) found that teachers who received appropriate training make a difference in the lives of gay, lesbian, and bisexual youths.

9. Develop and adopt antidiscrimination and harassment policies in your school (Chesir-Teran, 2003).

10. Encourage sexual minority adults to run for school boards (Wald, Rienzo, & Button, 2002). They will help promote change at the highest administrative level.

11. Consider training peer supporters with specialized knowledge of sexual minority youth (Bauman & Sachs-Kapp, 1998). Peer supporters can make a huge difference in promoting equitable treatment for sexual minorities.

12. Become familiar with local resources that assist sexual minority youths (Fisher, 1999).

13. Ensure that your school promotes safer sex by installing condom machines (Fisher, 1999). Research has shown that taking this step does not lead more students to become sexually active, but they do significantly increase condom use among teenagers who are (McKay, 2005).

CONCLUSIONS

"Although not all GLBTQ youth are in a crisis situation, we as a society are in a crisis situation" (Macgillivray, 2000, p. 321).

The time is long overdue that we begin to systematically address the problem of homophobia and heterosexism in urban schools. If one child takes his or her life because of a relationship breakup or clinical depression, then we as educators can relinquish our pain by realizing that we were not responsible. However, if a sexual minority child commits suicide because he or she was treated disrespectfully and punitively for years in a system that did not address his or her needs, then we must take responsibility—full responsibility. We cannot expect vulnerable children and teenagers to create an environment that protects themselves. For that, it is us adults who must create, monitor, and sustain safe environments.

Urban schools, for the most part, have remained negligent in their duty to protect children who are different because of their sexuality. While epithets directed at individuals designated as belonging to a sexual minority continue to occur with little if any censure or consequence, the cumulative damage to a youth's self-esteem and overall mental health can no longer be ignored. If school personnel do not work at ending or at least intervening in the prejudicial and discriminatory practices that continue to be directed at sexual minority youth, judicial systems will be forced to make the necessary changes for them.

Sexual minority youth are not Martians—they are themselves beautiful children. They have the same capacity to love other human beings as do heterosexual individuals. They are tired of being mentally and physically abused, and spiritually raped, by those who fail to understand them, and by those who understand them and hate them. It is time we all realize and take responsibility for the huge injustice that has been inflicted upon sexual minority youth. Let these young people flourish, and let them become visible in your urban schools. It is time that we all retract our antennas of invisibility.

REFERENCES

Alderson, K. (2000). *Beyond coming out: Experiences of positive gay identity.* Toronto, Ontatrio, Canada: Insomniac Press.

Alderson, K. G. (2001). Reflecting on shattered glass: Some thoughts about gay youth in schools. *The Alberta Counsellor, 27*(1), 1-8.

Alderson, K. G. (2003). The ecological model of gay male identity. *The Canadian Journal of Human Sexuality, 12,* 75-85.

Alderson, K. G. (2004a). A different kind of outing: Training counsellors to work with sexual minority clients. *Canadian Journal of Counselling, 38,* 193-210.

Alderson, K. G. (2004b). A phenomenological investigation of same-sex marriage. *Canadian Journal of Human Sexuality, 13,* 107-122.

Anderson, A. L. (1998). Strengths of gay male youth: An untold story. *Child and Adolescent Social Work, 15,* 55-71.

Athanases, S. Z., & Larrabee, T. G. (2003). Toward a consistent stance in teaching for equity: Learning to advocate for lesbian- and gay-identified youth. *Teaching and Teacher Education, 19,* 237-261.

Bagley, C., & Tremblay, P. (1998). On the prevalence of homosexuality and bisexuality, in a random community survey of 750 men aged 18 to 27. *Journal of Homosexuality, 36*(2), 1-18.

Bauman, S., & Sachs-Kapp, P. (1998). A school takes a stand: Promotion of sexual orientation workshops by counselors. *Professional School Counseling, 1,* 42-45. Retrieved June 4, 2005, from http://search.epnet.com.ezproxy.lib .ucalgary.ca:2048/login.aspx?direct=true&db=aph&an=288460

B.C. Court of Appeal supports bullied student (2005). Retrieved July 7, 2005, from http://www.proudparenting.com/page.cfm?Sectionid=58&typeofsite =snippetdetail&ID=1856&snippetset=yes

Blake, S. M., Ledsky, R., Lehman, T., Goodenow, C., Sawyer, R., & Hack, T. (2001). Preventing sexual risk behaviors among gay, lesbian, and bisexual adolescents: The benefits of gay-sensitive HIV instruction in schools. *American Journal of Public Health, 91,* 940-946.

Blumenfeld, W. J., & Raymond, D. (1993). *Looking at gay and lesbian life* (updated and expanded edition). Boston: Beacon Press.

Bohan, J. S. (1996). *Psychology and sexual orientation: Coming to terms.* New York: Routledge.

Bradford, J., Ryan, C., & Rothblum, E. (1994). National lesbian health care survey: Implications for mental health care. *Journal of Consulting and Clinical Psychology, 62,* 228-242.

Buckel, D. S. (2000). Legal perspective on ensuring a safe and nondiscriminatory school environment for lesbian, gay, bisexual, and transgendered students. *Education and Urban Society, 32,* 390-398.

Buston, K., & Hart, G. (2001). Heterosexism and homophobia in Scottish school sex education: Exploring the nature of the problem. *Journal of Adolescence, 24,* 95-109.

Callahan, C. J. (2001). Protecting and counseling gay and lesbian students. *Journal of Humanistic Counseling, 40,* 5-10. Retrieved June 4, 2005, from http:// search.epnet.com.ezproxy.lib.ucalgary.ca:2048/ login.aspx?direct=true&db=aph&an=4035825

Casper, V., Schultz, S., & Wickens, E. (1992). Breaking the silences: Lesbian and gay parents and the schools. *Teachers College Record, 94,* 109-137.

Chesir-Teran, D. (2003). Conceptualizing and assessing heterosexism in high schools: A setting-level approach. *American Journal of Community Psychology, 31,* 267-279.

Chung, Y. B., & Katayama, M. (1998). Ethnic and sexual identity development of Asian-American lesbian and gay adolescents. *Professional School Counseling, 3*(1), 21-25. Retrieved January 31, 2006, from Academic Search Premier database.: http://weblinks1.epnet.com.ezproxy.lib.ucalgary.ca/ citation.asp?tb=1&_ua=bo+B%5F+shn+1+db+aph- jnh+bt+TD++%222N2%22+A0EB&_ug=sid+2D1653F3%2D3516%2D40 02%2D8439%2D74CCB759093B%40sessionmgr2+dbs+aph+cp+1+68E4& _us=hd+False+fcl+Aut+or+Date+frn+1+sm+ES+sl+%2D1+dstb+ES+r i+KAAACBZD00015673+0E06&_uh=btn+N+6C9C&_uso=st%5B0+%2DJ N++%22Professional++School++Counsel- ing%22++and++DT++19980201+tg%5B0+%2D+db%5B0+%2Daph+h d+False+op%5B0+%2D+mdb%5B0+%2Dimh+B412&cf=1&fn=1&rn=4

Cody, P. J., & Welch, P. L. (1997). Rural gay men in northern New England: Life experiences and coping styles. *Journal of Homosexuality, 33*(1), 51-67.

Coleman, E. (1981-1982). Developmental stages of the coming out process. *Journal of Homosexuality, 7*(2-3), 31-43.

D'Augelli, A. R. (1991). Gay men in college: Identity processes and adaptations. *Journal of College Student Development, 32,* 140-146.

Dempsey, C. L. (1994). Health and social issues of gay, lesbian, and bisexual adolescents. *Families in Society, 75*(3), 160-167.

Department of Justice, Canada. (2005). Civil marriage and the legal recognition of same-sex unions. Retrieved October 12, 2005, from http://canada.justice.gc.ca/en/fs/ssm/

Elia, J. P. (1993). Homophobia in the high school: A problem in need of a resolution. *The High School Journal, 77,* 177-185.

Epstein, D. (1997). Boyz' own stories: Masculinities and sexualities in schools. *Gender & Education, 9,* 105-115. Retrieved June 4, 2005, from http://search.epnet.com.ezproxy.lib.ucalgary.ca:2048/login.aspx?direct=true&db=aph&an=9704113361

Fisher, J. (1999, February 23). *Reaching out: A report on lesbian, gay & bisexual youth issues in Canada.* Retrieved July 7, 2005 from http://www.egale.ca/printer.asp?lang=E&item=305&version=EN

Fisher, J. (2002). *Catholic School Board discrimination on trial.* Retrieved July 10, 2005, from http://www.samesexmarriage.ca/advocacy/marc_hall.htm

Flowers, P., & Buston, K. (2001). "I was terrified of being different": Exploring gay men's accounts of growing-up in a heterosexist society. *Journal of Adolescence, 24,* 51-65.

Floyd, F. J., & Stein, T. S. (2002). Sexual orientation identity formation among gay, lesbian, and bisexual youths: Multiple patterns of milestone experiences. *Journal of Research on Adolescence, 12,* 167-191.

Galliher, R. V., Rostosky, S. S., & Hughes, H. K. (2004). School belonging, self-esteem, and depressive symptoms in adolescents: An examination of sex, sexual attraction status, and urbanicity. *Journal of Youth and Adolescence, 33,* 235-245.

Gay, Lesbian and Straight Education Network (GLSEN). (2003). *The 2003 national school climate survey: The school related experiences of our nation's lesbian, gay, bisexual and transgender youth.* Retrieved June 26, 2005, from www.glsen.org/binary-data/GLSEN_ATTACHMENTS/file/274-3.pdf

Ginsberg, R. W. (1999). In the triangle/out of the circle: Gay and lesbian students facing the heterosexual paradigm. *The Educational Forum, 64,* 46-56. Retrieved June 4, 2005, from http://vnweb.hwwilsonweb.com.ezproxy.lib.ucalgary.ca:2048/hww/jumpstart.jhtml?recid=0bc05f7a67b1790e770910268787c473680e3e26a2b1ac5953e33823ddce7629a58ef3a01c6fbd43&fmt=H

Goldfried, M. R., & Goldfried, A. P. (2001). The importance of parental support in the lives of gay, lesbian, and bisexual individuals. *In Session: Psychotherapy in Practice, 57,* 681-693.

Green, J. (2005, July 1). Spain legalizes same-sex marriage. *Special to the Washington Post,* p. A14. Retrieved July 9, 2005, from http://www.washingtonpost.com/wp-dyn/content/article/2005/06/30/AR2005063000245_pf.html

Harison, J. H. (2005). *My Favorite Martian: A history of the show.* Retrieved July 9, 2005, from http://members.tripod.com/~jhh_2/TVMFM.htm

Hart, T. A., & Heimberg, R. G. (2001). Presenting problems among treatment-seeking gay, lesbian, and bisexual youth. *In Session: Psychotherapy in Practice, 57,* 615-627.

Henning-Stout, M., James, S., & Macintosh, S. (2000). Reducing harassment of lesbian, gay, bisexual, transgender, and questioning youth in schools. *School Psychology Review, 29,* 180-191.

Herdt, G. (1997). *Same sex, different cultures.* Boulder, CO: Westview Press.

Herring, R. D. (1998). *Career counseling in schools: Multicultural and developmental perspectives.* Alexandria, VA: American Counseling Association.

Hetrick, E. S., & Martin, A. D. (1987). Developmental issues and their resolution for gay and lesbian adolescents. *Journal of Homosexuality, 14*(1-2), 25-43.

Kiener, R. (2000, June). What teens really think. *Readers Digest, 156,* 50-57.

Kimmel, M. S., & Mahler, M. (2003). Adolescent masculinity, homophobia, and violence. *American Behaviorist Scientist, 46,* 1439-1458.

Kozik-Rosabal, G. (2000). "Well, we haven't noticed anything bad going on," said the principal: Parents speak about their gay families and schools. *Education and Urban Society, 32,* 368-389.

Lahey, K. A., & Alderson, K. (2004). *Same-sex marriage: The personal and the political.* Toronto, Canada: Insomniac Press.

Lasser, J., & Tharinger, D. (2003). Visibility management in school and beyond: A qualitative study of gay, lesbian, bisexual youth. *Journal of Adolescence, 26,* 233-244.

Little, J. N. (2001). Embracing gay, lesbian, bisexual, and transgendered youth in school-based settings. *Child & Youth Care Forum, 30,* 99-110.

Lock, J., & Steiner, H. (1999). Gay, lesbian, and bisexual youth risks for emotional, physical, and social problems: Results from a community-based survey. *Journal of the American Academy of Child and Adolescent Psychiatry, 38,* 297-304. Retrieved June 1, 2005, from http://find.galegroup.com.ezproxy.lib .ucalgary.ca:2048/itx/info-mark.do?&type=retrieve&tabID=T002&prodId=EAIM&docId=A54171868&source=gale&srcprod=EAIM&userGroupName=ucalgary&version=1.0

Macgillivray, I. K. (2000). Educational equity for gay, lesbian, bisexual, transgendered, and queer/questioning students: The demands of democracy and social justice for America's schools. *Education and Urban Society, 32,* 303-323.

Maguen, S., Floyd, F. J., Bakeman, R., & Armistead, L. (2002). Developmental milestones and disclosure of sexual orientation among gay, lesbian, and bisexual youths. *Journal of Applied Developmental Psychology, 23,* 219-233.

Marinoble, R. M. (1998). Homosexuality: A blind spot in the school mirror. *Professional School Counseling, 1*(3), 4-7.

McFarland, W. P. (1993). A developmental approach to gay and lesbian youth. *Journal of Humanistic Education and Development, 32,* 17-29.

McFarland, W. P. (2001). The legal duty to protect gay and lesbian students from violence in school. *Professional School Counseling, 4,* 171-179.

McKay, A. (2005). *Sexual health education in the schools: Questions & answers.* Retrieved July 7, 2005, from www.sieccan.org/pdf/sexual_health)_qs.pdf

McKirnan, D., Stokes, J., Doll, L., & Burzette, R. (1995). Bisexually active males: social characteristics and sexual behavior. *Journal of Sex Research, 32,* 65-76.

Money, J. (1988). *Gay, straight, and in-between: The sexology of erotic orientation.* New York: Oxford University Press.

Omizo, M. M., Omizo, S. A., & Okamoto, C. M. (1998). Gay and lesbian adolescents: A phenomenological study. *Professional School Counselling, 1*(3), 35-37. Retrieved June 4, 2005, from http://search.epnet.com.ezproxy.lib .ucalgary.ca:2048/login.aspx?direct=true&db=aph&an=288456

Orenstein, A. (2001). Substance use among gay and lesbian adolescents. *Journal of Homosexuality, 41,* 1-15.

Peters, A. J. (2003). Isolation or inclusion: Creating safe spaces for lesbian and gay youth. *Families in Society, 84,* 331-337.

Platt, L. (2001, January 1). Not your father's high school club. *The American Prospect, 1.* Retrieved June 1, 2005, from http://find.galegroup.com.ezproxy.lib .ucalgary.ca:2048/itx/infomark.do?&type=retrieve&tabID=T002&prodId =EAIM&docId=A69652767&source=gale&srcprod =EAIM&userGroupName=ucalgary&version=1.0

Pope, M. S., Prince, J. P., & Mitchell, K. (2000). Responsible career counseling with lesbian and gay students. In D. A. Luzzo (Ed.), *Career counseling of college students: An empirical guide to strategies that work* (pp. 267-282). Washington, DC: American Psychological Association.

Richardson, D., & Hart, J. (1981). The development and maintenance of a homosexual identity. In J. Hart & D. Richardson (Eds.), *The theory and practice of homosexuality* (pp. 73-92). Boston: Routledge & Kegan Paul.

Robinson, B. A. (2002). *Gay-Straight Alliances (GSAs) in public schools.* Retrieved July 7, 2005, from http://www.relgioustolerance.org/hom_psgr3.htm

Roffman, D. M. (2000). A model for helping schools address policy options regarding gay and lesbian youth. *Journal of Sex Education & Therapy, 25,* 130-136.

Rotheram-Borus, M. J., Murphy, D. A., Kennedy, M., Stanton, A., & Kuklinski, M. (2001). Health and risk behaviors over time among youth living with HIV. *Journal of Adolescence, 24,* 791-802.

Savin-Williams, R. C. (2001a). A critique of research on sexual-minority youth. *Journal of Adolescence, 24,* 5-13.

Savin-Williams, R. C. (2001b). *Mom, dad, I'm gay: How families negotiate coming out.* Washington, DC: American Psychological Association.

Schrader, A. M., & Wells, K. (2004). *Queer perspectives on social responsibility in Canadian schools and libraries.* Retrieved July 7, 2005, from http://www .schoollibraries.ca/articles/151.aspx

Spitzer, R. L. (2003). Reply: Study results should not be dismissed and justify further research on the efficacy of sexual reorientation therapy. *Archives of Sexual Behavior, 32,* 469-472.

Stein, T. S., & Burg, B. K. (1996). Teaching in mental health training programs about homosexuality, lesbians, gay men, and bisexuals. In R. P. Cabaj & T. S. Stein (Eds.), *Textbook of homosexuality and mental health* (pp. 621-631). Washington, DC: American Psychiatric Press.

Sussman, T., & Duffy, M. (1996). Are we forgetting about gay male adolescents in AIDS-related research and prevention? *Youth & Society, 27,* 379-393.

Taylor, H. E. (2000). Meeting the needs of lesbian and gay young adolescents. *The Clearing House, 73,* 221-224.

Thernstrom, M. (1999, March). The crucifixion of Matthew Shepard. *Vanity Fair,* *463,* 209-214, 267-275.

Totten, M. (2004). CPHA safe school study (Canadian Public Health Association). Retrieved July 7, 2005, from http://www.cpha.ca/antibullying/english/ backinfo/safe_school_study_final.pdf

Troiden, R. R. (1979). Becoming homosexual: A model of gay identity acquisition. *Psychiatry, 42,* 362-373.

Uribe, V. (1994). The silent minority: Rethinking our commitment to gay and lesbian youth. *Theory into Practice, 33,* 167-172.

Uribe, V., & Harbeck, K. M. (1991). Addressing the needs of lesbian, gay, and bisexual youth: The origins of PROJECT 10 and school-based intervention. *Journal of Homosexuality, 22*(3-4), 9-28.

Wald, K. D., Rienzo, B. A., & Button, J. W. (2002). Sexual orientation and education politics: Gay and lesbian representation in American schools. *Journal of Homosexuality, 42,* 145-168.

Warwick, I., Aggleton, P., & Douglas, N. (2001). Playing it safe: Addressing the emotional and physical health of lesbian and gay pupils in the U.K. *Journal of Adolescence, 24,* 129-140.

Williams, T., Connolly, J., Pepler, D., & Craig, W. (2003). Questioning and sexual minority adolescents: High school experiences of bullying, sexual harassment and physical abuse. *Canadian Journal of Community Mental Health, 22,* 47-58.

CHAPTER 9

URBAN GIRLS EMPOWERING THEMSELVES THROUGH EDUCATION

The Issue of Voice

Gunilla Holm and William W. Cobern

This chapter is focused on a 3-year evaluation and examination of the science curriculum in an all-girls charter middle and high school focused on math, science, and technology. The focus of the larger study is on whether these urban girls, who are ethnically very diverse and mostly poor, get an inquiry based science education that will provide them with a solid understanding of science as well as a foundation for continuing in nontraditional science related careers. However, the focus in this chapter is on a more specific issue, namely whether the girls in this inner city school have a voice. This is a population—urban, mostly poor and minority girls—that rarely gets a good education and even more rarely are they seriously listened to with regard to their needs, knowledge, and views. We explore what happens when well meaning school personnel try to listen to and build a well functioning school for these girls. The data on which we are

Inclusion in Urban Educational Environments:
Addressing Issues of Diversity, Equity, and Social Justice, 175–187
Copyright © 2006 by Information Age Publishing
All rights of reproduction in any form reserved.

basing our argument have been collected through classroom observations and in-depth open-ended interviews with administrators, teachers, and students over a 3-year period.

The literature on all girls schools claims that it is easier for teachers to teach in all girls schools because the classes are more focused and orderly (Herr & Arms, 2004). Many classrooms in all girls schools consist of tables instead of individual desks because girls are considered more social and work well together without discipline problems. There is some indication that girls do better in single sex science classes (DeBare, 2004; National Coalition of Girls Schools, 2005). These kinds of classes have also been found to have "significant positive effect on girls' ... science performance and persistence" (Shapka & Keating, 2003, p. 950). Previous studies also indicate that it can be especially important for middle-school girls to have single-sex instruction in math and science in order for their test scores and interest not to decline (Salomone, 2003).

Many studies (see for example, Fine, 2003, 2003b) also claim that girls, and especially poor girls, are being silenced in various ways in co-ed schools:

> In low-income schools, then, the process of inquiring into students' lived experience is assumed, a priori, unsafe territory for teachers and administrators. Silencing permeates classroom life so primitively as to render irrelevant the lived experiences, passions, concerns, communities, and biographies of low-income, minority students. In the process, the very voices of these students and their communities, which public education claims to enrich, shut down. (Fine, 2003b, p. 16)

Fine further argues that the students' communities are closed out of the school. This is partially the case at the studied charter school as well evidenced by the parents' lack of knowledge about the science curriculum and classes. However, unlike what Fine describes about suspensions and expulsions as a way to close out the troublemakers, at this school the troublemakers or the disturbing students continued in school except for in severe cases.

SCIENCE AND URBAN GIRLS

Girls tend to disengage from science if they do not find it personally relevant. Without the personal connection they engage in a particular situation related to science but do not develop a personal interest in science (Thompson & Windschitl, 2002). Furthermore, it is important for parents to support their daughters' science interests in order for the interest to withstand peer pressure not to engage in science (Hrabowski, Morton,

Greene, & Greif, 2002). Lee (2002) found that for girls not to become detached from and leave science studies they need to have rewarding social relationships in science studies. They need friends who find science interesting and talk about science as well as teachers who are caring and supportive. Girls will still do well in regular science course work but will not pursue careers in science without this kind of supportive atmosphere. Even though the achievement gap between boys and girls in science is decreasing there are several factors contributing to the gap that still exists (National Science Board, 2004; National Science Foundation, 2004). Often low-income schools have less qualified teachers, which was not the case in the school studied. In schools with high ratios of minority students standardized test preparation is emphasized, inquiry skills are deemphasized, and lower-order skills are emphasized (Oakes, Joseph, & Muir, 2004).

However, these things were not taking place in the school studied. In fact, the school was down playing standardized tests and strived for an inquiry-based curriculum (National Research Council, 2000). However, we also know that in general "without good social order in the organization, including respected leadership, good administration, and acceptance of teachers' authority, other factors—the amount of homework assigned, graduation requirements, or disciplinary routines-will not produce good results" (Useem & Goldstone, 2002, p. 522). In the studied school students clearly did not respect the teachers' authority and the teachers did not respect the coordinators. The issue of discipline was at the forefront every day in the school. The codirectors' respect for the teachers' authority was admirable but there were no larger policies and structures for maintaining order in the school. In this school there were certain values that were to be inculcated into the students. Self-respect and self-discipline were considered important for developing future leaders within math and science. Likewise, work habits were emphasized as can be seen in the internship program. Hennen (2005) argues that

> order, limits, firmness, and respect are qualities of a positive and effective school. Leaders make clear the boundaries of what is acceptable and what is not. They establish a hierarchy of sanctions—and rewards—and insist on their firm, fair, and consistent application. (p. 2)

The success of these measures is related to how well these rules are communicated to teachers, parents, and students. They need to be communicated in many different ways and repeatedly over time (Hennen, 2005; Ramsey, 2002).

Jones (2005) argues that school success requires school goals and a school culture where discipline is used not as an end in itself but a tool to enhance student development. In this school the goals were quite clear and even the expectations of students (called rights and responsibilities) with regard to their work habits were spelled out clearly and posted on walls. However, these expectations were created the summer before our last year at the school and we did not observe a single discussion about or reference to them after they were initially introduced. Hence, it was assumed that because they were stated, students would have the self-discipline to adhere by them. If these goals and expectations had been adhered to there would have been no discipline problems in the school. Hence, it is very clear that the lack of a follow-through in establishing a school culture where students respect each other, their work and their teachers led to chaotic classrooms because it left the teachers with nothing to fall back on since the school tried to avoid punitive actions to enforce appropriate behavior.

THE SCHOOL, THE STUDENTS, AND THE TEACHERS

In many ways this school sounds like the ideal school for urban girls. It was established by a group of powerful women in order to provide a solid and empowering education for urban girls. In this school all attempts are made by well-meaning administrators, teachers, supportive personnel, and outside supporters to provide an education and an environment that will allow the urban girls to empower themselves. The school raises about $100,000 per year to support extra programs. Girls who want to go to universities for summer programs or on science expeditions or an exchange program to Mexico can do so even if they have no financial support from home. In 2004, 68 students went to university or college programs. When equipment is needed for science classes, teachers will get it in most cases. The school provides special education services, access to a nurse and a doctor as well as a team of social workers. There is a college prep class to prepare students for applying to college. Hence, the school genuinely tries to care for the whole girl not just the academic achievement.

The student population is 70% African American, 15% Latina, 13% Caucasian, 1% Asian and 2% multiracial and 70% qualify for free or reduced lunch. Currently the school is located in an old beautiful building with classrooms and stairwells lit up by big windows. The school is very clean and the custodians are always available and have a good relationship with the girls. Since it is a charter school parents choose to send their daughters to this school, which means that at least initially the parents' and in most cases the students' attitudes towards the school are positive (except that some girls did not like the fact that there were no boys). The current enrollment is 325 with a waiting list of 290 girls. Despite the fairly low test scores for the first graduating class in 2004, 77% are attending 4-year colleges/ universities, 14% community colleges and 7% trade or transition programs. So considering typical inner-city schools in the United States, this school sounds ideal.

Unlike many other urban schools, this school has been able to hire formally competent science teachers every year. Many of the teachers have also had practical work experience as scientists working in labs and similar situations. At least one minority science teacher out of four has worked at the school each year. And more importantly since this is a girls' school, they have always been able to hire an almost entirely female staff. Hence, the girls have had female and minority science role models each year.

School Leadership

The two White, female codirectors are experienced urban educators who want to give the girls a solid education. They have progressive ideas about how the school should function. For example, they do not want to micromanage the teachers and their work. They want the teachers to be in charge of their own classrooms not only with regard to the subject matter but also with regard to discipline. The school goal is to care for the whole girl not just the academic side. Hence, the school has several social workers, a nurse, internship program for girls to become acquainted with the world of work, a special education teacher, and a variety of other support personnel. The school also has a unique grading policy. Instead of letter grades the girls' work is graded as not yet proficient, proficient, or high performance. A grade of not yet proficient (called "not-yet" for short) means that students get an incomplete rather than a failing grade on their work. They are allowed virtually unlimited time to make up their incomplete work.

Fine and Weis (2003) argue that schools continue to reproduce the societal inequalities as Bowles and Gintis articulated in 1976. Interestingly in this case the school board and the codirectors have designed a school that could contribute to changing those inequalities. The school with its leadership focus sets high academic standards in math, science, and technology for mostly poor and minority urban girls. Girls, who would normally not get a very strong education, nor go to 4-year colleges and universities now have the opportunities for a college prep education. Along this line of thinking, the classrooms are heterogeneously grouped based on the idea that *all* girls should get an education that prepares them for college. The school actively markets itself as a college preparatory school for all girls and most girls express a desire and plan to go to college.

So, What is the Problem?

The first spring semester of our study all three science teachers and the science director quit. Two of the teachers and the science director had been hired that year and the third science teacher had taught at the school for 2 years, in other words from the start of the school. The second year one teacher left. The third year of the study the science director and two of the three teachers left. The one remaining teacher considered leaving. Each time the teachers have left because they do not feel supported in their work by the codirectors and because of the so-called discipline problem. Unlike most other schools this school does not have a discipline system of detentions and suspensions. However, the science teachers would prefer this kind of traditional discipline system, because from their perspective there is no alternative. Because there is no other alternative system in place other than that the teachers are asked to take care of the problem in their classrooms and in severe cases write up the girls to be sent to the disciplinarian, the classrooms become chaotic. However, the codirectors argue that the lessons should be so interesting that the students do not want to misbehave. Unfortunately, this is not a sufficient plan to deal with the discipline problems. Even if lessons are interesting, there might be students misbehaving at times. From the teachers' perspective the students know that it does not really matter how they behave, because there are no repercussions. Teachers consider students disrespectful to them, other students and themselves as well as the subject matter. Students are considered very loud, talking all the time, not paying attention, not following directions, and disturbing students who want to work. However, as Fine and Weis (2003) point out, the voices could be considered in ways other than as inappropriate and disturbing. All the girls do not see the voices as inappropriate or disturbing. Many girls do not understand why the teachers are upset with them.

Our observations confirm that the classrooms are so loud with most girls talking all the time, that it is often difficult for the teachers to be heard. Students often engage in other activities as well, such as applying makeup, dancing, singing, eating, reading magazines, playing with various objects from their purses, and so forth. They also often get up and walk over to another table for socializing. The first 2 years there was a constant stream of girls going to the bathroom during class time, which was quite disruptive. However, this has been limited to some extent by the teachers, but still students often miss many minutes from, for example, directions for an experiment because of their bathroom visits. Likewise coming late to class is a major disruption. During the second year of the study often a fourth of the class trickled in late, sometimes up to 15-20 minutes late. The first half hour of school every day is devoted to reading, but it is not unusual to see students in the hallway or simply outside school instead of going to class for reading. Students are expected to be mature enough to go to class on their own and there is no consistent enforcement of the rule. The third year because there are more experiments in science classes a majority of students are at times engaged in the actual class activities. However, never are all students engaged.

During class time there are clearly girls who want to work and who are frustrated by the noise and the distractions. Often in one work group of four girls there are one or two who actually do the work, while the others play around and often copy the work at the end of class. In interviews the girls often state that they want to choose which girls to work with in order to get partners with whom they can work and who do work. However, even girls who complain in interviews about the noise and the distractions participate in them in class, because they think they might as well have some fun since no learning is taking place anyway. However, many girls also state that it is not disturbing for them if other girls talk quietly during class.

Why are the Classrooms Chaotic?

The obvious answer seems to be that the school does not have a consistent discipline policy. However, the problem goes beyond this straightforward and relatively simplistic answer. Some of the girls come from homes and communities where it might not be considered unusual for many individuals to talk at the same time, where being loud is not considered a problem; where moving around while talking is perfectly fine. However, this communication style does not fit the middle class culture of the school. The teachers are used to a straightforward give-and-take pattern where students listen when the teacher talks, where the room is otherwise quiet and relatively still, where students answer a question in an orderly and linear fashion. The students have not learnt that in order to be accepted and do well in this school they have to switch to a different mode of interacting once they enter the school building. Teachers try to be tolerant of the noise and ask the students kindly to be quiet. But many of the students might not be used to being asked but told to be quiet. As the students say "she needs to yell at us to be quiet." Hence, the teachers do not see a problem with their teaching style and that it might not be culturally congruent with the students' lives.

Furthermore, many students come from schools that do not have a serious academic culture. This can be seen from, for example, the very low reading levels of the students and their lack of study and work habits. It is not uncommon for the students to be a couple of reading levels below their grade level. The students have not gone to schools where they have been expected to produce and learn serious academic knowledge. Requiring urban girls to take science every semester as in this school is not the norm but the exception. As many of the girls say, they learn more in this school despite the chaotic classrooms. However, there has not been a sincere extended effort in this school to socialize the girls to a different mode of communication and self-discipline even though self-discipline is a goal of this school.

Since this school is concerned with the emotional and social development of the girls as well, it has led the administrators to not setting strict boundaries for acceptable behavior and speech. The codirectors want the girls to have all chances to succeed and develop. As experienced urban educators, they are wary of placing strict and excessive limits on the girls as is done in most urban schools. Most of the girls come from schools with traditional discipline procedures and where girls are not really expected to take a stand and defend their views. In other words, they come from schools where they have been silenced. The parents have chosen to remove their daughters from their assigned schools and send them to this charter school because they were dissatisfied with how the schools treated their daughters. They want the school to care about their daughters' intellectual and emotional needs. However, in encouraging the girls to develop their voice this school has gone to the other extreme where there is almost complete freedom, which in a way becomes both a terror and terrifying. Where are the limits? How far can students go? Teachers are constantly tested and pushed to their limits and sometimes beyond their limits. The girls admit that they know they misbehave terribly but continue to do so because the teachers let them continue to misbehave. The heterogeneously grouped classrooms exacerbate the misbehavior since the teachers push the academic limits of some of the students, but certainly not of the more advanced students. Teachers also like the heterogeneous groups, but are not very skilled in teaching these kinds of groups, which in turn leads to the fact that the classes do not run as smoothly as they could. The less advanced students cannot keep up with the pace and the more advanced students are bored.

The girls feel free and safe to express themselves. They state that it is much easier to ask questions and offer comments in this all girls' school than it is in a regular school with boys. The girls have developed their voice since coming to this school but it is an undisciplined voice that is hurting themselves as well as terrorizing others. The girls want and feel free to express themselves on most issues and often in opposition to a lot of activities. However, in this way they prevent those who do want to work from advancing. Unfortunately, this is the only way the girls know how to behave if they want to be noticed and heard. However, in this way they contribute to their own silencing because these kinds of voices do not fit the middle class culture of the school. In other words, the teachers try to shut them down because their voices are considered disturbing and distracting.

Teachers try to encourage students to do the work by allowing them to turn in work late and to take "not yets" as a grade. However, by turning in homework and class work late it also means that they, and often the entire class, are lagging behind despite the teachers' efforts to assist all students needing help with the subject matter. The teachers expect the students to finish their work and therefore work with them individually in class, during the daily homeroom as well as after school. Students do not understand the next project or segment because they have not finished the previous one. When students cannot follow what is going on and it is not interesting, they become more disruptive. For example, in one classroom the intention was to go over the homework in 5 minutes, but very few students (approximately 4 out of 30) had done the homework at home. The students got 40 minutes to do it in class, which meant that the few who had done it had nothing to do during the entire class. Students know that there are no consequences even if they do not do the homework or the work in class. Unfortunately this prevents the students who want to work from achieving at more than the minimum level. The instruction becomes even harder for the weaker students to follow since the basic knowledge level is quite low to start out with. For example, the eighth grade teacher was talking about pollution and a student asked if pollution is good or bad. Hence, she had no understanding of the basic concept or of the language used.

The teachers say that they genuinely care about the students but are only starting to develop an understanding of their educational and living backgrounds. Previous research indicates that it is essential for marginalized students to feel that the teachers know them as persons not just as students. High impact teachers make students feel they are part of the school. They use their authority instead of punitive measures for class discipline and make their classroom procedures and expectations very explicit (Ladson-Billings, 1994; Schlosser, 1992). Unlike what the teachers in this study believe, stricter discipline procedures might not be the solution. It is only a part of the solution. The science teachers in this school have no authority in the classroom. One of the questions emerging is of course, how do young, inexperienced teachers acquire authority? A simple strategy may be to start by making expectations very explicit and reinforcing them daily at the beginning of each class.

At this school the teachers do not know the students personally. Personal talk and discussions directly related to students' lives are not part of the classroom discourse. For example, teachers do not ask the students about their weekends, spring break, or how their mother or sister is doing. Personal tragedies are not part of the class time. Teachers have a sense that students have difficult home lives, but never pursue it with regard to what kind of support students might need in the classroom. Most of the teachers make themselves available to students before and after school, and many students come to work on the homework or work they did not do in class. But even on these occasions the talk is not personal. Most of the teachers never place a phone call to the parents regardless of whether the students are doing well or not. The teachers find it too difficult to call parents since they do not know them at all. Each teacher is responsible for an advisory group of about 20 students. They meet the parents of these students to discuss the overall school progress. However, there is no time or space during parent-teacher conferences for the science teachers to discuss the science progress with parents.

Virtually all parents interviewed said that they did not know much about what was going on in science classes. Interestingly, students also reported that they had much more homework in other subjects. They could always make up the science homework in class because the science teachers gave them extra time to do so. Hence, the parents did not learn about science through the homework either. Fuller (2000) found that charter schools, and especially those for poor and minority students, have difficulties sustaining parent involvement. Successful schools tend to have at least the parents' trust if not the involvement. Students bring in their lives to school, but they are not heard by the teachers. Students talk all the time but mostly not about science. Interestingly, the question becomes: Do the students have a voice in this school? They have a voice in the sense that they have managed to institute surface changes such as dances and eighth grade graduation ceremonies, the elimination of the dress code, a student council, and so forth. However, in the classrooms do students have a voice if they are not heard? In many ways the students have the power in the science classrooms. Through their disruptive behavior they set the stage for what can be done and what is accomplished with regard to science (See, for example, Gibson, 1988 and Willis, 1977 regarding student resistance and opposition). However, the teachers are closed to their voices, the teachers simply consider them disruptive and the end result is that many students are silenced by the disruptive students and all students' science learning suffers severely. As a consequence their future prospects with regard to college and job opportunities become limited since they do not get the science foundation they could acquire.

Another reason for student opposition is the teachers' inability to connect science to the everyday life of the students. For example, many of the girls are pregnant or teen mothers or at least they all know someone who is pregnant, but when they discussed the cell they did it more as an abstraction rather than connecting it to pregnancy. The curricula they use are in most cases inquiry based, but teachers need to have the courage to deviate from the curriculum to make it relevant and more intriguing by connecting it to their students' lives. This is of course difficult if you do not know the students' lives outside school. However, the curriculum could be connected to a relatively close physical environment very easily. For example, instead of examining invasive species and reproduction patterns in Lake Victoria as in the textbook they could examine the invasive species in the nearby lake. However, they never go to the lake which is just a few miles away for any science related project. This lack of exploration of the local physical environment is related to the girls' misbehavior on field trips. The teachers do not want to take the girls on field trips because it is impossible to convince them to pay attention and behave in appropriate ways. However, there is one field trip for most of the school related to a science project. In this case, in order to maintain control over the girls and the activities, all students have very specific tasks to accomplish and there is no real room for free exploration even though this is an outdoor field trip.

Researchers (Fine & Weis, 2003) tend to speak about students, and in particular poor and minority girls, as being silenced and about the issue of having a voice as very simple straightforward issues. However, this study indicates that having a voice is fairly complicated. In this study it is clear that students want and need to be heard, but some students contribute partially to the silencing of other students as well as of themselves by constantly using an undisciplined voice and a voice that is considered as disturbing by the school. In particular, because teachers lack an understanding of what the students' lives are really like, they hear students mostly as a disturbing noise. Teenagers need structures within which they can develop and be challenged. Too much choice and freedom becomes disorienting and challenging in an unproductive way since the limits have to be tested at all times. Finally do students have a voice if teachers do not hear them and is this kind of undisciplined voice empowering for the girls? We argue that by not requiring students to adhere to the rights and responsibilities as agreed on by students and staff, the school with the codirectors and the teachers contribute to the disempowerment of the girls they want to give a voice and empower.

CONCLUSION

The urban girls in this study feel safe and confident enough to speak up in this all girls' school. The founders and codirectors have made an attempt to create a middle and high school that make it possible for urban girls to go on to college and nontraditional careers. However, despite all the good intentions, support, resources, and qualified teachers the girls do not get the intended education because of, among other things, the exclusion of the girls' lives which ultimately disempowers them by delegitimizing them, their knowledge, and identities. The school has not created a curriculum and culture where science is personally relevant, and the girls do not have friends who are excited about science, which would help them become personally invested in science and a science career. Interestingly, being in an all girls' school does not necessarily mean that science is adapted to an all girls' student population. Furthermore, the science instruction is not adapted to an urban, mostly poor and minority, female student population. Teachers and codirectors acknowledge that there is a problem in the school, but the problem is seen mostly as limited to a discipline problem. The codirectors blame the teachers and the teachers blame the co-directors for being unsupportive. In neither case do they see the larger systemic issues. This means that any change will be a band-aid for an immediate visible problem without addressing the underlying issues of a lack of cultural understanding of the girls and their needs.

REFERENCES

DeBare, I. (2004). *Where girls come first: The rise, fall, and surprising revival of girls' School*. New York: Penguin.

Fine, M. (2003a). Sexuality, schooling, and adolescent females: the missing discourse of desire. In M. Fine & L. Weis (Eds.), *Silenced voices and extraordinary conversations ... reimagining schools* (pp. 38- 67). New York: Teachers College Press.

Fine, M. (2003b). Silencing and nurturing voice in an improbable context: urban adolescents in public school. In M. Fine & L. Weis (Eds.), *Silenced voices and extraordinary conversations ... reimagining schools* (pp. 13-27). New York: Teachers College Press.

Fine, M., & Weis, L. (Eds.). (2003). *Silenced voices and extraordinary conversations ... reimagining schools*. New York: Teachers College Press.

Fuller, B. (Ed). (2000). *Inside charter schools. The paradox of radical decentralization*. Cambridge, MA: Harvard University Press.

Gibson, M. A. (1988). *Accommodation without assimilation: Sikh immigrants in an American high school*. Ithaca, New York: Cornell University Press.

Hennen, C. (2005, February 14). Discipline or disorder: Building a healthy school climate. *Teachers College Record*. Retrieved March 29, 2005, from http://www.tcrecord.org ID Number:11747

Herr, K., & Arms, E. (2004). Accountability and single-sex schooling: A collision of reform agendas. *American Educational Research Journal, 41*, 527-555.

Hrabowski, F. A., Maton, K. I., Greene, M. L., & Greif, G. L. (2002). *Overcoming the odds. Raising academically successful African American young women*. Oxford, England: Oxford University Press.

Jones (2005, February 14). More discipline? *Teachers College Record*, R2005. Retrieved March 29, 2005, from http://www.tcrecord.org. ID Number: 11746

Ladson-Billings, G. (1994). *The dreamkeepers: Successful teachers of African American children*. San Francisco: Jossey-Bass.

National Coalition of Girls Schools. (2005). *The girls' school experience. A survey of alumnae of single-sex schools*. Retrieved January 28, 2006, from www.ncgs.org/public.pdf/2005_NCGS_Young-Alumnae_Survey.pdf

Lee, J. D. (2002). More than ability, gender and personal relationships influence science and technology involvement. *Sociology of Education, 75*, 349-373.

National Research Council. (2000). *Inquiry and the National Science Education Standards: A guide for teaching and learning*. Washington, DC: National Academy.

National Science Board. (2004). *National Science Board, Science and Engineering Indicators—2004, Vol. 1*. Washington, DC: National Science Foundation.

National Science Foundation. (2004). *Women, minorities, and persons with disabilities in science and engineering*. Arlington, VA: National Science Foundation, Division of Science Resources Statistics.

Oakes, J., Joseph, R., & Muir, K. (2004). Access and achievement in mathematics and science: Inequalities that endure and change. In J. A. Banks & C. A. Banks (Eds.), *Handbook of research on multicultural education* (2nd ed., pp. 69-90). San Francisco: Jossey-Bass.

Ramsey, R. D. (2002). *Administrator's complete school discipline guide: Techniques and materials for creating an environment where kids can learn*. San Francisco: Jossey-Bass.

Salomone, R. C. (2003). *Same, different, equal. Rethinking single-sex schooling*. New Haven, CT: Yale University Press.

Shapka, J. D., & Keating, D. P. (2003). Effects of girls-only curriculum during adolescence: Performance, persistence, and engagement in mathematics and science. *American Educational Research Journal, 40*, 929-960.

Schlosser, L. K. (1992). Teacher distance and student engagement: School lives on the margin. *Journal of Teacher Education, 43*(2), 128-140.

Thompson, J. J., & Windschitl, M. A. (2002). *Failing girls: Engagement in science learning among girls who are academically at-risk*. Paper presented at the National Association for Research in Science Teaching Conference, New Orleans, LA.

Useem, B., & Goldstone, J. A. (2002). Forging social order and its breakdown: Riot and reform in U.S. prisons. *American Sociological Review, 67*, 499-525.

Willis, P. (1977). *Learning to labour: How working class kids get working class jobs*. New York: Columbia University Press.

PART IV

RACE AND ETHNICITY

CHAPTER 10

BLACK BOYS THROUGH THE SCHOOL-PRISON PIPELINE

When "Racial Profiling" and "Zero Tolerance" Collide

R. Patrick Solomon and Howard Palmer

Current and projected demographic trends of racial minority growth rates that overtake dominant Whites in some Canadian cities[1] have rekindled the debate for equitable and democratic schooling of Black students in urban schools. Historically, such environments have proven to be uncompromising to socioracial groups in their struggle to escape a system of poverty, exploitation, and marginalization. Complicating such marginalization are ways the authority structure of schools and other institutions of power perceive and respond to such racial groups as Blacks. Recently, the popularized notion of "racial profiling" has focused attention on the surveillance and over-policing of Black life in urban communities,[2] but to what extent is such profiling a reality in schools, and how does it impact the lived experiences and life opportunities of Black youth?

In this chapter we argue that the institutional practice of negatively profiling Black youth is not only a reality in contemporary schooling, but

Inclusion in Urban Educational Environments:
Addressing Issues of Diversity, Equity, and Social Justice, 191–212
Copyright © 2006 by Information Age Publishing
All rights of reproduction in any form reserved.

is historically rooted; it predates the popular discourses of "racial profiling" and "zero tolerance" that dominate current public debates. We provide critical insights into how the volatile mix of stereotyping and intolerance lead to a disproportionate removal of Black youth from normal classroom learning with their eventual destination being secure custody institutions, a process Skiba, Simmons, Staudinger, Rausch, Dow, and Feggins (2003) conceptualize as the "school-prison pipeline." To conclude, we offer ideas for disrupting the "pipeline" and construct instead a critical, reflective, socially just praxis for Black youth in their schools and communities.

THE BLACK MALE AND AUTHORITY RELATIONS

In this review of the research we focus on how educational structures in Britain, the United States and Canada respond to Blacks as a racialized minority,[3] and how their responses to males, in particular, help to construct them as a group to be feared, monitored, and channelled to restrictive learning environments. Carby's (1982) British study uncovers strategies utilized by a network of institutions to intervene in all aspects of Black life. As a law enforcement agency, the police collaborated with the school and an army of youth workers, community workers, social workers, probation officers, school counsellors to intervene in the domestic, public, social, and educational lives of disenfranchised youth. Under the guise of developing good police-community relations, the police invaded the academic lives of students. This strategy is often referred to as a "soft-centred" form of control with the objective of reducing lawlessness in the community and developing law-abiding citizens out of Black youth. Carby concludes: "The construction of the 'fear' of crime by Black youth is used as a justification to police them in schools. Policing them in the classroom also aids with identifying and monitoring Black youth on the streets" (p. 207).

Subsequent British studies (Furlong, 1984; Gillborn, 1988; Mac an Ghaill, 1989; Sewell, 1997a, 1997b) document the continued negative attitudes and coercive behaviors of school personnel toward Black males. The characterization of these students as aggressive, violent, disruptive, and deviant grew out of a discourse of fear, as is evident in Sewell's (1997a) work: *Teacher Attitude: Who's Afraid of the big Black boy?* The presence of fear and social distancing between White teachers and Black youth creates an inhospitable climate for the teaching-learning process.

In the United States, the school environment is similarly inhospitable to Black students. They are marginalized in classroom social relations as teachers provide much greater learning opportunities, open encouragement, extended directions, rewards, praise and reinforcement to White students. The authority structure and power relations generated by mistrust and fear based on racial bias are well documented (Ferguson, 2000; Hopkins, 1997; Kreisberg, 1992, Kunjufu, 1983; Watson & Smitherman, 1992). Murray and Clark (1990) conclude, "(R)acism exists when school leaders down play the existence, gravity or the significance of acts of bias against minority students" (p. 24). Most of these studies focused on Black male culture of resistance and the system's coercive responses to it. As Black youths become alienated from a school structure they perceive as not representing their interest, they develop a vibrant, dynamic, nonconformist, counter-school culture that is threatening to the authority structures. The reallocation of resources from teaching to security personnel and sophisticated electronic surveillance systems reposition these institutions of learning as sites of control and containment. Blacks and other students from marginalized groups again find their educational and social growth as citizens in a democratic state seriously compromised.

In multiracial Canada, the authority relations within its institutions are mediated, to a large extent, by race. The influx of African Caribbean immigrants into Canada following the de-racialization of its immigration policies in the late 1960s made visible a brand of racism that escaped public scrutiny over the years. Established and entrenched European norms, values, traditions pervasive in Canadian institutions immediately cast new racialized minority immigrants as socioculturally dislocated, dysfunctional, and deviant in their family, community, and school life (da Costa, 1978; Dei, 1996; Solomon & Brown, 1998). To maintain some measure of power and control in their schools and communities these students developed distinct subcultural forms of behavior as a response to top-down, imposed control. Such a strident subculture collided with the authority of the school causing a spiralling of negative interactions that often led to the intervention of the police in schools (Solomon, 1992).

What has emerged from the literature is the construction of Blacks as fearful, deviant, socially dysfunctional, nonconformist and a threat to the safety and smooth functioning of the school as a social system. Moving from the sociological construction to applied profiling, the Ontario Human Rights Commission (2003) Inquiry Report: *Paying the Price: The Human Cost of Racial Profiling*, defines racial profiling as:

> any action undertaken for reason of safety, security or public protection that relies on stereotypes of race, colour, ethnicity, ancestry, religion, or place of origin rather than on reasonable suspicion, to single out an individual for greater scrutiny or different treatment. (p. 6)

The report provides examples of those in position of power and authority (i.e., law enforcement officials, private security guards, custom officers and school authorities) who practise racial profiling. This selected review captures the history and pervasiveness of profiling behavior in British, Canadian and Unites States institutions and societies, and its potential impact on social relations and the opportunity structure for Black youth. It is to the authority structure of schools and its supporting policies that we now turn.

Safe Schools Policies and "Zero Tolerance"

Rigid, "get tough" school discipline, codes of conduct and zero tolerance policies have brought a new dimension to the management of student behaviors in schools. A growing concern over the perceived increase in school violence and the prevalence of guns and drug use in U.S. schools in the 1980s and 90s led to more severe penalties with the hope that these would reduce intolerable behaviors in school. Zero tolerance policies for these and other school infractions were gradually implemented in school jurisdictions across the United States and Canada without the benefit of research confirming that such disciplinary measures result in safer schools (Ayers, Ayers, & Dohrn, 2001; Castella, 2001; Jull, 2000; Shannon & McCall, 2004; Skiba & Peterson, 1999).

These and other researchers have launched a wide-ranging critique of zero tolerance and its impact on schools and the students they serve. Such critique includes the growing popularity of zero tolerance as the approach that policy makers believe will secure schools as safe learning environments for students; media's contribution to such popularity through its sensationalization of violence and their misuse of statistics that vilify youth and their culture (Ayers et al., 2001; Jull, 2000; Skiba & Peterson, 1999); the displacement of troubled youth from the controlled social learning environment of the school to the less controlled neighborhoods where they engage in more serious offences (Ayers et al., 2001; Skiba et al., 2003; Thorson, 1996); school administrators' abdication of their responsibility for students' education and safety to security guards, law enforcement agencies and the juvenile court system (Ayers et al., 2001; Castella, 2001; Solomon, 1992); and zero tolerance policies' "one size fits all" approach based on the assumption that such policies are nondiscriminatory and treat all students equally (Jull, 2000; Cole, 1999; Epp, 1997; Larson & Ovando, 2001; Shannon & McCall, 2004; Skiba & Peterson, 1999).

The Canadian Association of Principals (CAP) report: *Zero tolerance policies in Context: A preliminary investigation to identify actions to improve school discipline and school safety* (Shannon & McCall, 2004) raises serious questions about the rigidity and prescriptive nature of zero tolerance policies, the variance in interpretation and implementation of such policies, and the unintended consequences of zero tolerance (pp. 3-4). These critiques all indicate the pervasiveness of the issue, but it is this last critique that is of most relevance to this paper. Zero tolerance policies do not take into consideration the social and environmental contexts of interpersonal interaction when deliberating youth's infraction of school rules and regulations. The emerging research appears to point to a zero tolerance policy that discriminates against Blacks more than any other racial groups (Jull, 2000).

Emerging from the research on Black students and institutional structures in Britain, the United States, and Canada are some conceptual and theoretical issues that inform the present study. The nature of power and power relations in institutional settings is top-down, impositional, and coercive and is imposed under the guise of maintenance of discipline. Essential to the maintenance of power and authority is a network of structures: the school, social service agencies in the community, and the criminal justice system that operate in symbiotic relationship with each other. Students who feel victimized by the system engage in this counter-hegemonic struggle using "cultural power," a creative use of popular subcultural forms generated from their ethnic heritages and their lived experiences of struggle. This collision of cultural empowerment and the institutional power of schools set up a spiralling negative interaction that leads to alienation and distancing between students and school authority. Such a conflict often results in the enforcement of the zero tolerance policy and the students' eventual exclusion from school. The rest of this paper provides students' accounts of how power and authority operate within schools and the communities in which they reside and how their lives were impacted in these settings. We analyze these narratives within the larger framework of racial profiling in multiracial societies and zero tolerance policies within schools. We conclude with some strategies for transforming schools into more equitable and accountable institutions for racialized minorities.

RESEARCH SETTING AND PARTICIPANTS

The study was conducted in 1995-96 in an urban residential school, Hopeful Village Youth Centre (pseudonym), a provincially operated institution for incarcerated youth. The school operates in conjunction with a treatment and correctional facility within the same physical complex. The Centre serves a large metropolitan area in Ontario and the students are young offenders with a history of behavioral problems in their home, school, and community who are sentenced to this institution. Under the Young Offenders Act of Canada, a young offender is one who has committed an offence and is convicted and sentenced to serve time in a secure setting. In addition to being removed from their home communities for a period of custody, youths who break the law are placed in a setting such as Hopeful Village where professionals are committed to identifying and responding to their needs, with the goal of fostering personal growth and ultimately achieving community reintegration.

At the time of the study, the Centre accommodated about 70 male and female students altogether, ranging in age from 14 to 18 years. There were approximately 75 residential counsellors, teachers, youth officers, clinicians, and other medical and therapeutic staff. All but seven were White, and of the seven, four were of African heritage. There was an over-representation of African Caribbean boys at the Centre; Whites as well as other ethnic minority youth reflected the diversity of the catchment area of the Centre but they were represented to a lesser extent. Participants in the study were 15 male students of African Caribbean heritage, ranging in age from 14 to 18 years in keeping with the age range in the school population. They were selected from students who were: in the 9th to 12th grade and who were in secure custody and detention within the facility; spending at least 6 months in the institution; and a mix of second generation African Caribbean and immigrant youth.

The official archival records of the Youth Centre (Ontario School Records and other institutional records) provide demographic profiles of youths' family constructs and residential localities, and their school and community deviance that contributed to their incarceration. Information gleaned from these official records fell into three categories: (a) home and family related social history: intrafamily relationships, family dysfunctionality, migration, and transplantation experiences; (b) schooling history: academic and social progress; psychological assessment, special education placements, behavior dysfunctionality, and (c) community functioning; information related to offences committed under the Young Offenders Act; involvement with such service providers as Children's Aid Society (CAS), probation and the courts, social workers, the police. From the documented history of these African Caribbean boys emerged a profile of frequent suspensions from school because of disobedience and non-conformity to classroom expectations, opposition to school authority, physical confrontations, and fighting in school. In the community these youth continued to engage in delinquent and nonconformist behaviors. They eventually came to the attention of law enforcement agencies and were subsequently incarcerated in secure custody institutions such as Hopeful Village Youth Centre. Reasons for incarceration were summarized as unmanageable and dysfunctional behaviors in the home, deviant and counter-school activities in school, and delinquent and law-breaking behaviors in the community. Missing from the above official documentation is the participants' own narratives of their reality. What emerges from this study are two scripts: the "official" as documented above and the "unofficial" self-report of the boys' lived experiences. We try to "make sense" of these contradictory perspectives and theorize about the power relations that mediate these realities.

The methodological approach used in this study provides insights into students' lived experiences in their schools and communities leading up to their incarceration. Lang and van des Molan, with Trower and Look (1990) and Linde (1981) suggest that by accepting informants' oral history, and by encouraging them to put their thoughts into words the researcher can form a picture of informants' experiential world; and the role of institutions and organizations in shaping the experiences of the informants. In this study the oral history focused specifically on the school and community dimensions of the informants' lives. Data collection was ongoing and accumulative. Themes emerging in the early stages were used as a basis for further exploration at subsequent "rap sessions" between the researcher and informants. This process of identifying common themes is what Polkinghorne (1993) terms "paradigmatic analysis." The principles of "constant comparative" method (Strauss, 1987) provided an approach whereby initial data from early informants generated probe questions for subsequent dialogues. The new data helped to strengthen emerging patterns and helped formulate generalizations. The findings that emerged from the study provide subjective views of authority structures and their arbitrary use of power in institutional settings.

Constructing the "School-Prison Pipeline"

From the perspective of the students, racial discrimination and negative authority relations in the schooling process became an obstacle to academic achievement. Further, the intervention of child welfare and law enforcement agencies in the schooling of Black youth sets up a "pipeline" that leads to incarceration in secure custody institutions.

Students' Experience of Racial Discrimination

An emerging theme in this study was students' lived experiences within racism, the antagonistic relationship this created between school authorities and themselves, and the potential impact on their academic achievement. Such perception was often generated from the differential treatment accorded Black and White students in areas of surveillance and monitoring within the school and exclusion from school. The following narratives reflect these perceptions:

> I fought with a guy and the principal gave me twenty days suspension. I am saying to myself, twenty days—that is very long. That's a lot of days missing [school] and they know that twenty days from school and I am not going to be able to pass [my year]. I am also saying to myself, why? Because two White youths in my class fought; they beat up one kid and they got only five days suspension. And then the teacher offered to give them [school] work to do at home. But me, they didn't offer me any. When I went to the school to ask them for schoolwork they refused and told me that I am not supposed to be on school property. I was saying, "Well, that's life." This happens to me all the time, so I'm used to it. I cared, but I didn't care because nothing's going to change anyway. (Brian)

> I got suspended one time for touching the glue without asking [the teacher]. We were doing art and I went to the back of the class and picked up the glue and brought it back to my table and started using it, and the teacher said, "Why did you touch the glue without asking?" I was then sent to the office and got two days suspension for that. (Tom)

Dissatisfaction with the principal's handling of his suspension was also expressed by Tom in this way: "The principal would not even say anything to me. He just told me to sit down and said, 'I am calling your mother and you are suspended.' He wouldn't even ask me what happened or nothing."

> I was suspended lots of time for the simplest thing. There were White kids that were involved, but I never seen them get suspended. There weren't many Black kids in school then anyway. The school was in a mostly a White neighbourhood. It was so hard because they didn't really look at me as someone that was gonna go anywhere. They think that I was a trouble-maker, so they just thought, "Okay, he's not really here to learn in school so what's the point of us helping him?" They just said, "Here's your work, do your work." When I asked for help, they would never come and help me, really. I was basically an outcast in the school. (David)

The narratives capture the extent of the social and authority relations within their schools. First, they express dissatisfaction with the arbitrary use of suspensions and additionally, its differential use based on race. Second, the school's geographical location within a predominantly White neighborhood and the limited number of Black students in attendance contributed to the feelings of isolation and marginalization. Finally, and most importantly, were the boys' perceived status within the social and academic structure of the school. David's label as a "trouble-maker" who did not take school seriously mediated the teaching-learning process and the pedagogical approach was perceived as one-directional and nontransactional.

Surveillance and Monitoring

The intrusive surveillance and monitoring of Black life increased their dissatisfaction with the schooling process. For example, consider James' experience:

> The school gave me a lock for my locker. They wouldn't let me put my own lock on. When I put my lock on they wanted the combination. They used to go through my locker all the time. I come in on Monday morning and my locker is ransacked, turned upside down, papers all over the place.

Many students perceived their experiences of arbitrary and differential treatment to be discriminatory and punitive. Peter explains:

> I was walking in the hallway going to the washroom. Then one teacher saw me and dragged me down to the principal's office saying that I was skipping class. She said, "Look at him, he has nothing, no books or anything. He is skipping last period." Then they called my teacher and he told them that he had given me permission to go to the washroom. The teacher who dragged me down to the office had to say sorry. But I know that she still hates me.

There have been arbitrary suspensions for being in the hallway, even with the permission of the teacher, for the type of dress they wear and for interacting with their friends. Harvey explains:

> I am walking in the hallways sometimes and the principal would pull me over and bring me straight down to the office and tell me that I am not going back to my class. He would suspend me for a day or two for that. He doesn't even ask my teacher if I had permission to be out in the hallway. He just went straight ahead and suspended me. He would pick on me for different reasons. Like, if I am talking to my friends, he'll come over and start saying some stuff like we can't do this and can't do that, or we can't dress like this. And they would suspend me for that reason. Like, we can't roll up our pant legs, or we can't put our pants in our socks, or we can't wear our shirts inside out.

> I went to a different high school, thinking that it would be all right because it is a new school, new principal and everything. When I went there the

principal knew every charge that I had on my record; everything. So right off the bat I knew things weren't going to work. I tried anyway, and got four credits first semester. But when second semester came around things started to get rough. They started putting me on some *Tracking Sheet*[4] for no reason. (James)

Such intense monitoring of Black life in schools is consistently documented in the research literature (Carby, 1982; Gillborn, 1988; Sewell, 1997a, b; Solomon, 1992). As a response to such authority structure students label teachers as "judgemental, vindictive, wicked, mean, authoritarian, prejudiced, racists, "crocked" [dishonest], and "scheming" [conspiratorial]" (Solomon, 1992, p. 52). Such negative labeling reflects the negative and disharmonious relationship that developed between school agents and Black boys, the widening of the "racial divide," and the potential social and academic exclusion of the boys from the schooling process.

Police Intervention in Schooling

The findings revealed collusion between the authority structure of the school and law enforcement agents in dealing with Black youth. From student narratives such interventions were coercive, punitive and often humiliating.

One day I skipped a class and went to the Mall and when I came back in the afternoon the principal came to my class and said that he wanted to speak with me. When I came out of the class, two police officers held me, put me up against the lockers, handcuffed me and carried me through the school the long way, so that when the bell rang everybody in the school saw me. Actually, they took me to the office that is in the front of the school, close to where the students wait for their buses. The police took me and stood in front of the office. One officer stood there and held me. At the same time all the students were lining up to take their buses and they kept asking me, "What happen, what happen, what did you do?" The whole school had seen me.[5] (James)

Other studies have also implicated the police as an extension of, or supplement to the school's discipline machine (Ayers et al., 2001; Carby, 1982; Solomon, 1992). Such interventions are potentially damaging to the reputation of schools' ability to maintain an independent authority structure. Students may perceive such relinquishing of its responsibility for maintaining control as a serious loss of power. Even more damaging in the long run is the negative social relations that are being incubated in the school between Black youth and the police.

The study also revealed a continuity of police surveillance and interrogation of Black youth from the school into the community. Student narratives express fear, dislike, and open antagonism toward the police. The following excerpts represent the general feeling of the informants in the study:

> I fought with a White guy who was bigger than me. But I got charged. My mom called the police and asked them to charge the guy I fought with. The police were acting like they did not want to charge the guy for what he did to me. It seems like the police wanted me badly. They kept on asking kids in the community, "Does Brian do anything to you guys? Does Brian take any money from you?" So now I go to court and got convicted for assault, right? And since all this time we know that the [White] youth still hasn't been charged. So then the police are on my case, on my back, every little thing, like trying to cause problems for me. I'm riding my bike, they'll go, "Oh, where did you get that bike?" Like, I'm some big criminal. (Brian)

Tom expresses his fears and perception of police racism.

> I don't know what's going on, but if I look out my window, I'll see two police officers chasing a Black guy, or a guy on the sidewalk being beaten by a police officer for no reason. The way it looks, if I don't move out of this neighbourhood I'm not going to live that long or last that long. I know that when I get older like them, the police are gonna do the same thing to me as they do to these people.

Peter sees the police as being on his case constantly. He gives the following example:

> One time I went behind a Budget [rent-a-car] parking lot to urinate, right? Somebody must have seen me and called the police. The police came and took me down to the station. But nothing was wrong with any of the cars 'cause I didn't touch any of them. So all that time [spent at the police station] for nothing.

Harvey expressed his dislike for the police based on his perception that the police constantly harass people. In fact, he compares the police with his school principal with whom he had a physical confrontation and by whom he was charged and finally convicted and sent to Hopeful Village Youth Centre.

> I don't really like them [police]. They behave like the principal; always on your case. But the police behave even worse. They handle you in a different way. Like if you don't tell them this or that, they will start beating you up for not telling them what they want to hear. And I don't like that. (Harvey)

In this section we provided the informants' perspectives on the police overzealous intervention into the lives of Blacks in their communities. Such perception of overpolicing was viewed with contempt as the boys interpret these acts as attempts to intimidate and criminalize them. The issue of criminalizing youth has been a matter of much debate within Black communities, commissioned studies and in the research literature (Gittens et al., 1995; Wordes & Bynum, 1995; Wordes, Bynum, & Corley, 1994). In the next section we theorize about the outcome of schooling for Black youth in rigid, authoritarian school structures.

When "Racial Profiling" and "Zero Tolerance" Collide

The reflective voices of Black youth in a secure custody institution raise serious questions about race and public schooling in multiracial societies. These narratives depict schools as repressive, coercive, undemocratic, authoritarian, and racist. The outcome of such racist schooling for Black students is often removal from the mainstream and placement in alternative institutions where opportunities for full and free participation in societal life is seriously diminished. What is the process for such marginalization? First, Black students respond to undemocratic and coercive schooling in many ways. Conflict theorists often locate students' counter-school behaviors within a sociopolitical context; schools become contested terrains in the struggle between the dominant and the marginalized over power and control (Collins, 1974; Bowles & Gintis, 1976). Black youth creatively utilize a potent mix of ethno-specific forms of behavior, popular youth culture, and aspects of their institutional life to create a vibrant counter culture (Foster, 1986; Furlong, 1984; Marotto, 1977; Solomon, 1992).

Even more detrimental to the youths' futures are the labels that lead to incarceration in secure custody institutions. The escalating negative spiral between authoritarian practices and students' resistance to them lead to "time out" at the principal's office, detention, in-school suspension, short term suspension, long term suspension, and finally, interventions by the criminal justice system. Here, the youth is faced with a new cadre of system agents: the police, the crown and legal counsel, the judiciary, probation officers, community workers, and eventually, institutional workers "behind bars." The nature and intensity of these involvements in the lives of the youths are well documented in their school records and clinical files analyzed for this study.

To what extent are our informants' perceptions of the authority structure of the school and police intervention corroborated by other research? For our response, we analyzed the results of three landmark Canadian studies. The first is the Report of the Commission on systemic racism in the Ontario Criminal Justice System that explores the practices, procedures, and policies of three major components of the system: the police, the courts and correctional institutions (Gittens et al., 1995). Perceptions, experiences and outcomes of the justice process were found to closely reflect the perceptions and experiences of the Black youths at Hopeful Village Youth Centre. Regarding racial discrimination in community policing the report concluded:

> Perceptions that the police discriminate against Black and other racialized people are widespread. A Commission survey shows that 74% of Black, 54% of Chinese, and 47% of White Metropolitan Toronto residents believe that the police do not treat Black people the same as White people. About nine in ten of those who perceive differential treatment believe the police treat Black people worse than White people, and more than seven in ten think it occurs about half the time or more. (Gittens et al., 1995, p. ix)

Regarding policing and school discipline, the report found school authority complicit in the differential policing of Black students in schools: "Some schools are quick to summon the police when Black lives are alleged perpetrators of harmful or inappropriate behavior, but are more likely to handle similar behaviour by White students or other racialized students internally" (Gittens et al., 1995, p. 361).

The second study also relates to the judiciary and its dealing with Black youth and the police. In an unprecedented turn of events, a Black female judge in the province of Nova Scotia, Canada, based on her understanding of a racist society and her personal experience of the social reality in Nova Scotia, acquitted a Black, 15-year-old boy of all charges brought against him by a White police officer. In her summative remarks she concluded, "Police officers had been known to mislead the court in the past, and they had been known to overreact particularly with non-White groups, and that would indicate a questionable state of mind" (Supreme Court of Canada, 1997, p. 6). Such a position was challenged by the police and crown attorney on the ground of a "reasonable apprehension of bias." Through a series of appeals her judgement was upheld by the Supreme Court of Canada. This ruling signalled, for the first time, the possibility of assigning credibility to Black youth and their experience of racist subordination in Canadian society.

A more recent study: *Paying the Price: The Human Cost of Racial Profiling*, by the Ontario Human Rights Commission (2003), concludes: "Racial profiling is a form of racial discrimination. As racial profiling exists in [Canadian] society, it also exists in institutions such as law enforcement agencies, the education system, the criminal justice system etc., which are a microcosm of broader society" (p. 13). The report moved beyond proof of the existence of racial profiling to point out that those most likely to engage in the practice are people in positions of authority who "may consciously or unconsciously exercise power differently when dealing with racialized persons" (p. 8). The most important message in this report is the negative psychological, physical, social, and economic cost of racial profiling on racial minority individuals and communities.

Recent media reports have provided insights into the ways Black students are differentially impacted by zero tolerance policies. For example, the CBC broadcast (Morrison, 2002), *Zero Tolerance: The Colour of Zero Tolerance* revealed that although safe schools policies are supposed to be "colour-blind," there is blatant differential treatment of Black and White students in punishment of behaviors defined by safe schools policies as disrespectful, disruptive and violent. The *Toronto Star's* article (March 18, 2003), "Blacks Don't Have a Margin of Error," confirms other reports that students of color are disproportionately suspended and expelled for behaviors deemed unacceptable by safe schools standards.

Beyond media reports, sustained research, as referenced in this study, has shown that in multiracial school systems Black students invariably become victims of zero tolerance policies. Such studies revealed that Black students are monitored, accosted, reprimanded, suspended and expelled more often than their non-Black colleagues. There appears to be a discourse of fear of Black people among White teachers. Such "Negrophobia" mediates the relationship between Black students (especially Black boys) and White. Some critics believe that teachers and school administrators strategically utilize zero tolerance policies to cleanse their institutions of the racial differences they fear (Ayers et al., 2001; Sewell, 1997a, 1997b; Solomon & Brown, 1998; Dei et al., 1997). Consequently, this socially and pedagogically unproductive relationship between Black youth and the schools' authority structure results in disrupted schooling and the eventual dropping out (or being pushed out) of school without the education to make them contributing members of Canadian society.

In this study the convergence of racial profiling of Black youth and a policy of zero tolerance that disproportionately penalizes them has created a well-beaten track from school to incarceration in a secure custody institution such as Hopeful Village Youth Centre. This movement of students is what Skiba et al. (2003) describe as "the school-prison pipeline." From their U.S. study of race, expulsion and incarceration they conclude: "There is evidence of a clear relationship between school suspension and juvenile incarceration ... [and] these relationships are by no means race neutral ... racial disparities in school discipline and corrections are in fact related" (pp. 17, 28-29). This study also suggests that school principals' beliefs and perspectives on discipline influence their practice. Those who believe in zero tolerance have higher suspension rates than those with contrasting perspectives on school discipline. In the next section we explore ways of disrupting the inequitable flow of Black youth through the school-prison pipeline.

Zero Tolerance for Racial Profiling: Disrupting the "School-Prison Pipeline"

How then may the school's authority structure be reconstituted to make it more equitable for racialized youth, especially Black youth? What roles and responsibilities may law enforcement agents have in the lives of Black youth in their school and community? How may schools develop social formations where Blacks have rights, privileges, and responsibilities equal to those of their White counterparts?

Traditionally, some school personnel operate on what King (1991) interprets as "dysconscious racism," that is "an uncritical habit of mind (including perceptions, attitudes, assumptions, and beliefs) that justifies inequity and exploitation by accepting the existing order of things as given" (p. 135). According to King and others, White teachers' privileged location within a race-stratified society provides them with skewed perceptions, subjective orientations, and flawed practices in their pedagogy. The findings of this study are an indication that the pedagogical practices of school personnel are predicated on assumptions about social difference; in this case, Black youth and their perceived subcultural behaviors that induce fear and require rigidity in discipline.

To tackle this "uncritical habit of mind," dominant group school personnel need to engage at a number of levels. First, they need to reflect upon their own racial identity development to uncover how their own formation as racial beings (i.e., White, middle class, heterosexual, able-bodied) has historically "colored their perceptions of the "racial other." Leonardo (2002) argues for the interrogation of "Whiteness" for a good understanding of how such a social construction marked by unearned privileges and claims to superiority has come about historically. He concludes that too often, "Whiteness remained cloaked in darkness while marking those with darker complexion for purposes of effective surveillance" (p. 41). From a position of "self-surveillance" White educators may start to develop a critical consciousness about race; one that helps them distance themselves from prescriptive, authoritative implementation of zero tolerance policies. They need to develop the analytic skills and the moral authority to apply such skills in disassembling preconceived notions about Black students.

As we have uncovered in this study, student resistance to perceived racism was too often interpreted as cultural deficit or social deviance; a pathological rather than a political response. Valencia (1997) connects these interpretations to the deficit mentality theory and ideology embraced by those in positions of power and authority as "a shift of blame from the structural deficits" to that of blaming the victim. Since educators' professional development historically over-emphasized technical knowledge at the expense of developing intuitive understanding of social difference, a more social justice based teacher education model must be developed. The inadequacies in educators' conceptions about race must be transformed, and the dialogical construction of meaning instituted. But given the ideological locations of race and other forms of social difference in social, political, and historical contexts, and the White privileges attached to such locations, teacher educators will be challenged to effect change. Evaluative studies carried out in Britain (Gillborn, 1995; Troyna, 1993), the United States (Cochran-Smith, 1995, Sleeter, 1992), and Canada (Carr & Klassen, 1997; Solomon & Levine-Rasky, 2003), have revealed that preservice and in-service teachers mount tremendous resistance to the inclusion of antiracism pedagogy in their practice. Antiracism ought to be the theory-practice discourse that interrogates the sociohistorical context of race, class, and gender; and one that develops strategies to make life equitable for oppressed, marginalized, and dehumanized groups. Its goal is to eradicate racism, an ideology and practice that has undermined, disenfranchised, disadvantaged, and marginalized people of color and other oppressed groups. Unlike multiculturalism that is often preoccupied with cultural identity projects, antiracism addresses the imbalances experienced by those affected by racist ideologies, policies, and practices. Teacher educators are therefore left with the urgent project of integrating antiracism scholarship and practices into their pedagogies.

Transformative antiracism teacher education will help educators move beyond the discourse of fear. To understand the deleterious effects of fear of social difference on their pedagogy educators should reflect on possible outcomes. First, fear of Black students, "negrophobia," may adversely affect teachers' social relationships with these students, curriculum content, instructional strategies, evaluative procedures, and cross-race conflict mediation and solution. Foster's (1986) concern that images of Black violence in urban settings accompanied by racist fantasies may result in the manipulation of behavior and academic standards for Black students. He concluded that this constitutes the most insidious form of racism.

Second, the paralysis of fear causes educators to relinquish their power and authority to an external force such as law enforcement agents. Such relocation may be perceived by students as a weakness in school authority structure, an inability to cope adequately with the affairs of the school. Marginalized students may exploit this power vacuum and institute the kind of power that may destabilize the regularities of the school. Since the external imposition of power and control is not emancipatory or demo-cratic for schools or their students any transformative work must be gen-erated from within. The project of antiracism education, therefore, is to promote social reconstruction within schools and to respect the political and power sharing capacities of Blacks and other marginalized students.[6] This should be the starting point for preparing students for democratic citizenship in the larger society. Paulo Freire's (1996) model is instructive here. In his work: *Pedagogy of the Oppressed*, he outlined the process for empowering the marginalized who struggle for voice and meaning in society, and proposes interaction that is dialogic, not one that fosters the top-down imposition of knowledge and social practices.

Finally, how do we get the police out of schools? The policy and prac-tice of police intervention into schools must be contested and reexamined on moral and legal grounds. Such intrusions have consistently trampled unabatedly on the rights of racialized groups. Concerns of school author-ity over violence in schools and the urgency to create "safe schools" have given administrators considerable freedom in summoning police inter-vention into the lives of students. Gittens et al. (1995) *Report of the Commis-sion on Systemic Racism in the Ontario Criminal Justice System*, concludes:

> Safety in schools is obviously a vital issue, and the criminal process is some-times an appropriate response to student behaviour. But the criminal law should be used with restraint so that "zero-tolerance" does not become a vehicle for over-criminalization of students. During the Commission's con-sultations across Ontario, many Black youths and their parents voiced seri-ous concerns that neither schools nor the police are exercising restraint. They said the police are often summoned for trivial incidents that schools once handled internally. (p. 351)

While the Commission recommends that schools inform parents and youths about school policing issues, we strongly suggest that Black stu-dents and their parents become integral participants in the development and implementation of any policy that potentially restricts their rights and responsibilities as citizens in a democracy. The advent of school coun-cils as an essential component of governance could readily facilitate the inclusion of community voices in the formulation of policies and proce-dures that control police intervention in the schooling process. For exam-ple, Ayers et al. (2001) suggest that marginalized groups on councils develop a network of legally-minded advisers to provide advice and repre-sent students and parents on matters of due process and human rights.

To conclude, for Black youth to become responsible citizens in western democratic societies, schools as socializing institutions must be liberating and empowering. In other words, Noguera (2003) suggests that schools need to invest in the "social capital" of youth and create a caring, trusting environment that provides a feeling of belonging. Blacks must be afforded equal rights and responsibilities and equitable opportunity to exercise them. For schools to produce informed, critical thinkers in a non-prejudiced, undifferentiated, democratic way, educators must set upon the painful project of unshackling themselves from the restrictive attitudes, assumptions and beliefs about the "racial other." This act will go a long way in demanding zero tolerance for racial profiling and disrupting the deregulated flow of Black youth through the "school-prison pipeline."[7]

NOTES

1. Recent StatsCan demographic data revealed that in urban centers such as Toronto, the racial minority population will surpass the dominant by the year 2017.

2. The Toronto Star's statistical investigation into race and crime (published October 19-27, 2002) revealed that the Toronto police engaged in the racial profiling of Blacks, treating them more harshly than Whites. In the debates that followed racial minority officers revealed that they themselves have been victims of racial profiling within their own force. A later study of the Kingston (Ontario) police "stop data" revealed a similar pattern of racial bias against Blacks (Rankin Toronto Star on-line, May 28, 2005). Indeed, racial profiling by police is not unique to Canada; this practice is pervasive in other western multiracial societies such as Britain and the United States.

3. The term "racialized minority" more accurately reflects the power relationship in the labelling process than the traditional descriptor "racial minority." In racially diverse societies such as Canada the dominant (White) group imposes labels or markers for those who are racially different than Whites. The process of "racializing" or "minoritizing" carries the effect of "marking" or "positioning" group status and social difference. In this article "racial minority" and "racialized minority" will be used interchangeably.

4. The *Tracking Sheet* is a monitoring device used by school personnel to verify the whereabouts of students. The sheet, carried by students, will indicate whether or not students are legitimately out-of- bounds during the school day.

5. School administrators who do not collude in the humiliation of racialized minority youth provide insights into police differential treatment of Black youth. For example, when non-Black kids are caught shoplifting they are often picked up by school personnel or taken home by the police and released to their parents. On the other hand, when Black kids are caught shoplifting, they are often escorted back to school in marked cruisers and released in the custody of the principal. If the school principal feels disinclined to accept this responsibility, the youth is taken to the police station for processing. This example provides insights into how Black youths are

differentially treated by the law enforcement agents and how school authority may collude in this process

6. An innovative system of student governance that is currently being built into authority structures in some secondary schools is an advisory group to the principal representing the racial, cultural and ethnic diversity of the school. Such a group functions independently of the student council but often collaborate with them on whole-school projects where the interests of non-mainstream students have to be represented.

7. An earlier version of the article was first published in *The Canadian Journal of Educational Administration and Policy*, Issue 33, Sept. 2004.

REFERENCES

Ayers, R., Ayers, W., & Dohrn, B. (Eds.). (2001). *Zero tolerance: Resisting the drive for punishment, a handbook for parents, students, educators, and citizens*. New York: New Press.

Bowles, S., & Gintis, H. (1976). *Schooling in capitalist America: Educational reform and the contradictions of economic life*. New York: Basic Books

Carby, V. H. (1982). Schooling in Babylon. In *Center for Contemporary Studies: The empire strikes back* (pp. 187-208). London: Hutchinson.

Carr, P. R., & Klassen, T. R. (1997). Different perceptions of race in education: Racial minority and White teachers. *Canadian Journal of Education, 22*(1), 67-81.

Castella, R. (2001). *At zero tolerance: Punishment, prevention and school violence*. New York: Lang.

Cochran-Smith, M. (1995). Colorblindness and basket-making are not the answers: Confronting the dilemmas of race, culture and language diversity in teacher education. *American Educational Research Journal, 32*(3), 493-522.

Cole, D. (1999). Discrimination and denial: Systemic racism in Ontario's legal and criminal justice system, 1892-1961. *Canadian Journal of Criminology, 41*, 428-432.

Collins, R. (1974). Functional and conflict theories of educational stratification. *American Sociological Review, 36*, 1002-1019.

da Costa, G. A. (1978). Orphans and outlaws: Some impacts of racism. *Multiculturalism, 2*(1), 4-7.

Dei, G. S., Mazzuca, J., McIsaac, E., & Zine, J. (1997). *Reconstructing "dropout": a critical ethnography of the dynamics of Black students' disengagement from school*. Toronto, Ontario, Canada: University of Toronto Press.

Dei, G. S. (1996). Black/African Canadian students perspectives on school racism. In I. M. Alladin (Ed.), *Racism in Canadian schools* (pp. 42-61). Toronto, Ontario, Canada: Harcourt Brace.

Epp, J. R. (1997). Authority, pedagogy, and violence, In J. R. Epp & A. M. Watkinson (Eds.), *Systemic violence in education: Promise broken* (pp. 25-36). Albany, NY: SUNY.

Ferguson, A. A. (2000). *Bad boys: Public schools in the making of Black masculinity*. Ann Arbour: University of Michigan Press.

Foster, H. L. (1986). *Ribbin', jivin', and playin' the dozen: The persistent dilemma in our schools* (2nd ed.). Cambridge, MA: Ballinger.

Freire, P. (1996). *Pedagogy of the oppressed.* New York: Continuum.

Furlong, J. (1984). Black resistance in the liberal comprehensive. In S. Delamont (Ed.), *Readings on interaction in the classroom* (pp. 212-236). London: Methuen.

Gillborn, D. A. (1988). Ethnicity and educational opportunity: Case studies of West Indian male/White teacher relationships. *British Journal of Sociology of Education, 9*(4), 371-385.

Gillborn, D. (1995). *Racism and antiracism in real schools.* Buckingham, England: Open University Press.

Gittens, M., Cole, D., Williams, T., Sri-Skanda, S., Tam, M., & Ratushny, E. (1995). *The Report of the Commission on Systemic Racism in the Ontario Criminal Justice System.* Toronto, Canada: The Queen's Printer for Ontario.

Hopkins, R. (1997). *Educating Black males: Critical lessons in schooling, community and power.* Albany, NY: SUNY.

Jull, S. (2000). *Youth violence, schools, and the management question: A discussion of zero tolerance and equity in public schooling.* Retrieved May 5, 2005, from http://www.umanitoba.ca/publications/cjeap/articles/jull.html

Kalinowski, T. (2003, March 18). Blacks don't have a margin of error. *Toronto Star,* p. B3.

King, J. E. (1991). Dysconscious racism: Ideology, identity, and the miseducation of teachers. *Journal of Negro Education, 60*(2), 133-146.

Kreisberg, S. (1992). *Transforming power: Domination, empowerment, and education.* Albany, NY: SUNY.

Kunjufu, J. (1983). *Countering the conspiracy to destroy Black boys.* Chicago: Afro-Am.

Lang, G. & van des Molen, H. with P. Trower & R. Look (1990). *Personal conversations: Roles and skills for counsellors.* London: Routledge.

Larson, C. L., & Ovando, C. J. (2001). *The color of bureaucracy: The politics of equity in multicultural communities.* Belmont, CA: Wadsworth.

Leonardo, Z. (2002). The souls of White folks: Critical pedagogy, Whiteness studies, and globalization discourse. *Race, Ethnicity and Education, 5*(1), 29-50.

Linde, C. (1981). The organization of discourse. In T. Shopen & J. M. Williams (Eds.), *Style and variables in English,* (pp. 84-114). Cambridge, MA: Winthorp.

Mac an Ghaill, M. (1989). Coming of Age in 1980s England: Reconceptualizing Black students' schooling experience. *British Journal of Sociology of Education, 10*(3), 274-286.

Marotto, R. A. (1977). Posin' to be chosen: An ethnographic study of ten lower class male adolescents in an urban high school. Unpublished doctoral dissertation, State University of New York at Buffalo.

McRobbie, A. (Ed.). (1978). Working class girls and the culture of femininity. In *The centre for contemporary studies, women studies group: Women take issue.* London: Hutchinson.

Morrison, N. (Producer). (2002, November 20). Zero tolerance: The colour of zero tolerance. *The Current.* [Radio broadcast] Toronto: Canadian Broadcasting Corporation.

Murray, C. B., & Clark, R. M. (1990, June). Targets of racism. *The American School Board Journal, 177*(6), 22-24.

Noguera, P. (2003). The trouble with Black boys: The role and influence of environmental and cultural factors on the academic performances of African American males. *Urban Education*, *38*(4), 431-459.

Ontario Human Rights Commission Inquiry Report (2003). *Paying the price: The human cost of racial profiling.* Toronto, Canada: Author.

Polkinghorne, D. E. (1995). Narrative configuration in qualitative analysis. In J. A. Hatch & R. Wisneiwski (Eds.), *Life history and narrative* (pp. 5-23). London: Falmer Press.

Rankin, J. (2005, May 28). Policing racial bias study stirs debate. *Toronto Star* [OnLine].

Sewell, T. (1997a, March). *Teacher attitude: Who's afraid of the big Black boy?* Paper presented at the Annual Meeting of the American Educational Research Association, Chicago.

Sewell, T. (1997b). *Black masculinities and schooling: How Black boys survive modern schooling.* Stoke on Trent, England: Trentham Books.

Shannon, M. M., & McCall, D. S. (2004). *Zero tolerance policies in context: A preliminary investigation to identify actions to improve school discipline and school safety.* Canadian Association of Principals. Retrieved July 3, 2004, from http://www.schoolife.com/safehealthyschools/whatsnew/capzerotolerance.html

Skiba, R., & Peterson, R. (1999). The dark side of zero tolerance: Can punishment lead to safe schools? *Phi Delta Kappan.* Retrieved February 29, 2004, from http://www.pdkintl.org/kappan/kski9901.html

Skiba, R., Simmons, A., Staudinger, L., Rausch, M., Dow, F., & Feggins, R. (2003, May). *Consistent removal: Contributions of school discipline to the school-prison pipeline.* School to Prison Conference, Harvard Civil Rights Project, Indiana Education Policy Center, Indiana University.

Sleeter, C. (1992). Resisting racial awareness: How teachers understand the racial order from their racial, gender, and social class locations. *Educational Foundations*, *6*, 7-32.

Solomon, R. P. (1992). *Black resistance in high school: Forging a separatist culture.* Albany, NY: SUNY.

Solomon, R. P., & Brown, D. A. (1998). From badness to sickness: Pathological conceptions of Black student culture and behaviour. In V. D'Oyley & C. James (Eds.), *Revisioning: Canadian perspectives on the education of Africans in the late 20th century* (pp. 104-119). North York, Canada: Captus Press.

Solomon, R. P., & Levine-Rasky, C. (2003). *Teaching for equity and diversity: Research to practice.* Toronto, Canada: Canadian Scholars.

Solomon, R. P., & Palmer, H. (2004, September). Schooling in Babylon, Babylon in school: When "racial profiling" and "zero tolerance" converge. *Canadian Journal of Educational Administration and Policy, 33* [Electronic Version], http://www.umanitoba.ca/publications/cjeap/issuesonline.html

Strauss, L. A. (1987). *Qualitative research for social scientists.* New York: Cambridge University Press.

Supreme Court of Canada (1997). R.D.S -v- Her Majesty the Queen. Ottawa, Canada.

Thorson, S. (1996). The missing link: Students discuss school discipline. *Focus on Exceptional Children, 29*, 9.

Troyna, B. (1993). *Race and education: Research perspectives*. Toronto, Canada: OISE Press.

Valencia, R. R. (Ed.). (1997). *The evolution of deficit thinking: Educational thought and practice*. London: Falmer Press.

Watson, C., & Smitherman, G. (1992). Educational equity and Detroit's male academy. *Equity and Excellence, 25*(2), 40-46.

Wordes, M., & Bynum, T. S. (1995). Policing juveniles: Is there bias against youths of color? In K. Kempt Leonard, C. E. Pope, & W. H. Feyerherm (Eds.), *Minorities in juvenile justice* (pp. 47-65). Thousand Oak, CA: Sage.

Wordes, M., Bynum, T. S., & Corley, C. J. (1994). Locking up youth: The impact of race on detention decisions. *Journal of Research in Crime and Delinquency, 31*, 149-164.

CHAPTER 11

"I'M LEAVING!"

White Fragility in Racial Dialogues

Robin J. DiAngelo

White people in North America live in a social environment which protects and insulates them from race-based stress.[1] Fine (1997b) identifies
this insulation when she observes, "how Whiteness accrues privilege and
status; gets itself surrounded by protective pillows of resources and/or
benefits of the doubt; how Whiteness repels gossip and voyeurism and
instead demands dignity" (p. 57). Whites are rarely without these "protective pillows," and when they are, it is usually temporary and by
choice. This insulated environment of racial privilege builds White
expectations for racial comfort while at the same time lowering the ability to tolerate racial discomfort. For many White preservice teachers, a
single required multicultural education course taken in their teacher
education program is the first time they encounter a direct challenge to
their racial viewpoints. This first exposure is frequently very uncomfortable, and common responses are anger, withdrawal, emotional incapacitation, guilt, argumentation, and cognitive dissonance. These reactions
are often seen in antiracist education endeavors as forms of resistance.
These reactions do function as resistance, but it may be useful to con-

Inclusion in Urban Educational Environments:
Addressing Issues of Diversity, Equity, and Social Justice, 213–240
Copyright © 2006 by Information Age Publishing
All rights of reproduction in any form reserved.

ceptualize them as the result of the reduced psychosocial stamina that racial insulation inculcates. I call this lack of racial stamina "White fragility." This chapter will explore the dynamics of White fragility, illustrated in action through a case study documenting a racial dialogue between White student teachers and students of color. I will close with a brief discussion of ways in which teacher educators might counter White fragility with their students.

WHITENESS

Whiteness refers to dimensions of racism that serve to elevate White people over people of color. Recognizing that the terms I am using are not "theory neutral 'descriptors' but theory-laden constructs inseparable from systems of injustice" (Allen, 1996, p. 95), I use the terms *White* and *Whiteness* to describe a social process. Frankenberg (1993) defines Whiteness as multi-dimensional:

> Whiteness is a location of structural advantage, of race privilege. Second, it is a "standpoint," a place from which White people look at ourselves, at others, and at society. Third, "Whiteness" refers to a set of cultural practices that are usually unmarked and unnamed. (p. 1)

Frankenberg and other theorists (Dyer, 1997; Fine, 1997a, 1997b; Sleeter, 1993; Van Dijk, 1993b) use Whiteness to signify a set of locations that are historically, socially, politically, and culturally produced, and which are intrinsically linked to dynamic relations of domination. Whiteness is thus conceptualized as a constellation of processes and practices rather than as a discrete entity (i.e., skin color alone). Because Whiteness is dynamic, relational, and operating at all times and on myriad levels, it is constantly propped up and protected. Whites are thus racially insulated daily and on multiple levels, resulting in the phenomenon of White fragility (Bonilla-Silva, 2003; Johnson & Shapiro, 2003). White fragility is a state in which even a minimum amount of racial stress becomes intolerable, triggering a range of defensive moves. These moves include the outward display of emotions such as anger, fear, and guilt, and behaviors such as argumentation, silence, and leaving the stress-inducing situation. These behaviors, in turn, function to reinstate White racial equilibrium.

Racial stress results from an interruption to what is racially familiar. These interruptions can take a variety of forms and come from a range of sources, including[2]:

- Suggesting that a White person's viewpoint comes from a racialized frame of reference (challenge to objectivity);
- People of color talking directly about their racial perspectives (challenge to White racial codes);
- People of color choosing not to protect the racial feelings of White people in regards to race (challenge to White racial expectations and need/entitlement to racial comfort);
- People of color not being willing to tell their stories or answer questions about their racial experiences (challenge to colonialist relations);
- A fellow White not providing agreement with one's interpretations (challenge to White solidarity);
- Receiving feedback that one's behavior had a racist impact (challenge to White liberalism);
- Suggesting that group membership is significant (challenge to individualism);
- An acknowledgment that access is unequal between racial groups (challenge to meritocracy);
- Being presented with a person of color in a position of leadership (challenge to White authority);
- Being presented with information about other racial groups through, for example, movies in which people of color drive the action but are not in stereotypical roles, or multicultural education (challenge to White centrality).

In a White dominant environment, each of these challenges become exceptional. In turn, Whites are often at a loss for how to respond in constructive ways. Many Whites have not had to build the cognitive or affective skills that would allow for constructive engagement across racial divides. In the following section, I provide an overview of factors that lead to this lack of skills and dispostions.

FACTORS OF WHITE FRAGILITY

The first factor leading to White fragility is the segregated lives which most Whites live (Helms, 1992; Tatum, 1997). Even if Whites live in physical proximity to people of color, segregation is occurring on multiple levels, including representational and informational. Growing up in segregated environments (schools, workplaces, neighborhoods, media images, and historical perspectives), White interests and perspectives are almost always central. Further, White people are taught not to feel any loss over the absence of people of color in their lives and in fact, this absence is what defines their schools and neighborhoods as "good". Whites come to understand that a "good school" or "good neighborhood" is coded language for "White" (Johnson & Shapiro, 2003). Because Whites live primarily segregated lives in a White dominated society, they receive little or no authentic information about racism and are thus unprepared to think about it critically or with complexity (Bonilla-Silva, 2003; Thandeka, 2000).

As a group, Whites are taught to see their perspectives as objective and representative of reality. The belief in objectivity, coupled with positioning White people as outside of culture (and thus the norm for humanity), allows Whites to view themselves as universal humans who can represent all of human experience. Within this construction, people of color can only represent their own racialized experience (Dyer, 1997). This is evidenced through an unracialized identity or location, which functions as a kind of blindness; an inability to think about Whiteness as an identity or as a "state" of being that would or could have an impact on one's life. In this position, Whiteness is not recognized or named by White people, and a universal reference point is assumed. A corollary to this unracialized identity is the ability to recognize Whiteness as something that is significant and that operates in society, but to not see how it relates to one's own life. In this form, a White person recognizes Whiteness as real, but as the individual problem of other "bad" White people (Helms, 1992; Tatum, 1997).

At the same time that Whites are taught to see their interests and perspectives as universal, they are also taught to value the individual and to see themselves as individuals rather than as part of a racially socialized group (Bonilla-Silva, 2003; McIntosh, 1988). Individualism erases history and hides the ways in which wealth has been distributed and accumulated over generations to benefit Whites today. It allows Whites to view themselves as unique and original, outside of socialization and unaffected by the relentless racial messages in the culture. Individualism also allows Whites to distance themselves from the actions of their racial group and demand to be granted the benefit of the doubt, as individuals, in all cases. Given the ideology of individualism, Whites often respond defensively when associated with other Whites as a group or "accused" of collectively benefiting from racism, because as individuals, each White person is "different" from any other White person and expects to be seen as such. Whites invoke these seemingly contradictory discourses—universalism and individualism—as needed. Both discourses work to deny the significance of their racial positions (Croteau, 1999; DiAngelo, 2004; Helms,

1990; Tatum, 1997). In the dominant position, Whites are almost always racially comfortable and expect to remain so (Helms, 1992). When racial discomfort arises, Whites typically respond as if something is "wrong," and blame the person or event that triggered the discomfort (usually a person of color). Since racism is necessarily uncomfortable in that it is oppressive, White insistence on racial comfort guarantees racism will not be faced except in the most superficial of ways.

Whites often confuse not understanding with not agreeing. Because most Whites have not been trained to think complexly about racism, and because it benefits White dominance not to do so, they have a very limited understanding of racism. Yet dominance leads to racial arrogance, and in this racial arrogance, Whites have no compunction about debating the knowledge of people who *have* thought complexly about race. Whites generally feel free to dismiss these informed perspectives rather than have the humility to acknowledge that they are unfamiliar, reflect on them further, or seek more information. This intelligence and expertise are often trivialized and countered with simplistic platitudes (e.g., "People just need to...") that serve to trivialize racism (DiAngelo, 2006). Because of White social, economic and political power within a White dominant culture, Whites are in the position to legitimize people of color's assertions of racism. Yet Whites are the least likely to see, understand, or be invested in validating those assertions and being honest about their consequences. This position, coupled with the need for racial comfort, has many Whites insisting that people of color explain White racism in the "right" way. The right way is generally politely and rationally, without any show of emotional upset. When racism is explained in a way that White people can see and understand, then its validity may be granted. However, Whites are usually more receptive to validating White racism if that racism is constructed as residing in an individual White person other than themselves (Croteau, 1999). When any of these dynamics are interrupted, White fragility makes the resulting disequilibrium intolerable. However, because White fragility finds its support through White privilege, fragility coupled with privilege will result in a response of resistance, indulgence in emotional incapacitation, exiting, or a combination of these. White fragility supported by White privilege makes it exceptional for Whites to respond with racial humility to any of the above challenges (Pierce, 2003).

The dynamics of White fragility are of concern in teacher education because the most recent data about U.S. teachers show that the majority of elementary and secondary school teachers are female and White. In 1999, the teacher population was 87% White (National Center for Educational Statistics, 2002) and 74% female (Suarez-Orozco, 2000). Recent estimates indicate that the percentage of White teachers in public schools is increasing (Snyder, 1999). In contrast, approximately 35% of students in classrooms are of color: 16% Black/African American, 14% Hispanic, 3.8% Asian/Pacific American, and 1% American Indian/Alaskan Native students (Snyder, 1999). It may be hypothesized from these statistics that although many White preservice teachers do not interact with people of color in any direct or sustained way in their preparation programs, they will likely be teaching students of color once they enter the public schools. Given this gap, I wanted to analyze their responses to the racial perspectives of people of color in order to anticipate how best to prepare preservice teachers for urban practice.

WHITE FRAGILITY IN ACTION

Methodology

The excerpt discussed here was part of a larger study which attended to documenting discourses and practices taken up in racial dialogues among student teachers that function to support White domination and privilege (modes of resistance to de-centering Whiteness). For this chapter, I am focusing on one dimension of the analysis from the larger study: White fragility.

Discourse Analysis

Discourse analysis is the study of language and the making of meaning in action and in social contexts. It is a method of investigating the back-and-forth dialogues which constitute social action, along with patterns of signification and representation which constitute culture (Gee, 1999). Gee (1999) states that "Meaning is not general and abstract, not something that resides in dictionaries, or even in general symbolic representations inside people's heads. Rather, it is situated in specific social and cultural practices, and it is continually transformed in those practices" (p. 63). Discourse analysis is attentive to the usages of language and how those usages position speakers in relation to others, both physically present others and larger categories of others (i.e., social groups). Language is not conceptualized as a transparent or neutral transmitter of one's core ideas or self. Rather, language is conceptualized as historically and socially situated, and discourse analysis is concerned with how ideologies are communicated and what the multiple effects might be (Evans, 2002). Discourse analysis is a useful tool in explicating Whiteness because it allows for a nuanced analysis of the socially and historically informed discourses that are available for negotiating racial positions. Discourse analysis can reveal processes of racism that otherwise would be difficult to establish, or that would be formally denied by the majority of participants (Van Dijk, 1993a, 1993b).

In differentiating discourse analysis from other forms, Van Dijk (1993b) states that "Although there are many directions in the study and critique of social inequality, the way we approach these questions and dimensions is by focusing on *the role of discourse in the (re)production and challenge of dominance*" (original emphasis, p. 300). I am interested in the social processes by which White people produce and maintain their racial position and power in situations in which their position is being challenged. Using Gee's definition of meaning as situated in specific social practices and transformed (or reinstated) through those practices and focusing on the production and interruption of Whiteness, my goal was to explicate how racialized meaning is generated, contested, and/or transformed in the practice of a facilitated, intergroup racial dialogue. Van Dijk, in describing critical discourse analysis, states:

> This does not mean that we see power and dominance merely as unilaterally "imposed" on others. On the contrary, in many situations, and sometimes paradoxically, power and even power abuse may seem "jointly produced," e.g., when dominated groups are persuaded, by whatever means, that dominance is "natural" or otherwise legitimate. Thus, although an analysis of strategies of resistance and challenge is crucial for our understanding of actual power and dominance relations in society, and although such an analysis needs to be included in a broader theory of power, and counter-power and discourse, our critical approach prefers to focus on the elites and their discursive strategies for the maintenance of inequality. (p. 300)

Because the majority of preservice teachers are White and thus the primary change-object, this analysis focused on elites and describes "top-down" relations of dominance rather than "bottom-up" relations of resistance, compliance, or acceptance.

Study Procedures

The study consisted of a 4-week, intergroup dialogue on racism among future teachers that I observed and videotaped. The dialogues took place in a large research institution in the Pacific Northwest of the United States. Participants were recruited from the College of Education Teacher Education Program (TEP) at a major research university located in the Northwest United States. Students were invited to participate via a third-party research announcement sent program-wide. The area or discipline of the students was not limited (i.e., elementary education students vs.

secondary students, science vs. social studies) because the analysis is tied to a wider, macrolevel analysis of how Whiteness functions overall in U.S. society (Dyer, 1997; Fine, 1997a, 1997b; Frankenberg, 2001; Roediger, 1998; Sleeter, 1993). Racial identity and ratio were the determining factors for inclusion in the study. The group consisted of 13 students: 8 students who identified as White (W) and 5 students who identified as people of color (POC), and was led by an interracial team of two facilitators, one facilitator of color (FOC) and one white facilitator (WF).

I observed four, 2-hour sessions. I was present during these sessions, taking notes on my observations, but I sat away from the group and did not participate in the dialogues in any way beyond my presence in the room. I did not have a prior relationship to the students. Each session was also videotaped. The videotapes allowed me to revisit sessions and to verify observation transcripts. Videotapes also allowed me to secure reliability via agreement from another content expert in Whiteness studies. The excerpt this chapter is based on occurred in the fourth and final session.

Participant key:

1.   Malena: Facilitator of color (FOC) (Biracial: Native American/ White)
2.   Becca: White Facilitator (WF)
3.   Jessica: White woman (W)
4.   Laura: woman of color (ChineseAmerican-POC)
5.   Barb: White woman (W)
6.   Ruth: White woman (W)
7.   Tiffany: White woman (W)
8.   Courtney: White woman (W)
9.   Jason: White man (W)
10.   Caroline: Woman of color (African American-POC)
11.   Marie: Woman of color (Biracial: Native American/White-POC)
12.   Amy: White woman (W)

WHITE FRAGILITY: I'M LEAVING

The following exchange, which occurred in the last session of the dialogue, is a cogent example of White fragility. The White participants had been repeatedly asked by the facilitators to consider how their racial locations (also referred to as *social identities*) inform their perspectives and responses. Following just such a request, Courtney initiates this interchange by asking Malena a rhetorical question:

COURTNEY (WF): Can I ask you something? Do you want White people to progress in their ideas about how they are racist?

MALENA (FOC): What do you think?

COURTNEY (W): I think so, but I hear contradicting things.

MALENA (FOC): How am I contradicting that?

COURTNEY (W): You know, I don't want to get into a personal argument, because it would still be between you and me, and I don't want to—

MALENA (FOC): Well, we still have forty minutes … so go ahead.

COURTNEY (W): I'm going to pass. I'm really ready to leave too, quite frankly.

BECCA (WF): So, how do you think that—I mean, just to tie this back into social identity: How do you think your social identity ties into the fact that, when things are getting really hot right here and you're faced with the stuff you don't want to look at, you want to leave?

COURTNEY (W): Well, I had something really important to go to tonight that I missed to be here. And so, that's part of what's going through my head too, is that, when I feel like—

MALENA (FOC): So, this isn't important?

COURTNEY (W): Not as important as what I—you know, it's important because I committed to it … so I, you know, missed the thing tonight to come here.

MALENA (FOC): Well, because you didn't say you felt like leaving earlier when you weren't having this difficult conversation?

COURTNEY (W): No. I did; I felt like leaving—or, like I kind of wished I could and I felt like I had a—I had committed to be here, so I'm here. So, that's part of why I feel like my threshold is lowered.

MALENA (FOC): what you're implying is that, because I don't trust you or any White people, I am also not for this change in White people about racism.

COURTNEY (W): No, I just asked you a question.

MALENA (FOC): And I'm also asking you a question right now if that's what you said. This dialogue we're having right now is me clarifying with you and asking

	you questions. And you continually refer to it as like me doing this difficult thing.
COURTNEY (W):	I'm leaving. I'm sorry that I'm—I'm the only one who is leaving, but really, I would rather not be here *(Courtney stands up and walks over to the exit)*.
BECCA (WF):	One of the things we talked about earlier was White people not calling other White people out, and I'm wondering if any White people in the group.
COURTNEY (W):	Yeah. Call me out. Anyone—before I leave, call me out.
RUTH (W):	Sure. I will. Do you want to stay? I mean, I'm—I'm confused as to why you're angry. And I understand—like, I don't know what this other important thing is. But I don't really understand, if you were committed to this—I mean, I have a problem with you—I have a problem with a lot of people in this room not understanding why—what the point of this is, you know. I can't—
COURTNEY (W):	I understand what the point is, but right now, it's —what I was saying before. Like I'm not—you know, I'm—I can be a fiery person, and right now I'm going to say a lot of things that aren't going to lead to really good discussions in this group. And I have something really important that I wanted to go to. So, I'm just going to leave, because I don't want it to be between you and me. I want other people in here to be talking. So, I'm just going to leave.
MALENA (FOC):	Courtney, I think you should stay. And I think that these things that—Ruth is trying to say something to you. And I know that you have goals for this group, and it's sort of what we talked about before. But we also have goals for this group. So, if it becomes this—if we spend the next half-hour between you and I, Becca and I have determined that that's okay. So, don't worry about what the purpose of the group is; like, we're handling that.
COURTNEY (W):	It's not okay with me. It's not okay with me. So, I'm leaving *(Courtney walks out)*.

As I start my analysis, it is important to keep in mind that a range of theoretical frameworks could be used to make sense of the dynamics. However, the analysis that I am offering for consideration is one of racial location. This analysis posits that racial group membership, rather than individual characteristics, is the salient force informing these well-documented patterns of interracial group dynamics (Dei, Karumanchery, & Karumanchery-Luik, 2004; Fine, 1997a, 1997b; Roman, 1993; Schofield, 2004; Sleeter, 1993; Van Dijk, 1992). Racial location is particularly salient in a context in which the stated purpose is building cross-racial understanding for Whites. I offer this analysis not as a claim of the definitive "truth" of the dynamics, but as a particular frame that has been useful within antiracist education for making sense of and responding to these familiar patterns (Adams, Bell, & Griffin, 1997; Derman-Sparks & Phillips, 1997; Levine-Rasky, 2000; Powell, 1997; Tatum, 1997).

Courtney's decision to walk out on the process, despite pleas from the facilitators and a participant not to do so, illustrates several dimensions of White fragility propped up by White privilege. Courtney displays both an inability to sustain even a minimal challenge to her racial position (White fragility), and the prerogative to remove herself from that challenge while locating the problem with others (White privilege) (Bonilla-Silva, 2003). Although there can be a range of reasons for Courtney's responses, within the context of the exchange and specific requests made of her, there is no indication that she can provide even the most elementary analysis of racism, or that she is willing or able to consider her role in the now polarized racial dynamics. First, Courtney's opening question in the above exchange: "Do you want White people to progress in their ideas about how they are racist?" is rhetorical and posed as a challenge. Malena takes the challenge and asks Courtney to be specific about her claim that Malena is contradicting herself. Courtney does not do this, and instead states that she wants to pass, adding the threat of leaving. This indicates that a critical state of White fragility has been reached and Courtney is retreating.

Courtney has a range of options at this point in the exchange. Malena, Becca, and Ruth have all expressed a desire for her to stay. If she does not want the exchange to be about "you and me" in relation to Malena, she could refrain from comment and listen. She could try to follow Malena's line of questioning and see where it led. She could consider Becca's request to explore how her Whiteness plays into her desire to leave. However, she chooses none of these options, perhaps because any one of them would require her to remain and face a racial challenge. When Becca appeals to the White participants to challenge Courtney's decision, Courtney agrees and asks to be "called out." Ruth rises to this challenge, but unfortunately, Ruth's White social position has ill prepared her to articulate a coherent counter argument, and her attempt is futile (it is significant to note that Ruth is the only White participant to respond to Becca's challenge. The other White participants appear immobilized). In Malena's final exchange with Courtney, she directly pleas with her to stay and to trust the facilitators' decision that it is acceptable for them to work through this moment. Courtney overrules the facilitators by stating, "It's not OK with me," and leaves. By refusing to engage any further, she ensures that her viewpoint will remain protected. Further, Courtney's refusal to take direction from a woman of color who holds leadership in the group and her very literal exit in the face of racial discomfort is a powerful message to the people of color in the group; Courtney positions herself to decide if, when, and how to engage in a discussion of race, and ultimately removes herself from the situation when the counter-pressure becomes intolerable. Although Courtney will make cursory acknowledgment of racism in the abstract, White fragility prevents her from acknowledging racism in the particular. Her inability to acknowledge racism in the particular is also evidenced in her response to the opening question of the dialogue: How have participants seen racism playing out in the group? Courtney's response to this question was to pass.

Courtney demonstrates White fragility most dramatically through her inability to move through her initial responses of anger and defensiveness. She has been angry and critical towards the facilitators from the opening session, and the facilitators have consistently responded with patience. Yet, in the final session, when the facilitators push back against her resistance, she literally walks out. She does this despite a commitment she has made to attend the sessions, a plea from the facilitators not to leave, and with full awareness that she is being videotaped. Although no other White participants walked out, Courtney's actions are not atypical and demonstrate a common form of White Fragility in the face of challenges to White racial comfort (Macedo & Bartolome, 1999; Sleeter, 1993). Using the concept of group-as-a-whole theory (Wells, 1985), Courtney can be seen as playing out a White desire on behalf of the other Whites in the group. As Malena will state later:

> MALENA (FOC):   I'm not surprised, and I think that, if I had pushed any of the White people in this group, they would have left. I don't think that Courtney did anything that's really that unique. And I think that a couple of you have been close already.

Malena's statement is met by nods of agreement from both White participants and those of color. This agreement indicates recognition that

Courtney represented the hostility and ambivalence that many other White participants felt but could not display. The agreement also indicates a familiarity with the move; while Courtney's departure may have been dramatic, it was not unusual or unexpected. She simply acted out a more explicit and composite representation of the White withdrawal from challenges to racial privilege that occurs in the larger society.

White Fragility: This Isn't my Problem

Aside from Ruth, no other White participants speak to Courtney's departure. The facilitators check in to see how these participants are responding. The ensuing discussion reveals another dimension of White fragility-narcissism supported by a deeply internalized sense of individualism (Patterson, 1998). These participants view Courtney's exit as a function of her right to choose; any interference would have been an infringement of her individual choice. After hours of dialogue, they do not understand that Courtney is seen by the participants of color to represent them as a fellow White person, nor do they comprehend the impact her departure has on the participants of color. This narcissism is not necessarily the result of a consciously held belief that Whites are superior to others (although that may play a role), but a result of the White racial insulation ubiquitous in dominant culture; a general White inability to see non-White perspectives as significant, except in sporadic and impotent reflexes, which have little or no long-term force or political usefulness (Rich, 1979).

In the following exchange, Malena and other participants of color struggle to lead another White participant, Barb, to an expanded interpretation of the racial dynamics operating in the incident, one that includes recognizing the impact Courtney's departure had on the them. The participants of color are unable to achieve their goal however, because Barb has the privilege of seeing herself as an individual rather than as a member of a racial group, and she relies upon this privilege to shield herself from their challenge (Dei et al., 2004; McIntosh, 1988).

MALENA (FOC): We're checking in with you too about what happened with Courtney.

BARB (W): Oh, I wanted to say, "Sit down, you little chicken shit White girl." I was so mad. I'm like, "I'm not saying anything. Let her little White ass leave; I don't care."

MALENA (FOC): How come you chose not to say anything?

BARB (W):	Because I don't care about her; I don't know.
MALENA (FOC):	What if you don't care about her, but in terms of racism, we care about her?
BARB (W):	She's—it's her choice. And I'm like—I was thinking, "You should sit down and be in pain with the rest of us."
MALENA (FOC):	But you decided not to call after her?
BARB (W):	Because I didn't think she'd listen. She had already decided; she had her coat, and I'm like, "Why are you still here?"
MALENA (FOC)	But she did stop, though and ask to be called out.
BARB (W):	And I'm thinking, "Why are you still here? Just leave if you don't like it. Fine; go run away. Fine."
MALENA (FOC):	But did you hear what I said, though; that she did stop and ask to be called out, and then started to come back?
BARB (W):	She did stop.
MALENA (FOC):	But you had already decided that she was going to leave, and so you decided…
BARB (W):	I had already decided that I didn't care what she did.
MALENA (FOC):	And what does it mean to you that I'm telling you that it matters to me that she stayed?
BARB (W):	I think that's really interesting. I didn't know that you cared if she stayed. Because why do you care if she stayed?
LAURA (POC):	What if we cared that White people—what if I cared that White people shouldn't give up on other White people because I think I kind of see this as, like, "Oh, well; who cares? Who cares if she leaves the room?; But it matters to me that White people give other White people a hand and—
BARB (W):	So, you would have preferred if we all had said, "Sit down?"
LAURA (POC):	(Nods head)
MALENA (FOC):	I think that the only person who could have reached her was a White person, and she asked for that explicitly, and nobody said anything but Ruth. And Ruth said something, and you chose not to.
BARB (W):	Yeah.

MALENA (FOC):	And we're telling you that it mattered, to us at least, that she stayed.
BARB (W):	And I—had you not told me that it mattered to you, I wouldn't know that it mattered to you.
MALENA (FOC):	So, but you kind of assumed for us that it didn't matter to us, because it didn't matter to you?
BARB (W):	I didn't … I didn't assume. I don't assume. I just—
MALENA (FOC):	You just didn't know? So, let me just be direct. I wish that you would have said something to her. I feel like you had the power to make her stay.
BARB (W):	Why?
MALENA (FOC):	Why?
BARB (W):	Why?
MALENA (FOC):	What do you mean, why?
BARB (W):	Why do you wish I had said something; because I'm White?
MALENA (FOC):	I just said, I think you had the power to make her stay, and she should have stayed. And so, I'm a little hurt and disappointed that you didn't say something.
BARB (W):	And I obviously think I have no power to make her stay. I don't -
MALENA (FOC):	But I think it doesn't matter how powerful you feel.
BARB (W):	You were disappointed—
MALENA (FOC):	I know that you had the power to make her stay.
BARB (W):	You know I had the power to make her stay, and I didn't know I had the power to make her stay. You wish that the White people had said, "Please stay," because we had the power to make her stay. Had all the White people said, "Please sit. Sit. Sit down, Courtney, please," and you're disappointed that we as White people did not say that.
MALENA (FOC):	And you in particular.
BARB (W):	And me in particular. And how do I feel about me in particular; is that what your question is?
MALENA (FOC)	Well, it wasn't really a question; I'm just telling you I felt that way.
BARB (W):	I—I'm sorry you feel that way. I don't know—I don't know—I don't have any big feelings about it. I don't feel compelled to go, "I'm so sorry."

MALENA (FOC):	I've never really seen, though, you be like this. It seems like you do have some big feelings right now.
BARB (W):	I have big feelings—yeah. But I don't know whether you want to hear them.
MALENA (FOC):	I want to hear what you have—
BARB (W):	What do you want to hear?
MALENA (FOC):	I'm not trying to guide you anywhere.
BARB (W):	Yes, you are; you're a facilitator.
MALENA (FOC):	But I'm not. Right now I want to know—
BARB (W):	You're asking pointed questions.
MALENA (FOC):	I don't want you to guess what I'm trying to get at. I want—I am asking you a question because I want to know what you actually think.
BARB (W):	About—
MALENA (FOC):	You.
BARB (W):	About - think about what? About the power I have and the power you don't to make her stay? I don't know. What do I feel about that? What do I think about that? It's new—it's a new thing for me to know that you even care about a person of White or color or anything.
MALENA (FOC):	It's new for—
BARB (W):	It's new for me to go, huh, people of color wish that White people had said something. That's new.
LAURA (POC):	I think—I was just going to say kind of the same thing you said. It's not debating about whether she would have stayed if the White people said something; it's more that the White people needed to say something, and what happens when the White people give up on each other.
BARB (W):	Oh.
CAROLINE (POC):	Mm-hmm—regardless of how you feel about it, that's how we perceive it as people of color when you don't say anything to her when she punked out—cause that's what she did.
BARB (W):	Okay.
CAROLINE (POC):	And I'm real—I was pissed off.
BARB (W):	Okay.

Throughout this exchange Barb distances herself from Courtney and her actions. Because Barb does not have a group framework from which to analyze racism, she does not see herself as implicated in Courtney's behavior as a fellow White person in a dialogue about race that is racially polarized (Marty, 1998; Roediger, 1998). In fact, she depicts Courtney as just some "chicken … White girl" whose actions have nothing to do with her. Although Barb refers to Courtney as White here, her positioning indicates that she ultimately sees Courtney as a separate individual. It did not occur to Barb to intervene because she did not view herself or Courtney as part of the White group, and therefore, given that Courtney was not acting on Barb's behalf, Barb "didn't care" what she did. She has positioned herself away from the play, maintaining distance and silence to rid herself of the problem, which she defines as Courtney: why doesn't Courtney just go away? Barb has also tuned out Malena's direct request to Courtney, stating that she didn't know Malena wanted Courtney to stay, as well as Becca's direct request for the White participants to intervene, claiming that she did not know she "should" have called Courtney back. White fragility has required Barb to literally block out racially stressful information and calls for action.

Although Barb does view Courtney's behavior as problematic, she does not see it as representative of any other White person. She uses "I" statements in her phrasing, positioning herself as a distinct individual standing on her own and responsible only for herself. In contrast, much of what the participants of color tell Barb is phrased in the collective voice of "we." This voice aligns people of color and positions them as a cohesive group, while Barb's language positions herself and the other Whites as individuals. Barb expresses astonishment that the participants of color wanted Courtney to stay and that they think she, as a White person, should have intervened. This astonishment is another indicator that even in the context of an interracial dialogue, she does not interpret from a framework of racial location. She does not see that other White people, their behaviors, or the impact of those behaviors on people of color should be her concern. Nor does Barb see herself as accountable to the participants of color for the impact her lack of intervention had on them. In fact, these perspectives are so unfamiliar to Barb that she seems to have difficulty even following the conversation.

White Fragility: I Don't Know How to Consider People of Color

The impact of White silence on people of color in the face of Courtney's move is expressed in the following responses:

MARIE (POC): Okay. I want to say that I think it was a really big value judgment that White people had to make when she left. They chose to appease one White woman and in turn let down at least five people of color. And her walking out and nobody saying anything, other than Ruth, was—it really said a very big thing to me, and maybe to other people of color: that "We value what this other—what this White woman thinks rather than what we value what—how you feel." And I felt devalued, so.

CAROLINE (POC): I would echo what Marie said, in terms of feeling devalued and kind of feeling, regardless of what—how you feel individually, the way it looked from the outside, and you really need to look at that in everyday life. And that to me was a huge example of a punk-out. And—yeah; she punked out big-time, and I really wanted to say something to her as she was walking out. But I didn't feel like it was going to come out like that, so I said, "I'm just going to—I'm going to hold back and see what anybody else is going to say." Nobody else spoke up, so—she's gone.

LAURA (POC): I think it's funny that, in the beginning go-around I said something about, you know, choosing when to engage and disengage. I think that was a perfect illustration of that and also a perfect illustration of response—what it means or what it looks like when White people don't take responsibility where they should.

These participants clearly see Courtney's departure and White inaction in response as representative of larger societal relations. However, after the discussion that followed Courtney's departure, and the direct feedback participants of color give to the White participants about how they interpreted that departure and the lack of White intervention, White participants still demonstrate that their initial interpretations remain largely intact. Further, they appear immobilized in their ability to either comprehend, or act upon, the explicit information provided to them by the participants of color, illustrating another dimension of White fragility, immobilization in the face of racial challenge. After the exchange with Barb, the facilitators attempt to pull other White participants into the discussion, but continue to meet ineptitude, if not direct resistance:

MALENA (FOC): Yes; Amy needs to say something.

AMY (W): Am I answering a specific question, or just—

MALENA (FOC): No. Why have you not talked?

AMY (W): Well, I feel like I should also say that I'm a really shy person. All my whole life I'm a person that doesn't—I know—I know that's how people might take that but that really—I'm a lot more comfortable when going around with the group and there's like a specific thing that I'm answering. I don't know if that's, you know, motivated by the racial dialogue. I'm sure it's a little bit, because it is uncomfortable to just interject [in the middle and be] talking directly with people.

MALENA (FOC): So, at this very moment, because of what Courtney did—because of the conversation I had with Barb, What was that like for you?

AMY (W) I did not feel like I—should have said something to her at the time that she was leaving, but now, after the conversation we just had, I can see, you know, that it would have been an appropriate time for people to say, you know, "Please" —just for support too, I mean, you know, "we want you here." Because I did; you know, I wanted to hear more of what she had to say and stuff too. But I can relate to Barb's feelings of, "Well, goodbye, you know. Forget it."

MALENA (FOC): So, do you feel like you let us down a little bit?

AMY (W): Yeah, but more because I don't talk more, not because I didn't say anything to Courtney then.

As with most of the White participants, to the end Amy is unable to racialize her responses. Although the issue of individual versus group identity has been raised in every session, Amy explains her silence in terms of her personality, positioning herself as a "shy person." She has also heard the exchange between Malena, Laura, Caroline, and Barb, in which they explain how they were hurt by Courtney's leaving and the lack of intervention from Whites. Still, Amy locates the person in need of support as Courtney. In so doing, she indicates a White allegiance and focus. Amy doesn't understand what the participants of color are trying to tell her—that asking Courtney to stay was not to support Courtney, but to

support them. Amy is unable to comprehend, much less engage constructively, across the racial lines offered to her. Jason articulates a somewhat
broader understanding of the dynamics based on the feedback he has
heard:

> JASON (W):   Clearly, I mean—you know, that learning curve:
> I'm still way at the beginning, because what I saw
> was purely on the surface. I saw a woman at the
> threshold of pain, and she couldn't take it any-
> more. And if —I mean, if she really was hurting
> that badly, she had to go. And was I letting her
> off the hook and letting everybody down? Yes.
> And the argument is, you've got to work through
> that pain and move on. I think she was—she was
> at white heat; I mean, she was done—sorry; bad
> analogy. She was at that point of pain and had to
> go. But again, I looked at it at the surface. And I
> didn't say, "How is this affecting the group?
> Where does it go from here?" So I've got a way to
> go.

Jason now recognizes that he was viewing the situation on a surface
level. Still, like Amy, he focuses on the individual White woman, not on
the dynamics of the group as a whole or in racial terms. He does not focus
on the impact of Courtney's departure and the lack of White intervention
on the participants of color, either as a group or as individuals. He also
does not indicate a sense of his own position as a White person in the
group and what role he might have played in supporting the participants
of color.

By the close of this 2 hour exchange, which occurred in the last of
four 2-hour sessions, Barb's interpretation has not been shifted enough
to cause her to do anything differently if she was in the same situation
again:

> BARB (W):   It honestly never occurred to me to tell her - to
> ask her to sit down and stay. Had I known every-
> one else wanted me to, or it was going to hurt
> anyone's feelings or form this idea that, wow,
> White people aren't allies, I probably would have
> said something, because it would have been an
> expectation, and I would have fulfilled that
> expectation, just to say the right thing. But I still,

> had—if it happened again, I probably still
> wouldn't say anything.

Barb holds a limited, single-incident understanding of what the participants of color are telling her. Her statement that if she had known that
not asking Courtney to stay would "form this idea that White people
aren't allies" indicates that she does not understand that this idea is
already formed for people of color, and that this latest enactment of
White inaction only verified it. For the participants of color, these are
common and familiar White patterns.

Even though Barb expresses some cursory understanding of the feedback she has received, she states that any future intervention she might
make in a similar situation would be disingenuous, and in fact she "probably still wouldn't say anything." As a White person, she does not demonstrate an investment in or sense of responsibility for interrupting racism.
Her claim that she would intervene to protect the feelings of people of
color is a form of White paternalism—she would help those in need but
does not see her own role in the creation of that need, or that intervening
could be for her advancement, not theirs (Sue, 2003). In the end, Barb
confesses that her interpretation has not shifted; she has not been rationally convinced that she has any role or responsibility in addressing the
behavior of other Whites.

This is the first time Barb and the other White participants have ever
encountered racial experiences in direct conflict with their own. This
one-time interaction, however, is not enough to overcome the need for
comfort that Whiteness has inculcated. If the pressure against White
centrality encountered in the dialogue is not sustained, Barb can continue to block out these counter-narratives; this dialogue is an anomaly
for her and the other White participants—a temporary situation. They
will soon regain the insulation that will greet them when the session
ends and they return to the familiar racial environment that waits outside the room.

White Fragility: I Am an Individual With My Own Rights

This final discussion illustrates another dimension of White fragility-
White individualism. The White participants in this study do not hold a
group framework and do not see themselves as responsible for each other.
The White participants consistently position Courtney as one individual
White woman. Interpreting from the discourse of individualism, the
White participants saw this individual White woman's decision to exit as
"her choice":

TIFFANY (W):   I think you said, "We'd like you to stay, and why are you leaving? Please don't leave." … and I thought, you know, this is her choice.

These participants seem unable to consider group dynamics, even in unracialized terms. Instead, they have an interpretive framework that positions each group member as a unique individual, each sharing their thoughts, feelings and opinions equally, and each with the right to engage however they choose. Although the stated goal of the dialogues was to provide White preservice teachers with an opportunity to gain an understanding of the racial perspectives of people of color, White fragility appears to have made this goal nearly impossible. This is notable given the limited exposure these future teachers have to these perspectives, both in the teacher education cohort and the culture at large.

At the same time that White participants do not have a sense of responsibility for one another in the goal of interrupting racism, they have not demonstrated a focus on or concern with people of color. This functions to keep Whiteness sheltered and guarded as people of color are left to deal with individual Whites, each of whom are operating from an individual framework and self-focus. The result is an unbridgeable gap between interpretive racial frameworks, for repeatedly the White participants demonstrate a White focus and an inability to move beyond individual White interest, needs, and perspectives. Positioning herself as an ally to the participants of color, Becca expresses great disappointment in the White participants:

BECCA (WF):   I am really disappointed right now. One of the things that we talked about earlier in this group was looking at how White people sat back in this group and about how that was a way that racism manifests itself. And I think that this was another example of that. And very specifically, both myself and Malena asked the group—asked the White people in the group to go there. And with a couple of exceptions, no one went there. I'm not entirely surprised, but it's frustrating and disappointing.

Becca's disappointment was inevitable, for one of the major discursive strategies in either the contestation or reinscription of racist relations occurs through the interpretation of race itself source. For Becca (who has practice in antiracist discourse), Malena, and the participants of color, talking about race means talking about racism; race and racism are inextricably linked because they work from an interpretive framework of race as a socially constructed category based in relations of domination and inequality. Race for these participants is not simply a signifier for differences in culture, place of origin, or skin color, and does not operate only at special times and places. Race is understood to shape every dimension of their lives and interactions. Talking about race is thus assumed to mean addressing and attempting to rectify these inequitable racist relations. Guided by this goal, these participants expect that attention will be paid to the way the conversation itself is held, and to the actions that will be taken within and beyond it. One's racial group position is understood as critical to these issues of attention, engagement and action. Their social locations have not insulated them from the ravages of racism; they have had to develop the stamina to face racism and do not expect, much less demand, exemption.

For the White participants, however, talking about race means something entirely different. Based on the evidence here, we can conclude that talking about race means little more than the equal sharing of opinions and past experiences. These opinions and experiences apparently do not need to be connected to race at all, as evidenced by the consistent inability of the White participants to connect their perspectives to race. Their racial positions were viewed as nonoperative or irrelevant to issues of attention, engagement or action; each person is seen as an ahistorical individual, standing only for themselves. When pressed to expand this framework, they do not have the interest or stamina to engage in, much less sustain, the effort.

IMPLICATIONS FOR TEACHER EDUCATION

Based on my observations, I have argued that the White preservice teachers in this study were unprepared to engage, even on a preliminary level, in an exploration of differences in racial perspectives that could lead to an observable shift in their understanding of race. Further, White fragility prevented them from responding constructively to other's racial perspectives (the silence from the majority of white participants in the group, in the face of repeated requests from participants of color for input, is included here as a form of nonconstructive response). The majority of these White preservice teachers did not appear able to withstand the stress of seeing themselves as raced subjects. This inability has several implications for the classroom, for if teachers choose to ignore racial location, they can only reinscribe White perspectives as universal. However, an assumption that they can choose to ignore racial location is somewhat misleading. White people do notice the racial locations of others and their refusal to acknowledge this, results in a kind of split consciousness that limits their ability to authentically connect to all of their students (Flax, 1998; Hooks, 1992; Morrison, 1992). This denial also guarantees that the racial misinformation that circulates in the culture and frames their perspectives will be left unexamined.

While preservice teachers often believe that multicultural education is only necessary for working with "minority" youth or in "diverse" schools, the exchange reported here suggests that it is critical to teach all children, particularly White middle class children, to engage complexly with race. For White middle class children who grow up to be White middle class teachers, the consequence of this misperception is particularly problematic. The ability to engage critically about race is all the more urgent in primarily White schools, for if students are not prepared to engage race, they will reinforce White fragility. When White teachers only notice "raced others," they reinscribe Whiteness by continuing to posit Whiteness as universal and non-Whiteness as other. Further, if they cannot listen to or comprehend the perspectives of people of color, they cannot validate the students of color in their classrooms. If they do not engage constructively with this contradiction, they have difficulty in guiding their future students through it. A continual retreat from discomfort of authentic racial engagement results in a perpetual cycle that works to hold racism in place (Marty, 1999).

While antiracist efforts ultimately seek to transform institutionalized racism, antiracist education requires an immediate focus on the micro-level. The goal is to generate the development of interpretations and skills that enable all people, regardless of racial location, to be active initiators of change (Ayvazain, 1995; Harro, 2000). Since all individuals who live within a racist system are enmeshed in its relations, this means that all are responsible for either perpetuating or transforming that system. However, although all individuals play a role in keeping the system active, the responsibility for change is not equally shared. White racism is ultimately a White problem and the primary responsibility for interrupting it must be carried by White people (Derman-Sparks & Phillips, 1997; Hooks, 1995; Wise, 2003). Teacher education programs should begin to have direct conversations about race with White preservice teachers (Adams, Bell, & Griffith, 1997). Conversations about Whiteness might best happen within the context of a larger conversation about racism. It is useful to start at the micro level of analysis, and move to the macro; from the individual out to the interpersonal, societal, and institutional. Starting with the individual and moving outward to the ultimate framework for racism —Whiteness—allows for the pacing that is necessary for many students in approaching the challenging study of race. In this way, a discourse on

Whiteness becomes part of a process rather than an event (Zúñiga, Nagda, & Sevig, 2002).

Many White people have never been given direct or complex information about racism before, and often cannot explicitly see, feel, or understand it (McIntosh, 1988; Weber, 2001). People of color are generally much more aware of racism on a personal level, but due to the wider society's silence and denial of it, often do not have a macrolevel framework from which to analyze their experiences (McIntosh, 1988). Further, dominant society "assigns" different roles to different groups of color, and a critical consciousness about racism varies not only between individuals within groups, but also between groups. For example, many African American students relate having been "prepared" by parents to live in a racist society, while many Asian heritage students say that racism was never directly discussed in their homes (Hooks, 1992; Lee, 1996). A macrolevel analysis may offer a framework to understand different interpretations and performances across and between racial groups. In this way, all students benefit and efforts are not solely focused on White students (which works to re-center Whiteness).

Talking directly about White power and privilege, in addition to providing much needed information and shared definitions, is also in itself a powerful interruption of common (and oppressive) discursive patterns around race (Arnold, Burke, James, & Martin, 1991; Powell, 1997). At the same time, students need to reflect upon racial information and be allowed to make connections between the information and their own lives. White fragility doesn't always manifest in overt ways; as we have seen, silence and withdrawal are also functions of fragility. Teachers can encourage and support students in making their social interactions a point of analysis. Viewing anger, defensiveness, silence, and withdrawal in response to issues of race through the framework of White fragility may help teachers see the problem as an issue of skill-building, as critical as any other social skill addressed in schools.

NOTES

1. Although White racial insulation is somewhat mediated by social class (with poor and working class urban Whites being generally less racially insulated than suburban or rural Whites), the larger social environment insulates and protects Whites as a group through institutions, cultural representations, media, school textbooks, movies, advertising, dominant discourses, and so forth.

2. All of the challenges that follow are consistent with scholarship in Whiteness—see Bonilla-Silva, (2003); Derman-Sparks & Phillips, (1997); Fine

(1997a, 1997b); Flax, (1998); Frankenberg, (1993); Helms, (1990); Morrison, (1992); Sue, (2003); Tatum, (1997).

REFERENCES

Adams, M., Bell, L., & Griffin, P. (1997). *Teaching for diversity and social justice: A sourcebook*. New York: Routledge.

Allen, D. (1996). Knowledge, politics, culture, and gender: A discourse perspective. *Canadian Journal of Nursing Research*, *28*(1), 95-102.

National Center for Education Statistics. (2002). Contexts of elementary and secondary school education [On-line]. Available: http://nces.ed.gov/programs/coe/2002/section4/tables/t30 3.asp

Arnold, R., Burke, B., James, C., & Martin, D. (1991). *Educating for a change*. Toronto, Canada: Between the Lines.

Ayvazain, A. (1995). *Oppression and empowerment: Essays on racism and social change activism: Selected writing, 1985-1995*. Los Angeles: Communitas Press.

Bonilla-Silva, E. (2003). *Racism without racists: Color-blind racism and the persistence of racial inequality in the United States*. Lanham, MD: Rowman & Littlefield.

Croteau, J. M. (1999). One struggle through individualism: Toward an antiracist white racial identity. *Journal of Counseling and Development*, *77*, 30-32.

Dei, G., Karumanchery, L., & Karumanchery-Luik, N. (2004). *Playing the race card: Exposing white power and privilege*. New York: Peter Lang

Derman-Sparks, L., & Phillips, C. (1997). *Teaching/learning anti-racism: A developmental approach*. New York: Teachers College Press.

DiAngelo, R. (2004). *Whiteness in racial dialogue: A discourse analysis*. Unpublished-doctoral dissertation, University of Washington, Seattle.

DiAngelo, R. (2006). My class didn't trump my race: Using oppression to face privilege. *Multicultural Perspectives*, *8*(1)

Dyer, R. (1997). *White*. New York: Routledge.

Evans, K. (2002). *Negotiating the self: Identity, sexuality, and emotion in learning to teach*. New York: Roultledge.

Fine, M. (1997a). Introduction. In M. Fine, L. Weis, C. Powell, & L. Wong (Eds.), *Off White: Readings on race, power and society* (pp. vii-xii). New York: Routledge.

Fine, M. (1997b). Witnessing Whiteness. In M. Fine, L. Weis, C. Powell, & L. Wong (Eds.), *Off White: Readings on race, power, and society* (pp. 57-65). New York: Routledge.

Flax, J. (1998). *American dream in Black and White: The Clarence Thomas hearings*. New York: Cornell University Press.

Frankenberg, R. (1993). *The social construction of Whiteness: White women, race matters*. Minneapolis: University of Minnesota Press.

Frankenberg, R. (1997). *Displacing Whiteness: Essays in social and cultural criticism* (pp. 1-33.). Durham, NC: Duke University Press.

Frankenberg, R. (2001). Mirage of an unmarked Whiteness. In B. Rasmussen, E. Klinerberg, I. Nexica, & M. Wray (Ed.), *The making and unmaking of Whiteness* (pp. 72-96). Durham, NC: Duke University Press.

Gee, J. P. (1999). *An introduction to discourse analysis: Theory and method*. London: Routledge.

Harro, B. (2000). The cycle of liberation. In M. Adams, W. Blumenfeld, R. Castaneda, H. Hackman, M. Peters, & X. Zuniga (Eds.), *Readings for diversity and social justice* (pp. 463-469). New York: Routledge.

Helms, J. E. (1990) (Ed.). *Black and White racial identity: Theory, research and practice*. Westport, CT: Greenwood Press.

Helms, J. E. (1992). *A race is a nice thing to have: A guide to being A White person or understanding the White persons in your life*. Topeka, KS: Content

Hooks, B. (1992). *Black looks: Race and representation*. Boston: South End Press.

Hooks, B. (1995). *Killing rage*. New York: Henry Holt & Company.

Johnson, H. B., & Shapiro, T. M. (2003). Good neighborhoods, good schools: Race and the "good choices" of White families. In A. W. Doane & E. Bonilla-Silva (Eds.), *White out: The continuing significance of racism* (pp. 173-187). New York: Routledge.

Lee, T. (1996). *Unraveling the "model-minority" stereotype: Listening to Asian-American youth*. New York: Teachers College Press.

Levine-Rasky, C. (2000). Framing Whiteness: Working through the tensions in introducing Whiteness to educators. *Race, Ethnicity and Education, 3*(3), 271-292).

Macedo, D., & Bartolome, L. (1999). *Dancing with bigotry: Beyond the politics of tolerance*. New York: St. Martin's Press.

Marty, D. (1999). White antiracist rhetoric as apologia: Wendell Berry's the hidden wound. In T. Nakayama & J. Martin (Eds.), *Whiteness: The communication of social identity* (pp. 51-68). Thousand Oaks, CA: Sage.

McIntosh, P. (1988). White privilege and male privilege: A personal account of coming to see correspondence through work in women's studies. In M. Anderson & P. Hill Collins (Eds.), *Race, class, and gender: An anthology* (pp. 94-105). Belmont, CA: Wadsworth.

Morrison, T. (1992). *Playing in the dark*. New York: Random House.

Nagda, B., Zuniga, X., & Sevig, T. (2002). Bridging differences through peer facilitated intergroup dialogues. In S. Hatcher (Ed.), *Peer programs on a college campus: Theory, training, and the voices of the peers* (pp. 25-41). San Diego, CA: New Resources.

Patterson, M. B. (1998). America's racial unconscious: The invisibility of Whiteness. In A. W. Doane & E. Bonilla-Silva (Eds.), *White out: The continuing significance of racism* (pp. 199-214). New York: Routledge.

Pierce, J. L. (2003). "Racing for Innocence": Corporate culture, and the backlash against affirmative action. In A. W. Doane & E. Bonilla-Silva (Eds.), *White out: The continuing significance of racism* (pp. 199-214). New York: Routledge.

Powell, L. (1997). The achievement (k)not: Whiteness and "Black Underachievement." In M. Fine, L. Powell, C. Weis, & L. Wong (Eds.), *Off White: Readings on race, power and society* (pp. 3-12). New York: Routledge.

Rich, A. (1979). *Disloyal to civilization: Feminism, racism, gynephobia*. New York: Morton.

Roediger, D. (1998). *Black on White: Black writers on what it means to be White*. New York: Schocken

Roman, L. (1993). White is a color!: White defensiveness, postmodernism, and anti-racist pedagogy. In C. McCarthy, & W. Crichlow (Eds.), *Race identity and representation in education* (pp. 135-146). New York: Routeledge.

Schofield, J. (2004). The colorblind perspective in schools: Cause and consequences. In J. A. Banks & C. A. M. Banks (Eds.), *Multicultural education: Issues & perspectives.* New York: Wiley & Sons.

Sleeter, C. (1993). How White teachers construct race. In C. McCarthy & W. Crichlow (Eds.), *Race identity and representation in education* (pp. 157-171). New York: Routledge.

Sleeter, C. (1993). White silence, White solidarity. In N. Ignatiev & J. Garvey (Eds.), *Race traitors* (pp. 257-265). New York: Routledge

Suarez-Orozco, C. (2000). Meeting the challenge: Schooling immigrant youth. *NABE News, 24*(2), 6–35.

Sue, D. W. (2003). *Overcoming our racism: The journey to liberation.* San Francisco: Jossey-Bass.

Tatum, B. (1997). *"Why are all the black kids sitting together in the cafeteria?": And other conversations about race.* New York: Basic Books.

Thandeka. (2000). *Learning to be White: Money, race and God in America.* New York: Continuum.

Van Dijk. T. A. (1992). Discourse and the denial of racism. *Discourse and Society, 3*(1), 87-118.

Van Dijk, T. A. (1993a). Principles of critical discourse analysis. *Discourse and Society, 4,* 249-283.

Van Dijk, T. A. (1993b). Analyzing racism through discourse analysis: Some methodological reflections. In J. H. Stanfield & R. M. Dennis (Eds.), *Race and ethnicity in research methods* London: Sage.

Weber, L. (2001). *Understanding race, class, gender, and sexuality: A conceptual framework.* New York: McGraw-Hill.

Wells, L. (1985). A group-as-a-whole perspective and its theoretical roots. In A. Coleman & M. Geller (Eds.), *Group relations reader 2* (pp. 22-34). Washington, D.C.: A. K. Rice Institute.

Wise, T. (2003). *Whites swim in racial preference.* Retrieved June 22, 2004. http://www.academic.udayton.edu/race/04needs/affirm20.htm

Zúñiga, X., Nagda, B., & Sevig, T. (2002). Intergroup dialogues: An educational model for cultivating engagement across differences. *Equity & Excellence in Education, 6*(1), 115-132.

CHAPTER 12

ANNE FRANK TEACHES TEACHERS ABOUT THE HOLOCAUST

Lesley Shore

We sit around a Toronto restaurant table, 37 years and a thousand miles away from the Grade 8 classroom at River Heights Junior High School in Winnipeg where "Wild Bill" Baker[1] was our social studies teacher. Suddenly a shared memory of Bill's classroom surfaces. Teaching a unit on World War II, our teacher posted a Nazi swastika on the bulletin board at the back of the classroom. Lucy, Dave, and Sarah seem as shocked today as they might have been in 1959 when they went home and reported this event to their parents who, in response, upbraided the teacher for his lack of sensitivity. It seemed "Wild Bill" had no idea this would be offensive, did not foresee an incendiary reaction, was appropriately, if not quite sincerely, apologetic. What followed was a sea-change in the relationships of the Jewish students with their once trusted and admired teacher.

Now that my former classmates are so voluble about remembering this moment, its pale shadow begins to seep through me. But given what I do now, teaching teachers at a faculty of education about the Holocaust, what does it mean that I did not remember this as a vivid memory of a time

Inclusion in Urban Educational Environments:
Addressing Issues of Diversity, Equity, and Social Justice, 241–254
Copyright © 2006 by Information Age Publishing

that has provided abundant inspiration and guidance for me as an educator? Where does this "absent presence" figure in my metamorphosis into a Holocaust teacher although I was officially hired to teach about high school English? How does it connect to my work with *The Diary of Anne Frank*? Did I judge my family's long-ago protest insufficient? Were we reluctant, perhaps embarrassed, to take a stand around being Jewish, to draw attention to ourselves as Jews? Is what I do today a way of expiating that submerged personal history?

I first read Anne's diary shortly after its North American publication, perhaps in 1956 or 1957, as a preadolescent, middle-class, assimilated Jewish girl growing up in respectfully diverse Winnipeg with its rich ethnic mix of Polish, Ukrainian, Scottish, Icelandic, German, and Jewish immigrants. My second-generation Canadian parents, good people to be sure, studiously avoided any discussion about the Holocaust. They said it was too difficult a subject for me but I suspect it was too difficult for them. Though I was always a thinker, this activity was not encouraged; it seemed unnecessary in a girl. My father took the more active role in my education, driving me to the library when I needed books for the many projects that characterized my "major work"[2] education. I can still see him hunched over the typewriter tapping away two-fingered as I dictated my essays to him. My mother pointedly absented herself from the arena of my education, her self-deprecating justification that she could not spell.

"I learned more about the Holocaust at your home than I did at mine," I admit to my once-best-friend Sarah in this leafy summer moment of 2005. "Your mother would talk about it. Your mother refused to buy anything that was made in Germany and when I asked her why, she took the time to explain it to me."

Now I teach teachers about the Holocaust, not as a historian or as an expert in the literature of the Holocaust. I teach about the Holocaust because few at my faculty of education are willing or able to teach about it and because the teacher candidates who study here want and need to learn about it.

"I don't really know how to say this," begins Diana, a student in a course on antiracist education whose instructor has invited me to visit their classroom. "I am a Master's student in Education but how can I think of myself as an educated person and a teacher when I know nothing about the Holocaust beyond the body count? And why didn't my education teach me anything about it?" Santayana's admonition that those who do not remember their own history are doomed to repeat it rings true all over our troubled planet. Education needs to remember.

Early last fall Rayanne, one of my preservice English teacher candidates, confessed to me before class one morning that she was troubled by the attitude of her "School and Society" (the compulsory course here with a dedicated focus on diversity issues) instructor around Jewishness. "We study every other kind of discrimination but anti-Semitism," she explained,

"Whenever I try to bring this up in class I get shot down. Jews are 'white' I am told and therefore, enjoy 'white privilege.' The proof of that is their obvious wealth and success." Rayanne was frustrated. "How can I tell him that for one entire year of my university education I lived on nothing but Kraft dinner?" She understood that in this instructor's world-view there were no poor, hungry, homeless Jews. Jewishness might even confer an unfair advantage. I imagine that Rayanne's instructor would never have suspected that his views were anti-Semitic. Labeling Jews wealthy and successful glossed over centuries of religious persecution and denied Rayanne's reality. But what about me? I had been a School and Society instructor. Had I taught about anti-Semitism? Was I convinced that there were no longer any struggles around being Jewish? I taught that course before and during 9/11 and not in its awesome aftermath. My current teaching about the Holocaust bears witness to how the world has changed since September 11, 2001 whose wake has spawned a resurgence of virulent anti-Semitic attacks across national and regional boundaries.

I teach about the Holocaust because it urgently needs to be done and because I have witnessed the power of this teaching in classrooms where the students were neither White nor Jewish. If the topic of the Holocaust is, in fact, as difficult a topic as it is claimed to be, teachers need to learn about it first themselves, in faculties of education, so that they may be prepared to teach about it in their own classrooms.

The course "Anne Frank, Holocaust Diaries and the Writing of the Adolescent Self" initially received approval, but not funding, along with feedback (reiterated by the various administrative committees who evaluated it) that I "broaden the notion of 'holocaust' to include the many genocides of history" (associate dean, personal communication, February 10, 2003). I removed "Holocaust diaries" from the course title and set my mind to interpreting the implications of "hatred based on difference" as broadly as I could. Then I persuaded the chair of my department to let me teach it. He wondered who would be interested in taking this course and expressed surprise when eleven students registered for it. All were young women. Nine of them were not Jewish. The majority taught in the Catholic system.

In setting the agenda for the course I was conscious of not making the Holocaust its singular focus because I had not been given institutional permission to do so. The initial readings provided historical context for the writing of Anne's Diary and more recent research on adolescence and the role of writing in it. Jane Miller's (1996) notion of the "autobiography of the question" (p. 258) alerted me to the importance of giving the students scope to follow their own needs and directions. "What brought you here?" I asked them in their first session. "What do you want to learn through the process of this course?" I insisted that all students read a companion text of war, revolution and/or genocide written by a young woman from a different time and place against Anne's diary. There was no shortage of choices.

Midway through the course, when students had begun selecting their preferred texts and readings, Jemille[3] asked "Do you think we could get a Holocaust survivor to visit our class?" The other students embraced her suggestion. "We may never have another opportunity to meet a Holocaust survivor." Since I had been directed to downplay the role of the Holocaust, their request caught me off guard. Now the students had chosen to make this an explicit part of their learning; moreover, they wanted to know how to translate what they had learned into action.

"The Holocaust began with words," Judy Cohen, survivor of Auschwitz, began her visit to our classroom. Against the riveting story of her survival, she offered the model of her social activism. The week before she retired, Judy decided to break the long silence about her wartime experiences after a confrontation with a white supremacist in front of her Toronto office. He told her that the Holocaust had not happened. She showed him the numbers tattooed on her arm. Then she understood that she had a moral obligation to speak to young people, to bear witness, to share her story.

The experience of the Anne Frank course and the readings around it provided a springboard into social activism for the teachers who participated in it. Jemille Chu Morrison, who teaches in a Catholic high school north of Toronto, convinced her principal to allow all the school's Grade 11 and 12 students watch the film *Hotel Rwanda* and have first period the following morning to write letters to the United Nations protesting their performance in Rwanda and demanding a more powerful role in Darfur. Jemille and her students traveled to New York City and hand-delivered 1,800 letters to Jan Egeland, U.N. Emergency Relief Coordinator. Their story was featured widely in the media; the students continue their efforts today in a variety of ways.

Tasha Boylan, a novice teacher in an urban public high school where student leadership is actively encouraged, was frustrated by the apathy of these same students. "How can I get my students to move outside the bubble of their own experience?" she asked. The readings of the course prompted her to research female leadership. Against the advice of her principal who deemed the situation a simple case of "boys will be boys," Tasha spoke up at a staff meeting to rally her fellow teachers around addressing the sexual harassment of female students in hallways and classrooms. She knew that she might be risking her chances of tenure by doing this. Listening to her tell her story during our last class together, her classmate Xiaohong Chi commented: "To change the world we must begin by changing ourselves."

Words have the power to inspire genocide and to deny it. Language is always a highly political artifact. Our students need to think critically around what language can do. Reflecting on how the experience of teaching this course has transformed me, I now understand myself as a teacher of "humane literacy" who thinks deeply about the power of words. But why begin with Anne's words? Why this particular text? In the summer of 2000, Richard Monette, artistic director of Ontario's Stratford Festival Theatre, announced that he did not want to "let the twentieth century go by without having something on the Stratford stages about the most important event of the twentieth century—the Holocaust" (Gould, 2002). He chose to represent that event by staging the *Diary of Anne Frank*. Sixty years after World War II, the two pivotal points of cultural reference for the existence of the Holocaust remain the extermination camp at Auschwitz and the Diary of a 14-year-old Jewish girl in hiding from the Nazis.

Anne Frank's Diary is the second best-selling nonfiction book in the history of publishing, next only to the Bible, with more than 31 million copies in 67 different languages. It articulates the adolescent's urgent need to be heard, respected, and understood by adults. Across the boundaries of time, culture, race, ethnicity, and gender, young people today still recognize Anne's name, know that she wrote a diary and want to read it. As such this text provides a worthwhile entry-point for approaching the difficult topic of the Holocaust across a variety of classroom subject areas. The teachers who were my students proposed that the English classroom might well be the best place to begin the study of the Holocaust, given the present Ontario curriculum where only one Grade 10 Canadian history credit is required for graduation. Four required English credits mean more scope for visiting and revisiting the Holocaust. Approaching the text in terms of sound bites, by choosing particular entries for reading, writing and discussion, is facilitated by the Diary's format. That it is a text written by a real (not a fictional) girl legitimates it for teenage boys who have a well-articulated preference for nonfiction and a natural curiosity about the workings of a young girl's mind.

Remarkably, the book was published first in The Netherlands in 1947 and soon after, in Germany in 1950. It is worth noting Alvin Rosenfeld's (1991) observations on German reaction to the Diary in light of the concerted (and understandable) postwar reluctance to "wrestle with the sense of their nation, especially when they felt compelled to do so by their conquerors" during the period of the Nuremberg trials. Rosenfeld reports:

Many of the early book reviews also make clear that the diary of Anne Frank broke through to German readers as almost nothing previously connected to the war had been able to do. In all of these respects, the emergence of Anne Frank as a factor in postwar German consciousness signaled something new—indeed, she was among the first prods to public memory and began a debate that continues, unresolved, to this day. (Rosenfeld, 1991, p. 264)

Deborah Britzman (1999) brilliantly explains the power of Anne's text as performing a "rescue fantasy." Falling in love with Anne through the medium of her Diary, good Christians (and Jews who lived outside the range of Hitler's grasp), absolve themselves of any guilt about their "bystander" status, how they let the Holocaust happen, how they did not love their brothers and sisters as themselves.

Curriculum theorist Marla Morris (2001) offers the model of a "dystopic curriculum"

that allows the shadow of the object, the shadow of the Holocaust, to darken perspectives. But darkening perspectives does not mean sliding into nihilism. A dystopic curriculum is an ethical one, a response to [Levinas'] "invocation" of the other. A dystopic curriculum is a promise of remembering that attempts to cut through lightness and inauthenticity toward the dark. (p. 11)

Nel Noddings observes that American curriculum veers away from treating anything that "smacks of suffering or grief." As she sees it "[e]ducation has at least in modern times been guided by optimism and notions of progress ... Perhaps we should now consider an education guided by a tragic sense of life" (as cited in Morris, 2001, p. 11). Maxine Greene (2001) would judge this reluctance to examine our darker side part of Dewey's legacy and the shortcoming of his vision.

Because she is a gifted writer who writes eloquently and with unprecedented openness about what she thinks and feels, we trust Anne and listen to what she has to say. Her text is not a diatribe; she does not preach. It is the puzzled voice of a child seeking to understand the mysterious adult world that she simply cannot decipher. It is other than what she, assiduously schooled in the philosophy of Western civilization, has been taught to believe. Even postwar Germans could tolerate questions Anne contended with in a passage like this one, written April 11, 1944:

We've been strongly reminded of the fact that we're Jews in chains, chained to one spot, without any rights, but with a thousand obligations ... one day this terrible war will be over. The time will come when we'll be people again and not just Jews!... Who has inflicted this on us? Who has set us apart from all the rest? Who has put us through such suffering?... Who knows, maybe our religion will teach the world and all the people in it about goodness, and that's the reason, the only reason, we have to suffer. We can never be just Dutch, or just English, or whatever, we will always be Jews as well. And we'll have to keep on being Jews, but then, we'll want to be. (Frank, 1991, p. 261)

Because young readers believe in Anne's rendering of their adolescent experience, they are prepared to engage seriously with her philosophical inquiry into what it is to be human. Asking students to write letters back to Anne in response to a passage like this one might be an interesting place to begin untangling the roots of anti-Semitism.

"To our great sorrow and dismay," Anne writes one month later,

we've heard that many people have changed their attitude toward us Jews. We've been told that anti-Semitism has cropped up in circles where once it would have been unthinkable. This fact has affected us all very, very deeply. The reason for hatred is understandable, maybe even human, but that doesn't make it right. (p. 302)

Still she understands that it would not be easy to "remain silent in the face of German pressure" (p. 302) to hate Jews and retains her hope that the goodness of the Dutch people will somehow manage to prevail, "that they'll never waver in their hearts from what they know to be just" (p. 303).

Moral decision making is critical to Holocaust education. Anne's signature sentence, "in spite of everything I still believe that people are really good at heart" (Frank, 1989, p. 694) reflects her moral choice to embrace goodness while completely understanding that we had not yet opened the conversation about the potential for evil residing within each one of us. While much is made of what critics have judged Anne's naïve (and misguided) faith in humanity, 60 years after her death, we have not even opened the conversation about the damage wrought by the dark impulses hidden in the deep recesses of our human hearts.

On May 3, 1944, Anne wrote:

I don't believe the war is simply the work of politicians and capitalists. Oh no, the common man is every bit as guilty; otherwise, people and nations would have rebelled long ago! There's a destructive urge in people, the urge to rage, murder and kill. And until all of humanity, without exception, undergoes a metamorphosis, wars will continue to be waged, and everything that has been carefully built up, cultivated and grown will be cut down and destroyed, only to start all over again! (Frank, 1991, pp. 280-281)

Invoking Anne Frank as a role model for the virtue of honesty and the concerted daily struggle of living a moral life, I urge teachers to begin a conversation about what it has meant and still means to hate Jews simply for being Jews, about how that hatred has been passed down (though perhaps never articulated as such) through hundreds of generations since the third century after Christ, about the various ways in which the repressed returns, about the human need to feel superior to someone else and how it might be possible to cloak that need in many garments.

Seldom in our "education" do we teach what it means to be fully human, what we need to sustain bodies and relationships, how to raise a family, how to make the world a more peaceful place, how to love, how to sustain hope, how to contain and disrupt that destructive urge within. Because she nakedly admits the wide range of her emotions, discussions can be opened up about topics that have rarely seen the light of the classroom's gaze. Reading this text can present a forum for discussions about the experience of growing up in a family, what it is like to feel rage for your mother at the same time as you feel guilty for that rage, what it means to be compared to brothers, sisters, cousins, or children of family friends, what it is like to make rational decisions against the stirrings of the adolescent body, what it means to live in a culture where expectations for the performance of gender are narrowly defined. Anchored in the emotional honesty required to begin such conversations, we can move on to the deeper questions. What it means to hate people when you are not even sure why you hate them. What it means to hate them just because your parents do.

In my view, there has been no more definitive insight into the persistence of evil in our world than Anne's naked call to individual responsibility. Anne alerts me to the potential within our students' hearts and minds to lead with conscience, to ask how "human nature" has changed for the better since Anne wrote her words, to question perhaps why it has not. And further, to consider in what ways the theories of "identity politics" have influenced the persistent reality of racial hatred, war, and genocide.

Whenever we target an individual as different, something that happens all the time in schools and often goes unexamined, we demonstrate through our behavior that the lessons of the Holocaust have not yet been learned. Whenever we witness, in the hallways of schools, scenes where students laugh at or mock or draw attention to or question another student's dress or behavior or skin color or cultural background or accent or appearance or sexual orientation and we, the teachers, remain silent, we are complicit in the same kinds of behavior that allowed the Holocaust to happen. We shut our eyes and close our ears to what we know and carry on. Carrying on is just what average Germans did, cold and hungry and without work during the war years, as they watched the smoke belching from the crematoria of Dachau and smelled human flesh burning and yet, did not know. Anne's story lends itself to examination of the roles of victim, perpetrator, bystander, collaborator, rescuer—set forth by the Oliners (1988) in their critical but, I believe, marginalized study of altruism, specifically the altruism of Holocaust rescuers and amplified in the *Facing History and Ourselves* (1994) curricula designed by American educator Margot Strom and her associates.

Still, in the institution of education where I teach, I hear echoes of the old stories, how we do not need to teach the Holocaust or *The Diary of Anne Frank* because all that is old news; we have been there and done that. And after all, it is a Jewish issue, is it not? In the contexts with which I am familiar in Ontario, Holocaust education is generally absent from the antiracist agenda or where it is present it is marginalized, the last item on the list. This is due, in some part, to the kind of education about the Holocaust that we have had in Ontario; we may have learned the body count but we have not learned the lessons. We need the kind of call to individual responsibility, the turning inward to examine the propensity for good and evil within each one of us that Anne makes again and again. Surely it is the role of education to engage precisely those topics which are the most difficult.

Anne's youth transcends the political. There is no need to situate her voice within any other system than the one which would ultimately murder her. In Wordsworthian terms this child's innocent morality of goodness is a guilty challenge to her adult readers, at the same time as it offers the possibility of rescuing us from our complicity with an adult world where our own youthful idealism has been tempered by a more sophisticated but less honest reality. And still she cannot save us. Though a cult of Anne Frank clubs has grown up in present-day Germany, it is too facile to infer from this that the deeper lessons of the Holocaust have been internalized in Europe, the Middle East, or on our own continent. Recent polls attest to a frightening revival of a new, reenergized strain of anti-Semitism which confounds age-old Jew hatred with anti-Zionism, anticapitalism, and antiglobalization.

We might wonder what force for the good Anne's text retains today against our own recent North American incidents of this revitalized anti-Semitism. Not that we have not been warned about the difficulty of teaching against the Holocaust.

"It may be comforting," wrote Tim Cole (1999), 6 years ago,

> to think that by encouraging school children to read *The Diary Of Anne Frank* and learn about the 'Holocaust', we can put an end to intolerance and discrimination. Yet if we ask ourselves 'had Anne Frank—an ordinary young Jewish girl—lived next door, could she have counted on us for help during the Nazi occupation?' and simply answer "yes," we betray a lack of humility which confrontation with the Holocaust demands. When faced with what "ordinary" men and women did to other "ordinary" men and women

because of their Jewishness, what other response is there but "I just don't know." It is too easy to say "yes" and thereby set up self-righteous categories of "us" and "them," meaning "we" would have helped, but "they," the "racists," the "intolerant," the "prejudiced," the "nationalists" would not have done so. (p. 43)

Is there a reader who does not read Anne's diary against precisely this question? As Chilean exile and poet Marjorie Agosin (1994) put it: "What would we have done if Anne Frank came to our door and asked us to hide her, asked us to lodge and feed her for one night or ten years?" (p. 8). Would I have risked my family to save another? Who might I have asked to save me? How exactly are such moral decisions made? How are such history lessons forgotten? Can we do a better job of teaching about the Holocaust?

I suggest that we might direct our students to begin by asking questions about their own school communities. What are the rules and laws operating in your school? What rights do students have? What are their obligations? Ask questions like: when has a right or freedom been taken away from you and how did you respond to that? What are the rights and obligations of the teachers in your school? Can you recall yourself as a child performing or bearing witness to a moral action? Can you remember an experience where an adult (perhaps a teacher) treated you with great kindness and empathy? How did that work for you? Have you experienced or witnessed incidents of racism, sexism or bullying in your school? How were they handled? How do you think your behavior has changed as a result of experiencing or witnessing these events? What are the characteristics of a hero?[4]

Beginning teacher Erin Gruwell (1999), in *The Freedom Writers Diary* describes how she used Anne's diary and the diary (modeled on Anne's) written by Zlata Filopovic (1994) in war-torn Sarajevo to motivate Gruwell's own low-achieving high school students. They kept diaries of their lives that showed the violence, homelessness, racism, illness, and abuse that surrounded them. With the published diaries as their model and a teacher who believed in them and held them to high expectations, these students, the Freedom Writers as they called themselves (in honor of the U.S. Freedom Riders of the 1960s), defied expectations and all graduated from high school. While teaching about anti-Semitism was not Gruwell's primary objective in using Anne's text, it became a part of what her students learned. They made connections between what happened during the Holocaust and their own traumatic lived experiences. Alvin Rosenfeld (2005) claims, and I agree, that it is impossible to be anti-Semitic if you have experienced good Holocaust education.

Curiously, anti-Semitism remains the last acceptable "ism" in our politically correct world. I wonder how Holocaust education can more fully inform the antiracist project. If "race" is discernable only through skin color and "racism" is the oppression only of people of color, students may not develop the critical thinking skills they will need to deconstruct future incarnations of racism. Dr. Carole Ann Reed, Codirector of the now-defunct Program for Holocaust and Genocide Education at OISE/UT, prefers Robert Miles' concept of "racialization":

> What rationalization racialization? refers to is how different groups have been named as a "race" at different times and in different places using different categories which include religion, culture, language, the concept of blood, skin colour—all of what anthropologists call phenotypical characteristics like skull shape, nose, hair, size. Racialization offers a broader historical scope. (C. A. Reed, personal correspondence, March 26, 2003)

This opens the door for building critical bridges with Holocaust and genocide education.

In time-worn phrases like "some of my best friends are Jewish" a subtle discrimination lurks just beneath the surface, as anti-Semitism often does. We must do more than pay lip service to "social justice" by laboring to contend with, interrogate, and amend the situated perspectives that would coopt this noble banner for purposes of exclusion rather than inclusion. If education is truly to be socially just and inclusive, it must approach that goal from the widest perspective not the most narrow. My vision of an inclusive classroom centers on daily practice that questions, upends, and reconceptualizes "received knowledges"—from home, from church, from culture, from media—to reveal the fault lines in our best-intentioned attempts to cross "the rackety bridge from self to Other" (Phelan, 1993, p. 174).

As part of the Canadian media's coverage of the 60th anniversary of the Liberation of Auschwitz, *National Post* reporter Mireille Silcoff (2005) described her reaction to a visit there:

> I should like to remember the victims of the Holocaust as human beings who had lives lived richly, often against all odds—for this is the truth. I do not want to remember them as brittle bones, totems of murder.... We might do better to spend more time remembering—and teaching our children about—the people that existed before the numbers and the life that existed prior to the descent into horror. (p. A14)

Anne provides the bridge for this kind of remembering. She shows us how life was lived in a close-knit, loving, cultured Jewish family, who valued friendship, lived their ethics and tried to make the world a better place. As Jews have often done. Let us remember the Holocaust in these terms too against the barbaric atrocities of what the Nazis did.

Let us remember with appropriate respect the magnificent achievement of this singular 14-year-old girl, only one of one and a half million innocent children brutally murdered in the Nazi plan to exterminate the Jews and mourn what more she and they might have given to the world. As teachers what we can do, and where we can stand is in the center of Anne's hope for humanity, working with our students, one by one, towards the self-knowledge that might reveal their own individual understandings of and commitment to the path of moral courage.

I began with a middle school memory and will end with another. Miss Colpitts, our Grade 8 homeroom teacher, teaches us French and music but it is music that is her passion. One day she writes on the blackboard the lyrics of a song which appears in the libretto of *South Pacific*, the musical sensation of the moment, but is not performed either in film or stage versions. She asks us to think about what might have prompted the producers to leave this song out. The song is called "You've Got To Be Carefully Taught":

> You've got to be taught to hate and fear,
> You've got to be taught from year to year,
> It's got to be drummed in your dear little ear,
> You've got to be carefully taught.
> You've got to be taught to be afraid
> Of people whose eyes are oddly made,
> And people whose skin is a different shade,
> You've got to be carefully taught.
> You've got to be taught before it's too late,
> Before you are six or seven or eight,
> To hate all the people your relatives hate,
> You've got to be carefully taught.

Suddenly, at the tender age of 13, we understand the subversive power of language.

I am stunned by the realization that hate is taught but it does not take long to realize that children can also be taught to love. In fact, that is precisely what Miss Colpitts teaches in our music class—how we can love one another across whatever boundaries of difference appear to separate us. In the late 1950s we sing Christmas carols in English, French, and Ukrainian, and Chanukah songs in Hebrew and Yiddish at our school's annual Christmas concert. We understand that all of this is intimately connected to the Second World War and what Miss Colpitts, outspoken as she is, can and cannot tell us about it.

Memories of Miss Colpitts' teaching eventually draw me to this profession; 40 years later her example inspires my teaching. I catch myself chuckling now and then as the images associated with one or another of her irreverent acts returns to me. The mind creates its own healing wisdom: scenes of her classroom come to gloss over that awkward suppressed memory of Mr. Baker's.

Miss Colpitts echoes Anne Frank's generous humanity to "join in loving not in hating" (Woolf, quoting Antigone, 1986, p. 190). Blurring the boundaries of time and space, of teacher and student, we dismantle hatred born simply of difference and share Anne Frank's "thousand obligations" in teaching about the Holocaust.

NOTES

1. Names have been changed to protect confidentiality except where otherwise indicated throughout the text of this paper.

2. The "major work" classes were an experiment in Winnipeg School District One where students designated as "gifted" by means of an IQ test were selected from various schools within neighborhoods to study with teachers specially trained to teach them. The experiment was disbanded after 20 years when studies showed that "major work" students had inordinate numbers of social problems which might have been the result of their prolonged segregation from the mainstream.

3. I have not used pseudonyms for Jemille and her fellow students in the Anne Frank course I offered in the winter of 2005 because I want to acknowledge their achievements here. Holocaust survivor Judy Cohen's name is her own as is the name of the late Marjorie Colpitts, the legendary teacher who most influenced my practice and who is lovingly remembered by thousands of her former students.

4. I am indebted to educator Joyce Apsel, former Director of Education Anne Frank Center USA, for raising provocative questions like these which stimulated my own thinking.

REFERENCES

Agosin, M. (1994). *Dear Anne Frank*. Washington, DC: Azul Editions.

Britzman, D. P. (1999). On the second history of Anne Frank. *Canadian Children's Literature, 25*(3), 120-140.

Cole, T. (1999). *Selling the Holocaust: From Auschwitz to Schindler. How history is bought, packaged and old*. New York: Routledge.

Filipovic, Z. (1994). *Zlata's diary: A child's life in Sarajevo*. New York: Viking.

Frank, A. (1989). *The diary of Anne Frank: The critical edition* (A. J. Pomerans & B. M. Mooyart-Doubleday, Trans.) New York: Doubleday.

Frank, A. (1991). *The diary of a young girl: The definitive edition* (S. Massotty, Trans.). New York: Doubleday.

Gruwell, E. (1999). *The Freedom Writers diary: How a teacher and 150 teens used writing to change themselves and the world around them*. New York: Broadway Books.

Gould, A. (2002, July). *My experience with Anne Frank*. Lecture given in TPS8002H Anne Frank in Life and Death, OISE/UT, Toronto, Ontario, Canada.

Greene, M. (2001, November). *The arts and social justice: A postscript*. R. Freeman Butts Lecture at the annual meeting of the American Educational Studies Association, Miami, FL.

Miller, J. (1996). *School for women*. London: Virago Press.

Morris, M. (2001). *Curriculum and the Holocaust: Competing sites of memory and representation*. Mahwah NJ: Erlbaum.

Oliner, S. P., & Oliner. P. M. (1988). *The altruistic personality: Rescuers of Jews in Nazi Europe*. New York: The Free Press.

Phelan, P. (1993). *Unmarked: The politics of performance*. New York: Routledge.

Rosenfeld, A. H. (1991). Popularization and memory: The case of Anne Frank. In P. Hayes (Ed.), *Lessons and legacies. The meaning of the Holocaust in a changing world* (pp. 243-278). Evanston, IL: Northwestern University Press.

Rosenfeld, A. H. (2005, May). *Remembering Anne Frank*. Lecture for Scholar-in-Residence program at Beth Tikvah Syngagogue, Toronto, Ontario, Canda.

Silcoff, M. (2005, January 25). Only the deaths, not the lives. *The National Post*, pp. A1, A14.

Strom. M. S. (1994). *Facing history and ourselves: Holocaust and human behavior*. Brookline, MA: Facing History and Ourselves National Organization.

Woolf, V. (1986). *Three guineas*. London: The Hogarth Press.

CHAPTER 13

ADDRESSING MULTICULTURAL AND ANTIRACIST THEORY AND PRACTICE WITH CANADIAN TEACHER ACTIVISTS

Darren E. Lund

I have long believed that teacher activists are ideally positioned to play an instrumental role in addressing social justice issues in contemporary Canadian society by virtue of their location in school settings. I feel fortunate in that my ongoing research has entailed much collaboration with those educators who have already begun to take up the challenge of addressing inequities in schools and society. Although individual commitment to social justice on issues is admirable, it is an inadequate end goal considering the significant reform needed in schools, school districts, and faculties of education in this country (Corson, 2000; James & Wood, 2005; Solomon & Levine-Rasky, 2003). Understanding how Canadian educators are currently addressing discrimination and other forms of oppression will inform the quest to ensure that both urban and rural schools provide equitable educational opportunities for all students regardless of their ethnic, cultural, racial or other identities.

Inclusion in Urban Educational Environments:
Addressing Issues of Diversity, Equity, and Social Justice, 255–274
Copyright © 2006 by Information Age Publishing
All rights of reproduction in any form reserved.

Aside from a few notable exceptions (Gillborn, 1995; Smith & Young, 1996) the voices of teacher activists currently engaging in social justice projects in real schools have often been excluded from this conversation. This chapter[1] addresses that silence by valuing those perspectives and engaging them directly with theory and research sources. The four teachers I interviewed as part of a larger research project[2] (Lund, 2001) speak as respected participants in this ongoing debate, their understandings grounded in the gritty terrain of daily activism and informed by their experiences in schools across Alberta, a province in western Canada.

A broad consideration of social justice encompasses a variety of concerns about the lived experiences of discrimination, oppression, and injustice, and seeks to understand the complex intersections of a number of often overlapping categories of social identity and conflict, including cultural, ethnic, and racialized identities, gender, sexual orientation, class, and physical ability. Attending to Hall's (1992) rejection of identity as "fixed transcultural or transcendental racial categories" (p. 254), I recognize *race* as a social construction while acknowledging the lived experience of the racialized context of contemporary schooling. My specific attention to antiracist and multicultural education does not deny the intersections between all forms of oppression, but is presented here as part of a broader field, a necessary limitation considering the wide scope of the literature in social justice education.

Below I offer a brief overview of the Canadian scene, followed by attention to particular relevant British and U.S. discussions in this field. There are a surprisingly few accounts of Canadian school-based antiracist and multicultural activism in educational academic literature, aside from a few anecdotal reports (Berlin & Alladin, 1996; Smith & Young, 1996), and this research represents an attempt to address that omission. Broadly speaking, my interest is in students and teachers who have organized events, projects, or coalitions to address diversity issues in their schools. Situating this research project in both urban and rural secondary schools in Alberta requires attention to public discourse and political developments. Conservative reforms to public policy over the past decade have significantly affected school and government multicultural policies and programming in Alberta. For example, many government, community and other organizations addressing diversity have faced dramatic reductions or elimination in recent years.

EXPLORING SOCIAL JUSTICE EDUCATION IN THE CANADIAN CONTEXT

In its relatively short history, the field of education attending to social justice issues in Canada has responded to a dynamic social context in which activists and educators must negotiate a balance between liberal notions of consensus-building and the critical need for significant societal and institutional reform to address inequities. Specifically on ethnocultural issues, social justice education has taken shape over the past few decades under the banner of multicultural education with significant influence from antiracist and other perspectives (Fleras & Elliot, 1992; James & Wood, 2005; Moodley, 1995). I conducted my interviews within the specific sociopolitical context of Alberta's public schools. However, with much of the research and theorizing in this area continuing to be informed by American conceptions of multicultural education and British formulations of antiracist education, I draw on insights from a selection of these sources as a backdrop for this chapter.

Canada remains the only nation with its multicultural ideals entrenched into its constitution and a range of national government policies (Joshee, 2004; Moodley, 1995), first introduced in policy statements by Prime Minister Trudeau in 1971, followed by each province enacting its own version of multicultural policy. Key documents include the 1982 *Canadian Charter of Rights and Freedoms* and the 1984 *Canadian Multiculturalism Act*. As well, this country's historical immigration patterns and policies, social and educational institutions, and public responses differ in significant ways from those of other countries, affecting the singular development of Canadian educational policies, research, and practices in this area (Fleras & Elliot, 1992; Kymlicka, 1998; Moodley, 1995).

Our national stereotype as Canadians includes a tendency toward conciliation and consensus rather than conflict. This complicates the current discourse on diversity, as does the pervasive and erroneous notion that Canada has always stood for harmony and acceptance. The purported absence of racism in Canada as experienced by White citizens is refuted by a long history of discriminatory government policies and practices, including racial segregation in schools, forced assimilation of First Nations Canadians, and racialized immigration restrictions (Baergen, 2000; Boyko, 1995). These and other racist aspects of Canadian history have either been excluded or inadequately challenged in current social studies school materials (Tupper, 2002), and denied by many in political and administrative positions.

There continues to be a vigorous public debate in Canada regarding the value of any form of antiracist or multicultural education, and indeed, of the concept of multiculturalism itself (Bissoondath, 1994). Arguments supporting the desired assimilation of newcomers to a mainstream culture and restricting immigration levels (from non-White countries, although this is rarely said directly) to uphold "traditional values" serve to entrench the status quo and ignore concerns around diversity issues. From within academic discourse, however, there is widespread consensus on the historical basis of racism in Canada, and on highlighting the benefits of cultural pluralism toward building a strong democracy. Unfortunately, much of the contention in this field still focuses on the recurrent disputes between supporters of two specific variants of social justice research and theory.

MULTICULTURAL AND ANTIRACIST EDUCATION IN CANADIAN EDUCATIONAL LITERATURE

About a decade ago, some Canadian researchers were depicting social justice education as a highly divisive field of study, describing conflicts between multicultural and antiracist camps using dichotomous, oppositional terms (Kehoe, 1994; McGregor & Ungerleider, 1993). In my own research and activist work I have sought to avoid simplified bipolar positions that deny the complexity of school-based social justice initiatives. Nevertheless, tracing the development of these two apparently contradictory strands of social justice education seems worthwhile toward understanding the experiences of school activists. Briefly, traditional multicultural education has been linked to notions of original federal multicultural policies that promoted ethnocultural retention. It is characterized as consisting of short-term programs and supplemental curricular material designed to cause attitudinal changes in individual students and teachers. The goal has been to foster appreciation of the cultural heritages of others toward increasing intergroup harmony; such models of multicultural education have been criticized as disregarding hidden forms of oppression (Dei, 1996a; James & Wood, 2005).

Antiracist education in Canada has emerged to explore more directly the embedded biases in learning materials and existing inequitable power sharing in schools (Thomas, 1984). As outlined below, much of this work has been informed by British and American sources. Some Canadian antiracist educators have complained that traditional multicultural programs fail to name and address racism and other discrimination, implicitly support assimilation to a mainstream, and may actually foster ethnic stereotyping by treating cultures as static and perpetually foreign (Dei, 1996a; Lee, 1994).

Social justice activists typically adopt a plurality of approaches, many of which incorporate both multicultural and antiracist ideals in their underlying intentions and implementation. Indeed, many Canadian multicultural education proponents have adopted a more critical and transformative stance (Ghosh, 1996; Moodley, 1995). Additionally, antiracism educators have been under fire from multicultural educators as well, for adopting too negative and oppositional a stance, for focusing on skin color only, and for downplaying the important race relations groundwork accomplished by multicultural educators (Friesen, 1991; McLeod, 1992). Of course, educational activists need not speak with a single, consensual voice. Through my research I seek a better understanding of strategic uses of conflicting terminology toward progressive ends, as it is experienced and expressed by school-based activists.

BRIEF NOTES ON MULTICULTURAL AND ANTIRACIST EDUCATION IN BRITAIN

Understanding how multicultural and antiracist education are framed differently in other countries will illuminate how these competing conceptions influence and complicate Canadian theorizing and activism in this field. For example, the work by antiracist educators in Britain has been highly influential in shaping notions of ethnic identity and racism in the ongoing redefining of multicultural policies in Canada for the past several years (Bonnett & Carrington, 1996; Troyna, 1993; Young, 1995). In contrast to the Canadian context, Britain's recent political history has included more restricted immigration policies, a strong national identity based on an assumed mono-cultural homogeneity, and no official national policies on multiculturalism. For decades, to be British meant to be White and Christian, and other ethnic groups were constructed as a threat to national cohesiveness (Gilroy, 1992). From this exclusivist context have emerged antiracist educational initiatives that have typically been highly oppositional to White racism and focused on Black resistance (Short & Carrington, 1996).

British scholars have described a form of "cultural racism" that has been flourishing as that nation has undergone a significant conservative resurgence. This "new racism" carefully masks references to race and skin color, replacing them with an absolutist ethnic argument for British national identity (Gilroy, 1992; Gundara & Jones, 1992). Briefly summarized, Thatcher's conservative government implemented policies and offered thinly veiled racist rhetoric in the largely conservative media surrounding notions of national identity. Just it has been in Canada, antiracism have been attacked as encouraging Black hatred and distrust of a White society, while social justice efforts in the schools have been dismissed as programs from the "loony left" (Bonnett & Carrington, 1996; Gillborn, 1995). Similarities to conservative reforms currently taking place in Canada makes the establishment of links between social justice practitioners and scholars across both countries both desirable and inevitable. Initiating this dialogue by talking with activists about specific issues in the academic literature is an important first step in establishing solidarity across national boundaries.

Both British and American scholars who have conducted thorough research reviews have noted that scholars and school activists in Canada have imported some key aspects of British antiracist activism into the multicultural education discourse (Bonnett & Carrington, 1996; Sleeter & Bernal, 2004). As revealed below, my interviews with activists confirm a more critical antiracist sensibility in activism on diversity issues. Reed (1995) reports that collaborative antiracist activism in schools attempts to "encompass understandings of the complex interplay of issues around 'race', class, gender, sexuality, disability and special educational needs" (p. 78). This broader vision for the future of social justice pedagogy shares a great deal with critical formulations of multicultural education that have developed recently in Canada, and over the past several decades in the United States.

A BRIEF LOOK AT AMERICAN MULTICULTURALISM

Educators concerned with social justice issues in the United States have used the term multicultural education to address a variety of social concerns regarding ethnic, class, gender, sexuality, and cultural issues. Many have avowed a "critical multicultural" stance toward education, specifically to allow for the interrogation of existing systemic inequities in curricular content, teaching practices, hiring procedures, and policies (Kincheloe & Steinberg, 1997; McCarthy, 1993). In this regard, the American use of the term *multicultural* automatically implies a uniting of cultural harmony concerns with antiracist educational goals. Without either the history of formal governmental policies on multiculturalism or the resultant decades of debate and backlash, the term carries far less of the ideological baggage as it does in Canada.

Even so, progressive educational reform activists and multicultural scholars in the United States, like their Canadian and British counterparts, have faced a great deal of public criticism over the years (e.g., Bernstein, 1994). As elsewhere, much of it emerges from conservative political positions by critics who wield phrases such as "educational standards" and "national pride" while dismissing multicultural education as divisive, anti-American, or left-wing "political correctness." My interest is in hearing how these debates play out in the work and understandings of school activists, whose views have been ignored by many scholars in this field.

In educational scholarship in the United States many theorists have criticized the confusion surrounding terminology in this field. As in Canada, a remarkable diversity in labeling exists, as a few examples from multicultural education literature illustrate. Banks (1995) broke the approaches down into content integration, knowledge construction, prejudice reduction, equity pedagogy, and an empowering school community. Kincheloe and Steinberg (1997) categorized the field as entailing conservative, liberal, pluralist, left-essentialist, and critical multiculturalism. McLaren (1997) went further to describe conservative, liberal, left-liberal, critical/resistance, and even revolutionary multiculturalism. This assortment of terms and concepts to describe and differentiate between similar approaches is identified as a source of frustration among social justice practitioners. Some school activists see this terminological splintering as a source of divisiveness in a field already under criticism from outside conservative political forces.

There is a growing recognition by many scholars and activists alike of the politicized nature of their work around pluralism, and of the pressing need for coalition building to influence educational policy and structural concerns. I have sought to understand ways in which school activists take up academic literature. Below are brief descriptions of four Alberta teachers, each one an activist working toward social justice within a public secondary school setting. In light of the additional time demands of extracurricular school involvement and the conservative political context in which they work, their engagement with academic work, research issues and scholarly literature seems especially laudable.

METHODOLOGY

I chose a qualitative, collaborative approach that allowed a necessary degree of openness and design flexibility. A team of longtime social justice activist colleagues assisted with formulating the initial research assumptions and questions. Issues emerging from these informal conversations were shaped into guiding hypotheses, "tools used to generate questions and to search for patterns" (Marshall & Rossman, 1995, p. 37). Among other hypotheses was the assumption that a general denial of racism and other forms of discrimination in their communities and in Canada as a whole by the majority of students and teachers presents a barrier to social justice activism in those communities. The student and teacher activists interviewed confirmed this. Their experiences remind us that we have much to learn about the creative responses that can be generated by collaborative school coalitions in overcoming seemingly insurmountable barriers to their ongoing work.

I sought to engage respectfully with the everyday activism of the participants, adopting elements of a critical ethnographic approach adapted from Carspecken (1996). Semistructured interviews took place over a period of 2 years, in a variety of settings of mutual convenience. Data gathering included site visits and at least 2 hours of in-depth conversation with each participant; these were tape-recorded, transcribed, and brought back to the participants for validation and revision for accuracy. Few changes were made to the original transcripts besides minor corrections for clarity. Transcripts and other data were coded and analyzed for embodied meaning and subjected to validity requirements as outlined by Carspecken (1996). I endeavored to understand participants' perspectives in their own terms, through a commitment to a collaborative process of discovery and analysis through interaction.

Selection of Research Participants

Existing social justice groups were identified using a *community nomination* method of selection. School coalitions were located through direct contact with a network of teacher colleagues, professional associations, government agencies, community activists, and the like. Participants in this research included four teacher activists from across the western Canadian province of Alberta. Their length of experience in this field ranged from one to over 25 years. Two of the participants lived and engaged in activism in larger cities, and two in rural or smaller urban settings.

TALKING WITH TEACHER ACTIVISTS

Bonnie[3] is an experienced diversity educator, with several years of service on volunteer community boards and committees that focus on ethnocultural and human rights issues. She has been the recipient of local and provincial awards for her leadership in antiracist education, and continues to serve on diversity-promoting committees in the province. She identifies herself as a Black educator of West Indian origin who has taught in Canada for greater than 25 years. Her current assignment is at a diverse junior high school in an urban setting, teaching language arts and social studies.

Ted is a senior language arts teacher and part-time administrator at a large academic high school in an urban center. He has taught for over 20 years and has an extensive background in the field of diversity education, having served on several multicultural education boards and committees over the past 15 years. He describes his identity as a married, able-bodied, White male. In the past Ted served on a committee that founded a well-regarded diversity leadership-training program for students.

Cathy is a single, White female educator in a high school in a small town in southern Alberta. She has taught overseas in Asia for 1 year and has taken courses in multicultural education as part of her university training. She has taught in Alberta for about 4 years in both the sciences and humanities and is currently the coordinator of a group of students who participate in an annual diversity leadership camp and organize the school's antiracist awareness activities. Although she says she has been mistaken for being of First Nations ancestry, Cathy reports her identity as an eighth generation Canadian of British heritage.

Gail has taught in several different schools in rural and smaller urban settings over the past 15 years. She has taught social studies, French, and language arts at the junior and senior high school levels. Her current interests around diversity have been shaped by her own itinerant life as a child of a military family living in the United States and across Canada. Gail describes herself as a "WASP" (White Anglo Saxon Protestant) with a strong interest in promoting the acceptance of differences. She is currently a senior high school teacher at a small urban setting where she coordinates a student action group that regularly tackles diversity issues.

Practitioners Engaging With Educational Literature

From the outset I strongly suspected that teacher activists would neither seek nor value academic and research-based sources to inform their activism. My interviews with these few educators show that to be an unsupported stereotype. In the daily practice of some activist educators, my research reveals, academic debates are not ignored. In fact, the teacher activists with whom I collaborated often read and discuss a range of professional and academic literature in this area. They routinely share sources with other activists and recommend a variety of readings as part of their education efforts. Some address this directly and share specific examples of their use of academic sources, while others offer weaker support for its relevance to their work; none report academic work as irrelevant to their activism.

Prior to undertaking this study, I assumed the debate between multicultural and antiracist education proponents would be largely irrelevant to most school-based activists. In fact, each of the teachers I interviewed discussed the conceptual and practical distinctions between these two stances in their own work in schools. As I outline above, some scholars have characterized the multicultural and antiracist positions as dichotomous and irreconcilable. The teachers I interviewed most often regarded the debate between these two approaches as important, and relevant to their daily practice in school-based activist groups.

Bonnie

The most experienced veteran of school-based activism, Bonnie expresses her interest in current educational research in the social justice field. Relatively little is known about the number of practitioners who regularly access academic studies and research materials from local university and college libraries and via the Internet. Bonnie's engagement with this body of work signifies a collaborative potential that has been under-researched until now. For example, as an African Canadian educator Bonnie pays special attention to the debates currently taking place around proposed models of Afrocentric education, citing recent work supporting Afrocentric schools in the Canadian public system (Dei, 1996b). Reflecting sentiments expressed by this author (Lund, 1998) Bonnie opposes his proposal for a number of specific reasons, and incorporates her understandings into curriculum for diversity units in her classes. Bonnie envisions public schools as having a mandate to foster social cohesion and sees Dei's model[4] working against that, saying "that solution to me seems flawed; I mean we've got to, at some point in time, learn to live in a society that's whole." She knows first hand the harmful effects of stereotyping and shares several poignant examples with me from her own life as a teacher in a predominantly Eurocentric system, and having two sons who have faced forms of racism both in and out of school. Despite the challenges, Bonnie says she is not willing to give up on the public school system as a site for progressive social change.

Bonnie considers practical ramifications of setting up a school system segregated along racialized lines, asking rhetorically, "the flip side is, then, is he saying that I as a Black teacher shouldn't be teaching in a White school? That all my kids aren't benefiting from having me as a teacher?" Bonnie wonders if Afrocentric schools represent giving up on pursuing an inclusive public system:

> That to me just reinforces that it can't work, and I don't think that we need to promote that it can't work. I refuse to accept it. It's such a complex issue that you can't package it, and say it's only [skin colour]. This is just one aspect of our lives. Let's not get caught up in these packaged little boxes. I'm trying to get out of a box and he wants to put me back in one!

Other research piques Bonnie's interest, and she brings up an example of a colleague in graduate studies who mentioned to her a recent study

showing, somewhat ironically, that "when multicultural or antiracist programs were run, the post-test showed more animosity than the pretests
show." She says that, rather than accepting the research at face value, she
immediately interrogated its validity; in a subsequent conversation with
Bonnie, she had indeed tracked down the study in question and given it
further scrutiny.

Her concern, she says, is to arrive at a valid means of assessing her
own efforts at mobilizing students around antiracist themes in her
school, but she resists simply dismissing researchers whose findings
might refute or devalue the impact of her own work in antiracist education. "I want to make sure," she says, "that our group is addressing that
research, rather than pretending that those studies don't take place. We
need to know what they mean to us here in our school." For Bonnie,
that means spending time at the university library, discussing and
debating problems and ideas with her colleagues, and making an effort
to incorporate new or contradictory ideas from the literature into their
activist group's plans for initiatives at the school and community levels.
She says she has, on occasion, been accused by colleagues of "rocking
the boat" on her staff, but continues to infuse social justice ideals in her
teaching. For example, her readings on Canada's segregated schools
found their way into a Grade 8 social studies lesson on inclusion, and
into a performance at a school assembly. Refuting a stereotype of teachers as somewhat anti-intellectual, Bonnie is a thoughtful and critical
consumer of academic production.

Ted

As a longtime social justice activist, Ted tells me that he had actively
attended to scholarly literature, and specifically to distinctions in the antiracist and multicultural perspectives, while studying school and district
policies for a national race relations organization a few years earlier. Ted
adds another dimension for his work that opens a space between curriculum and social policy, or what he calls "a fourth factor—an educational, a
learning and teaching basis for these policies." He says he has identified a
void in this area:

> I found that the majority of jurisdictions focused on the cultural retention
> idea and the "soft" multicultural idea that we should all love each other.
> Those were in every one of them. In Ontario and to a lesser extent in BC
> [British Columbia], antiracist education played a much larger role than in
> the rest of the country, and all of them had a certain degree of this Cana-
> dian identity bit. Surprisingly few of them had as a component of it that this

would enhance learning. One of the key recommendations out of this work was that policy makers needed to address that issue.

His findings point to a pedagogical need that, for him, is paramount in avoiding the problematic "boom and bust" cycle of social justice education.

In the example below, Ted recounts a recent academic Grade 11 English literature lesson with students of diverse cultural backgrounds. Suddenly the issue of the lack of ethno-culturally inclusive curricula in the course bubbled to the surface:

> What I find myself doing more now is applying [an inclusive curriculum] to my own teaching circumstances and situations. I had a student the other day say, "This is IB [International Baccalaureate] and we're looking at World Literature but what about Chinese literature?" and so we were able to have quite a good discussion. But he quickly back-tracked; he didn't want to push it. I said "Great, let's talk about it" [but he said], "Oh I know you can't do that," and he was de-legitimizing his own comment almost immediately. I had to underline that it was really a legitimate question, and why don't we [explore it], and what are the barriers to that? Because he would have something to contribute in a way that others wouldn't.

Ted's account shows a specific instance of how our systematic and internalized educational tradition of silencing marginalized voices in the curriculum can find its way into the classroom.

Cathy

Cathy is the only teacher in this study who had recently taken courses in multicultural and antiracist education as part of her teacher education program. She tells me that she sometimes feels a need to consult academic sources to enhance her efforts at combating racism in her school. For example, one of her former students who is currently at university will telephone Cathy and ask "Hey, what about this issue?" Their dialogue often provides ideas for Cathy's collaborative diversity projects with students. When asked for more specific examples of how she has incorporated academic literature on social justice in her activism, she admits to a number of frustrations.

She cites a difficulty with the typical academic style of writing that she believes is not ideally accessible to most school practitioners. Cathy says she believes that for students, the more theoretical material in social justice education can be especially daunting, and "a lot of time the written material goes right over everyone's head because you can interpret it in different ways when you read it." A solution she and her students recently came up with involved translating some statistics on racism into a more appealing format. She acknowledges that her students seem to understand how best to reach their peers with an antiracist message, including using multimedia presentations.

Regarding the conceptual distinctions between multicultural and antiracist education, Cathy says that, as a student, "I had never really thought of them as different things. Multicultural and antiracist were all, to me, the same idea." Her further study through university courses in the field and as a teacher-activist helped inform her of important distinctions between the two approaches. In our interview, Cathy articulates the push and pull that exists between them, observing, "it seems to me that if we're multicultural then we can challenge the racism, so it's got that connection in education."

She points to an example of the overlap of the two fields with her group's efforts to address discrimination against Aboriginal peoples. Stereotypes abound, and Cathy affirms that in rural schools this negative attitude toward Aboriginal peoples is readily apparent on a daily basis, and does not even enjoy the polite expression employed for other groups currently facing discrimination. Cathy says she thinks that this openly expressed racism toward First Nations students can be tackled by multicultural awareness programs but is, at the same time, emblematic of more hidden, systemic barriers to their engagement in mainstream Canadian society. She recognizes that it often takes both multicultural and antiracist forms of activism happening concurrently in her school, and is currently pursuing funding to bring in a performing group to share positive aspects of First Nations culture that are often underappreciated by mainstream White students in her homogeneous school. At the same time she tries to tap into historical and scholarly sources through research activities with her student activists to illuminate for them systemic forms of racism.

Cathy's group recently researched statistics and studies that addressed the plight facing Canada's Aboriginal population. She says "when we actually learned the history from a Native perspective, it sure made a difference for me and a bunch of my students." She says she believes that the transformative antiracist education she had offered her students was further enhanced by a week-long cultural diversity leadership camp that included multicultural education including experiential lessons by First Nations elders. Whether these efforts will culminate in more effective social justice activism is still uncertain, as the program is very much a work-in-progress for Cathy and her students. Though she struggles to incorporate scholarly material in her activism with students, she affirms its potential to inform the work of teachers and students striving to challenge racism.

Gail

In Gail's efforts to infuse social justice principles into her daily teaching practice, she refutes my initial assumption by incorporating theoretical and research literature in her lessons, though somewhat indirectly. As a social studies teacher, Gail encourages her students to consult a variety of academic and professional sources to address multiple levels of oppression in society, and has tried to model this approach by her own example. She explains that her motivation is born out of a realization that came about during her university studies of the ongoing devastating effects of White colonialism:

> The more I read and look at the White culture going in and dominating everywhere it goes, and forcing its culture and religion on everybody else, and all the problems that it causes, [I realize that] it's not over. I think, "Can't we learn and see what we're doing to these cultures?" but we don't, especially if there's a buck involved.

Her synopsis of her own studies of a few centuries of imperialism is one expression of her personal basis for including a critical study of history in her attempts to address social justice.

In her daily teaching, Gail says she tries to foster a critical sensibility in her students, enabling them to make links between contemporary and historical social issues. Though she did not offer this analysis, I believe her efforts have incorporated both the cultural interaction propounded by multicultural researchers and a political and structural sensibility more reflective of an antiracist stance. As an example, her activist group recently hosted a guest speaker to address current issues in Guatemala. Gail says she intended the experience of watching a Mayan woman speak Spanish through a translator to open the eyes of students in this homogeneous, rural town to a broader realization of diversity, in line with a traditional multicultural approach. Likewise, students in urban environments can be exposed to viewpoints from those in vastly different geographical, social and cultural settings as an educative way of expanding their understanding of a diversity of worldviews and life experiences.

In my view, Gail's efforts to extend the lesson show a practical case of a teacher striving to supplement this multicultural awareness with additional research toward an antiracist sensibility, with the goal of inciting them to politicized social action. Gail is "now convincing kids that there are things they can do, like not supporting a particular company because you know they exploit their workers, or writing a letter saying this is why I'm not supporting your company." She says: "There's still lots of education to do. But even if they recognize that they're making those choices, that's better than being totally ignorant of the situation."

She also makes efforts to include antiracist lessons seamlessly within the curriculum by educating students that many popular media stories and historical events are better viewed through a social justice filter. In a French language arts course, for example, Gail teaches a novel that addresses slavery in the United States from the personal perspective of a freed slave. A White man befriends him, but faces an internal struggle brought on by pressures from the Ku Klux Klan (KKK). These characters' plights reveal the overlapping that emerges between multicultural and antiracist perspectives; individual attitudes toward accepting differences are invariably set against a backdrop of systemic discrimination. In addition, Gail weaves into the unit an awareness in the students of their region's own shameful history of supporting the KKK and other blatantly racist organizations (see Baergen, 2000). Her choice to open this dialogue on overt and structural racism is riskier than the more common approach to diversity that entails well-meaning teachers simply telling their students to accept differences.

DISCUSSION

Bonnie's experiences as a Black educator in an ethnoculturally diverse urban school setting echo with themes from the research literature while at the same time countering claims from that same literature about the anti-intellectual nature of teachers. Resisting the stereotype that teachers eschew scholarly work, Bonnie actively engages with current themes in the antiracism literature, and lives out in her practice some of the ongoing tensions in the field. Her work within an urban school setting is necessarily political; Solomon and Levine-Rasky (2003) note the "rather conservative stance" taken by some school administrators on their teachers doing professional or community work that is perceived to be "political work" (p. 146). They reiterate Bonnie's unstated awareness that "it is essential that educators … start to perceive their work for equity, social justice and democratic schooling as a political process. Any struggle for representation of 'voice' in institutional settings must necessarily be political" (p. 146). This struggle for Bonnie takes place both within her planning of history lessons that incorporate her critical readings of current social justice research, and in her own ongoing intellectual engagement with the current discourse in the field of antiracist education. Teachers in urban settings could take an important lesson from Bonnie on enhancing the currency and relevancy of their activism through this engagement with leading theorists.

Likewise, Ted is a critical consumer of the antiracist literature and takes an analytical view of the past 2 decades of developments and cycles within the contested fields of multicultural and antiracist education (Sleeter & Bernal, 2004). He is aware of—but not paralyzed by—his own identity as a White educator within a diverse urban school setting. He pursues social justice in his teaching and community work where his own racial identity is necessarily often in the foreground. Recognizing the need for allies in the struggle to eliminate racism, Ted's efforts in the classroom to give voice to marginalized students offer strong guidance to other urban activist educators. Following the self-reflective model of scholars such as Howard (1999), Ted recognizes the identity politics that can characterize and complicate social justice efforts, and acknowledges his unearned White privilege and necessarily limited understanding of racism and other oppression.

With Cathy's initial efforts at implementing culturally relevant activities to reduce stereotyping and racism within a predominantly White rural setting, we see a teacher who is struggling to counter the assimilation and deficit models that have characterized education for decades (James, 2005). As James notes, "students whose 'differences' cannot be dismissed tend to be defined in terms of what they lack as opposed to their educational, cultural and social abilities, competences and accomplishments" (p. 18). Although her work takes place in a demographic setting that is not reflective of most urban secondary schools, Cathy's insight that students are the best resource for aiding in the development of activities for their peers may be instructive to any teacher activists. As other teacher activists have suggested, engaging students as participants in planning social justice activism in schools is an excellent means of building their feelings of ownership in the program and ensuring its relevancy to a greater number of their peers (Berlin & Alladin, 1996; Lund, 2001; Smith & Young, 1996).

Although Gail does not regularly access academic literature she shows openness to being informed by additional sources. From my perspective, she represents a rich potential audience for engagement with relevant scholarly work. Like Cathy, she works in a relatively homogeneous White small town, but her perseverance with creative ways to engage community speakers and antiracist lessons fluently within the curriculum can be instructive to any activist educators. Further, I believe the lessons she describes reveal a fluency in incorporating both multicultural and antiracist approaches into the curriculum, refuting the sharp distinctions identified between these approaches by earlier writers (Kehoe, 1994; McGregor & Ungerleider, 1993). In this sense her work both informs and extends scholarly understandings through her valuable grounded experiences where social justice theory comes to life and plays itself out in the classroom and community.

CONCLUSION

These interviews with teacher activists reveal a range of levels of support for entwining academic work with social justice activism. Addressing the complexity of labeling and political positioning in this field, the activists with whom I spoke often consciously used multicultural and antiracist labels simultaneously in strategic ways in their work. Their work in both urban and rural settings offers lessons that remind us of the need for pressing forward with progressive social change. In so many ways, educated and articulate activist teachers are ideally situated to explore analytically how various scholarly subjects are lived and understood within their classrooms. The participants in the study reported above offer support for the ability of educational research and theory to inform their daily school concerns, and each shows willingness to engage in further study of a variety of sources. From specific lesson plans on historical racism, to incorporating current debates into class discussions, to modifying their daily interactions with students, to shaping specific school activism around particular themes emerging from academic discourse and collaborations with students, these teachers reveal a complex and creative engagement with various bodies of educational literature.

I hope my ongoing research helps highlight the undervalued role of practitioners in taking up academic work, and might serve as incentive for engaging them more directly in future research. These participants show tremendous promise as critical consumers of—and contributors to—scholarly material that addresses practical concerns of relevance to their unique school settings. Finally, the moments of reflective analysis that emerge from interviews with the participants in this research, grounded in the understandings of daily teaching and activism, offer solid evidence of the possible mutual benefits of respectful collaborations to both reveal and share the wisdom of practitioners as social justice theorists.

NOTES

1. A revised version of this chapter was published as Lund (2003) and is used here with the kind permission of the editors. The author is grateful to anonymous reviewers of this chapter for their helpful suggestions.

2. I wish to acknowledge the generous support of my research by the *Social Sciences and Humanities Research Council of Canada*, the *Alberta Teachers' Association*, and the *Killam Trusts*.

3. The names of participants mentioned here are pseudonyms. These accounts are written in the present tense to enhance the immediacy of their words.

4. I need to note here that Dei's current position on Afrocentric schools has changed somewhat from his earlier writing. He contests the current Eurocentric ideological nature of all public schools regardless of the student and teacher populations and presents alternative Afrocentric schools as part of progressive social change in the public school system (Dei, 2005).

REFERENCES

Baergen, W. P. (2000). *The Ku Klux Klan in Central Alberta*. Red Deer, Canada: Central Alberta Historical Society.

Banks, J. A. (1995). Multicultural education: Historical development, dimensions, and practice. In J. A. Banks & C. A. McGee Banks (Eds.), *Handbook of research on multicultural education* (pp. 3-24). New York: Macmillan.

Berlin, M. L., & Alladin, M. I. (1996). The Kipling Collegiate Institute story: Towards positive race relations in the school. In M. I. Alladin (Ed.), *Racism in Canadian schools* (pp. 131-146). Toronto, Ontario, Canada: Harcourt Brace.

Bernstein, R. (1994). *Dictatorship of virtue: Multiculturalism, and the battle for America's future*. New York: Knopf.

Bissoondath, N. (1994). *Selling illusions: The cult of multiculturalism in Canada*. Toronto, Canada: Penguin.

Bonnett, A., & Carrington, B. (1996). Constructions of anti-racist education in Britain and Canada. *Comparative Education, 32*, 271-288.

Boyko, J. (1995). *Last steps to freedom: The evolution of Canadian racism*. Winnipeg, Manitoba, Canada: Watson & Dwyer.

Carspecken, P. F. (1996). *Critical ethnography in educational research: A theoretical and practical guide*. New York: Routledge.

Corson, D. (2000). A pan-Canadian research program for more inclusive schools in Canada: The diversity and equity research background. In Y. Lenoir, W. Hunter, D. Hodgkinson, P. de Broucker, & A. Dolbec (Eds.), *A Pan-Canadian Education Research Agenda* (pp. 167-191). Ottawa, Ontario: Canadian Society for Studies in Education.

Dei, G. J. S. (1996a). *Anti-racism education: Theory and practice*. Halifax, Nova Scotia, Canada: Fernwood.

Dei, G. J. S. (1996b). The role of Afrocentricity in the inclusive curriculum in Canadian schools. *Canadian Journal of Education, 21*, 170-186.

Dei, G. J. S. (2005, February 4). The case for Black schools. *Toronto Star* [on-line edition]. Retrieved November 26, 2004, from http://www.diversitywatch.ryerson.ca/media/cache/blackschoolsdei_star_feb4.htm

Fleras, A., & Elliot, J. L. (1992). *Multiculturalism in Canada: The challenge of diversity*. Scarborough, Ontario, Canada: Nelson.

Friesen, J. W. (1991). Multicultural education in Canada: From vision to treadmill. *Multiculturalism/Multiculturalisme, 14*(1), 5-11.

Ghosh, R. (1996). *Redefining multicultural education*. Toronto, Canada: Harcourt Brace.

Gillborn, D. (1995). *Racism and antiracism in real schools*. Buckingham, England: Open University Press.

Gilroy, P. (1992). The end of antiracism. In J. Donald & A. Rattansi (Eds.), *"Race", culture, and difference* (pp. 49-61). London: Sage.

Gundara, J., & Jones, C. (1992). Nation states, diversity and interculturalism: Issues for British education. In K. A. Moodley (Ed.), *Beyond multicultural education: International perspectives* (pp. 23-39). Calgary, Alberta, Canada: Detselig.

Howard, G. R. (1999). *We can't teach what we don't know: White teachers, multiracial schools.* New York: Teachers College Press.

Hall, S. (1992). New ethnicities. In J. Donald & A. Rattansi (Eds.), *"Race", culture, and difference* (pp. 252-259). London, England: Sage.

James, C. E. (2005). Perspectives on multiculturalism in Canada. In C. E. James (Ed.), *Possibilities and limitations: Multicultural policies and programs in Canada* (pp. 12-20). Winnipeg, Manitoba, Canada: Fernwood.

James, C. E., & Wood, M. (2005). Multicultural education in Canada: Opportunities, limitations and contradictions. In C. E. James (Ed.), *Possibilities and limitations: Multicultural policies and programs in Canada* (pp. 93-107). Winnipeg, Manitoba, Canada: Fernwood.

Joshee, R. (2004). Citizenship and multicultural education in Canada: From assimilation to social cohesion. In J. A. Banks (Ed.), *Diversity and citizenship education: Global perspectives* (pp. 127-156). San Francisco: Jossey-Bass.

Kehoe, J. W. (1994). Multicultural education vs. anti-racist education: The debate and the research in Canada. *Social Education, 58,* 354-358.

Kincheloe, J. L., & Steinberg, S. R. (1997). *Changing multiculturalism.* Philadelphia: Open University Press.

Kymlicka, W. (1998). *Finding our way: Rethinking ethnocultural relations in Canada.* Toronto, Ontario, Canada: Oxford University Press.

Lee, E. (1994). Anti-racist education: Panacea or palliative? *Orbit, 25,* 22-25.

Lund, D. E. (1998). Social justice and public education: A response to George J. Sefa Dei. *Canadian Journal of Education, 23,* 191-199.

Lund, D. E. (2001). *Social justice pedagogy and teacher-student activism: A collaborative study of school-based projects.* Unpublished doctoral dissertation, University of British Columbia, Vancouver, Canada.

Lund, D. E. (2003). Educating for social justice: Making sense of multicultural and antiracist theory and practice with Canadian teacher activists. *Intercultural Education, 14,* 3-16.

Marshall, C., & Rossman, G. B. (1995). *Designing qualitative research* (2nd ed.). Thousand Oaks, CA: Sage.

McCarthy, C. (1993). Multicultural approaches to racial inequality in the United States. In L. A. Castenell & W. F. Pinar (Eds.), *Understanding curriculum as racial text: Representations of identity and difference in education* (pp. 225-246). Albany, NY: State University of New York Press.

McGregor J., & Ungerleider, C. (1993). Multicultural and racism awareness programs for teachers: A meta-analysis of the research. In K. A. McLeod (Ed.), *Multicultural education: The state of the art national study, Report #1* (pp. 59-63). Winnipeg, Manitoba: Canadian Association of Second Language Teachers.

McLaren, P. (1997). *Revolutionary multiculturalism: Pedagogies of dissent for the new millennium.* Boulder, CO: Westview Press.

McLeod, K. A. (1992). Multiculturalism and multicultural education in Canada: Human rights and human rights in education. In K. A. Moodley (Ed.), *Beyond multicultural education: International perspectives* (pp. 215-242). Calgary, Alberta, Canada: Detselig.

Moodley, K. A. (1995). Multicultural education in Canada: Historical development and current status. In J. A. Banks & C. A. McGee Banks (Eds.), *Handbook of research on multicultural education* (pp. 801-820). New York: Macmillan.

Reed, L. R. (1995). Reconceptualising equal opportunities in the 1990s: A study of radical teacher culture in transition. In M. Griffiths & B. Troyna (Eds.), *Antiracism, culture and social justice in education* (pp. 77-95). Oakhill, England: Trentham.

Short, G., & Carrington, B. (1996). Anti-racist education, multiculturalism and the new racism. *Educational Review, 48*, 65-77.

Sleeter, C. E., & Bernal, D. D. (2004). Critical pedagogy, critical race theory, and antiracist education: Implications for multicultural education. In J. A. Banks & C. A. McGee Banks (Eds.), *Handbook of research on multicultural education* (2nd ed.) (pp. 240-258). San Francisco: Jossey-Bass.

Smith, J., & Young, J. (1996). Building an anti-racist school: The story of Victor Magel School. In K. A. McLeod (Ed.), *Multicultural education: The state of the art national study, Report #4* (pp. 57-66). Winnipeg, Manitoba: Canadian Association of Second Language Teachers.

Solomon, R. P., & Levine-Rasky, C. (2003). *Teaching for equity and diversity: Research to practice.* Toronto, Ontario: Canadian Scholars' Press.

Thomas, B. (1984). Principles of anti-racist education. *Currents: Readings in Race Relations, 2*, 20-24.

Troyna, B. (1993). *Racism and education: Research perspectives.* Buckingham, England: Open University Press.

Tupper, J. (2002). Silent voices, silent stories: Japanese Canadians in social studies textbooks. *Alberta Journal of Educational Research, 48*, 327-340.

Young, J. (1995). Multicultural and anti-racist teacher education: A comparison of Canadian and British experiences in the 1970s and 1980s. In R. Ng, P. Staton, & J. Scane (Eds.), *Anti-racism, feminism, and critical approaches to education* (pp. 45-63). Toronto, Canada: Ontario Institute for Studies in Education Press.

PART V

TOWARD INCLUSION IN
SCHOOLS AND COMMUNITIES

CHAPTER 14

SUPPORT THAT MATTERS

A Community-Based Response to the Challenge of Raising the Academic Achievement of Economically Vulnerable Youth

Norman Rowen and Kevin Gosine

The high school dropout rate in Ontario reached an alarming 32% in the 2003-04 academic year, a 22% jump from 2002-03 ("Editorial: School kids," 2005). Research indicates that young people from low socioeconomic backgrounds are more than twice as likely as their peers to drop out of school, and up to 4 times *less* likely to pursue postsecondary education (Gingras, Bowlby, & Robertson, 2000; Maynes, 2001). While the provincial government has made a down payment toward increased funding to support the success of the most at-risk students (November 2003 enhancement to the learning opportunities grant), school-based supports have, to this point, shown few demonstrable results likely owing to the fact that community and background factors have been shown to have far greater impact on achievement than school-based factors.[1] As well, results from numerous studies of federally sponsored youth programs in both Canada and the United States suggest that the costs of addressing the

Inclusion in Urban Educational Environments:
Addressing Issues of Diversity, Equity, and Social Justice, 277–299
Copyright © 2006 by Information Age Publishing

dropout problem after the fact are considerable and the effectiveness of such programs highly questionable. The lessons learned from the litany of previous attempts include the reality that dropout prevention is both programatically and cost effective.[2] In addition, the findings related to adopting a youth development approach amplify the need to consider the role of *communities* in student success. Specifically, evidence with respect to mentoring, academic support, recreation, and related programs suggest that key risk factors are present in the community and, as a consequence, the likelihood of successful outcomes is increased when protective factors are created in our communities.[3]

To illuminate the role that a community can play in enhancing the academic achievement and life chances of economically-vulnerable youth, this chapter describes the goals, services, structure, and successes of The Pathways to Education Program, a community-based youth initiative designed and implemented by the Regent Park Community Health Centre situated in downtown Toronto, Ontario. Pathways aims to help young people in an economically disadvantaged Toronto community known as Regent Park complete and succeed in high school by providing various forms of educational, social, advocacy, and financial support. The program is premised on the assumption that communities can play a role in promoting student academic achievement through the provision of social and substantive supports. The research reported in this chapter evaluates the effectiveness of the Pathways to Education Program in improving the educational attainments of program participants on two critical indicators of educational success: school attendance and course credit accumulation. These variables have been shown to be strong predictors of whether or not students complete high school and move on to postsecondary education (Brown, 2004). In assessing the effectiveness of the Pathways program in achieving its stated goals, this research employed three comparison groups as controls: two cohorts of Regent Park youth who went through high school prior to the establishment of the Pathways program and Pathways participants' peers from the secondary schools attended by most youth in the Regent Park community.

REGENT PARK AND THE PATHWAYS TO EDUCATION PROGRAM

Regent Park, the oldest and largest public housing project in Canada, continues to be one of the most economically disadvantaged communities in the city of Toronto. The challenges faced by this community are many: low incomes, high unemployment rates, low educational attainment, and a large proportion of single-parent families. The 2001 Canadian Census revealed that the median income for Regent Park is $16,954 compared with $25,593 for Toronto as a whole.[4] According to data compiled by the Metro Toronto Housing Authority (2000), 35% of residents receive general welfare, 25% receive Ontario Disabilities Support Plan, 28% are employed, with the remaining 12% in receipt of a pension or other income. According to 1996 Census information, Regent Park is home to twice as many single parent families as other parts of Toronto.

Ethnocultural diversity is one of Regent Park's most striking characteristics. The area is home to many new Canadians, many of whom speak little or no English. Currently, nearly 80% of Regent Park residents are visible minorities, with Asia, Africa, and Latin America being the predominant source regions. In addition, by 1996, 58% of the community's residents were born outside of Canada. Where educational attainment is concerned, the Regent Park community has historically experienced much higher drop out rates than the rest of Toronto. A cohort of students who entered Grade 9 in 1993 in the former Toronto Board of Education was tracked for a number of years to assess drop out rates. This analysis revealed that the drop out rate for Regent Park youth in this cohort was 56% compared with 29% for young people in the city as a whole.[5] Among immigrants in Toronto who had lived in Canada for 5 or more years, the drop out rate for the 1993 cohort in the rest of Toronto was 26% compared with 70% for Regent Park. Finally, among youth in this 1993 cohort from single parent, mother-led families, the drop out rate for the rest of this city was 42% compared with 77% for young people from the Regent Park community.

In light of the challenges faced by residents of Regent Park, along with the demonstrated relationship between education, income, and health (Raphael, 2002; Wilkinson & Marmot, 2003), the board of directors for the Regent Park Community Health Centre began to discuss a plan for the development of a program that could promote and support academic achievement in high school for Regent Park youth.[6] Specifically, the Centre sought to implement measures that would mitigate the drop out rate, heighten opportunities, and generally attenuate the achievement gap between youth in Regent Park and the broader population of young people in Toronto. As an outcome of its strategic planning process, which included extensive consultations with the community, the Health Centre adopted a strong vision to guide its work; namely,

> Our vision is of community succession: the children of the community will become the doctors, nurses, social workers, community health workers and administrators of the health centre. The vision challenges us to continue to strive for excellence (and) develop culturally relevant programs that

improve access and create a healthy community environment. Our tools are collaboration and activism.[7]

The Pathways to Education Program emerged from this vision. Based on a careful exploration of best practices, a review of the literature, and consultations with the community including a broad range of youth (across age and cultural groups; both in-school and dropouts), parents (in their first languages), agency staff, and educators, the Centre staff concluded that providing students with financial, academic, mentoring, and trained staff support would be the best means of promoting success in high school. The 2001-2002 academic year was the pilot year for the program, in which supports in the form of tutoring, mentoring, public transportation tickets, and school supplies were provided to approximately 115 students who attended two area Grade 8 schools. Enrollment climbed to 615 students in 2004-2005 (now from five elementary schools), and over 700 participants are anticipated for the 2005-2006 school year. Though participation in the program is voluntary, over 95% of the geographically eligible students and parents have signed "agreements" to participate in the first 3 years of the program. The rapid growth of the program stemmed from two related findings in the research and from the consultations with the community; namely, (a) that, to be effective, supports need to be provided over the full 4 or more years of high schools and, (b) that to have the desired impact on the community, the program must be available to all students, neither targeting nor creaming, as well as to each subsequent cohort.[8]

The Structure of the Pathways to Education Program

By 2004-05, Pathways consisted of 33 staff, 24 of which were employed full time. Given the number of students currently enrolled, there are 12 full time Student-Parent Support Workers reporting to a Student-Parent Support Worker coordinator. In addition, five part-time and two full-time program facilitators support tutoring and mentoring under the direction of a single coordinator of mentoring and tutoring, as well as over 200 volunteer tutors and mentors. An additional six part-time site support staff share responsibilities at the different sites in the community. In addition to a researcher, administrative assistant, and receptionist, the development and communication function has a director, development officer, and administrative assistant to support the significant fundraising required for the program. The office of the Pathways program is located on the second floor of a retail outlet on the northwest outskirts of the geographically defined Regent Park community.

Goals, Services, and Activities of Pathways to Education

The overall short-term goal of the Pathways to Education Program is to support academic achievement and success in high school among youth in the Regent Park and Moss Park communities. It is hoped that success in high school will encourage more Regent Park youth to pursue postsecondary education, thereby expanding their career opportunities and life chances. The long-term vision of the program is to achieve "community succession"—that is, having Pathways students become future professionals for the Health Centre and the Regent Park community as a whole (Rachlis, 2004). To accomplish this vision, the program has established the following as long-term goals:

1. increase the proportion of students graduating from high school; and,
2. increase the proportion of students applying to, accepted by, and enrolling in postsecondary institutions.

To achieve these goals, the specific objectives of the program are to:

1. increase school attendance;
2. improve grades;
3. increase the proportion of students achieving their credits in each year of high school, particularly in the earlier grades (9 and 10), where the lack of credit accumulation has been linked to subsequent school leaving; and,
4. increase the connections between the students and their parents, and the schools.

The Pathways to Education Program aims to meet these long-term and immediate goals through the provision of material supports, the enhancement of students' social capital through relationships with committed adults, advocacy, and the maintenance of a positive environment where norms of academic achievement prevail. Since there is no local high school servicing the community, students travel to over 40 schools and Pathways provides students with public transportation tickets and school supplies to lessen the financial burden of going to school[9] along with tutoring and mentoring services. In addition, the program sets aside $1,000 in Canadian funds each year for each student participant to a maximum of $4,000. Upon their graduation from high school, the funds accumulated for each student are used toward the individual's tuition and other expenses at a designated postsecondary educational institution.

Finally, students are provided a Student-Parent Support Worker who serves a liaison, advocacy, and informal mentoring function. All of these supports are provided for the full length of participants' secondary school education.

A key feature of the Pathways program is that it strives to be all-inclusive. That is, in contrast with most programs which only offer services and supports to some young people through "creaming" or "targeting" measures, Pathways aims to serve the entire geographically defined Regent Park community by enrolling *all* Grade 8 students in the area rather than those deemed to be most "deserving" to receive support.[10] Research (Kahane & Bailey, 1999; Maxfield, Schirm, & Rodriguez-Planas, 2003) indicates that the fostering of strong personal relationships between youth and program staff and volunteers is one characteristic of all successful youth programs. An example of this is the U.S.-based "I Have a Dream" (IHAD) program, which provides financial, academic, and social supports to inner-city public school students throughout the country. An evaluation of two IHAD programs (Kahne & Bailey, 1999) found them to be very successful, as the graduation rate of participants was almost twice that of students in a control group.[11] The researchers attribute this in large part to the IHAD emphasis on the creation of trust and understanding between participants, staff, and program sponsors, which furnishes youth with supports and guidance that can help them to negotiate various obstacles to their success (Kahne & Bailey, 1999). The establishment of positive and healthy relationships between students and program staff and volunteers is an important emphasis within the Pathways approach. The ultimate intent behind the nurturing of such relationships is to provide Regent Park youth with the social capital needed to succeed. The literature (Kahane & Bailey, 1999; Maeroff, 1998) suggests that social capital consists of two important elements: networks and social trust. Social networks refer to individuals' sense of connectedness to the larger community and social structures through participation in a network of relationships. Social trust facilitates participation in social networks by promoting interaction between actors and "reinforcing reciprocity" (Gilbert, 2002, p. 3). Within the Pathways programmatic model, the aim is for one-on-one relationships between students and volunteer tutors, mentors, and paid staff to provide youth with needed academic support as well as advocacy and access to information regarding academic and career opportunities.

Given the Pathways program's emphasis on building participants' social capital, mentoring, tutoring, the provision of professional advocacy and support for students and parents are key features of the program. Where the mentoring component of the program is concerned, a mentoring coordinator recruits and trains a group of volunteer mentors that includes university students (about two-thirds of the mentors), profession-als, and some community residents. Mentor groups for Grades 9 and 10 meet every 2 weeks. These biweekly meetings are structured by a set of activities developed by the mentoring coordinator as well as other activi-ties devised by individual mentors. Students in Grade 11 and 12 are eligi-ble to participate in Specialty Mentoring where they get involved in a variety of clubs and groups organized either at school or in the commu-nity designed to engage and encourage talent and skill development and to broaden opportunities to explore career options and experiences. Another vital pillar of the Pathways program is academic tutoring, which is provided to students 4 nights a week. The primary goal of the tutoring component of the program is to provide support for students in core aca-demic subject areas. In addition, tutors strive to improve participants' study skills, increase their general levels of literacy and numeracy, and help address the unique needs of students for whom English is a second language. Students whose grades fall below certain percentages set for each grade in the core subject areas of English, science, math, French, geography, and history are expected to attend tutoring at least twice dur-ing the week. The ratio of students to tutors is generally less than 5:1.

The Student Parent Support Workers (SPSWs) play a central role in the Pathways program. These paid members of the staff work to better engage students and parents with the secondary schools. Specifically, they track student attendance, distribute public transportation tickets to stu-dents based on their attendance, and assist students with school-related issues while working to keep parents connected with the program and the schools. The SPSW is acquainted with the policies, culture, and curricula of the schools, is connected to key personnel such as teachers, principals, and vice-principals, and is able to interpret policies and procedures of the school for the parent and student and, when necessary, advocate on behalf of the student and parent (Gilbert, 2002). An important goal of the program is to build the capacity of parents and students to become advo-cates within the school system. A 2005 in-program participant satisfaction survey revealed that Pathways students have overwhelmingly positive feel-ings about their relationship with their SPSWs.[13]

METHODOLOGY

Student data for this evaluation study were provided to the Pathways to Education Program by the Toronto District School Board (TDSB) in August 2004.[14] The TDSB provided Pathways with three electronic data files: one for Pathways program participants; one for Pathways partici-pants' peers who are not in the program, but who attend the same major schools attended by Pathways participants; and a historical data set which contains data for two Regent Park cohorts who began high school 1 and 2 years prior to the launch of Pathways and therefore did not participate in the program. All data files contained school-related variables for all students enrolled in TDSB schools, including courses taken, credits earned, grades, and absenteeism along with such demographic variables as age, gender, country of birth, mother tongue, grade level, and school attended at both the elementary and secondary levels. Where the Pathways data are concerned, Pathways students attending Catholic schools were not included in the TDSB file. Therefore, information for these students had to be entered into the data file manually by the Pathways research team. For the purpose of carrying out this analysis, all three data files were merged to create a single master data set.

As noted earlier, for the purposes of this evaluation, the historical Regent Park cohorts and the peers of the Pathways participants serve as controls. We believe that the most recent historical Regent Park cohort (what we call Regent Park Historical Cohort A) provides the strongest point of comparison. These students lived in the same community as Pathways participants, graduated from the same elementary schools and attended the same high schools, but are simply 1 year older than the first cohort of Pathways participants and began high school 1 year before Pathways was initiated.

The dependent variables used in this study are absenteeism rates[15] and credit accumulation. Where these outcomes are concerned, the first three cohorts of Pathways participants were compared year-over-year with the pre-Pathways Regent Park cohort A and, in some analyses, Regent Park cohort B. In addition, comparisons were made between the first three Pathways cohorts and their peers at the main schools attended by Pathways participants in the 2003-04 academic year.

A number of statistical procedures were used to analyze the data provided by the TDSB. Given that both dependent variables are continuous, one-sample t-tests and effect sizes were computed. The t-tests were used to determine whether the mean absenteeism rate and mean number of credits earned for Pathways participants was significantly different from that of the general population of TDSB students at the five main schools attended by Regent Park youth.[16] Where the means for these outcome variables are concerned, and where the required statistical information was available, effect sizes were computed to assess the magnitude of the difference between the population of Pathways students and their peers. For some analyses, the outcome variables were collapsed to ordinal categories to assess how successful Pathways has been in reducing the percentage of students most at risk of dropping out of school (for example, students who miss 15% or more of their school days and/or students in the lowest category on the ordinal credit accumulation variable for each grade level). For these particular analyses, simple cross-tabular tables were constructed.

FINDINGS

Differences In Attendance Between Pathways Participants and a Regent Park Historical Cohort

Study results demonstrate that the Pathways program has succeeded in promoting greater school attendance among Regent Park youth. Table 14.1 shows differences in absentee rates between the first three cohorts of Pathways participants and the historical cohorts of Regent Park students who began Grade 9 prior to the birth of the program. In their Grade 9 year (2000-01), the students in historical Regent Park cohort A missed an average of 10.8% of full school days.[17] The first Pathways cohort missed 3.4% *fewer* days (10.8% versus 7.4%) in its Grade 9 year (2001-02). Moreover, in the Grade 9 year, this figure steadily declined among subsequent Pathways cohorts, with the third Pathways cohort missing 4.3% of school days, less than half the mean of the historical cohort in its Grade 9 year (10.8% versus 4.3%).

Comparisons between Pathways students and the historical cohort in subsequent grades similarly attest to the success of the program in reducing student absenteeism. In Grade 10, the mean absenteeism rate of the first Pathways cohort is slightly less than half that of Historical Cohort A (18.6% for the historical cohort compared with 8.8% for Pathways cohort 1), with the second Pathways cohort showing an even lower mean for its

Table 14.1.   Mean Absenteeism Rates and the Proportion of Students Absent From 15% or More of School Days for Pathways Students and the Regent Park Historical Cohort A

Grade	Historical Regent Park Cohort A		Pathways Cohort 1		Pathways Cohort 2		Pathways Cohort 3	
	Mean	15+	Mean	15+	Mean	15+	Mean	15+
9	10.8%	24.4%	7.4%	13.2%	6.2%	13.0%	4.3%	5.6%
10	18.6%	35.3%	8.8%	19.8%	5.6%	10.4%		
11*	15.9%	35.1%	8.5%	20.2%				

*Historical Cohort B
Source: Toronto District School Board (2004).

Grade 10 year. In Grade 11, the mean absenteeism rate for the first Pathways cohort was 7.4% lower than that for Historical Cohort B (8.5% versus 15.9%).

Perhaps even more important than the results reported above is the finding that, at all grade levels, a substantially smaller percentage of participants from the three Pathways cohorts missed 15% or more full school days compared with students in the historical Regent Park cohorts. Table 14.1 reports that fewer Pathways participants in all three cohorts missed 15% or more school days in their Grade 9 year compared with students in the Regent Park Historical Cohort A (24.4% of students in the historical cohort missed 15% or more school days in Grade 9, compared with 13.2%, 13%, and 5.6% respectively for Pathways cohorts 1, 2, and 3). In addition, the table shows a dramatic decrease in the percentage of Pathways students who missed 15% or more school days in Grade 9 between the second and third program cohorts, with the percentage of students in this category dropping from 13% for the second cohort to 5.6% for the third cohort. The findings are similar for Grade 10, where the percentage of students in historical Regent Park group (35.3%) who missed 15% or more of school days is almost twice that of the first Pathways cohort in its Grade 10 year (19.8%), and more than three times that of the second Pathways cohort (10.4%). In Grade 11, the percentage of Pathways' cohort 1 students in this category is approximately 15% lower than that of the comparison group (Historical Regent Park Cohort B). These findings demonstrate that the Pathways program has succeeded in decreasing the percentage of Regent Park students who are most at risk of dropping out of school based on school attendance.

Differences in Attendance Between Pathways Participants and Their Peers

Where absenteeism rates are concerned, Tables 14.2, 14.3 and 14.4 show that Pathways participants compared favorably with their peers at the five main Toronto high schools attended by Regent Park youth in 2003-04. Table 14.2 presents the results of one-sample t-tests that compare the mean absenteeism rate of Pathways students at each grade level to that of the overall population of high school students at the five main schools. These analyses reveal that Pathways participants constitute a unique population of students, as the mean absenteeism rate for this group is significantly less than that of the general high school population at all three grade levels. The mean absenteeism rate for Grade 9 Pathways students was 4.4% less than that of the general Grade 9 population, with this result being significant at the .001 level (t = -9.65, $d.f.$ = 159, p =

**Table 14.2.   One-Sample t –Tests Comparing Pathways Students'
Absenteeism Rates With the General Student Population at
the Five Main Toronto High Schools, 2003-2004**

Grade	Population Mean	Pathways Mean	N	d.f.	Mean Difference	t
9	8.6%	4.3%	160	159	-4.4%	-9.65***
10	12.1%	5.6%	144	143	-6.5%	-10.04***
11*	11.4%	8.5%	89	88	-2.9%	-2.91**

***p < .001   **p < .01   *p < .05
Source: Toronto District School Board (2004).

**Table 14.3.   Mean Absenteeism Rates of Male and
Female Pathways Students and
Their Peers at the Five Main Schools, 2003-2004**

Grade	Male			Female		
	Pathways	Comparison	Effect Size	Pathways	Comparison	Effect Size
9	4.8%	9.9%	-.43	3.6%	9.0%	-.42
	(N = 86)	(N = 444)		(N = 74)	(N = 258)	
10	5.0%	15.0%	-.67	6.1%	10.8%	-.37
	(N = 63)	(N = 454)		(N = 81)	(N = 287)	
11	7.4%	12.1%	-.37	9.5%	11.2%	-.13
	(N = 41)	(N = 453)		(N = 48)	(N = 336)	

Source: Toronto District School Board (2004).

.000). Grade 10 Pathways students averaged 6.5% fewer full day absences than the general Grade 10 population in 2003-04, also significant at the .001 level ($t = -10.04$, *d.f.* $= 143$, $p = .000$). In Grade 11, the difference between Pathways students and the general high school population in terms of absenteeism rate was 3%, with this result achieving significance at the .01 alpha level ($t = -2.9$, *d.f.* $= 88$, $p = .005$).

Table 14.3 shows the differences in absenteeism rates between Pathways students and their peers broken down by gender. Male Pathways students attended school with slightly greater frequency than female Pathways students in Grades 9 and 10, with this trend being reversed in Grade 11. More importantly and echoing the *t*-test results, Table 14.3 shows that both male and female Pathways participants had substantively lower mean absenteeism rates than their peers at all three grade levels. This finding is particularly pronounced in Grades 9 and 10. In Grade 9, the mean absenteeism rate for male and female Pathways participants was

**Table 14.4.   Comparing the Proportions of Male and
Female Pathways Students in the 15%+ Category to That of
Their Peers at the Five Main Schools, 2003-04.**

	Male Students		Female Students	
Grade	Pathway	Comparison	Pathways	Comparison
9	7.0% (N = 86)	22.5% (N = 444)	4.1% (N = 74)	19.4% (N = 258)
10	7.9% (N = 63)	38.8% (N = 454)	12.3% (N = 81)	23.7% (N = 287)
11	14.6% (N = 41)	31.8% (N = 453)	25.0% (N = 48)	28.0% (N = 336)

Source: Toronto District School Board (2004).

approximately half that of their peers (4.8% versus 9.9% respectively for males, and 3.6% versus 9% for females). In Grade 10, among male students, the absenteeism rate for the comparison group is three times higher than that for Pathways students (15% for the comparison group versus 5% for Pathways students), with this difference yielding a moderate to large effect size of .67. Among female students in Grade 10, Pathways participants missed 4.7% fewer full school days than their peers (6.1% versus 10.8% respectively).

Table 14.4 provides further evidence of the success of the Pathways program in reducing the number of Regent Park youth who are most at risk of not completing high school. Specifically, the table shows that, at each grade level, a substantially *smaller* percentage of male and female Pathways students missed 15% or more school days in 2003-04 compared with their peers at the five schools primarily attended by Regent Park youth. Among male students, the percentage of non-Pathways students who missed 15% or more school days was 3 times that of Pathways' cohort 3 in Grade 9 (22.5% versus 7% respectively), and more than 4 times that of Pathways' cohort 2 in Grade 10 (38.8% versus 7.9% respectively). Among female students, there were 5 times as many students from the comparison group in this category in Grade 9 (19.4% of students in the comparison group missed 15% or more days compared with 4.1% of Pathways' participants), and almost twice as many as the Pathways population in Grade 10 (23.7% for the comparison group versus 12.3% for Pathways' participants).

Credit Accumulation

In addition to reducing student absenteeism rates, the data revealed that the Pathways program has been successful in helping participants to achieve their high school credits. Table 14.5 presents data that com-

**Table 14.5.   Comparing Credit Accumualtion of Pathways
Cohorts 1 and 2 to Pre-Pathways
Historical Regent Park Cohort A, Grades and 10**

Credits Accumulated	Cohort 2, Grs 9 & 10 (N = 141)	Cohort 1, Grs 9 & 10 (N = 86)	Pre-Pathways Regent Park Cohort A Grs 9 & 10 (N =108)
All credits (15.5+)	45.4% (N = 64)	45.3% (N = 39)	35.2% (N = 38)
1 credit short (14.5-15.0)	10.6% (N = 15)	11.6% (N = 10)	13.0% (N = 14)
2 credits short (13.5-14.0)	12.1% (N = 17)	10.5% (N = 9)	3.7% (N = 4)
3 credits short (12.5-13.0)	2.8% (N = 4)	8.1% (N= 7)	1.8% (N = 2)
4 credits short (11.5-12.0)	7.8% (N = 11)	4.7% (N = 4)	3.7% (N = 4)
5 credits short (10.5-11.0)	2.8% (N = 4)	4.7% (N = 4)	0
6+credits short (0 to 10 credits)	18.4% (N = 26)	15.1% (N = 13)	42.6% (N = 46)

Source: Toronto District School Board (2004).

pare the credit accumulation of Pathways students to the Regent Park
Historical Cohort A after the first 2 years of high school. As seen in
Table 14.5, a larger percentage of Pathways students accumulated all or
nearly all of the 16 credits they should have by the end of Grade 10
compared with the pre-Pathways Regent Park cohort. Specifically, the
table reveals that approximately 45% of Pathways students in both
cohorts achieved between 15 and 16 credits in cohorts 1 and 2 respectively, compared with 35% for the Regent Park historical cohort. More
importantly, the percentage of Pathways students who are 6 or more
credits short is substantially lower than that of the historical cohort.
Indeed, the percentage of cohort 2 Pathways students in this category is
less than half the percentage for the comparison group (18.4% versus
42.6% respectively). In the case of Pathways cohort 1, the percentage is
almost one-third that of the comparison group (15.1% versus 42.6%
respectively).

Table 14.6 reveals a similar trend for Grade 11. As seen in Table 14.6,
52.8% of Pathways students had acquired 22.5 or more credits compared
with 38.4% of their peers—a difference of approximately 15%. Conversely, the percentage of Pathways students eight or more credits short of

Table 14.6.   Comparing Credit Accumulation of Pathways Cohorts 1 and 2 to Pre-Pathways Historical Regent Park Cohort A, Grades 9 and 10

Credits Accumulated	Pathways Students Grade 11 (N = 89)	Regent Park Cohort B Grade 11 (N = 99)
22.5+ (all credits)	52.8% (N = 47)	38.4% (N = 38)
20.5 to 22 (1-2.5 credits short)	14.6% (N = 14)	7.1% (N = 7)
18.5 to 20 (3-4.5 credits short)	9.0% (N = 8)	10.1% (N = 7)
15.5 to 18 (5-7.5 credits short)	7.9% (N = 7)	14.1% (N = 14)
0 to 15 credits	15.7% (N = 14)	30.3% (N = 30)

Source: Toronto District School Board (2004).

Table 14.7.   One-Sample *t*–Tests Comparing Pathways Students' Credit Accumulation With the General Student Population at the Five Main Toronto High Schools, 2003-2004

Grade	Population Mean	Pathways Mean	N	d.f.	Mean Difference	t
9	6.0	7.1	160	159	1.0	8.40***
10	11.3	13.3	141	140	2.0	6.48***
11	18.2	20.5	89	88	2.3	4.28***

***$p \leq .001$ **$p \leq .01$ *$p \leq .05$
Source: Toronto District School Board (2004).

the total they should have by the end of Grade 11 (i.e., those who had between 0 and 15 credits) was almost half that of the historical comparison group (15.7% versus 30.3% respectively).

Table 14.7 reports the results of one-sample *t*-tests that show that Pathways students average more earned credits than the general student population at the five main high schools at all three grade levels. Specifically, the analysis revealed that Grade 9 Pathways students averaged one credit more than the general population of students, while Grade 10 and 11 Pathways students averaged slightly more than two credits beyond the mean number earned by the general population of students. The mean difference at all grade levels achieves statistical significance at the .001 alpha level.

Table 14.8.   Credit Accumulation Of Pathways Students and Their Peers at the Five Main Schools by Gender, Grade 11, 2003-2004

Credit Accumulation	Male Students			Female Students		
	Pathways (N = 41)	Comparison (N = 452)	Effect Size	Pathways (N = 48)	Comparison (N = 333)	Effect Size
Mean number of credits	20.3 (SD = 5.0)	17.7 (SD = 6.5)	.41	20.6 (SD = 5.2)	18.2 (SD = 6.6)	.37
All credits (22.5+)	48.8% (N = 20)	35.4% (N = 160)		56.3% (N = 27)	38.7% (N = 129)	
8+ credits short (0 – 15 credits)	17.1% (N = 7)	32.5% (N = 147)		14.6% (N = 7)	30.0% (N = 100)	

Source: Toronto District School Board (2004).

Table 14.9.   Credit Accumulation of Pathways Students and Their Peers at the Five Main Schools by Gender, Grade 10, 2003-2004

Credit Accumulation	Male students			Female Students		
	Pathways (N = 62)	Comparison (N = 451)	Effect Size	Pathways (N = 79)	Comparison (N = 287)	Effect Size
Mean number of credits	13.6 (SD = 3.0)	10.4 (SD = 5.4)	.62	13.1 (SD = 4.2)	11.7 (SD = 4.8)	.30
All credits (15.5+)	41.9% (N = 26)	29.1% (N = 131)		48.1% (N = 38)	33.4% (N = 96)	
6+ credits short (0–10 credits)	16.1% (N = 10)	43.8% (N = 197)		20.3% (N = 16)	35.9% (N = 103)	

Source: Toronto District School Board (2004).

Tables 14.8, 14.9, and 14.10 report data for the 2003-2004 school year grouped by gender for Pathways participants and their peers at the five main schools for cohorts 3, 2, and 1 respectively. The findings reported in these tables further illuminate the success of the Pathways program. In all three tables, for both male and female students, Pathways participants show slightly higher mean credit totals than their peers, illustrating that Pathways participants are on par with their peers where credit accumulation is concerned. For all three cohorts and for both males and females, a larger percentage of Pathways students achieved all or nearly all of their credits compared with their peers. More importantly, the percentage of Pathways students most at risk of not completing high school (i.e., students 8 or more credits short of where they should be in Grade 11, 6 or more credits short in Grade 10, and 3 or more credits short in Grade 9) is substantially lower than that of the comparison group for both male and

Table 14.10. Credit Accumulation of Pathways Students and Their Peers at the Five Main Schools by Gender, Grade 9, 2003-2004

Credit Accumulation	Male Students			Female Students		
	Pathways (N = 87)	Comparison (N = 410)	Effect Size	Pathways (N = 73)	Comparison (N = 236)	Effect Size
Mean number of credits	6.8 (SD = 1.8)	5.5 (SD = 3.0)	.46	7.4 (SD = 1.2)	6.2 (SD = 2.6)	.51
All credits (7.5+)	55.2% (N = 48)	45.6% (N = 187)		74.0% (N = 54)	54.7% (N = 129)	
3+ credits short (0 – 5 credits)	25.3% (N = 22)	38.8% (N = 159)		6.8% (N = 5)	29.2% (N = 69)	

Source   Toronto District School Board (2004).

female students at all three grade levels. All these differences show moderate effect sizes. Further analysis by school and gender show differences with larger effect sizes.

CONCLUDING THOUGHTS

A principal hypothesis behind the development and implementation of the Pathways to Education Program has clearly proven correct; namely, that a community-based initiative that builds a supportive environment and strong relationships combined with substantive supports can result in young people overcoming socioeconomic disadvantage to equal (if not surpass) the academic achievements of their peers. Given the extent of the disparity when the program began in 2001 (56% vs. 29% dropout rate for Regent Park and the city, respectively), the results are indeed impressive. The data show that Pathways students are outperforming their peers at the same schools and show significant positive differences compared to Regent Park youth who began school prior to the program. In light of the reported province-wide dropout rate of 32%, the young people in Toronto's most economically disadvantaged community are a strikingly successful group. By helping to improve the school attendance and credit accumulation rates of Regent Park high school students, Pathways has succeeded in reducing the percentage of youth in the community who are most at risk of dropping out of school. These results are made more impressive by the fact that these young people are overwhelmingly members of the ethnoracial groups who have historically been least successful within the educational system.

Second, the program's results suggest that recent policy questions may need to be approached in ways contrary to prevailing wisdom. In particular, the discussion of whether an "alternative" credential is necessary for those who are struggling with the current curriculum should be informed by the data; and the data for over 600 Pathways students suggest that this may not be necessary *if* (and this is an important qualification) the supports are in place to ensure that students will succeed (Maynes, 2001). The young people of Regent Park and, by extension, other similar communities do not require a credential that may come to be considered "second class." Rather, they need and benefit from strong relationships with committed adults and the provision of substantive supports.[18]

Third and related, one of the community's main hypotheses has been largely born out; that is, the impact of the program will be greatest by having *all* students participate. This universal dimension (the only criterion for participation is geographic eligibility) ensures that those who might struggle the most are not singled out to receive special treatment, that these students will not be stigmatized further, and will benefit from being included in the "normal" life of the community that seeks to support increased achievement for all its young people. That over 95% of eligible young people and their parents participate affirms the community's wisdom.

Fourth, expert opinion on youth development programs suggests that there is an important tension between school-based and community-based approaches and that these approaches need to be better linked. In particular, there is a need to increase accountability and for "stable infrastructures for funding, planning and capacity building" in addition to "good monitoring tools (including) ... the need for baseline and annual tracking data at the individual and aggregate levels" (Pittman, Irby, & Ferber, 2000, pp. 41, 43, 48). The authors additionally suggest the need to expand offerings beyond the pilot level to include more of those in the community. These issues are clearly present in the development and implementation of the Pathways to Education Program, though the inclusion of 95% of eligible youth is another unique feature of the program.

Fifth, there is a range of systemic issues within the Ontario educational system that the program is not equipped to address, though the program is engaged by them, as are the young people. The Safe Schools Act and its unequal implementation and consequences is a factor for some students and, while the program can support staff and students to contest some of its application and mitigate some of its effects, the changes needed are clearly beyond the scope of our efforts (though the program continues to collect data, both qualitative an quantitative, on its effects). Similarly, there is a need to ensure special education support for those in need of it and which can provide genuine opportunities for success, rather than limiting the expectations for our young people by assuming that there is little point in, for example, assigning them homework. In terms of accommodating the special needs of students within the educational system, the programmatic scope of Pathways does not encompass the curricular and policy changes that need to be considered. There is no doubt that it might benefit our young people to have a broader range of curricular options including content more reflective of their backgrounds and experiences and, hopefully, more engaging. Similarly, increasing the diversity of school staffs might benefit some young people. But neither of these changes will address the need for a more inclusive pedagogy, which is also required.[19] Community-based interventions such as Pathways must be complemented by systemic changes within the school system if the opportunities and life chances of diverse youth from Regent Park and similar communities are to be maximized. Sixth, given the variety and scope of recent changes and student initiatives it is hoped that similar research will be undertaken to examine the effectiveness of these approaches.

Finally, it is inescapable that the young people in Pathways take pride in their achievements and those of the program as a whole. They identify with the community and, in many instances, have rejected the stigma attached to the space in which they live. Their identification with the community is important and urges educators to develop partnerships with community agencies and programs that support our young people. The assumption that the responsibility for educational attainments rests solely with the schools is not merely erroneous, it is unproductive. As Rozanski (2002) argues,

> [i]t is unfair to require the Ministry of Education alone to provide all the funding necessary for the additional supports.... Other ministries, other levels of government, and community agencies must share the responsibility for ensuring that students have an equitable opportunity to succeed in school. (p. 19)

It is clear that, through the Pathways to Education Program, a community agency has accepted considerable responsibility and, having effectively engaged numerous external partners, now requires a public presence to sustain the program. This is *not* to suggest that school-based reforms are immaterial. Rather, it is to acknowledge that community-based approaches are central if we are to provide effective supports that generate demonstrable results.

That noted, the capacity to provide these supports in communities must increase substantially. The absence of coherent youth development approaches hinders all of our efforts. Increasing this capacity, through funding, organizational development, and deliberate interventions based on clear evidence, remains a central challenge if we are to effectively address the needs of our young people. The Pathways to Education Program is but one important and effective approach.

ACKNOWLEDGMENTS

The authors are grateful to Rob Brown, Petrona Duhaney, Karen Hayward, and Esther Rootham for their invaluable contributions to the research reported here. Pathways research has been supported in part by the Ontario Ministry of Education and the Wellesley Central Health Corporation, as well as through program funding provided through the Regent Park Community Health Centre. Finally, we are grateful to Executive Director Carolyn Acker and to the Board of Directors at the Regent Park Community Health Centre for their ongoing support of The Pathways to Education Program. Any errors that remain, of either omission or commission, are those of the authors.

NOTES

1. This finding has been most recently demonstrated with respect to Grade 9 test results in Ontario (Educational Quality and Accoutability Office, EQAO, 2003), and is amplified for other jurisdictions in Raptis and Fleming (2003) and studies cited therein. For the City of Toronto, historical evidence to this effect has now been updated to include recent data which demonstrates a clear relationship between high school achievement and family income. For example, the 2000-01 data suggests a graduate rate difference of more than 30% between lowest and highest deciles, with more than 3 times the proportion dropping out from the lowest compared to the highest decile. (See TDSB, *Student Success Indicators*, May 2002.) Additional support for the importance of community-based approaches, given the persistence of risk factors in the community, can be found in the presentations of numerous panelists at the *Symposium on Children and Youth at Risk* (Pan Canadian Education and Research Agenda; Council of Ministers of Education and Statistics Canada; 2001 Canadian Education Statistics Council).

2. See, in particular, Human Resources Development Canada (HRDC) (2000) and HRDC (1997). The questionable effectiveness of such remedial programs includes their comparatively high cost (ranging from $8,000 to $20,000 per participant compared to $4200 for P2E), as well as the lack of demonstrable results for significant numbers of participants. See also Greenwood, (1996), Long (1996) and Audas and Willms (2001).

3. Connell, Gambone and Smith (2000) suggest three broad developmental goals: youth must "learn to be productive" at school or work, "learn to connect" with adults, peers, and the community; and "learn to navigate

among changing conditions in their multiple worlds" (p. 287). Also see, for example, the need for "connectedness" as a condition for youth development as articulated in Maeroff (1998), Benson and Saito (1999), Pittman et al. (2000) and Connell, Gambone, and Smith (2000). A list of "resilience and protective factors" provided by the U.S. National Clearinghouse for Alcohol and Drug Information demonstrate the importance of family, community and economic factors in addressing the needs of at-risk youth. See also *Serving High-Risk Youth: Lessons From Research and Practice* (Public/Private Ventures, 2002) which notes that "today, we seem no closer to productively engaging these young people than we were over 30 years ago." Benson and Saito (2000) note that "the initial publication of the National Longitudinal Study of Adolescent Health concludes that youth's connection to multiple support networks of family, school and community serves as an important protective factor across multiple domains" (p. 132).

4. Regent Park is listed as the community with the second lowest income. The lowest is Moss Park at $15,357, which is also part of the catchment area for youth enrolled in Pathways.

5. The data for Regent Park were prepared by Rob Brown of the Toronto District School Board as part of the development of the Pathways to Education Program.

6. Community succession planning began in the fall of 2001 after considerable ground work over several years.

7. Other programs at the Regent Park Community Health Centre are also directed toward realizing this vision including the work of clinical and community health practitioners as well as Parents for Better Beginnings which delivers pre and postnatal support and preschool readiness programs, as well as a number of integrated Early Years initiatives in conjunction with Health Centre and external clinicians.

8. The growth, however, required a major financial commitment. The program has, from its inception, been funded almost exclusively from private contributions from foundations, corporations, and individuals. In the Fall 2004, the provincial Ministry of Education provided a grant of approximately 15% of the program's budget. However, the balance of the 2005/06 budget of $2.9M continues to be raised privately.

9. The amalgamation of local school boards to create the Toronto District School Board, coupled with changes in the Ontario funding formula, put the onus on families to provide public transportation tickets for children. The cost of a student metropass is $80 per month, with monthly costs for tickets averaging $50. In 2004/05 the program spent approximately $35,000 per month to meet this basic need.

10. We are aware of no other similar program which provides these kinds of support to an entire community or to the numbers included in Pathways. Indeed, an important finding of the program may be that the increased attainments which have resulted from the program are a result, at least in part, of its inclusion of all students.

11. While IHAD programs have been mounted in many U.S. communities, Kahane and Bailey is the only research identified which demonstrated the effectiveness of the program. It may be that other examples of IHAD have been equally effective, but no other published research can be cited for other local examples of this program.

12. Group mentoring is one of four models for the 21st century identified by Jaffe (1999). However, little evidence of the effectiveness of group mentoring has been available. See Herrera, Vang, and Gale (2002) as one such study.

13. According to this survey (N = 441) conducted in April and May of 2005, more than two-thirds of Pathways participants at all grade levels indicated being "very satisfied" with their SPSW. A clear majority of students indicated that their SPSW helped them either very much or somewhat with the following issues in the order in which students ranked the support to be strongest: school attendance, problems at school, communicating feedback from teachers, and selecting courses. In each of these areas, less than 10% of students reported that their SPSW was not helpful. When asked how often they spoke with their SPSW one-to-one (either by telephone or in person), 87.5% of students reported speaking with their SPSW at least every 2 weeks, while over half (54.6%) reported speaking with their SPSW at least once a week. Only 7% indicated that they speak with their SPSW approximately once a month, and 5.6% reported rarely or never communicating with their SPSW.

14. In order to conduct ongoing evaluation research, the Pathways to Education Program has established a data sharing relationship with the TDSB that continues to evolve. First, the research staff at the TDSB extract data from student records. Separate data files are created for (a) Pathways to Education participants; (b) the peers of Pathways students; (c) students from two historical Regent Park cohorts; and, for the 2004-05 academic year, (d) three comparison communities in Toronto, namely Jane and Finch, Rexdale, and Malvern. These data extracts are produced in accordance with requirements specified through written documentation by the program director and researcher at Pathways. Upon receipt of these data sets from the TDSB, the data are cleaned and analyzed by the Pathways research team. The results of this evaluation research are reported to the variety of funders of the program, including a range of foundation and corporate supporters as well as, most recently, the Ontario Ministry of Education. Upon receipt of data, a Data Protocol Report is submitted to the TDSB that outlines in detail what Pathways does with the data after receiving it. Also submitted to the TDSB is a list documenting any problems with the data so that these issues might be dealt with in future data received. In addition, periodic meetings are arranged between representatives (specifically, the program director and the program researcher) from Pathways and representatives from TDSB to review requirements and concerns regarding the data.

15. The TDSB data sets contained a variable indicating the number of half days absent for each case. In the SPSS computer program used to analyze the data, this variable was divided by 2; this quotient, in turn, was divided by the total number of school days in the given academic year and multiplied by 100 to produce the absenteeism rate variable used in the analyses reported here.

16. This population included Pathways participants.

17. Since the TDSB provided only aggregate data on the historical communities, it was not possible to employ t-tests or effect sizes in the analysis of these data.

18.   This is particularly true of applied level students and particularly true of young men. These are among the youth who have been unsuccessful in large numbers, who have been racialized in the outcomes they demonstrate and in the processes that affect them.

19.   For example, a pilot program at one high school provided a more integrated, project-based, team taught approach which demonstrably engaged students more than the curricular organization which separates learning opportunities into eight subjects. This approach seemed feasible and, more important, effective for some students (and not only Pathways) and yet was not sustained in the particular school. Where schooling structures are concerned, some commentators (e.g., Dei, Holmes, Mazzuca, McIsaac, & Zine, 1997; Solomon, 1992) have highlighted the ways in which discriminatory streaming practices, Eurocentric curricula, and the underrepresentation of faculty from certain minority groups work to marginalize and alienate certain groups of students, particularly racialized minorities and those from working class backgrounds. The Pathways Program is not designed to achieve the systemic structural change needed to ameliorate such problems.

REFERENCES

Audas, R., & Williams, J. D. (2001). *Engagement and dropping out of school: A life-course perspective*. Ottawa, Ontario, Canada: Applied Research Branch, HRDC.

Benson, P., & Saito, R. (2000). The scientific foundation of youth development. In Public/Private Ventures (Ed.), *Youth development: Issues, challenges, directions*. Philadelphia: Public/Private Ventures.

Brown, R. S. (2004). *TDSB secondary student success indicators, 2003-04*. Toronto, Ontario, Canada: Organizational Development Department, Research and Information Services.

Connell, J. P., Gambone, M. A., & Smith, T. J. (2000). Youth development in community settings: Challenges to our field and our approach. In Private /Public Ventures (Ed.), *Youth Development: Issues, challenges and directions* (pp. 281-300). Philadelphia: Private/Public Ventures.

Dei, G. S., Holmes, L., Mazzuca, J., McIsaac, E., & Zine, J. (1997). *Reconstructing "drop-out": A critical ethnography of the dynamics of Black students' disengagement from school*. Toronto, Ontario, Canada: University of Toronto Press.

Educational Quality and Accountability Office, EQAO. (2003, November). *Grade 9 assessment of mathematics 2002-03 report of provincial results*. Toronto, Canada: Queen's Printer for Ontario.

Gilbert, J. (2002). *Toward a conceptual framework for the Pathways to Education Program*. Unpublished manuscript.

Gingras, Y., Bowlby, J., & Robertson, H. (2000). *Dropping out of high school: Definitions and costs*. Ottawa, Ontario, Canada: Applied Research Branch.

Greenwood, J. (1996, November). *Lessons learned on the effectiveness of programs and services for youth*. Background paper presented on the effectiveness of employment-related programs for youth: Lessons learned from past experience, at Human Resources and Development Canada (HRDC).

Herrera, C., Vang, Z., & Gale, L.Y. (2002). *Group mentoring: A study of mentoring groups in three programs.* Philadelphia: Public/Private Ventures and National Mentoring Partnership.

Human Resources Development Canada. (1997). *Lessons learned: Effectiveness of employment-related programs for youth.* Ottawa: Applied Research Branch, Human Resources Development Canada.

Human Resources Development Canada. (2000). *Dropping out of high school: Definitions and costs.* Ottawa: Applied Research Branch, Human Resources Development Canada.

Jaffe, N. (1999). Mentoring in 1998: Four models for the 21st century. In J. B. Grossman (Ed.), *Contemporary issues in mentoring.* Philadelphia: Public/Private Ventures.

Kahne, J., & Bailey, K. (1999). The role of social capital in youth development: The case of "I Have a Dream." *Educational Policy and Prevention, 21*(3), 321-343.

Long, D. A. (1996, Fall). *What works? Evidence from evaluation research on programs for disadvantaged youths in the United States.* Background paper presented on the effectiveness of employment-related programs for youth: Lessons learned from past experience at Human Resources and Development Canada (HRDC).

Maeroff, G. (1998). *Altered destinies: Making life better for school children in need.* New York: St. Martins.

Maxfield, M, Schirm, A., & Rodriguez-Planas, N. (2003). *The quantum opportunity program demonstration: Implementation and short-term impacts.* Washington, DC: Mathematica Policy Research.

Maynes, B. (2001). Educational programming for children living in poverty: Possibilities and challenges. In J. P. Portelli & P. Solomon (Eds.), *The erosion of democracy in education: From critique to possibilities* (pp. 269-296). Calgary, Alberta, Canada: Detselig.

Pittman, K. J., Irby, M., & Ferber, T. (2000). Unfinished business: Further reflections on a decade of promoting youth development. In Public/Private Ventures (Ed.), *Youth development: Issues, challenges, and directions.* Philadelphia: Public/Private Ventures.

Rozanski, M. (2002). *Investing in public education: Advancing the goal of continuous improvement in student learning and achievement: Report of the Education Equality Task Force.* Toronto, Canada: Ontario Ministry of Education.

Public/Private Ventures (2002). *Serving high-risk youth: Lessons from research and programming.* Philadelphia: Authors.

Rachlis, M. (2004). *Prescription for excellence: How innovation is saving Canada's health care system.* Toronto, Ontario, Canada: HarperCollins.

Raphael, D. (2002). *Poverty, income inequality and health in Canada.* Toronto, Canada: CSJ Foundation for Research and Education.

Solomon, P. (1992). *Black resistance in high school: Forging a separatist culture.* Albany, NY: SUNY.

Editorial: School kids for success. (2005, August 22). *The Toronto Star,* p. A18.

Wilkinson, R., & Marmot, M. (Eds.). (2003). *Social determinants of health: The solid facts* (2nd ed.). Copenhagen, Denmark: WHO Regional Office for Europe.

CHAPTER 15

FRAMING EQUITABLE PRAXIS

Systematic Approaches to Building Socially Just and Inclusionary Educational Communities

Brenda J. McMahon and Denise E. Armstrong

In spite of the fact that Western democratic societies implicitly and explicitly promise equal educational opportunities and the benefits of "the good life" for all, research on the state of education in Canada (Leithwood, Fullan, & Watson, 2003; MacKinnon, 2001; Taylor, 2001); the United States (Haberman, 2004a, 2004b; Nieto, 1992) and; England (Gillborn & Youdell, 2000) consistently indicates that reforms have failed to deliver their espoused targets of excellence, equality, and high achievement for urban students, particularly as they relate to social class, race, ethnicity, language, and gender. A considerable amount of controversy has been generated regarding this unfilled promise and the failure of students and parents to take advantage of the benefits of the system. Conversely, a number of theorists have pointed to deep hegemonic structures and discursive practices within education, and the larger society that ensure that dominant interests are served, and students who do not fit

Inclusion in Urban Educational Environments:
Addressing Issues of Diversity, Equity, and Social Justice, 301–322
Copyright © 2006 by Information Age Publishing

into the norm remain on the margins of society (Capper, 1993; Dei, 1996, 2002; Dei & Karumanchery, 2001; Giroux, 1993; Portelli & Solomon, 2001).

Research consistently demonstrates that the achievement gap between disadvantaged and affluent populations has widened over the past 4 decades (Haberman, 2004b). This chasm is particularly glaring in urban schools, which have consistently failed to implement the structural changes required to address inequities related to power and social difference, and have contributed to the disenfranchisement of significant proportions of minoritized youth and their communities (Dei & Karumanchery, 2001; Haberman, 2004a, 2004b). Recent policy audits of Ontario educational reforms by Leithwood et al. (2003) point to a situation of crisis, where incoherent and overwhelming policy environments, increases in class and school size, combined with decreases in resources and support have created "unintended negative consequences" and more difficult and harsher school environments for less advantaged and diverse student populations (p. 10). Within urban communities, marginalized students embody the collateral damage resulting from recent reform initiatives, as these so-called unintended consequences have long-term negative ramifications for their lives and their chances for success.

This paper focuses on the exclusionary impacts of reform on urban students, and the ways in which school communities can work towards inclusion. Using Foster's (1986) and Eisner's (2002) analogies of the schools as artistic endeavors, it examines how narrow monofocal visions and dominant metanarratives of schooling include or exclude the polyphonic voices of students and parents due to intersections of difference related to academic and physical (dis)abilities, race, class, sexuality, gender, and religion. Using our experiences as urban educators and researchers as a base, we argue for reflective polyfocal approaches to equity and social justice which encompass issues related to people, program, policies, and procedures. We propose the Aspire framework as a systematic approach to inclusionary praxis, and provide examples to illustrate how the multiple narratives of urban students and their parents can be re-inscribed into the drama of schooling.

MONOFOCAL VISIONS: EXCLUSIONARY IMPACTS OF REFORM

Narrow visions of what constitute reforms present normative and political obstacles to the institutionalization of equitable practices in schools (Oakes, Wells, Yonezawa, & Ray, 2000). These subtle and complex mechanisms, masquerading as efficiency and effectiveness operate at the macro and micro levels, and reproduce, extend, and legitimize inequalities by "rationing education" (Gillborn & Youdell, 2000, p. 1), which further compounds inequalities associated with ethnic origin, social class, and gender. Embedded within this social efficiency agenda is the push towards uniformity in aims, content, assessment, and outcomes so that "intentions can be efficiently realized" (Eisner, 2002, p. 5). Within the current climate, efficiency is manifested in an obsession with measurable, elitist standards, publication of school results, heightened surveillance of schools and competition for resources (Gillborn & Youdell, 2000). School reforms framed within notions of efficiency misunderstand the nature of effective schools. As Hertzberger (2001) points out since effectiveness does not necessarily equate with efficiency (Hertzberger, 2001). Extreme specificity, motivated by a fear of chaos and the perceived deficits of urban schools, produces a command-control orientation. This approach leads to a focus on regulations over relationships and results in more "fragmentation than integration" (p. 46). Attempts to create system conformity by constraining diverse urban populations within a "one-size-fits-all" die cast are myopic because they ignore their unique dynamics and needs.

This phenomenon is documented in recent analyses of Canadian, American and British contexts, which consistently implicate educational reforms in the failure of schools to support students who differ from the dominant majority in terms of social class, race/ethnicity, first language, and gender (Gillborn & Youdell, 2000; Murphy, 2001; Nieto, 1992). Dei and Karunmanchery (2001) identify top-down educational reforms that focus on standards, efficiency, accountability and high stakes testing as factors contributing to poor schooling for Canadian students. Based on their accumulated academic credits under the current reform initiative, King (2004) projects that 49% of all secondary school students in the province of Ontario will not graduate within the designated time frame, if at all. Similarly in the United States where at least 50% of students in urban U.S. districts do not graduate, Haberman (2004b) indicts dysfunctional bureaucracies within urban school districts that intentionally employ blocking strategies in order to "protect the present distribution of financial rewards, power, status, and unearned privileges for themselves and their constituents who benefit from maintaining the present failed systems" (p. 2).

The exclusionary impacts of this efficiency paradigm is further obfuscated by unitary discourses of equality, effectiveness, and improvement that espouse a neutral, deracialized position while contributing to the erasure of issues of economics, race, sexuality, and equity from current educational policy (Dei & Karumanchery, 2001; Gillborn, & Youdell, 2000; McCaskell & Russell, 2003; Murphy, 2001). By co-opting the discourse of equity and social justice through the rhetoric of quality, common standards, high achievement, accountability, and effectiveness, dominant groups have furthered their reform agenda while reinforcing the existing status quo. Rizvi (1993) maintains that this "universalist curriculum" functions to protect dominant interests, and "is inimical to the notions of social justice" (p. 207). These issues are not neutral, independent variables external to policy, but are "constitutive of curricular, pedagogic and administrative relations in schools" and as such, it is impossible to assume a position of neutrality (Rizvi, 1993, p. 215).

Monofocal reforms that are framed by myopic views of efficiency narrowly define the purposes and goals of effective schools, which result in piece-meal interventions that are influenced by the current "flavour of the month." This proliferation of programs often leads to passive resistance from veteran teachers, who under the guise of contrived or negative collegiality sabotage changes, thus ensuring equity does not take place (Haberman, 2004a; Hargreaves, 1994). Although seemingly well-intentioned, these initiatives are short-sighted, because they do not comprehend the complex interlocking realities of students' lives. Students who do not conform to preimposed dominant heterosexual, White, middle-class norms are labeled as "problems" that need to be fixed. Such treatment models often serve to further marginalize and alienate the very students that were designed to include because core issues of exclusion have not been addressed at a deeper systemic level (Capper, Frattura, & Keyes, 2000).

POLYFOCAL VISIONS: INCLUSIONARY PARADIGMS

Singular visions which frame current reforms reduce education to a basic essential quantifiable format and ignore the fact that urban schooling is a complex human enterprise whose core is mediated by qualitative relationships. Monofocal visions ignore the depth and breadth of urban landscapes. An alternative to narrow approaches to inclusion is the instutionalization of genuinely polyfocal perspectives that embrace diverse identities.[1] These paradigms take into consideration the complex refractions of the urban kaleidoscope and the intricate interplay resonating between individual, cultural, and institutional systems. In addition, they are polyphonous because they listen to, respect, invite resistance, and take seriously the multiple collaborative, and at times competing and conflicting voices of students, parents, teachers, support staff, and community members. Foster's (1986) analogy of schools as multifaceted entities that that tell a story, complete with characters, plot, and setting, enhances our understanding of schools as living organisms. Applying the literary metaphor to school programs, issues of inclusion and exclusion encompass the plot and setting of the articulated as well as hidden curriculum.

Characters, in the form of students, teachers, support staff, and administrators enter and exit the school stage and function as actors, critics, directors, authors, and spectators. As political, economic, cultural, and racial locatedness change within the school communities, the co-created plot by necessity either evolves or fails to tell the story.

Foster's metaphor can be extended with the recognition that there is not one plot for all students. Instead several interwoven texts and subtexts in the form of explicit and implicit curriculum coexist and intermingle. Similar connections can be made with Eisner's (2002) analogy of education as a musical work. Like an orchestra, each instrument is valued for its contribution and synthesized to create a masterpiece. In this way, contrasting voices provide valuable point and counterpoint to enrich the melody of the discourses that inform people, programs, and policies. Polyscopic and polyphonic visions are consistent with paradigms of democratic transformative leadership that conceptualize education as an artistic endeavour (Eisner, 2002; Foster, 1986). The conceptions of school leadership most congruent with this ideology are articulated by theorists such as Freire (1998), Foster (1986), Marshall and Oliva (2003), and Ryan (2003). Variously called transformative, leadership for social justice, or emancipatory, they are based on hope, action, inclusion, and shared, democratic processes, and challenge formal and informal leaders to counter endemic trends which maintain oppression and privilege such as classism, racism, sexism, and heterosexism.

THE ASPIRE MODEL: INSTITUTIONALIZING EQUITY, SOCIAL JUSTICE AND INCLUSION

Although there are many excellent models that frame urban practice the approach that has best informs our work as educators and leaders within urban environments has been the ASPIRE model (Figure 15.1). As an example of a polyfocal approach to school leadership, the ASPIRE framework proposes a comprehensive systematic model whereby individuals, schools, and systems can generate positive, sustainable change in their daily interactions with minoritized students and their families within urban schools. It interrogate the core ideologies and practices of schooling in order to determine how educational programs, policies, and procedures include or exclude urban communities. Polyfocal visions use multiple lenses to examine equity practices at the individual, institutional, and system levels. They continually scrutinize, focus on, and synchronize the three overlapping areas of people, programs, and policies to ensure social justice and equity by always putting students at the centre of decision-making processes.

Our model focuses on cognitive, political, and socioemotional processes. It speaks to the importance of building relationships across the permeable boundaries of communities, institutions, and systems and to the moral nature of schooling. While traditional hierarchical reform notions of leadership privilege principals as sole leaders, this framework sees leadership as existing at all levels of the organization. Leaders include not only school staff but also students, their parents and guardians, and members of the local community and leadership is embedded in relations between and among actors. Our approach departs from hierarchical functionalist organizational models that configure schools as static entities and students as cogs that must fit into a postindustrial wheel. Rather, it conceptualizes schools as dynamic polyarchical environments which accommodate the diversity of individual and group interpretations, and are engaged in a continuous cycle of accommodation, change and transformation. This process is premised on a framework of equity and social justice and recognizes that inclusionary practice is complex, nonlinear and relational and can only be addressed through in-depth, thoughtful, creative, and systematic approaches that go to the core of these issues. Therefore, it allows for recursive and iterative processes within and across the spheres of difference while acknowledging their multiple intersecting layers and textures. Embedded within a paradigm of critical reflective practice and research, ASPIRE is multileveled and multilayered and encompasses the following six overlapping phases of *Assessment, Synthesis, Planning, Implementation, Review,* and *Evaluation* that are critical to successful and systematic change processes. The following sections describe the ASPIRE model and provide suggestions and questions which can assist in the implementation of inclusionary practices.

Assessment and Synthesis

Assessment and Synthesis are interrelated processes which interrogate how issues of equity and social justice are enacted within the school environment. Assessment is the process of gathering discrete units of information about people, program, policies, and procedures while synthesis collates them. The Assessment phase provides an opportunity for the entire school community to engage in critical reflection and dialogue about issues pertaining to individual, institutional, and community beliefs and practices. Although it is often used as an important first step, it is critical that assessment audits are conducted on a continuous basis to determine the extent to which the school is inclusionary or exclusionary. These audits can be done formally and informally through written checklists, questionnaires, and survey sheets, or through individual and group conversations, interviews, forums, and focus group discussions.

As an extension of the Assessment phase, Synthesis brings together multiple voices to determine the common themes, areas of divergence, patterns, and omissions. The key challenge for Assessment is to open up the conversation and to facilitate in-depth examinations of school practices related to equity and social justice, while keeping the needs of all students at the front stage. The objective of Synthesis is to collate information in order to develop a comprehensive picture of the current state of affairs. The challenges are to listen to what is said and unstated, not privilege some voices over others, not rush too quickly to conclusions

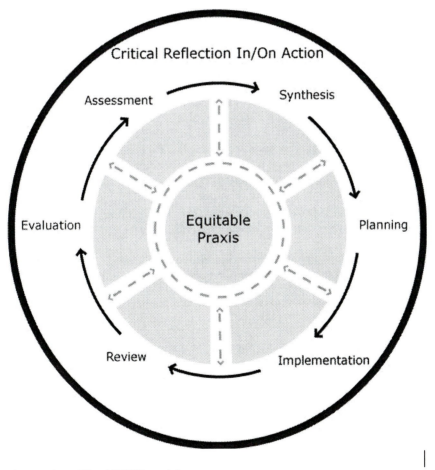

Figure 15.1.   The ASPIRE model.

or agreement, and not become overwhelmed by the enormity of the task. During this phase it is critical that a democratically chosen committee of representatives clarify any areas of potential misunderstanding and terms of reference, and prioritize the key issues that are identified. Providing feedback that is timely and accessible and allowing for additional input are important for keeping school community members informed and actively involved in the process. During Assessment and Synthesis, meta-narratives within the institution are critiqued, illuminating the contours, shadows and plotlines which frame the institutional, individual, and cultural stories of urban schooling.

People

Principals are legislated to initiate assessments and accountability models generally assume that this is a top-down process. While we believe that administrators have a critical role to play in assessing the equitable nature of their schools, it is impossible to create in-depth change unless all levels of the school hierarchy are meaningfully involved in this process. A polyfocal perspective respects and brings together multiple viewpoints irrespective of status. It actively seeks to include teachers, lunch room supervisors, hall monitors, caretakers, and secretarial staff since they see the school from different perspectives and can pinpoint "best practices" as well as gaps and improvements. Similar processes need to occur with students, parents, and community members. Participants need to be convinced that this is an honest and genuine undertaking so that parents, students, and staff are aware of the purposes of the assessment and do not feel threatened.

Yonezawa and Oakes (1999) stress the importance of genuine and transparent assessments of school personnel, policies and practices.

> Honest statements by administrators about the inequities in the educational system and, more important, about how they intend to address these inequities might give skeptical families greater confidence and would enhance information flow between school and the families who desperately need it. (p. 36)

Although students and their parents are constantly assessing the system for inclusionary or exclusionary practices on an ongoing basis, their voices are seldom included in the Assessment phase of most reforms. Meetings are often held at the convenience of school personnel and take place on school premises without consideration of parents' work schedules and access by public transportation. In addition, many parents feel intimidated by schools, particularly if they were alienated as students or are unfamiliar with a particular school system. Parental involvement needs to move beyond superficial levels which "can only be accomplished if and when school systems display alternate structural arrangements that give parents a voice in governance" (Ryan, 2003, p. 190). Within schools, educators are called upon to create space for, listen to the voices of, and share power with traditionally powerless parents. Commitments to authentic collaboration can be demonstrated by: holding meetings within community and cultural centers in accessible locations at times when parents are available to attend; extending personal invitations; providing childcare and translators; and fostering a positive, welcoming, supportive environment where their ideas are respected. Actively listening to all voices communicates respect and encourages a culture where community members feel accountable for themselves and the harm or good that they do to each other.

The Assessment and Synthesis Phases of equity and inclusion require that educational leaders ask: What are the needs of students strengths, staff, parents, and community? What successful inclusionary practices are in place? Which school community members occupy which roles? How is the assignment of roles currently determined? How is the staff representative of the student populations? Are teacher and administrator expectations for academic success and behavior consistent for all groups of students? What would they like to change? How are they willing to commit to the changes? What supports do they need and how do they foresee working with others?

Program

School programs include not only the content (what is taught), but also the process (how it is taught), and the outcomes (what students learn and what they can do). They extend beyond the playbill of the espoused curriculum to include the use of power, time, space, structures, resources, and rewards. Haberman's (2004b) critical analysis provides a starting point for assessing school practices. The four levels illustrate the multilayered and political nature of curricula operating in schools.

> The first is the broadest. It is the written mission of the school district. The second curriculum is what the teachers actually teach. The third operative curriculum is what the students actually learn which is considerably less than what the district claims or what the teachers teach. The fourth curriculum is what is tested for and this is the narrowest of the four. The tested curriculum frequently supports the narrowing and lowering of expectations. (p. 10)

Studies (Armstrong & McMahon, 2002; McMahon & Armstrong, 2003; Ryan, 2003) identify both the overt and covert curricula, which extend beyond the classroom to experiences within the larger school culture, as exclusionary and as hindering possibilities for success for minoritized students. The existing elitist curriculum serves to normalize White, middle-class, male, hetereosexual, and able-bodied experiences and world-views while marginalizing the lived realities of urban students (Capper, Frattura, & Keyes, 2000; McCaskell & Russell, 2003; Miner, 1995). This is supported by Coelho's (1998) observation that "[a]spects of the 'hidden curriculum' such as the images and events that are celebrated in the school, also give strong messages about the relevance or importance of the different racial and cultural groups in the school" (p. 37). Similarly, Brathwaite and James (1996) and Solomon (1992) cite curriculum as a source of cultural dissonance for Black students since it does not reflect their presence, experiences, or values.

Maynes' (2001) study of a successful Toronto project school shows that curriculum cannot be disembodied from the sociopolitical context from the urban schools in which it is enacted. Teachers identify curriculum as broader than traditional conceptualizations expressed in the syllabus and "recognize that, in the context of traditional 'middle class' schooling, the children they serve are marginalized because such schooling reflects neither these children's life experiences nor their diversity." At the Assessment and Synthesis phases, school constituents need to ask the following questions related to the program: What ideologies permeate programs? Which physical, psychological, and curricular structures set the stage for forms of inclusion and exclusion? What are the programs' goals and purposes? How are they aligned with inclusionary practice? What are the overt and covert curricula? What are the expectations of students and parents? How are expectations of students and their parents communicated? How do curricular resources include the voices and multiple perspectives of the school communities? How are underlying assumptions within texts and other resources deconstructed?

Policy

Policy represents the written texts and unwritten codes that guide practices and shape experiences within schools. Although often articulating inclusion, policy within school environments draws lines around urban communities and serves as scripts to further confine and marginalize urban students. Haberman (2004a) speaks to the oppressive nature of policy in describing the failure of urban American districts to create success for all students. He indicates that "the policies and procedures of the system punish schools that treat parents as equal, cooperating partners and reward schools that treat them as part of the problem" (p. 6). Ryan (2003) also contends that although parental involvement in Ontario schools is legislated, within urban environments this form of inclusion is superficial because "parents still remain relatively powerless" (p. 192). For example, parental involvement in policy decisions tends to be limited to the creation of behavioral codes which emphasize individual student "deviant" acts but ignore educator practices and systemic structures that maintain oppression.

As part of the Assessment and Synthesis phases school communities need to critically analyze policies to determine: What constitutes policy? How are policies created and implemented? What are the underlying beliefs and implicit messages in policies? What are the inclusionary and exclusionary functions of existing policy scripts? How are ministry and district policies implemented? How are they aligned with school cultures and practices? Who benefits and who is disadvantaged by existing policies? How do policies relate to the (in)equitable distribution of resources? How do policies distribute power? How do policies define school improvement? To whom are educators accountable?

Planning and Implementation Phases

The Planning and Implementation phases involve stakeholders in meaningful activities to create possibilities for urban student success, by using the knowledge gathered through individual, institutional, and system audits. During the Planning phase, to extend the literary and artistic metaphors, the play or score that depicts the school communities is rewritten. Students, parents, community members, and school staff are involved in the development of the vision for the school. In addition, goals and procedures are articulated as communities "develop an action plan to move from their current perspectives or status to another status or level that will make them more effective" (Solomon, 2002, p. 191). Measurable courses of action are based on a solid research foundation as well as successful inclusionary practices. Within this phase, participants consider the short and long-term effects of decisions within and outside of the school for students with multiple and intersecting identities. Steps are structured so as to embed equitable approaches and strategies at the individual, institution, and system levels, with care taken to avoid totally relegating any of the players to starring or supportive roles. In addition, procedures and policies are clearly delineated and checks are made at all stages to ensure that actions are consistent with polyfocal perspectives. Comprehensive approaches ensure that targets, timelines, resources, responsibilities, accountability measures, and review and evaluation processes are clearly articulated. Decisions are made about who is responsible for what, by when and according to which criteria.

In keeping with their moral obligation to all students within their care, during the Implementation phase, educational leaders move beyond articulations regarding inclusion and take authentic action to ensure equitable processes and outcomes. Consistent with theorists' (Fernandez-Balboa, 1993; Hooks, 1994; Martin, 1992) definitions of critical thinking as inseparable from action, educational leaders, in conjunction with other members of the school community, put initiatives into play and implement strategies which focus on historically and socially located inequities. Issues of equity are brought to the forefront of practice as the polyphonic scripts are enacted within the arenas of people, program, and policy.

People

Within the planning and implementation processes it is essential that students' needs and strengths are placed at the center of all decisions. Strategic planning, using collaborative and transparent processes which consider the impacts and consequences of decisions, focuses on professional development, partnership, and staffing matters. Cutbacks in professional development to increase teaching time by reform governments challenge administrators to create opportunities for the examination of sociopolitical and historical contexts of urban education. Reports from the England (Gillborn & Youdell, 2000), the United States (Haberman, 2004b) and Canada (Dei, 1997; Griffith & Reynolds, 2002) indicate that the teaching populace is not reflective of student populations in urban environments. Specifically, the teachers are primarily female, White, middle class, and heterosexual while the students are mainly members of minoritized groups. Racism, classism, sexism, and heterosexism existing within school communities, largely a result of ignorance of lived experiences of the "other" can be alleviated through appropriate professional development initiatives.

In view of the fact that teachers bring their cultural perspectives to the classroom just as they bring their prejudices, stereotypes, and misconceptions, administrators need to model critical reflective practice as they implement professional development initiatives. Although in an effort to appear equitable, educators may say they treat all students all students equally and they do not see race, class, and sexuality, this denial has the effect of making students' identities invisible and therefore invalidates them (McMahon & Armstrong, 2003). Since sustainable changes begin with individual growth and development, school leaders' reflection in and on their own action is important in the development of equitable learning environments (Darling-Hammond, 2002a, 2002b). Moodley (1992) emphasizes the significance of self-examination processes for educators:

> Because the teacher mediates the messages and symbols communicated to the students through the curriculum, it is important for teachers to come to grips with their own personal and cultural values and identities in order for them to help students from diverse racial, ethnic and cultural groups to

develop clarified cultural identities and to relate positively to each other. (p. 167)

Reflecting individually and deconstructing behaviors with others, enables educators to bring to consciousness their feelings about people from other backgrounds and to constantly reflect on their reactions to, and interactions with, them. This critical reflection can be facilitated at the individual level with existing school staff with reference to Helms' (1995) and Tatum's (1992) racial awareness developmental theories which can be extended to all forms of locatedness. These frameworks may help principals and teachers further develop the self-understanding crucial to overcome discomfort, ignorance, fears, and prejudices about difference.

We recognize that staffing issues are subject to contract restraints due to union contracts and issues of due process, and that these are sensitive areas. However, in order to plan for inclusion schools need to interrogate issues of representation, access, resources, integration, student, family and community participation, and local knowledges. This fulfils a need to move away from professional development initiatives that perpetuate essentialist views of students and their families without examining institutional structures. These formal and informal processes should include meaningful interaction and dialogue with a variety students, parents, and community members. Working for shared understandings and interacting with community members introduces a personal dimension, and extends parents' and teachers' learnings about each other and confirms that they are working toward common goals. Additionally, in order to generate sustainable changes, processes and structures need to be in place where individuals can explore these issues and receive the necessary support and training to enhance their equity literacy, identify their own sphere of influence, and build coalitions with a broad range of community groups and institutions.

The development of equitable school communities is enriched through interactions with teachers in other schools and professional development faculties. School leaders are in an ideal position to collaborate with pre-service and leadership education instructors within a climate that values researcher and practitioner knowledge. Individual, collective, and alliance building professional development alliances can help alleviate some of the "unintended negative consequences" of color-blind school improvement initiatives for minoritized students. In Ryan's (2003) study, administrators speak to the importance of making connections with community organizations such as "religious, cultural, social service and business groups" (Ryan, 2003, p. 204). Solomon (2002) reminds us that, "since schools are interdependent with other institutions in society, administrators must build alliances and coalitions with other equity conscious groups and agencies" (p. 194). Similarly, Young and Laible (2000) point to a need to develop partnerships with members of oppressed groups to develop understanding and bring about political and social change.

Schools which emphasize reflective professional development and community building initiatives typify Darling-Hammond's (2002a) contention that, "teachers do not have to be members of the same racial/ethnic community as their students to teach them well" (p. 205). At the same time, representative staffing is important to equitable and inclusive educational environments. In planning for and taking action on issues related to academic achievement, administrators have an obligation to ensure that their recruitment, hiring, and promotion practices generate staff that is representative of their student populations. Making space by bringing different actors to enrich the cast of urban schools may entail shifting roles so that diversity is reflected not only within support staffs, but is evident in teaching and administrative staff that have the power to effect change. Solomon (1996) refers to a vast body of research which asserts that:

> representative role models from various racial and ethnocultural groups serve not only as examples of accomplishment and success, but as teachers who are ideally positioned to enrich the curriculum with pertinent cultural and cognitive strategies that may lead to higher functioning for students of colour. (p. 217)

Short term initiatives include the aggressive recruitment of teachers who are members of minoritized groups, the creation of supportive environments, and the preparation of those educators to assume leadership positions within the school community. Long term planning includes the creation, implementation, and maintenance of programs which demonstrate that a career in teaching is a possibility for urban students who are socioeconomically, ethnoculturally, and sexually marginalized.

In order for educators to work effectively with students in urban educational environments, it is important for them to extend this process of self-examination and reflection by asking: How does my multifaceted identity influence my beliefs, assumptions, expectations, and attitudes? What are my attitudes towards students who are different from me? In addition to this individual critical reflection, the following questions about the school as an institution need to be addressed by multiple stakeholders, for example: How can the organization move beyond superficial and surface responses to equity? What is the staff's capacity to implement inclusive practice? How this can be supported to ensure that equity processes are sustainable? What hiring, recruitment, and promotion practices need to be institutionalized to ensure a more representative staff at all levels? How do staff development initiatives adopt antiracist perspectives which deconstruct essentialist views and include multiple perspectives? What structures and processes need to be in place to ensure meaningful staff, student, and parent involvement? How can internal relationships be sustained? How can meaningful partnerships external to the school community be created and maintained?

Program

The Planning and Implementation phases revise approaches to curriculum in its broadest senses. At the classroom level, these phases move beyond superficial inclusionary practices and require that teachers communicate high expectations for urban students. This entails providing challenging curriculum and academic, social, and emotional support to engender possibilities for equitable outcomes. In framing their approaches to teaching, educators need to incorporate "the cultural contexts within which students develop and learn, and understand how those contexts are tapped or ignored within schools and classrooms as well as how they influence students' experiences in society and school" (Darling-Hammond, 2002a, p. 206). Consistent with *concepts* of engaged pedagogy (Armstrong & McMahon, 2002), and "curriculum of life," Portelli and Vibert (2001) emphasize the need for equitable programming to be:

> grounded in the immediate daily worlds of students as well as in the larger social and political contexts of their lives. As such, students' worlds and lives are not addressed as factors that need to be excused, pitied, mediated, or fixed in order to get on with the curriculum, but as vital ground of or for learning. (pp. 78-79)

This is not a matter of simply modifying existing curriculum to accommodate some students, nor is it accepting state, board, and school level curriculum as given but it includes an understanding of overt and covert curricular pedagogy which "addresses the histories and experiences of people who have been left out of the curriculum" (Miner, 1995, p. 9). Instead it asks all teachers to be instrumental in envisioning curriculum as interactive and to be questioned and challenged by adopting approaches which connect "the diverse experiences of their students to challenging curriculum goals" (Darling-Hammond, 2002a, p. 150). These perspectives affirm diversity within a politics of cultural criticism and a commitment to social justice as important to engendering student achievement. At the same time this is juxtaposed with a recognition that there are oppressive structures in place and that educators have an obligation to teach urban students how to read social and political situations, familiarize themselves with power interests, and connect ethical values with political actions in order to bring about change (Nehaul, 1996).

As instructional leaders, principals' status within the school community enables them to plan for and implement equitable perspectives "in forms that ensure its longevity and protect against wider changes in educational policy" (Ryan, 2003, p. 182). At the school level, this amounts to planning for and implementing academic pathways or streaming programs so that they do not disadvantage students on the basis of racial, economic, gender, and sexual orientation group membership. A number of theorists (Darling-Hammond, 2002b; Lee, 2002; Moodley, 1992; Ryan, 2003; Solomon, 2002) offer suggestions which assist educators in the Planning and Implementation phases. A commitment to an equitable climate involves providing meaningful opportunities for student participation and leadership, inside and outside of the classroom. Beyond the classroom, student involvement in clubs, extracurricular activities, and leadership opportunities is important for building self-esteem and fostering student engagement and academic achievement (Portelli & Vibert, 2001). Inclusionary tutorial and mentoring programs and practices are most effective when they are based on individual and group needs of students and established in conjunction with parents, community organizations and agencies.

The following questions raise critical issues related to program planning and implementation: What practices need to be instituted to ensure high academic and social expectations for all students? What programs can be adopted to guarantee equity of access and outcome? Are all academic streams or pathways legitimate choices for all students? What procedures can be implemented to ensure that students and their parents are involved decision-makers? How can on-going assessments of course content and delivery be conducted to guarantee delivery of equitable, inclusive course materials? How can resources be allocated across programs in equitable ways? How can a broad spectrum of extracurricular and co-curricular activities be operational?

Policy

The Planning and Implementation phases require schools to carefully evaluate policies and to determine how they cohere with existing practices. In addition, it is incumbent on them to adopt existing Ministry and district policies which promote equity and social justice, and resist policies that reinforce societal inequities. Human rights and equity legislation and protocols within national and provincial jurisdictions must be augmented with approaches which challenge exclusionary belief systems, policies and practices as they relate to educators' interactions with students, parents and other community members. At the same time, policies and procedures need to be implemented which mitigate the marginalization of urban students by high-stakes testing. At the school level, creative interpretations and subversive implementation of so-called safe-school or zero tolerance policies need to ensure safe schools while circumventing aspects of these policies which disadvantage urban students. These efforts to redress inequitable policies are reinforced by working with parents, students, and community groups to challenge them and the underlying ideologies which configure urban youth as violent. Questions to be addressed include: How does policy support the work of equitable schooling? What are some of the unintended effects of policy? How can these be mitigated for students? How can policies be interpreted creatively? How can schools work with students and parents in developing humane and equitable policies at the school level? How can students, parents, schools and community members work together as political actors at the larger system level to ensure equity and social justice?

Review and Evaluation Phases

The Review and Evaluation phases are a reiteration of Assessment and Synthesis and the processes of inclusion are similar. They involve all of the schools' constituents as well as external reviewers who are familiar with urban environments to include a wide spectrum of experiences. The Review phase consists of a series of ongoing processes which are infused throughout the entire model at the individual, institutional, and system levels. Plans, approaches, and strategies are revised to address emerging issues and concerns and additional resources are accessed. The Evaluation phase includes making quantitative and qualitative judgments regarding performance during the course of which individual, institutional, and system are called upon to demonstrate equitable perspectives, approaches, and strategies. Similar to the Assessment phase, an audit of students, parents, teachers, and community members is conducted to determine the extent to which the baseline targets of the earlier stages have been achieved.

It is critical that evaluations are conducted both internally and externally, focusing on processes and products to prove the power of inclusionary interventions in urban schools. This is reinforcing for the staff, the communities, and external bodies and is used to show the efficiency and effectiveness of genuine polyfocal approaches that involve the whole spectrum of urban communities. In reporting on Toronto's Project School initiative, Maynes (2001) study demonstrates the importance of both of these forms of review and evaluation. He finds that in conjunction with feelings of connectedness and belonging for students and their parents, "careful evaluations conducted by the Toronto School Board's Academic Accountability Unit have demonstrated that project schools have been successful in improving academic outcomes" (Maynes, 2001, p. 273). When accountability to the community was demonstrated by a commitment to equity, school improvement was also demonstrated on externally generated standardized tests. Such evaluation shows that inclusionary practices are consistent with excellence in the form of high academic achievement for marginalized students. It is within such environments that it is possible for urban students in particular, and for all students from diverse racial, ethnic, and social-class groups to "experience educational equality and a sense of empowerment" (Banks, 1993, p. 27).

School communities need to consider the following questions when implementing formal and informal evaluative tools ask participants to consider the following questions: How are test results indicative of progress? What gains have students made? What evidence is there that the school has adopted equitable and inclusionary perspectives? How are goals and practices aligned? Does the school demonstrate its commitment to social justice through consistently proportional student representation in all types, levels and streams of courses? How are individuals, schools, and systems guaranteeing success for urban students? How are partnerships meaningful and beneficial to students? How are partnerships furthering equity and social justice agendas? What is the level of implementation of democratic practices? How is democratic transformation actualized? What else needs to be done? Who are identifiable allies, protagonists, and antagonists?

CONCLUSION

The above discussion provides an alternative to the paradox of working to fit an eclectic dynamic urban population into a singular script which is generated from within a unitary efficiency paradigm. We recognize that many urban teachers are doing a tremendous job, but because they often represent an oasis of hope in the wasteland of reform, their efforts are not powerful enough to counter the negative impact and to sustain inclusive environments. For many educators, teaching and leading according to a prescribed script creates a tremendous amount of frustration and often leads to anger and hopeless to the detriment of the students who can least afford it. Conversely, polyfocal models provide an organic structure that is flexible enough to accommodate a variety of interpretations without compromising the fundamental goals of equity and inclusion for all students. It is important to recognize that all stakeholders within the school and its extended community have the potential to make important contributions to inclusionary, socially just schools. In order to envision multiple possibilities for success for students, social justice reformers need to listen to the silences generated by the untold stories of diverse populations. The muted and sometimes nameless characters are often relegated to the sole purpose of providing a contrast to or backdrop for the major characters. When viewed as problems through monocular lenses, urban schooling presents a tableau of bleak prospects. Alternatively, when conceptualized as a work of art, urban education comes alive with promises of infinite possibilities. Shifting these dynamics by providing space for all players to act as critic, actor, director, coauthor, and spectator is key to the drama of urban schooling.

We recognize that as with a literary piece, all the words have been used before, some in the same order and with similar themes. This was clearly articulated by Edmonds (1986):

> We can whenever and wherever we choose, successfully teach all children whose education is of interest to us. We already know more than we need in order to do that. Whether or not we do it must finally depend on how we feel about the fact that we haven't so far. (p. 103)

This injunction does not absolve individuals, institutions and systems of their accountability for students' success. In taking informed action based on their moral and legal responsibilities, educators can fulfill the promise of social justice and inclusion for urban student populations who have erased from the equation of equitable schooling. Reenacting the script of equitable education to create possibilities for students and their communities is an act of courage that requires the faith and creative energy of all and is dependent on the multiple visions and talents of the communities. It requires a critical analysis of the urban landscape and the skill and will to work with others to reconfigure it on behalf of students. By looking at the varied topography, we can develop a comprehensive and honest picture of the challenges and the possibilities. In a sense, this represents a paradigmatic shift that requires us to hold multiple constructs in place and to balance form and function, process and product, ends and means depending on the context. It is our hope that the ASPIRE model will create a usable framework for urban educators and theorists to harness existing potential and to achieve the unfulfilled promise of an inclusive education.

NOTES

1. Within this chapter, we interchange the terms polyfocal, polyphonic, and polyscopic in order to represent the richness of multiple perspectives, visions, and voices.

REFERENCES

Anderson, G. L., & Herr, K. (1993). The micro-politics of students' voices: Moving from diversity of bodies to diversity of voices in schools. In C. Marshall (Ed.), *The new politics of race and gender* (pp. 58-68). Washington, DC: Falmer Press.

Armstrong, D., & McMahon, B. (2002). Engaged pedagogy: Valuing the strengths of students on the margins. *Journal of Thought, 37*(1), 53-65.

Banks, J. (1993, September). Multicultural education: Development, dimensions, and challenges. *Phi Delta Kappan, 75*, 22-28.

Brathwaite, K. S., & James, C. E. (Eds.). (1996). *Educating African Canadians.* Toronto, Canada: James Lorimer.

Capper, C. (Ed.). (1993). *Educational administration in a pluralistic society.* Albany, NY: SUNY.

Capper, C., Frattura, E., & Keyes, M. (2000). *Meeting the needs of students of all abilities: How leaders go beyond inclusion.* Thousand Oaks, CA: Corwin.

Coelho, E. (1998). *Teaching and learning in multicultural schools.* Toronto, Ontario, Canada: Multilingual Matters.

Darling-Hammond, L. (2002a). Educating a profession for equitable practice. In L. Darling-Hammond, J. French, & Garcia-Lopez, S. (Eds.), *Learning to teach for social justice* (pp. 204-225). New York: Teachers College.

Darling-Hammond, L. (2002b). What is the problem and what can we do about it? In L. Darling-Hammond, J. French, & S. Garcia-Lopez (Eds.), *Learning to teach for social justice* (pp. 149-152). New York: Teachers College.

Dei, G. (1996). Listening to voices: Developing a pedagogy of change from the narratives of African-Canadian students and their parents. In K. Brathwaite & C. James (Eds.), *Educating African Canadians* (pp. 32-57). Toronto, Canada: James Lorimer.

Dei, G. (1997). *Drop out or push out? The dynamics of Black students' disengagement from school.* Toronto, Canada: OISE.

Dei, G. (2002). Situating race and equity concerns in school effectiveness discourse. In C. Reynolds & A. Griffith (Eds.), *Equity and globalization in education* (pp. 165-182). Calgary, Alberta, Canada. Detselig.

Dei, G., & Karunmanchery, L. (2001). School reforms in Ontario: The marketization of education and the resulting silence on equity. In J. P. Portelli & P. Solomon (Eds.), *The erosion of democracy in education* (pp. 189–215). Calgary, Canada: Detselig.

Edmonds, R. (1986). Characteristics of effective schools. In U. Neisser (Ed.), *The school achievement of minority children: New perspectives* (pp. 93-104). Hillsdale, NJ: Erlbaum.

Eisner, E. (2002). What can education learn form the arts about the practice of education? *The Encyclopedia of Informal Education.* Retrieved August 15, 2004, from www.infed.org/biblio/eisner_arts_and_the_practice_of_edcuation.htm

Fernandez-Balboa, J. (1993). Critical pedagogy: Making critical thinking really critical. *Analytic Teaching, 13*(2), 61-72.

Foster, W. (1986). *Paradigms and promises: New approaches to educational administration.* Amherst, NY: Prometheus Books.

Freire, P. (1998). *Pedagogy of freedom: Ethics, democracy, and civic courage*. New York: Rowman & Littlefield.

Gillborn, D., & Youdell, D. (2000). *Rationing education: Policy, practice, reform and equity*. Philadelphia: Open University.

Giroux, H. (1993). *Border crossings: Cultural workers and the politics of education*. New York: Routledge & Kegan Paul.

Haberman, M. (2004a). Creating effective schools in failed school districts. *EducationNews.org*. Retrieved August 25, 2005, from http:www.educationnews.org/creating-efffective-schools-in-fa.htm

Haberman, M. (2004b). Urban education: The state of urban schooling at the start of the 21st century. *EducationNews.org*. Retrieved April 23, 2005, from http:www.educationnews.org/urban-edcuation-the-state-o-furb.htm

Hargreaves, A. (1994). *Changing teachers, changing times: Teachers work and culture in the postmodern age*. London: Cassell.

Helms, J. (1995). An update of Helms's White and people of color racial identity models. In J. Panterotto, J. M. Casas, L. Suzuki, & C. Alexander (Eds.), *Handbook of multicultural counseling* (pp. 181-198). Thousand Oaks, CA: Sage.

Hertzberger, H. (2001). *Lessons for students in architecture* (4th ed.). Rotterdam, Netherlands: 010.

Hooks, B. (1994). *Teaching to transgress: Education as the practice of freedom*. New York: Routledge.

King, A. (2004). *Double cohort study: Phase 3 report*. Toronto, Ontario, Canada: Ontario Ministry of Education.

Lee, E. (2002, May). *Still at the bottom*. Paper presented at the Canadian Society for Studies in Education Conference. Toronto, Canada.

Leithwood, K., Fullan, M., & Watson, N. (2003). *The schools we need: Recent education policy in Ontario and recommendations for moving forward*. Toronto, Canada: OISE/UT.

MacKinnon, D. (2001). A wolf in sheep's clothing: A critique of the Atlantic provinces education foundation program. In J. P. Portelli & R. P. Solomon (Eds.), *The erosion of democracy in education* (pp. 117-144). Calgary, Canada: Detselig.

Marshall, C., & Oliva, C. (Eds.). (2003). *Leadership for social justice: Making revolutions in education*. New York: Pearson.

Martin, J. (1992). Critical thinking for a humane world. In J. Norris (Ed.), *The generalizability of critical thinking* (pp. 163-180). Boston: Teachers College Press.

Maynes, B. (2001). Educational programming for children living in poverty: Possibilities and challenges. In J. P. Portelli & R. P. Solomon (Eds.), *The erosion of democracy in education* (pp. 63-82). Calgary, Canada: Detlselig.

McCaskell, T., & Russell, V. (2003). Anti-homophobia initiatives at the former Toronto board of education. In T. Goldstein & D. Selby (Eds.), *Weaving connections: Educating for peace, social and environmental justice* (pp. 27-55). Toronto, Ontario, Canada: Sumack.

McMahon, B., & Armstrong, D. (2003). Racism, resistance, resilience: The 3Rs of educating Caribbean students in a Canadian context. In T. Bastick & A. Ezenne (Eds.), *Teaching Caribbean students: Research on social issues in the Carib-*

bean and abroad (pp. 249-284). Kingston, Jamaica: University of the West Indies.

Miner, B. (1995). Taking multicultural, anti-racist education seriously: An interview with Enid Lee. In D. Levine (Ed.), *Rethinking schools* (pp. 9-15). New York: The New Press.

Moodley, K. A. (1992). Ethnicity, power, politics and minority education. In K. A. Moodley (Ed.), *Beyond multicultural education: International perspectives* (pp. 79-93). Calgary, Canada: Detselig.

Murphy, S. (2001). No-one has ever grown taller as a result of being measured revisited: More educational measurement lessons for Canadians. In J. P. Portelli & R. P. Solomon (Eds.), *The erosion of democracy in education* (pp. 145-167). Calgary, Canada: Detselsig.

Nehaul, K. (1996). *The schooling of children of Caribbean heritage*. London: Trentham.

Nieto, S. (1992). *Affirming diversity: The sociopolitical context of multicultural education*. New York: Longman.

Oakes, J., Wells, A., Yonezawa, S., & Ray, K. (2000). Change agentry and the quest for equity: Lessons from detracking schools. In N. Bascia & A. Hargreaves (Eds.), *The sharp edge of educational change* (pp. 156-177). New York: Routledge Falmer.

Portelli, J. P., & Solomon, P. (Eds.). (2001). *The erosion of democracy in education*. Calgary, Canada: Detselig.

Portelli, J. P., & Vibert, A. B. (2001). Beyond common educational standards: Towards a curriculum of life. In J. P. Portelli & R. P. Solomon (Eds.), *The erosion of democracy in education* (pp. 63-82). Calgary, Canada: Detselig.

Rizvi, F. (1993). Race, gender and the cultural assumptions of schooling. In C. Marshall (Ed.), *The new politics of race and gender* (pp. 203-317). Washington, DC: Falmer.

Ryan, J. (2003). *Principals and inclusive leadership for diverse schools: Studies in educational leadership*. Hingham, MA: Kluwer.

Solomon, R. P. (1992). *Black resistance in high school: Forging a separatist culture*. Albany, NY: SUNY.

Solomon, R. P. (1996). Creating an opportunity structure for Blacks and other teachers of colour. In K. S. Brathwaite & C. E. James. (Eds.), *Educating African Canadians* (pp. 216-133). Toronto, Canada: James Lorimer.

Solomon, R. P. (2002). School leaders and antiracism: Overcoming pedagogical and political obstacles. *Journal of School Leadership, 12*, 174-197.

Tatum, B. (1992). Talking about race, learning about racism: The application of racial identity development theory in the classroom. *Harvard Educational Review, 62*(1), pp. 1-24.

Taylor, A. (2001). *The politics of educational reform in Alberta*. Toronto, Canada: University of Toronto Press.

Yonezawa, S., & Oakes, J. (1999, April). Making parents partners in the placement process. *Educational Leadership, 56*(2), 33-36.

Young, M., & Liable, J. (2000). White racism, antiracism, and school leadership-preparation. *Journal of School Leadership, 10*, 374-407.

ABOUT THE AUTHORS

Kevin G. Alderson is an assistant professor in the Division of Applied Psychology, Faculty of Education, University of Calgary. He was the head of counseling and health services at Mount Royal College in Calgary and has been a licensed psychologist since 1986. He has authored four books, including *Beyond Coming Out: Experiences of Positive Gay Identity; Breaking out: The Complete Guide to Building and Enhancing a Positive Gay Identity for Men and Women; Same-sex Marriage: The Personal and the Political (coauthored with Kathleen A. Lahey); and Grade Power: The Complete Guide to Improving Our Grades Through Self-Hypnosis.* Most of his published journal articles are in the area of gay and lesbian studies. Kevin may be reached at alderson@ucalgary.ca

René Antrop-González is an assistant professor of Curriculum and Instruction/Second Language Education at the University of Wisconsin-Milwaukee. His research interests are in critical pedagogy in second language education, small high school reform, Puerto Rican/Latino sociology of education, and qualitative inquiry. René may be reached at antrop@uwm. edu

Denise E. Armstrong is an assistant professor, in the Faculty of Education at Brock University. She brings over 30 years of educational experience in elementary, secondary, and tertiary institutions in Canada and the Caribbean, where she has worked as a teacher education instructor, school principal, and teacher-counsellor. Her research focuses on personal, professional, and organizational change and transitions, values and educational leadership, social justice, equity and diversity, and student success. She has authored publications in the areas of student engagement, professional transitions, and antiracist practice including: *Constructing Moral Pathways in the Transition From Teaching to Administration; Leadership at the Crossroads: Negotiating Challenges, Tensions and Ambiguities in the Transition from Teaching to Administration; and Resistance, Resilience and Racism: The 3Rs of Educating Caribbean Students in a Canadian Context.* Denise may be reached at denise.armstrong@brocku.ca

Amy Barnhill is an assistant professor in the Department of Education and Human Development at SUNY College at Brockport in New York. She teaches literacy courses and is leading the implementation of the MS in Childhood Literacy program at SUNY Brockport. Prior to teaching at SUNY College at Brockport, Amy taught literacy courses at Central Missouri State University in Warrensburg, MO. She has also taught at the middle school level and has served as a reading specialist for grades K-5 in the Missouri area. Amy's research interests include higher level thinking, gender links to literacy and sibling literacy. The manuscript presented here is a product of Amy's dissertation, *The Effects of Gender Schema and Gender Orientation of Text on Cognitive Complexity of Responses to Fictional Stories.* Amy is currently pursuing the topic of sibling literacy and has been presenting her work at local and national conferences. Amy can be reached at abarnhil@brockport.edu

William W. Cobern is professor of biology and science education, and director of the Mallinson Institute for Science Education, Western Michigan University. His interests include the cultural factors that influence the K-12 teaching and learning of science. The premise of his research is that science educators must understand the fundamental, culturally based beliefs about the world that students, teachers, and curricula bring to the classroom, and how these beliefs are supported by culture. His publications include: *World View Theory and Science Education Research; Everyday Thoughts About Nature: An Interpretive Study of 16 Ninth Graders' Conceptualizations of Nature;* and *Defining "Science" in a Multicultural World: Implications Science Education.* Bill may be reached at bill.cobern@wmich.edu

Leigh Kale D'Amico is a doctoral candidate in curriculum and instruction at the University of South Carolina. She serves as a research assistant to the faculty in her program and has focused her work on race and class issues as they relate to educational policy. Prior to her current role, she worked with The Mecklenburg Partnership for Children in Charlotte, North Carolina implementing programs to improve the quality of early childhood education and eliminate achievement gaps among students from diverse backgrounds.

Robin DiAngelo is adjunct faculty in the College of Education at the University of Washington. She teaches courses in Multicultural Teaching, Intergroup Dialogue Facilitation, and Cultural Diversity & Social Justice. Her research is in Whiteness Studies. She has been a workplace consultant and mediator in race relations for over 10 Years. Recent Publications Include *The Production Of Whiteness In Education: Asian International Students in a College Classroom*, and *My Race Didn't Trump my Class: Using Oppression to Face Privilege.* Robin may be reached at rjd@u.Washington.edu

Pey-chewn Duo graduated from Chinese Culture University (Taipei, Taiwan) with a bachelor degree in english language and literature in 1998. She earned her master degree and PhD degree respectively in the Department of Curriculum and Instruction from the Pennsylvania State University. She has taught at the Department of Applied Foreign Languages at Cheng-Hsiu University (Kaohsiung, Taiwan) and is currently, she is an assistant professor at the Applied English Department at Ming Chuan University in Taipei, Taiwan. She has coauthored and published the following papers: *Different Word Meanings Between Chinese and English; and Curriculum Standards in the Foreign Language* and *I Wouldn't Want to be a Woman in the Middle East: White Pre-service Teachers and the Discourse of the Oppressed Muslim Woman*.

Debra Freedman is a member of the Educational Leadership Program and the secondary education faculty in the Department of Curriculum and Instruction at the Pennsylvania State University. Two foci direct Debra's program of research: (1) teacher identity and beliefs in relation to classroom practices, pedagogy, and curriculum, and (2) the development of curriculum and pedagogical practices that sustain democratic communities. Her research appears in such journals as, *The Journal of Teacher Education, Teaching and Teacher Education, The Journal of Curriculum Theorizing, Race Ethnicity and Education,* and *Teachers and Teaching Theory and Practice.* Debra can be reached at dfreedman@psu.edu

Kevin Gosine is the researcher for the Pathways to Education Program™. He grew up in the Regent Park community before going on to obtain a master of social work from the University of Toronto and a PhD in sociology from York University. In addition to working at Pathways, he currently teaches an undergraduate course in research methodology at York.

Catherine Hands is an associate faculty member within the department of Theory and Policy Studies at The Ontario Institute for Studies in Education of the University of Toronto. She has been an elementary teacher, a college instructor and university lecturer, and has worked as an educational consultant with independent school administration and teachers in the areas of curriculum and policy. Catherine's research interests include school-community relations, parent involvement in schooling, social justice and equity, values and ethics in educational leadership, schools as communities, and educational reform. Her publications include: *It's who you know AND what you know: The Process Of Creating Partnerships Between Schools and Communities*; and *Creating Community: A Real Possibility for Schools in Culturally Diverse Societies.* Catherine may be contacted at c.hands@utoronto.ca

Gunilla Holm is a professor of sociology and education, Department of Educational Studies, Western Michigan University. Professor Holm's research interests are focused on qualitative research methods as well as issues related to race, ethnicity, class, and gender. She has published widely on adolescent cultures and on schooling in popular culture. Her publications include: *Contemporary Youth Research: Local Expressions and Global Connections; Imagining Higher Education: The Academy in Popular Culture; Schooling in the Light of Popular Culture; Teaching in the Dark: The Geopolitical Knowledge and Global Awareness of the Next Generation of American Teachers; The Sky is Always Falling: [Un]changing Views on Youth in the U.S.* Gunilla may be reached at gunilla.holm@wmich.edu.

Hsiu-Ping Huang is an assistant professor in the Department of Education at the National Taitung University, Taiwan. Her research focuses on curriculum theory and development, curriculum evaluation, designing integrated curriculum, and teacher education. She has authored publications in the areas of curriculum development and evaluation including: *A Content Analysis Study of the Civics Law-textbook in Junior High School; Transforming and Innovating: A Project for Construction, Practicing, and Evaluation of the Fundament Curriculums of the Taitung University; Curriculum Evaluation: Stake's Countenance Model;* and *The Analysis on the Effects of Death Education Course in Taiwan (1991-2004).* Hsiu-Ping may be reached at hsiuping999@yahoo.com

Rhonda Jeffries is associate professor of curriculum studies in the Department of Instruction & Teacher Education at the University of South Carolina. She has taught in the areas of cultural foundations, urban and community education, curriculum studies, and qualitative research methods. Her research interests include understanding the educational experiences of marginalized people, and her work often examines educational phenomena through a performance theory lens. She is the author of *Performance Traditions Among African American Teachers* and is coeditor of *Black Women in the Field: Experiencing Ourselves and Others Through Qualitative Research.*

Dominique Johnson is the founding executive director of The Joseph Beam Youth Collaborative, focusing her work on LGBT youth, gender, and social justice in schools, with particular emphasis upon developmental benefits for LGBT youth of color. She is an assistant editor of the *Journal of Gay and Lesbian Issues in Education.* She has authored and coauthored publications on social justice in schooling, gender, educational policy, and LGBT students including: *Fragmented Safety: Envisioning Just Schools for Transgender and Gender Nonconforming Students; Leaving our Children Behind: The No Child Left Behind Act of 2001;* and *Liberation Through Community: The Impacts of Mentoring on LGB Youth.* She can be reached at djohnson@beamyouth.org

Darren E. Lund is assistant professor and Killam Resident Fellow in the Faculty of Education, Graduate Division of Educational Research at the University of Calgary. Darren helped found the long-running Students and Teachers Opposing Prejudice *(STOP)* program. He has published more than 120 articles and book chapters in the field of social justice pedagogy and activism. Darren's current research and teaching focus on school-based social justice activism, student and teacher collaborations, responding to hate, and teacher education for diversity. He received the *2002 Outstanding Dissertation Award* from the American Educational Research Association (Div. B-Curriculum Studies), the *2004 Educational Research Award* from the Alberta Teachers' Association, and the *2004 Exemplary Multicultural Educator's Award* from the Canadian Council for Multicultural and Intercultural Education. Darren may be reached at dlund@ucalgary.ca

Brenda J. McMahon is an assistant professor, in the Faculty of Education, Department of Graduate Studies Leadership at Nipissing University. Prior to this appointment she was an instructor with the Ontario Institute for Studies in Education (OISE/UT) Initial Teacher Education Program. She has been a teacher and administrator in a variety of school settings within metropolitan Toronto for more than 20 years. She has authored publications related to conceptions of risk, resilience, and engagement and their impact on urban students including: *Engagement for What? Beyond Popular Discourses of Student Engagement; Putting the Elephant Into the Refrigerator: Student Engagement, Critical Pedagogy and Antiracist Education;*

Engaged Pedagogy: Valuing the Strengths of Students on the Margins; and Conceptions of Resilience: Compliance or Transformation? Brenda may be reached at brendam@nipissingu.ca

Howard Palmer graduated from Mico Teachers College, Jamaica, where he founded and directed a youth club program in urban, inner-city Kingston. In 1997 he earned a PhD in Sociology of Education at State University of New York. His professional work in Ontario includes working with incarcerated young offenders in an urban residential high school and youth centre. He is currently involved with the cultural and tutorial program for African Canadian students run by the Jamaican Canadian Association (JCA), Toronto, and is also an interpreter of Jamaican dialect for the Ontario courts. He has extensive research and work experience with African Caribbean male students and their academic underachievement in the Canadian school system. His thesis work investigated the home, school, and community-related factors that contribute to such underachievement.

Norman Rowen is the developer and has been program director of the Pathways to Education Program™ of the Regent Park Community Health Centre since the program's inception. His background includes work in community development, literacy, and more than 25 years in educational research, evaluation. and policy analysis. He was a consultant and senior policy analyst for the Ontario Council of Regents' Vision 2000 exercise, and was principal investigator for several projects including Metro Toronto Movement for Literacy, Ontario Literacy Coalition, and several Ontario colleges and government departments. His publications include: *Renewing Entry Assessment, More Walls Than Doors, People Over Programs,* and *Terribly Obvious, Awfully Complex.* The challenges of developing more effective community and organizational relationships to achieve demonstrable outcomes continue to inform his work and are integral to the work of the Regent Park Community Health Centre. Norman can be reached at NormanR@regentparkchc.org

Jim Ryan is a professor and codirector of the Centre for Leadership and Diversity in the Department of Theory and Policy Studies at OISE/UT. His research interests—leadership, diversity and inclusion—are represented in his two most recent books, *Leading Diverse Schools* and *Inclusive Leadership.* Jim can be reached at jryan@oise.utoronto.ca

Susan L. Schramm-Pate is associate professor of curriculum studies in the Department of Instruction & Teacher Education at the University of South Carolina. Her teaching concentration and research interests revolve around history, gender studies, cultural studies, staff diversity development, and integrated curriculum, and enhancing the communication skills and the virtues necessary to more effectively educate people of color and women. Her research appears in *High School Journal, Journal of Curriculum Theorizing, International Journal of Educational Research, Journal of Communications and Minority Issues, Art Education Journal, Southern Studies Journal*, and *Journal of Secondary Education*. Her books include *Transforming the Curriculum: Thinking Outside the Box; A Separate Sisterhood: Women Who Shaped Southern Educational Reform in the Progressive Era;* and *Grappling With Diversity: Readings on Civil Rights Pedagogy and Critical Multiculturalism.*

Lesley Z. Shore is an assistant professor, in the Department of Curriculum, Teaching and Learning at OISE/University of Toronto. Lesley has taught most grades from K-12 in public, private, and Jewish schools in Ontario. Her research and teaching interests include: the influence of reading/culture on adolescent female development, Holocaust education through literature, narrative inquiry, and integrated arts education. Her publications include: *A Thousand Obligations: Anne Frank, Holocaust Education and Anti-semitism in Changing Times; Self-Writing, Sex Ed and the Creation of Adolescent Identity; Sound Bites From Anne Frank; Good/Bad Girls and the Women who Teach Them: A Renewed Call for Media Literacy; Girls Learning, Women Teaching: Dancing to Different Drummers;* and *"I kept my mouth shut": Anne Frank on Sexuality and the Body.* Lesley may be reached at lshore@oise.utoronto.ca

Anne Slonaker is an assistant professor in language and literacy education at Penn State Berks. She was hired to help start up a new urban elementary teacher education program and is interested in studying literacy learning as a centerpiece for working toward more public democratic ways of living together.

Jennifer L. Snow-Gerono is an assistant professor in the College of Education, Department of Curriculum, Instruction, and Foundational Studies at Boise State University in Boise, Idaho. Her research focus is teacher development, including an emphasis on diversity, social justice, and curriculum. She has authored publications and lead conference presentations in the areas of teacher inquiry, school-university partnerships, and social justice through literacy, including *Naming Inquiry: PDS Teachers' Perceptions of Teacher Research and Living an Inquiry Stance Toward Teaching; A Factious Analogous Analysis of No Child Left Behind Through the Lens of Harry Potter and the Order of the Phoenix; Finding our Discursive Selves: Examining Positionality and (Silent) Voices in School-University Partnerships; Literacy* *as Transformative Practice: Teachers' Inquiry into Social Justice.* Jennifer may be reached at jennifersnow@boisestate.edu.

Patrick Solomon is an associate professor in the Faculty of Education, York University. He developed and coordinates the Faculty's Urban Diversity Teacher Education Initiative. He previously served as a school-community liaison with an urban public school district, providing better access to schooling for new and minoritized immigrant groups. His publications include: *Black Resistance in High School; The Erosion of Democracy in Education; Teaching for Equity and Diversity*; and *Urban Teacher Education and Teaching: Innovative Practices in Diversity and Social Justice* (in press). His current research includes a longitudinal study of graduate teachers, their strategies and challenges of implementing diversity and social justice pedagogy in urban schools and communities. Patrick may be reached at psolomon@edu.yorku.ca.

Lindy Zaretsky is superintendent of special education and leadership development with the Simcoe County District School Board. She has been an educator for 15 years as a regular and special education teacher in both the elementary and secondary panels and a special education consultant. Her publications include: *Parent Advocates' and Principals' Perceptions of Professional Knowledge and Identity in Special Education; Reaction to Policymakers' Perceptions of Social Justice Training for Leadership; Responding Ethically to Complex School-based Issues in Special Education; Democratic School Leadership in Canada's Public School Systems: Professional Value and Social Ethic; Advocacy and Administration: From Conflict to Collaboration: Principals and Parent Advocates as Partners in Learning; Using the High Stakes Testing Debate to Advance the Conversation of Equity and Excellence in Education for All Learners; Voices from the Field: School leadership in Special Education.* Lindy can be reached at zaretskyl@rogers.com